SIMON & SCHUSTER

New York

London

Toronto

Sydney

Tokyo

Singapore

DANIEL POOL

What Jane Austen Ate and Charles Dickens Knew

FROM FOX HUNTING TO WHIST —
THE FACTS OF DAILY LIFE
IN NINETEENTH-CENTURY ENGLAND

SIMON & SCHUSTER
SIMON & SCHUSTER BUILDING
ROCKEFELLER CENTER
1230 AVENUE OF THE AMERICAS
NEW YORK, NEW YORK 10020

DESIGNED BY MARYSARAH QUINN
MANUFACTURED IN THE UNITED STATES OF AMERICA

7 9 10 8 6

LIBRARY OF CONGRESS CATALOGING-IN-PUBLICATION DATA
POOL, DANIEL.
WHAT JANE AUSTEN ATE AND CHARLES DICKENS KNEW: FROM FOX HUNTING
TO WHIST—THE FACTS OF DAILY LIFE IN NINETEENTH-CENTURY ENGLAND/
DANIEL POOL.
P.   CM.
INCLUDES BIBLIOGRAPHICAL REFERENCES (P.) AND INDEX.
1. ENGLISH LITERATURE—19TH CENTURY—HISTORY AND CRITICISM.
2. LITERATURE AND SOCIETY—ENGLAND—HISTORY—19TH CENTURY.
3. DICKENS, CHARLES, 1812–1870—CONTEMPORARY ENGLAND.   4. AUSTEN,
JANE, 1775–1817—CONTEMPORARY ENGLAND.   5. ENGLAND—SOCIAL LIFE
AND CUSTOMS—19TH CENTURY.   6. MANNERS AND CUSTOMS IN LITERATURE.
I. TITLE.
PR468.S6P66   1993
820.9'008—DC20   93–16240
                                                      CIP

ISBN 0–671–79337–3

FOR MY PARENTS
AND
FOR LISA S.

Acknowledgments

This book would not have been possible without the aid of a number of individuals. The staff of the General Research Division of the New York Public Library were of enormous assistance in suggesting materials that might answer the author's questions and in helping to locate rare or arcane publications. He is particularly in debt to Ms. Catharine Halls, whose extensive knowledge, unfailing resourcefulness, and patient good humor turned his fruitless inquiries into productive ones, lengthy searches into short hunts, and hesitant queries into research infinitely more informed and efficient than it could otherwise possibly have been. The reference staff of the Butler Library at Columbia University were also uniformly painstaking and imaginative in helping him to find ways to locate sources of information and answer troublesome questions.

He owes special gratitude to his parents and brother Eugene for reading the manuscript of this book at various stages. It is a pleasure, in addition, to acknowledge the assistance of Peyton Houston, who not only read the manuscript but commented in detail on it with his characteristic shrewdness and practicality.

Malaga Baldi proved that all the terrible things the writer had heard about literary agents were untrue, at least in her case, and she has been untiring in her backing for the book. To Bettina Berch he owes great support *ab initio* and an introduction to Malaga. His editor, Gary Luke, read the manuscript, edited it, offered useful advice and understanding and still remained enthusiastic about it.

Jeffrey Miller had the brilliant idea for the book in the first place, which is perhaps only to be expected of a man whose cookie always has the best fortune in it. Without the generous financial support of the David S. Korzenik Foundation, this book would not have appeared at all. Margaret Hornick taught both by example and by patient questioning how to complete a project as daunting as this seemed at the outset. The author is in debt to her consistent good cheer and kindness.

Finally, Jill Bennett has been unfailingly supportive and encouraging about this volume. It is not the first such project of the author's that she has supported, and if it can afford her a pleasure in some small way equal to that which her friendship has given him since the days when she managed to get the piano at Highland Avenue for all of $10, the author will be very pleased.

Contents

CONTENTS.....11

PART TWO

Introduction

What were the assizes?

Would Trollope's Gerald Palliser, the duke of Omnium, have been outranked by an earl—or a countess?

What was ague?

Why did Miss Havisham keep wax and not tallow candles burning in her house during her long vigil?

What was in the gruel that Scrooge ate to ease his cold?

What were the steps of the country-dances that Elizabeth Bennet and Mr. Darcy danced?

How did you play whist, publish the banns—or tell a housemaid from a parlormaid?

This book grew from a wish to answer some of the questions that nag any half-curious reader of the great nineteenth-century English novels, those sometimes daunting but enjoyable works of Dickens, Jane Austen, the Brontës, or Trollope. Today's reader is apt to find himself or herself puzzling over references to aspects of everyday English life that are now long vanished but that the contemporary author took for granted that his—contemporary—audience knew.

Such a reader, typically, wants either to know a quick bit of information—what was a dormouse, or a costermonger, or the lord chancellor?—or else background on some nineteenth-century English institution or set of practices that figure in the novel, fox hunting perhaps, or marriage, or the rites of the Church of England or the seasons in farming.

The book is divided into two parts. In the first section aspects of

English life that figure significantly in the major nineteenth-century English novels are treated at a length of several pages or more. These are the sections for the reader who wishes to know more, say, about farming, or whether canons outranked deacons or vicars in the Church of England, or why people wound up in debtor's prison when they were bankrupt, and so on. In short, it describes the major institutions and practices of nineteenth-century English life that are likely to be unfamiliar to today's reader. At the same time, the reader or student of nineteenth-century English life or literature often has a question about a very specific matter that turns up in his or her reading—what were the "assizes" referred to in *Far from the Madding Crowd,* for example, or the "articles" by which Oliver Twist is "bound" to the cruel undertaker in Dickens's great novel. Such words are explained in the second half of the book in a glossary that explicates their meanings and connotations with specific reference to the needs of the contemporary reader.

In the course of research and writing, the book by its nature evolved into a partial picture of certain aspects of nineteenth-century English life and customs. Fox hunting, farming, marriage, sex, the conduct of business affairs, or parliamentary practice—the specific details of these and other social practices or customs of the era are provided here to the reader who may have as much interest in the history and habits of the time as in its literature. Because the book addresses primarily the interests of the reader of literature, it ignores some of the prominent concerns of the day—the student of Chartism, factory conditions, or the Crimean War, for example, will find little or nothing on these matters here because they are not treated in the "great" nineteenth-century novels.

"Now, what I want is Facts."

CHARLES DICKENS:

Hard Times (1854)

PART ONE

The Basics

CURRENCY

𝒢uineas, shillings, half-pence. You know what they are?" Mr. Dombey asks his little son Paul. Paul, Dickens tells us, knew, but the average reader of today is not always likely to be so knowledgeable.

In the 1800s, British money was calculated in units of pounds, shillings, and pence. These were the units of *value*—like the American mill, cent, and dollar—in which all transactions were reckoned, regardless of whether the value was represented by a bookkeeping entry, by coin, by bank notes, or by notations written on a check. The actual *physical* instruments of currency were paper bank notes and gold, silver, copper, and bronze coins like the sixpence, the crown, the sovereign, the shilling piece, and the penny. Thus, for example, the physical units called pennies were used to measure the value created by an equivalent number of pence. (The guinea, uniquely, was a unit of physical currency that *also* became an abstract measure of value as well; that is, long after the actual guinea coin itself stopped being minted in the early 1800s, prices for luxury items like good horses and expensive clothes continued to be quoted in guineas as if it were some independent unit of value like the pound.)

Sovereigns and half sovereigns were gold; crowns, half crowns, florins, shillings, sixpences, and threepences were silver; pence, ha'pence, and farthings were copper until 1860, after which they were bronze. The coins were issued by the Royal Mint, but the bank notes got their names from the fact that they were not issued by a government agency but by a bank, in fact—after the mid-1800s— only by *the* bank—the Bank of England. Until then banks all over

BASIC UNITS	Value	Coin	Paper	Slang Term
	1,000 pounds		1,000-pound note	
	500 pounds		500-pound note	
	200 pounds		200-pound note	
	100 pounds		100-pound note	
	50 pounds		50-pound note	
	20 pounds		20-pound note	
	10 pounds		10-pound note	tenner
	5 pounds		5-pound note	fiver
	21 shillings	guinea		
One Pound	20 shillings	sovereign	1-pound note	quid
	10 shillings	half sovereign	½-pound note	
	5 shillings	crown		bull
	2½ shillings	half crown	half a crown	
	2 shillings	florin		
One Shilling	12 pence	shilling		bob, hog
	6 pence	sixpence		tanner, bender
	4 pence	groat		
	3 pence	threepence		thruppence
	2 pence	twopence		tuppence
	1 pence	penny		copper
	½ pence	halfpenny		ha'pence
	¼ pence	farthing		
	⅛ pence	half farthing		

the country issued their own bank notes (or promises to pay), which circulated more or less like money. Private banks in the provinces are by one estimate believed to have cranked out about £20,000,000 worth of notes between 1810 and 1815. With the Bank Charter Act of 1844, however, the government gave the Bank of England a monopoly on the issuance of bank notes. As the currency of other banks subsequently disappeared from circulation, "bank note" or "note" in consequence became synonymous with the paper issued by the Bank of England.

To abbreviate their money, Britons used the symbol £ for pound, *s.* for shilling, and *d.* for pence, although five pounds, ten shillings, sixpence could be written £5.10.6. "Five and six" meant five shillings and sixpence, and it would have been written "5/6."

It is very difficult to know what a pound or shilling from 1800 to 1859 is worth in 1990s America, and, as any economist will volubly inform you, the fact that the Victorians had no Hondas and we have no candles, i.e., we don't buy the same goods and don't have the same economic needs, makes the purchasing power of the two currencies fundamentally incommensurable. Nonetheless, intrepid estimates in the last ten years have put the pound's worth in the neighborhood of $20, $50 or $200.

THE CALENDAR

*L*ondon. Michaelmas Term lately over, and the Lord Chancellor sitting in Lincoln's Inn Hall. . . . Fog everywhere."

Yes.

And fog enveloping the reader of *Bleak House* trying to make out when on earth Michaelmas Term was—to say nothing of Boxing Day, Lady Day, Hilary Term, Whitsunday, Twelfth Night, and all the rest of those nettlesome English holidays. Yes. Well—church feasts, folk festivals, law terms, and academic terms at Oxford and Cambridge—here they all are:

Twelfth Night	January 5
Epiphany	January 6
Plough Monday	First Monday after Epiphany
Hilary Term (law courts)	Begins in January
Hilary Term (Cambridge)	Begins in January
Hilary Term (Oxford)	Begins in January
Candlemas	February 2
Lady Day (a quarter day)	March 25
Easter Term (Oxford)	
Easter Term (Cambridge)	
Easter	In March or April
Easter Term (law courts)	Begins after Easter
Ascension	40 days after Easter
Whitsunday (Pentecost)	50 days after Easter
May Day	May 1
Midsummer (a quarter day)	June 24
Trinity Term (law term)	Begins after Whitsunday
Trinity Term (Oxford)	Begins in June
Lammas (Loaf Mass)	August 1
Michaelmas (a quarter day)	September 29
Michaelmas Term	Begins in October
Michaelmas Term	Begins in October

Michaelmas Term	Begins in November
All Hallows, All Saints	November 1
All Souls	November 2
Guy Fawkes Day	November 5
Martinmas	November 11
Christmas (a quarter day)	December 25
Boxing Day	Generally, first weekday after Christmas

A few words of explanation:

1. The word *term* designated alike the academic sessions of Oxford and Cambridge and the periods during which the high courts (King's Bench, Exchequer, and Common Pleas) sat; *vacation* the time when they were not in session. The academic terms appear to have lacked fixed dates from year to year, and Cambridge, as the calendar indicates, had one less term than Oxford. Beginning in 1831, the law terms were fixed at January 11–31 for Hilary Term, April 15–May 8 for Easter, May 22–June 12 for Trinity, and November 2–25 for Michaelmas. The law terms were abolished in favor of sessions in 1873.

2. In 1752 the British joined the rest of Europe by switching from the Julian (thereafter called Old Style) to the Gregorian calendar. This meant going from Wednesday, September 2, 1752, directly to Thursday, September 14, 1752, and dropping eleven days permanently. In *Tess of the d'Urbervilles,* we are thus told that "Lady Day was at hand, and would soon be followed by Old Lady Day, the end of her term here," the incidence of the same quarter day being calculated differently under the two systems of figuring.

3. Quarter days marked off three-month periods of the year on which rents were traditionally due, servants might be hired to begin a term of labor, and so on, as the passage above from *Tess* indicates. Dickens in *The Pickwick Papers* describes the renters in Southwark as "migratory, usually disappearing the verge of quarter-day."

4. Since there are occasional, sometimes rather knowing, references to the reigning monarch in some of the novels, it may be helpful to be reminded of the dates of their reigns.

George III   1760–1820
George IV   1820–30
William IV   1830–37
Victoria   1837–1901

For the last ten years of his life George III was insane. His son, later George IV, was declared prince regent during this period, which was accordingly known as the Regency era.

HOGSHEADS AND DRAMS: ENGLISH MEASUREMENT

Until 1826 Britain stumbled along with a variety of quaint Anglo-Saxon measurement systems like the quartern, the hogshead, or the furlong that were harder and harder to use as industry and commerce grew more modern and widespread. Accordingly, Parliament drew itself up and promulgated the Imperial Statute System of Weights and Measures. The Imperial system of measurement left basically unchanged the units for measuring weight and distance but altered others, resulting in a queer patchwork of modern and archaic means of measurement. Like the corresponding American measurements, the English foot was twelve inches, and the mile, 5,280 feet. There were some additional units of measurement specific to England, however. Thus, in between the foot and the mile came the furlong, equal to 660 feet. (It was the old measure of a standard plowed field's length, i.e., one "furrow long".) The pound was an equivalent unit of weight in both England and the United States, too. However, the British both before and after 1826 also used the stone (fourteen pounds) as a unit of weight. Eight stone in turn constituted a hundredweight (abbreviated cwt). (In *The Return of the Native* Susan Nunsuch uses wax from the hundredweight of honey she has to make a doll of Eustacia Vye into which to stick pins.)

The reform of 1826 introduced the quarter, which weighed 28 pounds—one quarter of a hundredweight. (Not to be confused with a quartern—"quartern" with an "n" on the end being a more general term referring to a quarter measurement of an ounce, a stone, a peck, or a pint. A quartern loaf was a sort of standard bread size equal to a four-pound loaf.) More significantly, the Imperial system standardized the measurement of volume for both liquid and dry goods. 8.655 cubic inches constituted a gill, of which four made a pint. As in the United States, there were two pints to a quart and four quarts to a gallon (except that the English gallon was somewhat larger than that of the United States) and then came pecks, bushels, and so on. (288 gallons = 144 pecks = 36 bushels = 4.5 quarters.)

Notwithstanding the advent of the new system, many goods continued to be measured in their own peculiar units even after 1826. Cloth, for example, was often measured in ells, each 1¼ yards long. Port and madeira wines were measured in pipes (about 100 gallons a pipe) and other wines were measured in hogsheads, as was ale, the hogshead being the equivalent of 1½ barrels or 54 gallons. The practice of measuring wine by butts and tuns seems to have faded by the century's end.

A minor note: the dram was a unit of weight equivalent to one-sixteenth of an ounce. When, however, Abel Magwitch confesses to the soldiers who catch him on the marshes in *Great Expectations* that he stole "some broken wittles—that's what it was—and a dram of liquor, and a pie," he is referring not to this minuscule portion but to the amount of liquor one can down in one swallow.

ENGLAND

*E*ngland and Wales were divided into fifty-two counties, units of both governmental and residential significance to the average English person. Many of the counties had names ending in "—shire"; the counties were *called* shires until William the Conqueror changed the name of the old regional designation. Much of Jane Austen's novels was set in the counties not far north and south of London. George Eliot's novels are often set in the Midlands, the area of fox hunting and enclosures north of London. Dickens, of course, cen-

England and Wales.

tered most of his books in London itself; often, however, their locale
may wander, as in *Pickwick*, *Great Expectations*, and *David Copperfield*, southeast of London to the coastal region of Rochester and
Chatham, where Dickens spent part of his childhood. A good portion
of *Vanity Fair* is set in and around "Queen's Crawley, Hants.," the
latter being an abbreviation for Hampshire county, not far southwest of London.

In the far north, there was Yorkshire, where a good part of the second half of *Jane Eyre* takes place. *Wuthering Heights,* of course, is set in western Yorkshire in the area of the county known as the "west riding." And lastly, there was the Wessex of the great Hardy novels, a region in the southwest of England whose name the novelist borrowed from the old Saxon kingdom that had once occupied the area, territory Hardy described as "bounded on the north by the Thames, on the south by the English Channel, on the east by a line running from Hayling Island to Windsor Forest, and on the west by the Cornish coast," of which Dorset was the heart.

The names of certain cities would also have conjured up vivid associations for the nineteenth-century Englishman. Industry, of course, was centered in the north. Thus, Birmingham (sometimes "Brummagem") was the center of metal manufacturing; Manchester of the cotton industry; Newcastle, of course, supplied coal to the country; and Bath was a social center that developed to meet the needs of rich, gouty invalids who came there to take the waters. Liverpool, where Mr. Earnshaw finds and takes pity on the boy Heathcliff, "starving, and houseless, and as good as dumb, in the streets," was the main port of connection in northern England with the Atlantic and the West Indies. Portsmouth, on the southern coast and important in *Mansfield Park,* was a major naval base.

And then there was London. . . .

LONDON

*L*ondon geography was determined by the Thames. The great river ran from west to east through the city after a dogleg north past Westminster—so, too, did the city itself, its two great thoroughfares being the Strand–Fleet Street and Oxford Street–Holborn–Cheapside.

At its core was the old City of London—known as "the City" as the century wore on—an entity consisting of the roughly square mile making up the area that had once been inside the old walls of the medieval city of London, bounded by the Thames on the south, the Inns of Court and Temple Bar on the west, and the Tower in the

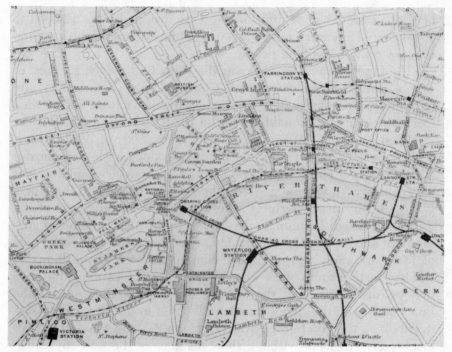

Sketch plan of London.

east, with its seven gates (Newgate of prison fame being one), which had all been torn down save for "that leaden-headed old obstruction," as Dickens calls it at the beginning of *Bleak House,* "appropriate ornament for the threshold of a leaden-headed corporation, Temple Bar."

Within the City lay the Royal Exchange (the 'Change upon which Scrooge's word in *A Christmas Carol* is said to be so good), which was a gathering place for merchants in different trades, and the Bank of England, the financial nucleus of the nation, together with the financial offices and activities that naturally clustered around them. In fact, the term "the City" was also used to denote the financial heart of England in the way that "Wall Street" is used to describe the financial heart of the United States. In Jane Austen's day, it was still customary for some merchants to live in the City, but as railroads were thrust through it and commuting became more feasible, even poor clerks began commuting to work from fringe or suburban areas the way we are told that Bob Cratchit does from Camdentown. In the first eighty years of the nineteenth century, in fact, the resident population in the City dropped from 128,000 to 50,000, while greater London as a whole mushroomed from a million to more than 4.5 million people.

The fancy area of London was the West End, which lay west of Temple Bar and London's center, Charing Cross. (Bloomsbury, site of the Russell Square where the Sedleys live in *Vanity Fair*, became increasingly less fashionable after the 1820s.) At the historic core of the West End lay what had once been the royal city of Westminster, with its palaces of St. James and Whitehall, along with Westminster Abbey and the Houses of Parliament. The Treasury building was here, along with Downing Street, the Foreign Office and the Horse Guards (army headquarters). These had now become part of the larger, expanded London, and adjacent to this nerve center of government and royalty the ultrafashionable West End residential area of Mayfair (and, later, Belgrave Square and the nonfashionable Chelsea farther south) grew up. Mayfair was the location of the posh men's clubs on Pall Mall, the exclusive shops on Bond Street and the fancy houses on the ritziest residential street in the city, Park Lane, overlooking the great greensward of Hyde Park on Mayfair's western border. All were within a short distance of the new royal residence, Buckingham Palace.

Predictably, the rest of the city became less fashionable and to the east, in particular, degenerated into slums, the East End along the docks beyond the area of the Tower becoming synonymous by the end of the century with poverty and misery. There were other areas as desperately poor, however; the notorious St. Giles and Seven Dials that sheltered Fagin's gang were located not far from Charing Cross. Across the Thames lay Southwark, sometimes referred to as "the Borough" but part of London, where Little Dorrit's father was imprisoned in the Marshalsea. The pleasure grounds of the Vauxhall Gardens where Joe Sedley was too drunk to pop the question to Becky Sharp lay here, and on the area's west bank was Lambeth Palace, the official residence of the archbishop of Canterbury. Greenwich, with its royal hospital for old sailors, lay downstream to the southeast, as did Woolwich, one of the army's two main arsenals. West were Kensington, Fulham, and Hammersmith; Whitechapel and Bethnal Green were to the city's east; and north were St. Pancras, Islington, Clerkenwell, and Hampstead, where the distracted Sikes wandered after murdering Nancy.

As they swelled in population, many of these areas also became terminals for the great railroads coming in from all over England.

The reader of Victorian fiction will recognize the names of some of the big stations a mile or so northwest of the city's center that connected London with the north, Marylebone (1899) being farthest west, and then, in increasing proximity, Euston Station (1838), St. Pancras (1867), and King's Cross (1852). A bit north of Hyde Park was Paddington Station (1854), which connected London with the west. Victoria Station (1862), a few blocks southwest of Buckingham Palace, ran to the south and southwest, and across the Thames River near the bridge of the same name Waterloo Station (1848) also brought in southerly traffic.

The Thames was some 800 to 1,500 feet wide as it flowed through the city. Originating far upstream from London, it flowed down past Henley and Windsor as clear water, and, although the Thames was a tidal river, it was seldom brackish in London unless tides were unusually high and the wind had been from the east for a long time. In 1800, one could travel from the "Middlesex" (county) or London side to the "Surrey" side (Southwark) via London Bridge, the ancient stone bridge just west of the Tower, via Blackfriars Bridge near the Temple, or by way of Westminster Bridge near the great Abbey. "It was Old London Bridge in those days," says Pip in *Great Expectations*, "and at certain states of the tide there was a race and a fall of water there which gave it a bad reputation." Pip masters the trick of negotiating its waters, but the bridge's architecture made the current sufficiently dangerous to be a factor in its replacement later in the century. In 1819, Southwark Bridge, the "Iron Bridge," as Dickens calls it in contrast to London Bridge, was built between London Bridge and Blackfriars, and in 1817 Waterloo Bridge was constructed between the Blackfriars and Westminster bridges. We are occasionally reminded that in those days even foot passengers had to pay to cross the river. In a visit to the "Patriarchal Tent," Dickens tells us, Little Dorrit "went by the Iron Bridge, though it cost her a penny." (The wherries of the watermen and, later, the short-distance steamers might have taken her up or down the river for a fee as well.)

From the standpoint of the riverfront, London Bridge really marked the entrance to the city; indeed, directions on the river were frequently given with reference to it as "above bridge" or "below bridge." Large ships found London Bridge impassable so the great companies constructed several hundred acres' worth of "the Docks," as they were called (that of the East India Company alone covered 250 acres) to its south. "The Docks" were inshore from the

Pool, the stretch of water south of the bridge where the colliers and other shipping massed, waiting for the signal to come in and unload their cargo.

From there it was south some fifty miles—past Gravesend and the long, flat marshy stretches of Kent and Essex—to the river's entrance at the Channel. "The river below," wrote the author of a London guidebook in the 1870s, "and nearly all the way to the mouth, lies between flat marshes, over which the ships appear sailing across the grass, as in a Dutch picture."

Such was London.

But what was it like to live in?

The fog in London was very real. Just why it was the color it was no one has ever been able to ascertain for sure, but at a certain time of the year—it was worst in November—a great yellowness reigned everywhere, and lamps were lit inside even during the day. In November, December, and January the yellow fog extended out some three or four miles from the heart of the city, causing "pain in the lungs" and "uneasy sensations" in the head. It has been blamed in part on the coal stoves. At eight o'clock in the morning on an average day over London, an observer reported the sky began to turn black with the smoke from thousands of coal fires, presumably for morning fires to warm dining rooms and bedrooms and to cook breakfast. Ladies going to the opera at night with white shawls returned with them gray. It has been suggested that the black umbrella put in its appearance because it did not show the effects of these London atmospherics. The fog was so thick, observed a foreigner at mid-century, that you could take a man by the hand and not be able to see his face, and people literally lost their way and drowned in the Thames. In a very bad week in 1873 more than 700 people above the normal average for the period died in the city, and cattle at an exhibition suffocated to death.

There were problems underfoot as well as in the air. One hundred tons of horse manure dropped on the streets of London each day, and a report to Parliament said that "strangers coming from the country frequently describe the streets of London as smelling of dung like a stable-yard." Originally, many streets were not paved; by mid-century, however, the dust from the pulverized stone with which London streets were paved coated furniture in good weather and turned to mud when it rained. An etiquette book advised gentlemen to walk on the outside of the pavement when accompanying a lady to ensure that they walked on the filthiest part of it, and every major street had a crossing sweeper like Jo in *Bleak House,* who for a penny swept the street before you made your way across it on rainy days so your boots did not become impossibly filthy. Nor was the Thames any better. London sewage, some 278,000 tons *daily* at mid-century, as well as pollutants from the factories along the river's banks, was dumped untreated into the water, presumably helping to fuel the cholera epidemics that swept the city in the early part of the century. The smell was bad enough in the summer of 1858 to cause Parliament to end its session early.

There was what we would surely call noise pollution, too—the incessant sound of wheels and horses' hooves clacking over the pavement, the click of women's pattens on the sidewalks in the rain, the bell of the muffin man, and the cries of the street peddlers selling such items as dolls, matches, books, knives, eels, pens, rat poison, key rings, eggs, and china, to say nothing of the German bands, the itinerant clarinet players, and the hurdy-gurdies.

The children who added their din to that of the costermongers remind us that London was an overwhelmingly young city, as we are apt to realize when we read, say, *Oliver Twist,* a city of multitudinous street arabs, young costermongers, crossing sweepers like Jo, or the mud larks who scavenged the bed of the Thames—all playing in the streets or crying their wares, holding horses for gentlemen, fetching cabs for theatergoers on rainy nights, carrying packages or opening cab doors or doing cartwheels or handstands in the street in the hope of earning a ha'penny or penny. There was no compulsory school until 1880, and children under fourteen made up 30 to 40 percent of the population. A girl like Lizzie Hexam in *Our Mutual Friend* was thus free all day to help her father drag for lost items— or bodies—in the Thames.

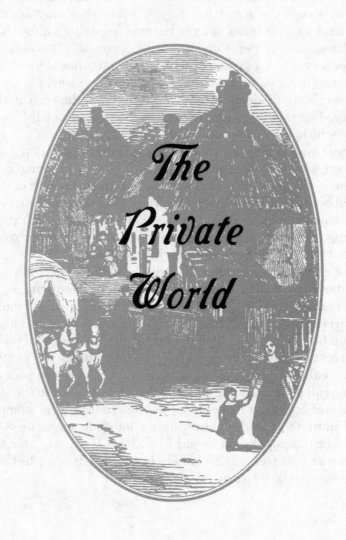

The Private World

PRECEDENCE:
OF BISHOPS,
BARRISTERS, AND
BARONETS

a good deal of the social hierarchy in England was made explicit in the order of precedence, a more or less official ranking of honors, ranks, lineage, and occupational statuses in the kingdom. It was certainly a ranking of which no nineteenth-century hostess would have dreamed of being ignorant, for by mid-century it had become the custom in almost every household of any pretension for the guests at a dinner party to gather in the drawing room before the meal, the ladies then being escorted in to the dining room by the gentlemen one at a time in strict order of both their ranks, the personages of greatest rank or distinction going first. The good hostess at any dinner party ascertained everyone's rank in advance and then quietly arranged the guests in order of precedence while the party mingled informally in the drawing room before the meal: "If the society is of a distinguished kind," observed an etiquette book soberly, "she [the hostess] will do well to consult Debrett or Burke, before arranging her visitors."

Trollope, the infallible guide to social distinction and nuance, tells us both what a headache this could be and the social weapon it could become in the hands of the skillful. In *The Last Chronicle*

ORDER OF PRECEDENCE AMONG MEN.

All † Peers rank among themselves by date of creation, in the following order :—English, Scotch, of Great Britain, Irish, of the United Kingdom.

THE SOVEREIGN.
Prince of Wales, Sons of the Sovereign, in order of birth. Grandsons, Brothers, Nephews, and Uncles of the Sovereign, Younger Princes of Blood Royal.

Archbp. of Canterbury.
Lord Chancellor.
Archbps. of York, Armagh, Dublin.
President of Council.
Lord Privy Seal.
Lord Great Chamberlain.
The Earl Marshal.
Lord Steward of Household.
Lord Chamberlain of Household.
Dukes†
Lord Great Chamberlain, ⎫
Lord High Constable, ⎬ if a Marquis.
Earl Marshal, ⎪
Lord Steward of House- ⎪
hold, ⎪
Lord Chamberlain of ⎪
Household, ⎭
Marquises.†
Dukes' eldest sons.
Lord Great Chamberlain, ⎫
Lord High Constable, ⎬ if an Earl.
Earl Marshal, ⎪
Lord Steward, ⎪
Lord Chamberlain, ⎭
Earls.†
Eldest sons of Marquises.
Younger sons of Dukes.
Lord Great Chamber- ⎫
lain, ⎬ if a Vis-
Lord High Constable, ⎪ count.
Lord Steward, ⎪
Lord Chamberlain, ⎭
Viscounts.†

Eldest sons of Earls.
Younger sons of Marquises.
The Bishops of London, Durham, and Winchester.
English Bishops according to date of consecration.
The Bishop of Meath.
Other Irish Bishops, in order of consecration.
Lord Great Chamberlain, ⎫
Lord High Constable, ⎪
Lord Steward, ⎬ if a Baron.
Lord Chamberlain of the ⎪
Household, ⎭
Secretary of State,
Barons.†
Speaker of House of Commons.
Commissioners of the Great Seal (when they have no claim to higher rank).
Treasurer of the Household, ⎫
Comptroller of the ⎬ if of no higher
Household, ⎪ rank.
Master of the Horse, ⎪
Vice-Chamberlain of ⎪
Household, ⎪
Secretary of State, if below ⎭
the rank of Baron.
Eldest sons of Viscounts.
Younger sons of Earls.
Eldest sons of Barons.
Knights of the Garter, if of no higher rank.

Privy Councillors, in order of appointment, when with no higher precedence.
Chancellor of the Garter.
Chancellor of Exchequer.
Chancellor of Duchy of Lancaster.
Chief Justice of Queen's Bench.
Master of the Rolls.
Chief Justice of Common Pleas.
Chief Baron of Exchequer.
Vice-Chancellors, according to seniority.
Puisne Judges of Queen's Bench.
Puisne Justices of Common Pleas.
Puisne Barons of Exchequer.
Commissioners of Bankruptcy.
Younger sons of Viscounts.
Younger sons of Barons.
Baronets of England, Scotland, Great Britain, Ireland, & United Kingdom, in order of their respective patents.
Knights of the Thistle, if of no higher rank.
Knights of St. Patrick, if of no higher rank.
Knights Grand Cross of the Bath; and of St. Michael and St. George.
Knights Commanders of the Bath; and St. Michael and St. George.
Knights Bachelors.
Companions of the Bath; and of St. Michael and St. George.

Eldest sons of younger sons of Peers.
Eldest sons of Baronets.
Eldest sons of Knights Grand Cross of the Bath.
Eldest sons of Knights Grand Cross of St. Michael and St. George.
Eldest sons of Knights Commander of the Bath.
Eldest sons of Knights Commander of St. Michael and St. George.
Eldest sons of Knights Bachelors.
Younger sons of the younger sons of Peers.
Younger sons of Baronets.
Esquires of the Sovereign's body.
Gentlemen of Privy-chamber.
Esquires of Knights of the Bath.
Esquires by creation, and by office.
Younger sons of Knights Grand Cross of the Bath; of Knights Grand Cross of St. Michael and St. George; of Knights Commanders of the Bath; of Knights Commanders of St. Michael and St. George; and of Knights Bachelors.
General and Flag Officers.
Colonels in the Army, Captains in the Navy.
Gentlemen entitled to bear arms.

Order of precedence among men.

of Barset he asks, "Amidst the intricacies of rank how is it possible for a woman to learn and remember everything? If Providence would only send Mrs. Dobbs Broughton a Peer for every dinner-party, the thing would go more easily; but what woman will tell me, off-hand, which should go out of the room first; a C.B., an Admiral of the Blue, the Dean of Barchester, or the Dean of Arches?" In *Can You Forgive Her?* one of the suitors for Mrs. Greenow's hand is allowed to take her in to dinner, while the other, grinding his teeth, must follow with another lady. "There was no doubt as to Mrs. Greenow's correctness," says Trollope. "As Captain Bellfield held, or had held, her Majesty's commission, he was clearly entitled to take the mistress of the festival down to dinner." And the loser's companion points out to him briskly, "If you were a magistrate, Mr. Cheesacre, you would have rank; but I believe you are not."

In the order of precedence the peerage (dukes, marquesses, earls, viscounts, and barons) soared above virtually everyone else, including baronets and knights, who were creatures of relatively low distinction. A bishop, too, ranked very high, which is why the battles over the post (see *Barchester Towers*) could be so ferocious, while the high position accorded the lord chancellor and the archbishop of Canterbury suggests why those personages are alluded to in novels as beings of such consequence. As we shall see, official rank and actual social clout in the case of any particular individual might be two different things, but any effort to come to grips with the world embodied in the nineteenth-century novel must begin with precedence.

THE TITLED

*T*here were two orders of titled folk in England. Dukes, marquesses, earls, viscounts, and barons (who ranked in that order) were known as the peerage. Considerably below them on the social scale and *not* peers came the baronets and knights, easily recognizable because they were always addressed as "Sir."

Together with the bishops and the archbishops of the Church of England, the peers composed the House of Lords, and, indeed, a reference to a "lord" almost always meant a peer or one of his children. They were invariably hugely wealthy and possessed of gigantic landed estates, but their only privilege of any significance was the right to be tried for a felony by the House of Lords rather than by a court. In addition, on extremely formal ceremonial occasions peers got to wear coronets. Search the Palliser novels and you will probably find a reference somewhere to "strawberry leaves." These were the flora (in the form of precious stones, of course) that ornamented the ducal coronet; lower ranks in the peerage had their distinctive coronets as well.

The title was always hereditary, with the exception of a very few "life peerages" created late in the 1800s, whose honors died with them. The title generally passed to the eldest son; in some families, if there were no male heir, the peerage ended. However, children stepped into their father's shoes for purposes of inheritance, so that if the heir left a male child, the child would inherit the title. If the child died or there were no child, the title would pass to a brother of the title's holder. Failing that, it would pass to another male still in the line of direct descent from the first holder of the title. In *Can You Forgive Her?*, this means that Jeffrey Palliser has a chance at the title once his cousin Plantagenet dies, as Plantagenet's wife, Lady Glencora, calmly explains to a friend: "If I have no child, and Mr. Palliser were not to marry again, Jeffrey would be the heir." This also accounts for the classic denouement of Victorian melodrama in which the impoverished American street urchin is discovered to be the new earl of Foxglove. Branches of the family might have ramified endlessly since the title was first bestowed, but if the urchin were the closest living male heir—even if he were from a very junior or "cadet" branch of the original family—he would inherit the title and usually the manor.

A lady marrying a peer took his noble status, which is why the socially ambitious Lizzie Eustace pursues Lord Fawn in *The Eustace Diamonds,* even though she has already acquired a bundle of money with her first marriage and Lord Fawn is both dreary and penniless. "How could she have done better?" cries Mme. Goesler. "He is a peer and her son would be a peer." That is, a man who married a widowed viscountess could only send out cards inviting you to dinner in the name of Mr. Smith and Viscountess Warwick. If Miss Smith married Viscount Warwick, however, she became Viscountess Warwick.

But why would a peer marry beneath him? Partly, no doubt, because the landed estate that went with his title was often tied up in an entail that prevented him from selling any of it to raise money and was, in addition, often burdened with legal requirements to pay jointure and portions to various members of the family, so that a peer might be as interested in trying to land a rich heiress as she was in trying to land him. This was especially true because it was firmly believed that to be a peer required a fairly expensive keeping up of appearances, so much so, indeed, that at one time military heroes awarded a peerage were often granted great landed estates simultaneously to allow them to maintain the title in proper style. Lord Fawn, as Trollope points out, had estates that brought him very little, and, indeed, he "was always thinking, not exactly how he might make both ends meet, but how to reconcile the strictest personal economy with the proper bearing of an English nobleman. Such a man almost naturally looks to marriage as an assistance in the dreary fight. It soon becomes clear to him that he cannot marry without money, and he learns to think that heiresses have been invented exactly to suit his case. . . . He has got himself, his position, and, perhaps, his title to dispose of, and they are surely worth so much per annum." "A rich heiress can buy a coronet any day,"

wrote a shrewd American observer in the 1880s. "There are march-
ionesses now living whose fortunes fresh from trade saved the ancient estates of the aristocracy from the hammer."

Although titles like duke, earl, and viscount conjure up images of
armored figures with maces and swords clashing on horseback, a
great many peerages were not of very long standing. A peerage—
which was always granted by the monarch—was given perhaps
most often for service to the political party then in power at the
behest of the prime minister. (Disraeli's becoming earl of Beaconsfield comes to mind in this connection.) In addition, very wealthy
lawyers, brewers (perhaps surprisingly), and lord chancellors (almost invariably) became peers, as did military heroes, like the duke
of Wellington. To keep the peerage small and sought after, commoners were seldom made peers unless they were old and lacking in
male children so that the title would die with them and keep the
aristocracy unsoiled from contact with the plebs. (This exclusivity
and the consequent desirability of the honor were strengthened by
the fact that in each generation only one child, the heir, was enno-
bled, and the others all became commoners.) Titles were sometimes
called patents of nobility because they were originally granted by
"letters of patent," that is, letters that were open to the whole world
to see. In the case of two peers of the same rank, the one with the
oldest patent took precedence. "His rank in the peerage was not
high," Trollope remarks of Lord Popplecourt in *The Duke's Children*, "but his barony was of an old date." Brand-new peerages
were considered tacky. When a new lord chancellor was proposed
for the peerage in the 1880s, he requested that the title be granted
to his *father* so that the chancellor himself would be the *second*
Lord———. Promotions could be made from within the peerage,
with the titles previously attained trailing along after the new one.
Accordingly, one might be Baron Little one year; Viscount More,
Baron Little the next; Earl Stillmore, Viscount More, Baron Little
the year after; and so forth.

Below the peerage came the baronets and knights, who were
much more numerous in nineteenth-century English fiction and
were much less influential, at least at a national level, in English
society. These ranks, if the word doesn't have too disrespectful a
sound, were the middle-class English titles, though, in the case of
baronets, it is admittedly a very upper middle class that is at issue.
A baronetage was hereditary like a peerage, but baronets were not
peers and they did not sit in the House of Lords. Sir James Dedlock

in *Bleak House*, Sir James Chettam in *Middlemarch*, Sir Walter Elliot in *Persuasion*, and Sir Pitt Crawley in *Vanity Fair*—all are baronets. They constituted the upper reaches of that somewhat amorphous group called the gentry, and while they might sit in the House of Commons, they were more often preoccupied with local, "county" affairs.

At the bottom of the titled ranks was knighthood. Knighthood was not hereditary, perhaps one reason it lacked some of the grandeur of a baronetcy. In addition, distinguished doctors or lawyers tended to become baronets, while knighthoods, the novelists tell us, were bestowed for reasons bordering on the comical on persons who were often—heaven forfend—"in trade." Trollope speaks in *The Warden* of the pleasure of "a city tallow-chandler in becoming Sir John on the occasion of a Queen's visit to a new bridge," while in *Great Expectations* Dickens tells us how Mrs. Pocket's father "had been knighted himself for storming the English grammar at the point of a pen, in a desperate address engrossed on vellum, on the occasion of the laying of the first stone of some building or other, and for handing some Royal Personage either the trowel or the mortar."

How to Address Your Betters

*L*ife was full of perplexities for the nineteenth-century English gentleperson, perhaps never more so than when dealing with the aristocracy and other worthies. First there was the problem of addressing them in conversation; second, that of writing them a friendly note or sending them a properly addressed invitation to one's ball. Both situations were complicated by the "faux-noble" nomenclature problem, that is, the use of such titles as lord and lady for members of the upper crust who *did* have status but were not *real* lords and ladies and were given these titles only as "courtesy titles." How did one keep all this straight?

By using these forms of address:

I. In Direct Conversation:
Your Majesty—to the king or queen.

Your Royal Highness—to the monarch's spouse, children, and siblings.

Your Highness—to the nephews, nieces, and cousins of the sovereign.

Duke or Duchess—to a duke or duchess if one were a member of the nobility or gentry.

Your Grace—to a duke or duchess if one were below the gentry, and to an archbishop of the Church of England.

My Lord—to a peer below the rank of duke and to a bishop of the Church of England.

Lord—to address an earl, marquis, or viscount. The first two were often marquis or earl *of* someplace; e.g., "the earl of Derby." They were not addressed this way in conversation but, rather, one dropped the "of" and put "lord" in front of the geographical locale designated in the title; e.g., "the earl of Derby" became "Lord Derby." A viscount had no "of" in his title but was simply "Viscount Palmerston"; however, he was likewise addressed as "Lord Palmerston." A baron was virtually *never* spoken of or addressed as "Baron"; "Lord Tennyson" (as in the case of the poet who was created a baron) was the invariable way of addressing a peer of the lowest rank.

Lady—to a marchioness, countess, viscountess, or baroness. It worked as it did for the males; e.g., the "marchioness of Derby" became "Lady Derby."

Sir—to a baronet or knight with his first name; e.g., "Sir Thomas Bertram."

Baron—to a judge of the Exchequer Court or, on extremely formal occasions, a baron in the peerage.

Lady—to the wife of a baronet or knight. Here, in contrast to the way "Lady" was used for a peeress in the manner described above, Jane Fairfax, the wife of Sir John Fairfax, was addressed as "Lady Fairfax." That is, Sir Thomas Bertram's wife in *Mansfield Park* is referred to as "Lady Bertram," and Sir Leicester Dedlock's wife in *Bleak House* is "Lady Dedlock." It is not merely contemporary readers who may find it difficult to distinguish between peeresses on the one hand and the wives of knights and baronets on the other when both groups use the title Lady. The female peerage were said to find the usurpation of the title by the lower ranks quite annoying; some apparently wished the wives of knights would resume their old title of Dame.

My Lord—to a lord mayor, and to judges of the King's Bench and Common Pleas courts.

Your Worship—to a justice of the peace but probably only by his inferiors.

Doctor—in the early part of the century, i.e., in Jane Austen's era, the term would probably have been used for a doctor of divinity; it was still so used in *Tess* in 1891. Otherwise, it would probably have been applied to a physician but not to a surgeon, who would have been styled "Mr." At the beginning of *Dombey and Son*, Paul's birth is attended by "Doctor Parker Peps, one of the Court Physicians" and by "the family Surgeon," who is addressed as "Mr. Pilkins." In addressing a medical doctor, it was mandatory to use the surname after the title; it was thus considered rude to say simply, "Yes, doctor."

Squire—a term with no legal significance at all. Though they were often justices of the peace, squires per se were merely substantial landowners with a long residence in a particular country area, no more.

II. In Direct Written Communication:

the Most Reverend—to an archbishop.

His Grace—to a duke or an archbishop.

the Most Noble—to a marquis.

the Right Honourable—to an earl, viscount, or baron.

the Right Reverend—to a bishop.

the Right Honourable—to a member of the Privy Council and, hence, to all cabinet members since they were privy councillors ex officio. Also, to a peer's eldest son bearing an inferior, courtesy title of his father's.

the Venerable—to an archdeacon.

the Very Reverend—to a dean.

the Reverend—to a rector, a vicar, a canon, and all other clergy of the Church of England not covered under the above titles.

the Honourable—to a member of Parliament.

III. Courtesy Titles

As noted above, these were titles given to the children of peers and some of their spouses as a matter of politeness, not because they conveyed any legal rights with them the way a genuine peerage did. That is, all the children of peers were commoners, including the eldest son, until he—or one of the others—inherited the title from his father or was otherwise granted a title when he became a peer himself. However, to distinguish socially the children and—in the case of male children—their wives, they were all granted courtesy titles, as follows:

Lord—to the eldest son of a duke, marquis, or earl, who was also entitled to use the inferior title of his father, that is to say, a peer customarily bore several titles (duke of X, marquis of Y, earl of Z, etc.), using only the highest, and his eldest son took the next title down as a courtesy title until he inherited the highest title from his father. In *Middlemarch*, Celia Brooke, after marrying the baronet Sir James Chettam, reflects that it is nice her son is who he is, but "it would be nice, though, if he were a Viscount. . . . He might have been, if James had been an Earl." And the oldest son of Plantagenet Palliser, the duke of Omnium, is called the earl of Silverbridge in *The Duke's Children*, even though he does not sit in Parliament and is not really an earl. He is addressed as "Lord Silverbridge," after the name of a borough associated with the family.

Lord—to a younger son of a duke or marquis. Presumably because the younger son was not an heir, the "Lord" was simply tacked on to his Christian name and surname; e.g., Lord Silverbridge's younger brother in *The Duke's Children* is called "Lord Gerald Palliser." There was no borrowing of one of father's titles.

Lady—to the daughter of a duke, marquis, or earl, with her Christian name and surname; that is, for naming purposes she was treated like a peer's younger son. Thus, in *Vanity Fair*, we first encounter young Pitt Crawley as he is "said to be paying his addresses to Lady Jane Sheepshanks, Lord Southdown's third daughter." Just to confuse things a little more, "Lady" would also be the courtesy title of the spouse of a peer's son bearing the courtesy title "Lord." She would have been known as Lady John Fairfax, in contrast to the two no-courtesy style usages of "Lady" listed above.

the Honourable—to all children, male and female, of the lower peers, that is, viscounts and barons, and to the younger sons of earls. In *Persuasion*, Sir Walter Elliot madly pursues an acquaintance with his cousins, "the Dowager Viscountess Dalrymple, and her daughter, the Honourable Miss Carteret." The housekeeper, Mrs. Fairfax, in describing Mr. Rochester's current womanfriend in *Jane Eyre*, alludes to the woman we come to know as Miss Ingram as the "Hon. Blanche." Her father, deceased, was Baron Ingram.

One occasionally sees the word "dowager" introduced into a title; e.g., the "Dowager Lady Ingram," as Charlotte Brontë calls Blanche's mother. This was neither a courtesy nor legal title but simply designated the widow of the titled male implied by the title, e.g., Lord Ingram, or, in the case of Viscountess Dalrymple, Viscount Dalrymple. After a certain point, the custom also developed of referring to a dowager simply as "Joan, countess of Warwick," the first name being used to differentiate her from the current earl's wife.

In a not dissimilar fashion, you called yourself "Alfred, Lord Tennyson" to distinguish yourself from other Lord Tennysons in the lineage. Tennyson's title also illustrates the tendency in the lower reaches of the peerage for names in titles to be drawn from surnames as well as from places. That is, dukes were *always* dukes of some *geographical area*—e.g., Omnium, Windsor, Rutland, Edinburgh—as were, generally speaking, marquesses. Earls, however, might be either geographical (Disraeli was earl of Beaconsfield) or use their family name (like Prime Minister John Russell, who became Earl Russell). The same was true of viscounts and barons.

The contemporary reader may be confused by the different uses of the title of Lady. To summarize what has been said above, there were four distinct usages. If you married the baronet or knight Sir John Drudge, you became Lady Drudge (husband's last name). If Sir John, who is, we shall say, a resident of Chiswick near the noble river Avon, then became an earl and subsequently a marquis, he would probably be known, assuming he chose a territorial designation, as the marquis of Chiswick and earl of Avon, and he would then be addressed as Lord Chiswick and his wife would become Lady Chiswick (husband's territorial designation). Their eldest son, Horace Drudge, would now have the courtesy title Lord Avon, and *his* wife, by analogy to a real peerage, would be Lady Avon (husband's territorial designation). Horace's younger brother would be known as Lord Albert Drudge, and *his* wife, the former Gwendolyn Sprockett, would be known as Lady Albert Drudge (husband's Christian name and surname). Finally, Hypatia—Horace and Albert's sister—would be known as Lady Hypatia Drudge (own Christian name and family surname).

If all this was simply too confusing, it was always comforting to remember that an overly ostentatious use of formalities and titles was frowned on anyway. After all, the queen sometimes made do with Ma'am as a formal title of address and the Prince of Wales with Sir. Only servants, suggested a contemporary book touching on usage, said "My Lord" and "My Lady" in every other sentence. It added: "It is, however, well to show that you remember the station of your interlocutor, by now and then introducing some such phrases as, 'I think your Grace was observing,' or, 'I believe, madam, I was pointing out to you—'" Among themselves, and with friends and relatives, except perhaps on a first introduction, the nobility even dropped the "Lord" in front of their names in conversation, so that, for example, to his friends "Lord Derby" was simply "Derby." (He would have remained "Lord Derby," however, to servants, business and tradespeople.)

Star, collar, and badge of the Order of the Garter.

Esq., Gent., K.C.B., etc.

What did it mean to put "Bart." or "Esq." after one's name, to style oneself "K.C." or "Q.C.," or, like Lady Macleod in *Can You Forgive Her?*, be "the widow of a Sir Archibald Macleod, K.C.B."? What did the mysterious letters signify?

Here is a guide to the meaning and significance of those that were among the more common:

Bart., Bt.—Abbreviations for baronet.

Esq. (Esquire)—Originally, an esquire was the young man who attended on a knight and was in training to be a knight himself. The name, then, was a job description rather than, as knight, a title of honor. By the nineteenth century, the term had become somewhat casual in application, although denoting in theory that one was a member of the gentry, ranking below a knight and above a mere "gentleman." There were subsequent, doomed attempts to maintain that it should be used only by justices of the peace, military men, barristers and physicians, and certain sons of knights and peers, but eventually it became merely a title of indeterminate respectability. Thus, after the farmer's wife has mingled with the quality at Squire Thorne's "fete champetre" in *Barchester Towers*, "it might fairly be expected that from this time forward the tradesmen of Barchester would, with undoubting pens, address her husband as T. Lookaloft, Esquire."

Gent.—Short for gentleman, in social terms an increasingly imprecise status, though it carried an unmistakable air of gentility. A gentleman was defined by the law as someone with no regular trade or occupation.

B.A.—Abbreviation for bachelor of arts, a degree apparently often associated with clergymen who had gone straight from Oxford or Cambridge to an incumbency.

D.D.—Abbreviation for doctor of divinity.

K.C.—King's Counsel, an honor given to a senior, distinguished barrister in recognition of an outstanding career. Toward the middle of the nineteenth century, K.C. replaced serjeant as the highest honor within the bar to which a barrister could aspire.

Q.C.—Queen's Counsel, the equivalent during Victoria's reign of the K.C.

C.B.—Companion of the Bath. Lowest of the three honors within the Order of the Bath. In *Vanity Fair,* the renewed campaign against Napoleon means that before the fighting ended, Thackeray says, "Mrs. Major O'Dowd hoped to write herself Mrs. Colonel O'Dowd, C.B."

G.C.B.—Grand Commander of the Order of the Bath. A high distinction of knighthood often conferred for distinguished military service. One of Jane Austen's brothers was a G.C.B. Originally, part of the ceremony of becoming a knight involved bathing in order to purify oneself.

K.C.B.—Knight Commander of the Bath (less status than a G.C.B.). The honor held by Sir Archibald Macleod, "who had been a soldier."

Kt.—A knight.

K.B.—A knight bachelor, same status as the plain knight with no trimmings. (In another context, K.B. was an abbreviation for the Court of King's Bench.)

K.G.—Knight of the Garter. The highest order of knighthood, given, as a rule, only to peers.

M.P.—Member of Parliament.

R.A.—Member of the Royal Academy, the officially sanctioned institute of painting founded by George III as an art school and a forum for annual exhibits of work by contemporary artists.

V.C.—The Victoria Cross. A very high military award and not an honor of knighthood like the Bath. It was first given in 1857 to Crimean War heroes and was traditionally manufactured by a London jewelers' firm out of metal from captured Russian guns. Not to be confused with the D.S.O., the Distinguished Service Order, an award for officers only that came into being in 1886.

S T A T U S :
G E N T L E M E N   A N D
L E S S E R   F O L K

*T*he order of precedence explained whether a bishop's wife had precedence over the daughter of a peer and whether a duke outranked the archbishop of Canterbury and other easy-to-grasp distinctions. On a daily basis, however, the average Englishman would also have had to deal with more subtle distinctions of class and status for which there was no readily available guide.

At the beginning of the century everyone knew where he or she stood. Dukes, marquises, and earls were on top, except that possession of a distinguished family name and great landholdings for generations would outrank a paltry title of lesser age, as witness the immense deference accorded by everyone to the titleless Mr. Darcy in *Pride and Prejudice.* Below the great nobles and landowners were the gentry, the locally based "county families" of squires, clergy, baronets, and knights with properties not as great as those of the dukes but large enough to have tenants. Bishops and physicians and barristers would rank somewhere in here, and then came the yeoman farmers, the independent landowners with their large or small holdings, and the bankers, and then the lesser tradesfolk, artisans, and at the very bottom the working poor and farm laborers.

The changes in English society in the 1800s altered this somewhat static hierarchy. To begin with, industry and manufacturing created new sources of wealth that could compete with land, even though its holders frequently had to put some of their wealth into landownership of a country estate to be really "accepted." Second, the professions became both more influential and more respected: doctors acquired real scientific training for a change; the clergy became more conscientious about its duties and education; and suddenly there was a new class of people, like Lydgate in *Middlemarch*, demanding to be taken seriously—socially and professionally. Meanwhile, a lower middle class made up of Bob Cratchits and Sue Brideheads and Eugene Hexams popped up to serve in the counting houses and the great bureaucracies of government, such as the educational system. At the same time, the enclosure acts and the mechanization of agriculture dramatized so vividly in novels like *Tess* drove many off the land and destroyed the traditional village life that had sustained the cottager and the rural laborer.

In effect, these vast and rapid changes meant that status was more and more what you yourself could make it. If you were Eugene Hexam, you tried to have people treat you as a solid member of the middle class. If you were Ferdinand Lopez or Pip, you asked to be taken seriously as a gentleman. Progress into a higher class necessitated mastery of various social rituals, speech patterns, and even habits of spending. Estella makes fun of Pip in *Great Expectations* for his "coarse hands," and we are told of Lizzie Eustace in *The Eustace Diamonds* that to be "lady-like" she insists on never combing her own hair or doing even the most trivial of tasks associated with putting on or maintaining her wardrobe. These were part of the prejudice against manual labor that marked someone as having aspirations to gentility. In fact, the resolute display of a hopeless inability to do anything oneself became increasingly the distinguishing mark of a lady or gentleman as the century wore on, and along with it, of course, went a growing reliance on servants.

Indeed, the first thing any household with pretensions to middle-class status did was to hire a housemaid or even a maid-of-all-work. When you really arrived, you hired a manservant, an index of social propriety that reassures the timid maidens of the ladies' boarding school into whose midst Mr. Pickwick makes his erring way: " 'He must be respectable—he keeps a man-servant,' said Miss Tomkins to the writing and ciphering governess." This was something of a change, as Jane Austen's nephew pointed out in a memoir of his aunt written in 1870. "Less was left to the charge and discretion of servants, and more was done, or superintended, by the masters and mistresses," he writes of her era. "Ladies did not disdain to spin the thread of which the household linen was woven. . . . A young man who expected to have his things packed or unpacked for him by a servant, when he travelled, would have been thought exceptionally fine, or exceptionally lazy. When my uncle undertook to teach me to shoot, his first lesson was how to clean my own gun."

But as the century wore on, more and more of the attributes of status fell into the category of behavior to be avoided—and things that could be "acquired." One had at all costs to avoid doing manual labor, and also one could not be "in trade." And what things should one try to acquire? Stated baldly, if you were well-off, you had to have a carriage and servants, and, if you had real pretensions, you had to have land, an ancient family, and a title—probably in that order.

If you already *had* a carriage and servants and were socially ambitious, then you wanted land and—hopefully—a distinguished and ancient pedigree. "She has no fair pretence of family or blood," observes Mr. Weston crushingly of Mrs. Churchill in *Emma*. An ancient pretension to family grandeur in and of itself, of course, was ridiculous if there were nothing to back it up; this is the moral of the absurd pretensions of Tess Durbeyfield's father, but they are echoed in the aspirations of Alec's father, Mr. Simon Stoke, the imitation d'Urberville in *Tess* who digs the name d'Urberville out of a book in the British Museum while looking for "a name that would not readily identify him with the smart tradesman of the past." Minimally, it would seem, descent from a Norman family was imperative. The parson tells Durbeyfield "that you are the lineal representative of the ancient and knightly family of the d'Urbervilles, who derive their descent from Sir Pagan d'Urberville, that renowned knight who came from Normandy with William the Conqueror." The Normans, after all, had created the whole system of lords of the manor whose descendants continued down through the nineteenth century to exact fealty from their social inferiors. Is it an accident that Mr. Darcy—was it not probably d'Arcy at one point?—and his relative, Lady Catherine de Bourgh, have a suggestion of something French about their names?

Land was perhaps more the key than anything else to real social distinction. You certainly needed land to support a peerage with the appropriate style, and at one time it was fashionable to reward poor but impoverished military heroes with great chunks of land along with their titles so they wouldn't disgrace the peerage. "A Countess living at an inn is a ruined woman," as Sir Pitt Crawley sneers of his mother-in-law in *Vanity Fair*. Not that you would expect to get a peerage right away if you bought land, but if you were middle class it was vital to the attainment of any genuine social status. "Mr. Bingley," we are informed in *Pride and Prejudice*, "inherited property to the amount of nearly a hundred thousand pounds from his father, who had intended to purchase an estate, but did not live to do it. Mr. Bingley intended likewise, and sometimes made choice of his county," but then changed his mind—which drove his social-climbing siblings crazy: "his sisters were very anxious for his having an estate of his own." Once settled, it was recommended by a contemporary that one try to marry a daughter to one of the county gentry and at the same time try to become a justice of the peace.

Above all, people craved a title, the problem being that as you got down among the lower reaches of the gentry there was a danger that *anybody* could become a baronet or knight—as Jane Austen is quick to point out. That friend of the Bennets', for example, "Sir William Lucas had been formerly in trade in Meryton, where he had made a tolerable fortune and risen to the honour of knighthood by an address to the King, during his mayoralty. The distinction," Austen adds loftily, "had perhaps been felt too strongly."

But no one ever said it would all be easy. The easiest way to be in this enviable position was to have a huge estate, the sort of property that went with all old feudal families and obviated the necessity for working because you simply collected the rents from your tenant farmers. "You misled me by the term *gentleman*," observes a character in *Persuasion*. "I thought you were speaking of some man of property."

Nor did the socially hopeful wish to be in trade. Why? Because being a gentleman or lady denoted freedom, in true aristocratic fashion, from the need to earn a living. As George Eliot observes of Dorothea Brooke's forbears in *Middlemarch*, "the Brooke connections, though not exactly aristocratic, were unquestionably 'good': if you inquired backward for a generation or two, you would not find any yard-measuring or parcel-tying forefathers."

A barrister's wife could be presented at court while a solicitor's could not. Surely, this was in some measure because the solicitor took fees directly, i.e., was in trade, while the barrister only received an honorarium. Doctors, it was said, could rarely rise to the peerage, and at least one contemporary observer noted approvingly that this made sense in view of the fact that they actually accepted money from people, i.e., seemed to be in trade.

One should not be in trade, and one should avoid manual labor. Hence, for status one needed servants. There was one other minimal prerequisite to respectable middle-class status besides servants. "Lady Fawn and her daughters," says Trollope in *The Eustace Diamonds*, "were poor rich people. . . . The old family carriage and the two lady's maids were there—as necessaries of life." "Your father's only a merchant, Osborne," says the long-suffering Dobbin to the unbearable George Osborne one day at school in *Vanity Fair*.

"My father's a gentleman, and keeps his carriage," retorts the obnoxious boy. Carriages were an enormous status symbol; it is a measure of the devotion felt by some Victorian heroines for their husbands that they submit when all looks black to the prospect of being able to live with only one carriage.

Education and upbringing were important to gentlemanly status, too. "A clergyman is a gentleman by profession and education," observes Mr. Riley in *The Mill on the Floss*. The story of the nineteenth century is, in fact, that of the efforts of many to obliterate their humble origins in an ascent to gentlemanly status with*out* a great landed estate. This upward mobility through education is, in some measure, the story of *Great Expectations*, where Magwitch determines to make a "gentleman" of Pip.

SOCIETY
Society and "The Season"

*T*he chief target of the socially ambitious—and the main arena of those who had already arrived—was London. The fancy London

In the season.

society that swirls on the outskirts of Trollope's Palliser novels and glitters just beyond the reach of the social-climbing Veneerings in *Our Mutual Friend* was composed of perhaps some 1,500 families in all, totaling among them some 10,000 people.

In London, "Society" dwelt within a relatively small area of the West End. The most desirable residences were right next to Hyde Park on Park Lane, the western border of Mayfair and the residence in *Vanity Fair* of the selfish old Miss Crawley whose £70,000 Becky Sharp schemes to obtain. Then, just east of the park, came Grosvenor Square and Berkeley Square in Mayfair itself. Farther south and west was the still respectable area of St. James, where Pall Mall and its clubs were, and Buckingham Palace, and even farther south was the slightly less desirable but still fashionable area of Belgrave Square. Society shopped on Bond Street and Regent Street, and the latter—for men, after the theater and dinner—was the place to meet unmarried ladies of a more forthcoming sexuality than those whose prospects and futures were so carefully chaperoned by the anxious mammas and papas of the regions farther north. This was "the Belgrave-cum-Pimlico life, the scene of which might extend itself to South Kensington, enveloping the parks and coming round over Park Lane, and through Grosvenor Square and Berkeley Square back to Piccadilly. Within this," thinks the young Frank Greystock, trying to decide on a course of life in *The Eustace Diamonds*, "he might live with lords and countesses and rich folk generally, going out to the very best dinner-parties, having everything the world could give."

As a rule, the nobility and gentry began coming to town to the West End from their country estates sometime around Christmas to prepare for the opening of Parliament. "The season depends on Parliament," wrote a contemporary, "and Parliament depends upon sport." Until then shooting and fox hunting made leaving the countryside more or less unthinkable, or, as an observer put it, "the sessions of Parliament cannot be held til the frost is out of the ground and the foxes begin to breed."

In London, it was up early to go riding in Hyde Park, preferably on the sandy track known as Rotten Row (there was also the Ladies' Mile for the women), then home for breakfast. Shopping and paying bills for the ladies and making calls on those one knew extremely well came next. Then lunch, followed for men by the club—if they were not in Parliament or it was not in session just then—while the ladies took to their carriages to leave cards and to pay still more calls.

Dinner followed at around six or seven and in the evening there were soirees or the opera (dinner parties, too, especially on the Wednesdays and Saturdays when there were no evening parliamentary sessions) and then balls or dances starting at ten or later that could go until three o'clock in the morning.

The height of the season, however, did not come until sometime after the opening of Parliament, and through midwinter, indeed, up through March, many families still remained in the country. Drawing rooms and levees at St. James's Palace were rarely crowded as yet, people actually *went* to the opera or the theater, and you could still afford the luxury of stopping to chat if you encountered a friend on your way up Piccadilly. It was not until after a short Easter holiday—during which Parliament adjourned and families returned briefly to the country—that the real season began, a dizzying three-month whirlwind of parties, balls, and sporting events. In May came the annual exhibition at the Royal Academy of Art, the first of the gala court balls and concerts, and the beginning of the round of debutante-delighting private balls and dances. Despite all the surface gaiety, these latter gatherings revolved around the deadly serious business of marrying off the young girls of the family to eligible and wealthy young men in what Trollope and others referred to as the "marriage market." This could be done only with difficulty in the country, given the relative paucity of prospects, but at the round of balls, concerts, and gay parties which the London season offered, there were such great numbers of wealthy and titled young men and women brought together from all over England that it was inconceivable that demure young Lady Elizabeth wouldn't catch *some-body's* eye once she was "out." In fact, her first season marked a dramatic turning point in the life of a well-bred young girl. Until she was seventeen or eighteen, she was not considered socially alive and, in a telling phrase of the era, was deemed to be "in the schoolroom"; at dinners when guests were present she did not speak unless spoken to and then it was only to answer questions yes or no. "A girl not out, has always the same sort of dress," observes Miss Crawford in *Mansfield Park*, "a close bonnet for instance, looks demure, and never says a word." She was not to encourage or entertain romantic attentions from the opposite sex. Then, overnight, everything changed: she was suddenly expected to dress and wear her hair in an adult fashion, and she "came out," which meant that she was formally presented along with a host of other young debutantes to the sovereign in a formal drawing room at St. James.

It was, naturally, a momentous and eagerly anticipated event in a girl's life. "Before the carriage arrived in Russell Square," Thackeray tells us as Amelia Sedley and Becky Sharp leave Miss Pinkerton's Academy for the great world at the start of *Vanity Fair*, "a great deal of conversation had taken place about the Drawing-room, and whether or not young ladies wore powder as well as hoops when presented."

Having once been presented, the young girl embarked on an extraordinary round of balls and dances and similarly festive affairs—when she came out in 1849 Lady Dorothy Neville attended "50 balls, 60 parties, 30 dinners and 25 breakfasts." All this was with a serious goal in mind. If the girl did not get herself married within two to three seasons she was considered a failure; at thirty a hopeless, permanent spinster. Men, even a man like the crass Thomas Bertram in *Mansfield Park*, were apparently aware that they were supposed to focus only on the "eligible" girls. Recounting a stroll with two sisters, he says, "I afterwards found out that I had been giving all my attention to the youngest, who was not *out*, and had most excessively offended the eldest. Miss Augusta ought not to have been noticed for the next six months, and Miss Sneyd, I believe, has never forgiven me." Someone else commiserates with the absent Miss Sneyd: "To be neglected before one's time must be very vexatious," adding, "But it was entirely the mother's fault. Miss Augusta should have been with her governess."

In May or June came the two great annual sporting events of the season—the Derby, which had to be shared with the masses because of its overwhelming popularity and for which Parliament always adjourned, and then Ascot, some thirty miles from London, a much more exclusive horse race altogether. July witnessed the Henley Regatta along with various climactic cricket contests—notably between Oxford and Cambridge, and between Eton and Harrow—at "Lord's" on the outskirts of London. And now, suddenly, as the eponymous young M.P. and hero of *Phineas Finn* notices, a new air of expectancy would begin to manifest itself in society, for "everyone around him seemed to be looking forward to pleasant leisure days in the country. Men talked about grouse, and of the ladies at the houses to which they were going and of the people whom they were to meet." Naturally, for it was only a short time until August 12, which, when it came, signaled alike the end of the season, the adjournment of Parliament, and the retreat of everyone who was anyone to the north—August 12 marked the opening of the grouse season. The fashionable deserted London altogether at this point. If you were lucky, you went north to your "grouse moor" in Scotland or else wangled an invitation from someone who *had* one, thereby inaugurating a period of some months devoted to the persecution of small animals that would last until people went "up" to "town" again the next winter. Partridge shooting began on September 1, and the pheasant season opened October 1, while "cub hunting," the preseason practice hunting of immature foxes with inexperienced riders, got under way at approximately the same time. On the first Monday of November there came the traditional opening of the fox-hunting season.

And then it was back to town to start the whole thing all over again.

Basic Etiquette

The Gentleman

1. In riding horseback or walking along the street, the lady always has the wall.
2. Meeting a lady in the street or in the park whom you know only slightly, you wait for her acknowledging bow—then and only then may you tip your hat to her, which is done using the hand farthest away from her to raise the hat. You do not speak to her—or to any other lady—unless she speaks to you first.
3. If you meet a lady who is a good friend and who signifies that she wishes to talk to you, you turn and walk with her if you wish to converse. It is not "done" to make a lady stand talking in a street.
4. In going up a flight of stairs, you precede the lady (running, according to one authority); in going down, you follow.
5. In a carriage, a gentlemen takes the seat facing backward. If he is alone in a carriage with a lady, he does not sit next to her unless he is her husband, brother, father, or son. He alights from the carriage first so he may hand her down. He takes care not to step on her dress.
6. At a public exhibition or concert, if accompanied by a lady, he

goes in first in order to find her a seat. If he enters such an exhibition alone and there are ladies or older gentlemen present he removes his hat.

7. A gentleman is always introduced to a lady—never the other way around. It is presumed to be an honor for the gentleman to meet her. Likewise (and it is the more general rule of which this is only a specific example), a social inferior is always introduced to a superior—and only with the latter's acquiescence. Elizabeth Bennet is horrified when the obtuse Mr. Collins insists on *introducing himself* to Mr. Darcy in *Pride and Prejudice*. She tries to persuade "him that Mr. Darcy would consider his addressing him without introduction as an impertinent freedom, rather than a compliment to his aunt; that it was not in the least necessary there should be any notice on either side, and that if it were, it must belong to Mr. Darcy, the superior in consequence, to begin the acquaintance."

8. A gentleman never smokes in the presence of ladies.

The Lady

Her rules of conduct are perhaps simpler.

1. If unmarried and under thirty, she is never to be in the company of a man without a chaperone. Except for a walk to church or a park in the early morning, she may not walk alone but should always be accompanied by another lady, a man, or a servant. An even more restrictive view is that "if she cannot walk with her younger sisters and their governess, or the maid cannot be spared to walk with her, she had better stay at home or confine herself to the square garden."

2. Under no circumstances may a lady call on a gentleman alone unless she is consulting that gentleman on a professional or business matter.

3. A lady does not wear pearls or diamonds in the morning.

4. A lady never dances more than three dances with the same partner.

5. A lady should never "cut" someone, that is to say, fail to acknowledge their presence after encountering them socially, unless it is absolutely necessary. By the same token, only a lady is ever truly justified in cutting someone: "a cut is only excusable when men persist in bowing whose acquaintance a lady does not wish to keep up." Upon the approach of the offender, a simple stare of silent iciness should suffice; followed, if necessary, by a

"cold bow, which discourages familiarity without offering insult," and departure forthwith. To remark, "Sir, I have not the honour of your acquaintance" is a very extreme measure and is a weapon that should be deployed only as a last resort.

How to Address the Nontitled

*I*t must not be Lucy any longer, Lord Lufton; I was madly foolish when I first allowed it." This quote from Trollope's *Framley Parsonage* shows that it was just as problematic to converse with people informally as it was to get their titles straight. That is, there were rules even within the family and among friends as to how you addressed people, titled or not, and a breach of these rules could be a blunder in etiquette as severe as sending the wrong lady down to dinner first at a dinner party.

To his wife, the man of the house was quite often "Mr. ————," just as he called her "Mrs.————." (To call one's husband "Thompson" was not a sign of good breeding, however; to call him "T." was hopelessly vulgar.) Daughters customarily addressed their parents as "mama" and "papa" (the accent in well-bred circles being always on the second syllable); as the unspeakable Mrs. General instructs the heroine in *Little Dorrit*, "Papa is a preferable form of address. . . . Father is rather vulgar, my dear." However, this was not true for males. The boys would call their parents "father" and "mother." When outsiders spoke of the family, the eldest daughter was differentiated from the other daughters by being called "Miss" followed only by her surname, while the other daughters were spoken of by "Miss" and the Christian name, if not by both Christian name and surname. Thus, the traveling Dorrits are entered on a hotel register as William Dorrit, Esquire; Frederick Dorrit, Esquire; Edward Dorrit, Esquire; Miss Dorrit; Miss Amy Dorrit.

Outsiders, even women friends, at least in Jane Austen's time, generally addressed the women of the family as "Mrs." or "Miss," as the case might be, followed by the surname, until a great deal of intimacy had been achieved. It was sufficiently rare for these formalities to be dropped that in *Vanity Fair* Thackeray mentions as a sign of remarkable sudden sympathy that "the girls Christian-named each other at once." If the speaker were male and the lady—young or not—an unmarried woman, use of a first name was unpardonable, as poor Lucy instructs Lord Lufton, unless the two were—or were about to be—engaged. "Mrs. Greenow—may I say Arabella?" begs Farmer Cheesacre in *Can You Forgive Her?* "Mr. Cheesacre!" says Mrs. Greenow. "But mayn't I? Come, Mrs. Greenow. You know well enough by this time what it is I mean." "My dear young lady—Miss Brooke—Dorothea!" gushes Mr. Casaubon in atypical rapture when Dorothea accepts his marriage proposal, "this is a happiness greater than I had ever imagined to be in reserve for me."

When Casaubon subsequently introduces Dorothea to his cousin, Will Ladislaw, Casaubon as we would expect, observes the proper formalities. "Dorothea, let me introduce to you my cousin, Mr. Ladislaw. Will, this is Miss Brooke." The introduction by Casaubon of Ladislaw as "Mr.," notwithstanding Will and Dorothea's youth, is not excessively formal. In *Pride and Prejudice,* Mrs. Bennet habitually refers to the men of the younger generation courting her daughters as "Mr." Darcy and "Mr." Bingham. (Not unlike the formality of "Miss" for young women.) Young males enjoyed a peculiarly informal yet potentially intimate relationship with their female cousins. As Trollope noted, "Cousins are Tom, and Jack, and George, and Dick . . . cousins are about the same as brothers, and yet they may be lovers." Among themselves gentlemen would habitually address one another by surname only. Someone like Casaubon would normally deviate from this observance only when, as in his introduction of "Will," the person addressed was within the family circle.

To the servants the master and mistress of the house were "sir" and "madam," and the unmarried daughters would be "miss," the boys—depending on age—usually either "master" or "sir." Catherine Linton is confused on her first visit to Wuthering Heights when she meets Hareton Earnshaw and—uncouth though he is—he seems to act as if he has some right of proprietorship to the place. "I thought he had been the owner's son. And he never said, Miss: he should have done, shouldn't he, if he's a servant?" she asks. The family, on the other hand, would address the butler by his surname ("Horrocks" is Sir Pitt Crawley's butler in *Vanity Fair*), and the housekeeper as "Mrs.," even if she were unmarried. The cook in grander households was also "Mrs."; otherwise just "Cook." Other indoor servants were generally called by their first names only, and

sometimes even that dignity was denied them. In some families, a
string of underservants in succession in the same position all might
be called by the same first name because the family did not want to
be bothered learning a new one each time a replacement was hired.
(Footmen were invariably John, Charles, or James.) Or a serving
woman named Mary might become Alice if a wife or daughter in the
employer's household were named Mary, and sometimes the reason
for a name change seems to have been pure whim. When Mr.
Dombey hires Mrs. Toodle as a wetnurse, he instructs her, "While
you are here, I must stipulate that you are always known as—say as
Richards—an ordinary name, and convenient. Have you any objec-
tion to be known as Richards?"

The first quadrille.

"May I Have This Dance?"

I consider a country-dance as an emblem of marriage," says John Thorpe to Catherine Morland in *Northanger Abbey*.

"But they are such very different things!" she says.

"—That you think they cannot be compared together."

"To be sure not. People that marry can never part, but must go and keep house together. People that dance only stand opposite each other in a long room for half an hour."

This peculiar business of standing around during a country-dance—likewise, in *Pride and Prejudice*, during the Netherfield ball Elizabeth Bennet and Mr. Darcy get up to dance and then "they stood for some time without speaking a word; and she began to imagine that their silence was to last through the two dances." is a good deal less puzzling if we realize these were glorified square dances. Although the country-dance dated back to the 1600s in one form or another, by Jane Austen's time the dance had assumed its quintessential nineteenth-century form, in which three or more couples, the men and women in separate lines some four feet apart, facing one another, danced their way through a series of figures.

A figure was merely a sequence of movements, like those in square dances in which men and ladies opposite one another advanced and then retreated, or locked arms and swung around, or do-si-doed (from the French *dos-à-dos*), or wove their way through the other dancers. Depending on the nature of the figures, all the couples might be in motion at once, or only one or two, with the rest following the leading or "top couple" in sequence—each dance could vary considerably in form at the pleasure of the dancers. Those danced by the partners in *Northanger Abbey* at the Bath Assembly rooms and by Elizabeth Bennet and Mr. Darcy at Meryton evidently involved the other couples standing idly by while the top couple or their successors were in motion. This period of inactivity is what allowed time for the long, bantering Austenian conversations. In the case of *Emma*, it enabled the heroine to eavesdrop on Mr. Elton: "she was not yet dancing; she was working her way up from the bottom, and had therefore leisure to look around, and by only turning her head a little, she saw it all. When she was half-way up the set, the whole group were exactly behind her, and she would no longer allow her eyes to watch; but Mr. Elton was so near that she heard every syllable of a dialogue which just then took place between him and Mrs. Weston." The number of couples also affected the length of a dance (and, thereby, conversations while dancing). If there were only three couples—the minimum—you might be able to whiz through a dance in five minutes. If there were twenty or more in the "set" of dancers, however, it might take an hour.

At the other extreme is the country dancing at Mr. Fezziwig's party for his family and apprentices which the Ghost of Christmas Past conjures up from Scrooge's part (in which constant movement rather than standing around predominated): "Away they all went, twenty couple at once, hands half round and back again the other way; down the middle and up again; round and round in various stages of affectionate grouping; old top couple always turning up in the wrong place; new top couple starting off again, as soon as they got there; all top couples at last, and not a bottom one to help them."

A sure-fire crowd-pleaser that was almost invariably the last dance on a formal program was the "Sir Roger de Coverley." It also seems to have become associated with Christmas. In *Silas Marner*, it is the signal to begin the dance at Squire Cass's annual Christmas party; in *A Christmas Carol*, as was probably more common, it closes out the evening's festivities, with the Fezziwigs once again top couple, going through all the figures: "advance and retire, hold hands with your partner; bow and curtsey; corkscrew; thread-the-needle, and back to your place."

Dickens could describe the "Roger de Coverley" in such detail because it was the one country-dance whose figures never changed. It was, in fact, the dance American square dancers know as the Virginia reel. Bottom man and top lady retire and advance, bottom lady and top man do the same, the couples then repeat the steps, linking arms, and then the top man and top lady weave their way in and out down their sex's line, join hands at the bottom and promenade on up—with the next couple repeating the figures until all the couples have gone through the same sequence. It was a natural for sending everyone off into the night in a convivial and neighborly frame of mind.

As the new century wore on, however, the country dancing of couples dancing in a group gave way to the more intimate—and socially isolating—waltz.

The waltz was no doubt more suited to the anonymous, citified society that England was increasingly becoming, a society where

even the partners—let alone the other couples—were often unknown to each other. The social logic of the waltz, indeed, lay in a
direction other than that of the country-dance—attention was
focussed exclusively on the couple rather than on the group—and
conversation became secondary to the intoxication of the now constant, swirling movement (so unlike that of the country-dance), as
we see in *Can You Forgive Her?* when Lady Glencora Palliser's old
flame, Burgo Fitzgerald, shows up at Lady Monk's ball to try quite
literally to sweep Lady Glencora off her feet and out of her marriage—" 'I will go up to her at once, and ask her to waltz,' Burgo said
to himself." So he does. "And then they were actually dancing,
whirling around the room together. . . . Burgo waltzed excellently,
and in old days, before her marriage, Lady Glencora had been
passionately fond of dancing. She seemed to give herself up to it now
as though the old days had come back to her. Lady Monk, creeping
to the intermediate door between her den and the dancing room,
looked in on them and then crept back again. Mrs. Marsham and
Mr. Bott standing together just inside the other door, near to the
staircase, looked on also—in horror." By the 1850s the country-
dance and the minuet had been replaced by the waltz and the only
real survivor of the collective dancing of the old days was a descendant of the country-dance named the quadrille. This was a dance
performed by four couples, each of which occupied one point of a
diamond. The quadrille was used to open virtually every fashionable
ball until almost the end of the century—it could be varied in theory,
like the country-dance, but in practice it usually consisted of five
figures, which collectively incorporated such square-dance figures as
the do-si-do. (There was also a complicated variant known as the
lancers, after the cavalry units of the same name, which never
rivaled the original quadrille in popularity.)

It would seem, however, that the quadrille rapidly became a
chore to be got through while you waited for the waltz to begin. A
mid-century etiquette book advised that a young lady need know
only the figures—not the steps—as she prepared to "walk" through
it. It took so long, moreover, that a gentleman was advised to lay in
a half hour's store of conversation while the tedious figures were
gone through. *Punch* noted in a satirical piece on the coquette that
"she will walk a quadrille with a county member, but will not, if
possible, waltz with any thing under a peer."

The Rules of Whist
and Other Card Games

*O*ne cannot seem to make it through any Jane Austen book without a brush with whist, speculation, quadrille, or casino. And not only Jane Austen. Dickens's people play all-fours and Pope Joan, Trollope's characters play whist, and in *Vanity Fair* Rawdon Crawley turns out to be an ecarte man. And what would the drawing rooms and card parties of nineteenth-century England have been without loo?

What were these games like?

Many games, such as whist, were to be played with a specific number of players. Others, however, like loo, commerce, and speculation, were "round games"; that is, theoretically, any number could play. The player on the dealer's right was sometimes called the "pony," the person on his left the "elder hand." When the dealer dealt, say, five cards to every player, that was the player's "hand." (The dealer's leftover cards were sometimes called the "stock.") When each of the players played one of his or her cards in sequence in a round of play with everyone else, it was often called a "trick." A "rubber" usually consisted of three or more games. As for the cards themselves, the highest suit in a game—sometimes determined at the game's outset by simply turning over a card—was the "trump" suit. The little clubs or hearts or other emblems that marked the particular suit of a card were called the "pips"; in whist the jack, king, queen, or ace of the trump suit were sometimes called "honors."

All-Fours—Known as high-low-jack in America, in Dickens it seems to turn up as a game for somewhat raffish characters, like the doctor and his scruffy friend who play it in the Marshalsea Prison in *Little Dorrit*. There are two, sometimes four, players. The idea is to get the highest score with your six cards, the game being to ten or eleven points. The high trump, the low trump, the jack of trumps, and the highest number of pips each counts as one.

Beggar My Neighbor—The game played by Pip, appropriately, the first time he encounters Estella at Miss Havisham's. The two players divide the cards between them and then turn over their top cards in sequence. When one of them turns up an ace, king, queen, or jack, the other must give up, respectively, four, three, two, or one of his own cards, except that if in doing so *he* turns up an ace, king, queen, or jack, the other must play to him. The winner is the person who ends up with all the cards. The players begin to play in *Great Expectations*, and Miss Havisham's vengeful delight can scarcely be contained—"Beggar him," she cries, and at the end, says Pip, Estella "threw the cards down on the table when she had won them all, as if she despised them for having been won of me."

Casino—(also spelled cassino)—In *Sense and Sensibility*, a game played by Lady Middleton, who is somewhat lacking in inner resources. David Copperfield "used to go back to the prison, and walk up and down the parade with Mr. Micawber; or play casino with Mrs. Micawber" when her husband was thrown in the King's Bench Prison. Each of the two players (each may have one partner) is dealt four cards down. Beginning with the eldest hand, each player must match—and take—the card face up; or else build on it, e.g., play a 4 to a 3, so on the next round—if no one else can—he matches and takes them with a 7, or just puts down a card and takes nothing. You play until all the cards are used up or one player gets 21.

Commerce—Basically, an old form of poker. Three cards are dealt down, which you can discard if you wish, and then you try to get three of a kind, a three-card straight flush, a flush of three, a pair and "point," the latter being the biggest number of pips in one hand.

Cribbage—A game that seems to have been associated with lengthy, subdued evenings of recreation among the elderly. Two players (generally) are each dealt six cards and then discard or "lay out" two of them into a "crib." Cards are turned over, with each player in putting down his card trying to get a 15, a pair, a "sequence" (a straight), or 31. Points are recorded by moving pegs around a board with tiny little holes in it.

Ecarte—A popular gambling game, played, not surprisingly, by Rawdon Crawley in *Vanity Fair*. Generally, a two-person game, though at one time played with spectators betting on the game. You deal five cards to each player after removing the 2s through 6s from the deck. Players may try to discard if they wish.

Euchre—For two to four players. The 2s through 6s are removed from the deck and then five cards are dealt to each player. To be "euchred" is to get fewer than three tricks.

Faro—A gambling game in which players bet on the order in which cards will turn up when dealt off the bottom of a deck. Except that they are not exactly "dealt." The dealer uses a faro box—a machine with a spring in it that pops up the cards.

Loo—A round game in which, apparently, play is best restricted to five to seven participants. Everyone gets three cards down, and an extra hand is dealt down for the benefit of all called a "miss." The players make their bets before dealing is completed and then may put down their hand and take up the miss, pass, or play from their hand, the high card of the suit led or highest trump winning the trick.

Ombre—An old-fashioned card game, probably already out of fashion in Jane Austen's time, that took its name from the Spanish word for "man." The ombre plays against the other two, each being dealt nine cards from a forty-card deck which has had the 8s, 9s, and 10s removed. The ombre gets to discard and also to designate the trump suit. The play is like whist.

Patience—The game of solitaire.

Piquet (also spelled picquet)—Two players are each dealt twelve cards from a pack with no 2s, 3s, 4s, 5s, or 6s, the remaining eight cards being available for exchange. The elder hand then enumerates the cards in his hands, first by "point" (being the highest number of cards of one slot he holds and, if the other player has an equal number, "point" going to the player with the highest value in pips in those cards), then by a flush of three or more (e.g., "tierce," "quart," "quint"), then how many 4s or 3s of a kind he has, his opponent each time responding "not good," "good," or "equal," corresponding to whether he can do better, worse, or the same. A number of tricks are played thus.

Pope Joan—Apparently a convivial, cheerful game to be played on festive occasions—Christmas in *The Last Chronicle of Barset*—or within the family circle, as with the merry-makers at Dingley Dell in *Pickwick*. A round game, it drew its name from a supposed ninth-century female pope and was played with a deck that had no 8 of diamonds and with a board with divisions marked "Pope Joan," "Intrigue," "Matrimony," "Ace," "King," "Queen," "Knave," and "Game." The idea was to play the card next highest to the one that had just been placed on the table, those with various winning combinations getting stakes that had been placed in the different divisions of the board. At Dingley Dell, "when the spinster aunt got 'matrimony,' the young ladies laughed afresh, and the spinster aunt seemed disposed to be pettish; till, feeling Mr. Tupman squeezing her hand under the table, she brightened up."

Quadrille—"Mrs. Bates," we are told in *Emma*, "was a very old lady, almost past everything but tea and quadrille." It was a variation of ombre, which it replaced in popularity in the early 1700s. It was played by four people with a deck from which the 8s, 9s, and 10s had been removed.

Speculation—A round game in which you ante up a set amount, the dealer anteing up double. Each player gets three cards, and another is turned face up to determine the trump. The players take turns turning up cards until someone has a higher card than the trump. He may then sell it, if he wishes. The holder of the highest trump takes the pot. In *Mansfield Park* Mary Crawford characteristically, while playing, "made a hasty finish of her dealings with William Price, and securing his knave at an exorbitant rate, exclaimed, 'There, I will stake my last like a woman of spirit. No cold prudence for me. I am not born to sit still and do nothing. If I lose the game, it shall not be from not striving for it.'"

Vingt-et-un—Basically, the American game of 21, in which players try to get cards whose face value is 21 or as close to that number as possible without going over it.

Whist—A game for two couples, the partners sitting opposite one another and each player being dealt thirteen cards. The first person puts down a card which the next person must match in suit if he can. Otherwise, he must play the trump suit or discard. The person who plays the highest trump or the highest card of the suit led wins the trick and leads for the next trick. Points are won according to the number of tricks played and, sometimes, the number of honors held, and a game is won by getting 5 or 10 points, depending on whether "short" or "long" whist is played. A "rubber" usually consists of the best two out of three games. Whist is the ancestor of bridge.

Whist and round games seem to have been viewed, respectively, as instances of rather stodgy, reflective card playing on the one hand and a more lighthearted, boisterous sort of play on the other, as in the speculation game in *Mansfield Park* when "the round table was altogether a very comfortable contrast to the steady sobriety and orderly silence of the [whist players]." In *Pickwick*, similarly, "the rubber was conducted with all that gravity of deportment and sedateness of demeanour which befit the pursuit entitled 'whist'—a solemn observance, to which, it appears to us, the title of 'game' has been very irreverently and ignominiously applied. The round-game table, on the other hand, was so boisterously merry as materially to interrupt the contemplations of [one of the whist players]."

Calling Cards and Calls

*I*n the 1800s suddenly more people were trying to get into "society," people who wanted to claim members of the elite as their friends or at least be acknowledged by them; people, in short, who wanted to be part of the social world of those who *were* the social world. What could the upper crust do with these pretenders?

The calling card and the "morning calls" served as nice ways, if not to keep these social aspirants forever at a distance, at least to hold them off for a while and perhaps to screen those who would be allowed some entree from those who would not. Accordingly, the calling card and the morning call, or visit, flourished during most of the nineteenth century.

The protocol for leaving cards was as follows: when you came to town, you drove around with your footman to the houses of those you wished to notify of your presence. ("The morning was chiefly spent," we are told in *Sense and Sensibility* of Mrs. Jennings's first day back in London, "in leaving cards at the houses of Mrs. Jennings's acquaintance to inform them of her being in town.") This was principally an activity of ladies. At each house, the footman took a small card bearing your name and two cards of your husband's (yours for the mistress of the house and one of his for both the master and the mistress) and gave them to the butler, who would put them on a salver inside the front hall or, in less fancy establishments, perhaps on the mantelpiece. Visitors then had a chance to see whom the family numbered among its social circle and be suitably impressed. In *Persuasion*, for example, the anxious social climbers took care for "the cards of Dowager Viscountess Dalrymple, and the

Hon. Miss Carteret, to be arranged where they might be most visible," and when Becky Sharp receives cards from the marchioness of Steyne and the countess of Gaunt, "you may be sure they occupied a conspicuous place in the china bowl on the drawing-room table, where Becky kept the cards of her visitors." (Mr. Gunter insults Mr. Noddy in *The Pickwick Papers* by refusing him his card "because you'll stick it up over your chimney-piece, and delude your visitors into the false belief that a gentleman has been to see you, sir.") If there were daughters living at the home you were calling on, you might leave separate cards for them and for any guests of the household, too. If you were calling with an unmarried daughter or daughters in tow, they did not generally leave cards of their own but you wrote their name or names under your own name on your card before handing it to the footman to be delivered. The object of all this, of course, was to renew—or solicit—acquaintance, and, of course, those who were suddenly wealthy or famous could expect to receive a deluge of cards, like Mr. Dorrit, who becomes suddenly allied with the fraudulent but immensely sought-after Mr. Merdle. "Cards," says Dickens, "descended on Mr. Dorrit like theatrical snow. As the friend and relative by marriage of the illustrious Merdle, Bar, Bishop, Treasury, Chorus, Everybody wanted to make or improve Mr. Dorrit's acquaintance." In *Our Mutual Friend* the humble dustman Mr. Boffin is suddenly bequeathed an immense fortune: "Foremost among those leaving cards at the eminently aristocratic door before it is quite painted are the Veneerings—out of breath, one might imagine, from the impetuosity of their rush to the eminently aristocratic steps." In addition, "the enchanting Lady Tippins leaves a card. Twemlow leaves cards. A tall custard-coloured phaeton tooling up in a solemn manner leaves four cards, to wit, a couple of Mr. Podsnaps, a Mrs. Podsnap, and a Miss Podsnap. All the world and his wife and daughter leave cards."

It was understood that the lady of the house was then socially obliged to return a card to you, or, if she wished, she could make a call and actually visit you. A call, of course, counted for more than the mere leaving of a card. Indeed, you might try to "call" in the first instance rather than merely leave a card, although in doing so, naturally, you took a risk of rejection that you didn't when you merely left a card. Suppose you are bold, however; with a call, instead of merely leaving your card, you inquired if the lady were "at home." She was free to peer out of her drawing-room window on the second floor, see you and then whisper an emphatic "no" to her servant. This was perfectly acceptable, and it was understood that many people were *physically* at home when they were not *socially* "at home," although it was crass if they got caught. "She reached the house without any impediment, looked at the number, and inquired for Miss Tilney," we are told in *Northanger Abbey.* "The man believed Miss Tilney to be at home, but was not quite certain. Would she be pleased to send up her name? She gave her card. In a few minutes the servant returned, and with a look which did not quite confirm his words, said he had been mistaken, for that she was walked out." Catherine Morland leaves, we are told, "with a blush of mortification," but "at the bottom of the street, however, she looked back again, and then, not at the window, but issuing from the door, she saw Miss Tilney herself."

If the lady of the house wished to see you, however, you were invited to come inside and enter the drawing room (on the first floor in town houses, the ground floor in country mansions), the room in which a lady always received her visitors. If you were a gentleman, you took your hat and riding whip with you (umbrellas could be left downstairs), presumably to show you did not intend to stay long.

And nobody did, as a rule. If you were calling purely for the sake of formality (weddings, for example, demanded calls; "not to wait upon a bride," says Mr. Woodhouse in *Emma,* "is very remiss") you were expected to stay no more than fifteen minutes, and your call could be returned merely with a card. If another visitor appeared while you were making the polite chit-chat calls required, you eased your way slowly out, after an introduction—presuming it was to a socially inferior person, a social equal agreeable to being introduced, or a social superior who didn't mind—had been effected. No refreshments were offered, at least until the advent of afternoon tea in the latter part of the century. Conversation was supposed to be light and touch on safe, general topics like the weather and certainly not on friends whom another, strange caller might not be presumed to know. If you were not well acquainted with the callee, you made your call between three and four o'clock. If you were somewhat better acquainted, between four and five, and a good friend received you between five and six. These were all referred to as morning calls, notwithstanding the fact that they occurred in the afternoon or early evening, a carryover from the eighteenth century when "morning" often denoted the time before dinner, and dinner was often not until three or four in the afternoon. Certainly, no one but a great intimate would presume to actually call in the *real* morning, i.e., before one o'clock.

When you left town, you submitted a card with PPC written on it, short for *pour prendre congé,* French for "I'm leaving," and, if you were really new in town, you might sidestep this whole process by getting a letter of introduction from a friend to someone of prominence in the community. These were sometimes referred to as "tickets for soup" since they required as a minimum, generally, that the person receiving the letter invite the bearer to dinner.

It will have been apparent that paying and receiving calls was largely a female enterprise, in large part because many men were at work, hunting or shooting (in the country), or at their clubs during the day. Men could pay calls as well; however, they did not receive them from ladies, unless those ladies were of dubious reputation. It was a very strict rule that no lady ever called on a gentleman except upon a business or professional matter. To do otherwise, as a mid-century etiquette book stiffly put it, "would be, not only a breach of good manners, but of strict propriety." Thus, well as she knows Gabriel Oak, Bathsheba Everdene is in some doubt of the propriety of going to talk to him at the end of *Far from the Madding Crowd* after he announces he won't work for her anymore. At his door, "she tapped nervously, and then thought it doubtful if it were right for a single woman to call upon a bachelor who lived alone, although he was her manager, and she might be supposed to call on business without any real impropriety." The one obligatory time for a man to send out his own cards was upon his marriage, the receipt of the card signaling that you were respectable enough to be retained as a friend even though the new groom's bachelor days were now over. "When a man marries, it is understood that all former acquaintance *ends,* unless he intimates a desire to renew it, by sending you his own and his wife's card."

St. James's Street—Her Majesty's drawing room.

THE MAJOR RITUALS
Presentation at Court

*I*t marked the formal entrance of a young girl into fashionable society, her "coming out"—after which she was free, indeed, required, to marry. Young men were presented, too, after they left Oxford or Cambridge or had outgrown the awkwardness of adolescence. It might also mark a great occasion in your life, such as getting married, and, as presentation was a prerequisite to attending a court ball or concert, you had to be presented at some point if you were socially active, since everyone who was anyone attended at least one court function a year. In addition, Thackeray suggests, it was a means of certification for the morally dubious, such as Becky Sharp: "If she did not wish to lead a virtuous life, at least she desired to enjoy a character for virtue, and we know that no lady in the genteel world can possess this desideratum, until she has put on a train and feathers and has been presented to her Sovereign at Court. From that august interview they come out stamped as honest women."

Ladies were presented at "drawing rooms," men at "levees," both of them held at St. James's Palace. The requirements for presentation were very strict. Persons of rank could be presented; so, too, could the wives of clergy, military men, naval officers, physicians, and barristers, "these being the aristocratic professions." Wives of general practitioners, solicitors, businessmen, or merchants (except bankers) could *not* be presented, and at least during Victoria's reign, no divorcees or other ladies of a questionable past.

Men had to wear buckle shoes, knee breeches, and a sword. For ladies, dress was to include a train precisely three yards long and feathers to be placed at the back of the lady's head but that "must be high enough to be visible to Her Majesty when the lady enters the room." Neck and shoulders were to be bare no matter how cold the weather or august (or elderly) the lady unless a doctor's certificate had been obtained.

And when the great day actually came—?

Her train folded over her left arm, her wraps left behind in her carriage, a lady about to be presented was ushered into the long gallery at St. James's, where she awaited the summons to the Presence Chamber. When the time came, she entered the room by the door pointed out to her and made her way to the throne, having let down her train, which was spread out immediately by the attendant lords-in-waiting. A card bearing her name was handed to another lord-in-waiting, who announced her to Her Majesty. The lady then curtsied until she was almost kneeling, whereupon she kissed the queen's hand, unless the lady were a peer's daughter or a peeress, in which case the queen kissed her on the forehead. The lady then arose, curtsying once more to the queen and also to any other members of the royal family present, and then backed out of the room, not turning her face away from the queen.

Fitting a fire screen between a gentleman and the fire.

The Dinner Party

*T*his evening the Veneerings give a banquet," announces Dickens in *Our Mutual Friend.* "Fourteen in company, all told. Four pigeon-breasted retainers in plain clothes stand in line in the hall. A fifth retainer, preceding up the stair-case with a mournful air—as who should say, 'Here is another wretched creature come to dinner; such is life!'—announces, 'Mis-ter Twemlow!' "

Dinner parties were an ordeal—if not for the guests, then certainly for the hostess. They were given enormous space and attention in contemporary etiquette books for the upwardly anxious, perhaps with good reason, given the opportunities dinner parties offered for improving the acquaintance of those who could be helpful in one's way up the social ladder in a society whose middle class was increasingly upwardly mobile.

The dinner party began, naturally, with the selection of guests, a process that involved choosing people who would not fight or be socially uncomfortable together—the poor curate and the titled M.P., for example, could be expected to be an unhappy mix. Since the purpose of the enterprise was conversation, perhaps a total of ten guests all told would be fixed upon as a good number. The invitations were sent out (two days to two weeks in advance, depending on the grandeur of the event) by the lady of the house, and some form of reply was expected in return.

At the appointed hour, generally in the neighborhood of 7 P.M., on the appointed day, the guests arrived, although, after mid-century it was mandatory that one be precisely fifteen minutes late. The guests were then shown into the drawing room. (Note that the Veneering servant escorted Twemlow "up" the stairs, since the drawing room in a London town house was always on the first—our second—floor.) Everyone stood about making polite chitchat while waiting for the late arrivals. There was no shilly-shallying here, since this was a staging area for an assault on the food and not a cocktail party. Drinks were not served, and loquacity was not encouraged. The host and hostess circulated discreetly to make sure that the appropriate gentlemen were paired off with ladies of appropriate status and then arranged in order of precedence for purposes of the formal promenade in to dinner. This, since it often involved very tricky questions of status and rank, was probably in many cases the hostess's most nerve-ranking moment during the whole evening, and, if she were uncertain, she would be well advised to consult Debrett's or Burke's at this point to get her ranks straight. In *The Prime Minister*, the problem is complicated by the fact that two "young" people are of the party, and Mr. Wharton, the father of the girl, dislikes the boy, her suitor. Trollope tells us that Mrs. Roby pairs off several couples with no difficulty. "All that had been easy,—so easy that fate had good-naturedly arranged things which are sometimes difficult of management. But then there came an embarassment. Of course it would in a usual way be right that a married man such as Mr. Happerton should be assigned to the widow Mrs. Leslie, and that the only two 'young' people,—in the usual sense of the word,—should go down to dinner together. But Mrs. Roby was at first afraid of Mr. Wharton, and planned it otherwise. When, however, the last moment came she plucked up courage, gave Mrs. Leslie to the great commercial man, and with a brave smile asked Lopez to give his arm to the lady he loved. It is sometimes so hard to manage these 'little things,' said she to Lord Mongrober as she put her hand upon his arm." While this was going on, the guests would be able to check discreetly that their formal attire—black pants, waistcoat and jacket, with white tie, shirt, and gloves for the gentlemen; formal evening dress for the ladies—was in order.

The servant then announced that dinner was served.

The couples in order of status then proceeded "down" (in the town house the dining room would be on the ground, or entry-level, floor) or "in" (in the country house, dining and drawing rooms were generally both on the ground floor) to the dinner that would follow. Typically, the hostess would have arranged it so that the man of the house took the highest-ranking lady by the arm. Mrs. Roby, the hostess, takes the arm of the highest-ranking gentleman, Lord Mongrober, in *The Prime Minister*. They then led a grand procession of couples into the dining room, where, with any luck, a damasked tablecloth awaited them along with a butler and two footmen.

The man of the house seated his escort on his right, it having already been arranged, of course, for men and women to alternate down the table. They would not necessarily be able to see each other once seated; the epergne might have made its appearance in polite society by now, a great heavy, many-armed candlesticklike thing which sits ornamentally in the center of the table to add an "accent." Like the plate and various other objects and pieces of furniture, e.g., the sideboard, it might well serve the purpose of conspicuous display that the dinner party has, perhaps, in part been given to fulfill. "Hideous solidity was the characteristic of the Podsnap plate," says Dickens of their dinner party in *Our Mutual Friend*. "Everything was made to look as heavy as it could and to take up as much room as possible. Everything said boastfully, 'Here you have as much of me in my ugliness as if I were only lead; but I am so many ounces of precious metal worth so much an ounce—wouldn't you like to melt me down?' A corpulent straddling epergne, blotched all over as if it had broken out in an eruption rather than been ornamented, delivered this address from an unsightly silver platform in the centre of the table."

In the event it were summer or there were only a little chill in the air, a fire lit in the room some hours earlier might have been allowed to die down; in the event it were freezing, a roaring fire might be needed throughout dinner. To avoid roasting half the guests and freezing the other half in this latter event, a fire screen would be placed in front of the fire to shield those nearest from its direct blaze, or, probably less frequently, a horseshoe table might be used, with the open part of the shoe encircling the fire itself. Sometimes a guest was simply neglected, however. At Plantagenet Pal-

liser's Matching Priory in *Can You Forgive Her?* we are told Alice
Vasavor "occupied one side of the table by herself, away from the
fire, where she felt cold and desolate, in the gloom of the large
half-lighted room."

Then the eating began.

In *Can You Forgive Her?* Trollope describes a modest country
repast for a much humbler gathering than that assembled at Matching Priory, a group numbering the unattached Mrs. Greenow and
the rustic Farmer Cheesacre among its members. "The dinner was
exactly what a dinner ought to be for four persons. There was soup,
fish, a cutlet, a roast fowl, and some game." They got off easy. A
typical dinner given for a substantial group of, say, twelve, could
easily run to ten courses—not counting dessert, coffee, and wal-
nuts—and would probably be on the order of the repast described
by the contemporary author of *London at Dinner*. "A delicate soup
and turtle are handed round—nothing on the tables except flowers
and preserved fruits in old Dresden baskets, a bill of fare placed next
to every person, a turbot with lobster and Dutch sauces, carved by
an able domestic on the side-board, and a portion of red mullet with
Cardinal sauce are offered to every guest; cucumber and the essen-
tial cruet stands bringing up the rear. The 'flying dishes,' as the
modern cooks call the oyster or marrow *pates,* follow the fish. The
entrees are carried round, a *supreme de volaille aux truffes*, a sweet-
bread *au jus,* lamb cutlets, with asparagus, peas, a *fricandeau à
l'oseille.* . . . Either venison, roast saddle of mutton, or stewed beef
à la jardinière, are then produced, the accessories being salad, beetroot, vegetables, French and English mustard. A Turkey poult,
duckling, or green goose, commences the second course, peas and
asparagus following in their course; plovers' eggs in aspic jelly, a
mayonaise of fowl succeeding; a *macédoine* of fruit, *meringues à la
crème,* a marasquino jelly, and a chocolate cream, form the sweets.
Sardines, salad, beetroot, celery, anchovies, plain butter and cheese,
for those who are gothic enough to eat it. Two ices, cherry-water and
pineapple cream, with the fruit of the season, furnish the dessert.
Two servants or more, according to the number of the party, must
attend exclusively to the wine; sherry, Madeira, and champagne,
must ever be flowing during dinner."

Service was either *à la française* or—increasingly as the century
wore on—*à la russe.* The former meant that the dishes were left on
the table for the guests to serve themselves, which, among other
things, posed embarassing difficulties for the gentlemen who had not

mastered the mandatory art of carving. *A la russe*, on the other hand, involved having the footman appear discreetly at your elbow with the dish of the moment, from which you could then serve yourself, whereupon the footman retired, leaving the table free of serving dishes.

As the gentlemen began on their first course (or awaited its delivery by the silent footman), they were supposed to embark on polite conversation with the lady on their right. They then tucked themselves into the soup, after which the first of the wines was served, perhaps claret. The custom of "taking wine"—which called for catching the eye of someone else, looking meaningfully at them, and raising one's glass in their direction while they raised theirs eloquently back—would have vanished by the 1860s except in eccentric rustic households. In *Pickwick*, on the other hand, which, the author informs us, takes place in 1827, the custom was still apparently going strong. "Glass of wine, sir," says the "stranger" at dinner, to which Mr. Pickwick replies, "With pleasure," "and the stranger took wine, first with him, and then with Mr. Snodgrass, and then with Mr. Tupman, and then with Mr. Winkle, and then with the whole party together, almost as rapidly as he talked."

It was hard to get good help, as everyone sadly acknowledged. However, if the hostess had adequately prepared for the evening, the help should have been able to rise to the occasion. (The need of having *men* to serve at dinner sometimes necessitated pressing the gardener or groom into service when there were few male indoor staff, occasionally with inelegant or disastrous results.) The butler was in charge of the actual service of the meal, seeing to the wine himself and overseeing the carrying of the plates by the footmen. (They might often have had to carry dishes a considerable distance in a great country house, sometimes with silver covers to keep them warm, since the Victorians hated kitchen smells and—where possible—located their kitchens so far away from dining areas that it was no small trick to keep the food warm in transit.) There was no noise. The dining room would have been carpeted to eliminate the sound of the footmen's feet clattering against the oak floors; special noncreaking shoes for the help were also suggested in this connection. The footmen did not need to be told what to do—all this had been thoroughly explained earlier so that the main purpose of the evening—food and conversation—might proceed uninterrupted. If there *were* problems with the service, too bad. One did not *ever* talk to or about the servants during dinner.

Notwithstanding the vast number of dishes, guests were not expected to eat everything. It was understood that the board groaned under a plentitude of dishes and that even the fattest and most overstuffed red-faced Victorian could not ingest everything offered him. However, one was to eat certain things in a certain *way*. "In London it is not the custom to put the knife in the mouth," says Herbert Pocket to Pip in *Great Expectations* when he first arrives in London. This may seem like Pocket's facetious banter to a present-day reader, but the advice was echoed perfectly seriously by contemporary etiquette books. It had evidently been customary to eat peas, for example, in this manner. When Pocket tells Pip not to do so, it is because the custom still lingered in certain country areas. Fish was always eaten with a fork in the right hand, a piece of bread in the left—no knives. (Both fish and after-dinner fruit knives—the good hostess knew this—had to be of silver. In this pre-stainless-steel age it was found that fish and fruit juices discolored steel.)

Eventually the main courses came to an end. Now the tablecloth would be removed and dessert and champagne wines would be served. After the dessert, the ladies withdrew to the drawing room. Thus, Mortimer, we are told, leaves the Veneering dinner party to get a message after the meal "as the disappearing skirts of the ladies ascended the Veneering staircase." The ladies would proceed to the drawing room for coffee or tea, while the gentlemen circulated the port clockwise (or "way of the sun—through the button-hole" (that being on the left), as the "stranger" puts it in *Pickwick*).

The gentlemen might even smoke, something that was *never* done by a gentleman in the presence of a lady, even with her permission. This period of separation of the two sexes was not necessarily a long one—perhaps only half an hour. Weighty subjects might be touched on or racy stories told by the men, and an American guest was horrified in 1810 to discover a chamber pot being withdrawn from the sideboard and put to use—the conversation flowing freely all the while—during this period.

Eventually, however, the host would perceive that his guests were becoming too free in their speech and suggest that it was time to join the ladies. They then made their way to the drawing room where they would enjoy coffee, tea, and mixed conversation for perhaps an hour. It then being about eleven o'clock, the carriages were called for, the ladies handed down by the gentlemen and—if it were the London season and they were "in town"—it was now time for the main event of the evening—the ball.

The Ball

*T*he ball was one of the highlights of the social season. Precisely how it differed from an ordinary dance does not seem to have been a matter on which there was general agreement; one commentator suggested it had to do with the number of people in attendance: 200 to 500 participants made an event a ball, fewer made it merely a "dance." Perhaps having an orchestra rather than just a piano player was key, too, and having more elaborate decorations. In any event, people had them and seemed generally to recognize them when they did.

Invitations from the lady of the house went out three to six weeks in advance:

<blockquote>
𝔐𝔬𝔫𝔡𝔞𝔶, 𝔍𝔞𝔫𝔲𝔞𝔯𝔶 4

𝔐𝔯𝔰. 𝔖𝔱. 𝔍𝔬𝔥𝔫 𝔆𝔥𝔬𝔩𝔪𝔬𝔫𝔡𝔢𝔩𝔢𝔶 requests the pleasure of 𝔐𝔯. 𝔆𝔥𝔞𝔯𝔩𝔢𝔰 𝔅𝔢𝔞𝔲𝔠𝔥𝔞𝔪𝔭'𝔰 company at a 𝔈𝔳𝔢𝔫𝔦𝔫𝔤 𝔓𝔞𝔯𝔱𝔶, on 𝔐𝔬𝔫𝔡𝔞𝔶, 𝔍𝔞𝔫𝔲𝔞𝔯𝔶 28.

𝔄𝔫 𝔞𝔫𝔰𝔴𝔢𝔯 𝔴𝔦𝔩𝔩 𝔬𝔟𝔩𝔦𝔤𝔢.

𝔇𝔞𝔫𝔠𝔦𝔫𝔤.
</blockquote>

A reply within twenty-four hours was considered mandatory. In London, the town house would then be prepared by turning everything upside down. "In the houses of the aristocracy," said *The Ball-room Guide* in 1868, "hours are often spent in polishing a floor with bees'wax and a brush where a ball is to be given." Failing that, a "crumb cloth or linen diaper" might be stretched over the carpet. (In *The Pickwick Papers* the hero attends the Bath assembly with its "chalked floors.") In a large house a suite of rooms opening one onto another on the "first" floor would be arranged with a refreshment room nearby so ladies would not get chilled passing down drafty staircases on their way for tea or lemonade between dances. Mrs. Weston, we are told in *Emma*, worried about putting the supper room at the other end of the hall from the ballroom, for she "was afraid of draughts for the young people in that passage." Smaller houses had to jam the same things into a small room at the front of the house with a place for refreshments at the back, the ballroom itself being ideally squarish rather than long and narrow. There also had to be cloakrooms where men and women could park their wraps (or retire to, in the ladies' case, so the maids could mend any damage to their dresses). And a supper room was necessary downstairs to which people could repair for the main meal. When old people were asked to be part of the festivities, there had to be a cardroom set aside for them in which to play whist, loo, vingt-et-un, or speculation while the young danced. At "one of the Miss Guests' thoroughly condescending parties," described in *The Mill on the Floss*, "the focus of brilliancy was the long drawing-room, where the dancing went forward, under the inspiration of the grand piano; the library into which it opened at one end had the more sober illumination of maturity, with caps and cards; and at the other end the pretty sitting-room with conservatory attached, was left as an occasional cool retreat."

Things generally got under way around 8 P.M. It was often the practice for the hostess and her daughter(s) to receive the guests as they came in the front door. Or after they'd gotten something to eat. Social courtesies out of the way, guests made their way to the ballroom, the men in formal black trousers, black jacket, and black waistcoat with white tie and shirt, and the ladies in white, wearing the jewelry that was considered *de trop* during the day. Floral decorations were popular in the 1850s and 1860s, but—at least until the 1890s—too much décolletage would be frowned on by the governess or married woman friend of the family who sat in as chaperone of each young lady who attended and endeavored to ensure that no breath of scandal could attach to her reputation. Both sexes wore gloves at all times.

At the "top" of the room—usually the area farthest away from the door—was the orchestra, sometimes discreetly hidden behind ornamental shrubbery or placed just outside the room, but with an opening through which the music could be heard. At a large ball in the middle of the century one would wish to have a cornet, a piano, a violin, and a cello, the cornet sometimes being omitted for smaller affairs.

Protocol for these events varied. In the early part of the century, when public balls and assemblies were not uncommon, an august personage known as the master of the ceremonies was often charged with maintaining proper decorum and at a minimum generally made the introductions between a strange man desiring to dance and the lady waiting patiently in her seat at the side of the floor. In *Pickwick* an unfamiliar member of the party decides to go after a widow at an assembly. "The stranger walked boldly up to, and returned with, the master of the ceremonies; a little introductory pantomime; and the stranger and Mrs. Budger took their places in a quadrille." At the increasingly popular private balls that took the place of these events, the chaperone or perhaps a good friend or the lady of the house performed this office instead. Sometimes the ladies would have dance cards on one side of which the dances would be listed, with spaces on the other in which they or their partners would write in their names for the dances they preferred with the helpful little pencil that was attached to the card by a ribbon, a useful memory aid when there were many dances.

When the dance began, the first dancers were the hostess or her daughter and the gentleman of highest rank present. This could apparently occasion some genteel teeth-grinding; in *Emma* the obnoxious Mrs. Elton, being a new bride, "must be asked to begin the ball." Emma is quite displeased, we learn. "It was almost enough to make her think of marrying." At the beginning of the century a ball would have begun with a minuet and been followed by various country-dances. By mid-century, however, the average dance would have started with a quadrille and then been followed by some fourteen waltzes, galops, and polkas, after which there would have come a time out for supper. There would then have been another ten or so dances, which meant that a fancy ball might not wind up until one in the morning.

There was also a prescribed etiquette for the commencement of each individual dance. Early in the century, at least, the gentleman would bow and the lady curtsy to her partner. A customary conclusion to dancing evolved, too. The gentleman was expected to promenade at least halfway around the room at the conclusion of each dance with his partner on his right arm. At the conclusion of the quadrilles at the birthday party given by the Veneerings for their daughter in *Our Mutual Friend*, the dancers, "two and two, took a walk among the furniture," and we are told "the procession of sixteen . . . slowly circled about, like a revolving funeral." The gentleman then inquired if his partner desired refreshments, and if she said yes, he escorted her to the refreshments room, where they partook of wine, lemonade, ices, biscuits, tea, or coffee. In Jane Austen's time, there was soup spiked with negus at many balls. Fanny Price weaves her way up to bed after the great dance in *Mansfield Park*, "feverish with hopes and fears, soup and negus." If a gentleman were dancing with someone when the break for supper came, he took her down to supper and stood by while she ate but did not himself partake (he was to do that only later, alone), although he might permit himself a glass of wine while she dug into the turkey and ham. And there was always supper. Mrs. Weston suggests in *Emma* "having no regular supper; merely sandwiches, etc., set out in the little room," but "a private dance without sitting down to supper was pronounced an infamous fraud upon the rights of men and women."

The dances were not without their downside notwithstanding all their glitter and gaiety. Quite apart from any damage to hearts or reputations, wax dripped from the overhead candelabra and chandeliers onto the dancers with some regularity. The wilder dances involved mad sorties across the floor (one etiquette book found it necessary to warn cavalry officers not to wear spurs in the ballroom) and with the bracelets that some ladies wore, in at least one instance someone slammed into another girl cutting her arm and sending blood spurting all over.

The Country House Visit

*O*ne of the most important social rituals of nineteenth-century England was the house party at a large country estate. In embryonic form, it appears in Jane Austen's novels when the affectionate friends or relatives come for long stays in the country. Mr. Rochester throws open the doors of Thornfield Hall for a visit by his perhaps intended, Blanche Ingram, and in Trollope, guests come to pass the days or weeks at a great house and connive, flirt, and transact business as the plot of the novel goes forward.

Can You Forgive Her? paints a vivid portrait of this era at midpoint in its description of a long party arranged by Lady Glencora Palliser and her husband, Plantagenet, during which Alice Vasavor comes to stay at Matching Priory for a few weeks. There are several designs afoot; Plantagenet is angling to become Chancellor of the Exchequer, and he has invited a party leader, the duke of St. Bungay, in order to get in good with him. ("When it was known among outside politicians that the Duke of St. Bungay was staying at Matching Priory, outside politicians became more sure than ever that Mr. Palliser would be the new Chancellor of the Exchequer.")

In addition, Lady Glencora has asked her friend Alice Vasavor to join the group in order to have some company, while the dreadful Mr. Bott and Jeffrey Palliser are there to take part in whatever shooting and hunting there is to be had—and, in the intervals, it seems, to pursue more or less equivocal flirtations with Alice. Sport, romance, political intrigue, and socializing—these were all characteristic elements of the country house visit.

Transportation at the beginning of the century was very poor, which is one reason visits were often so long. It was so much trouble to travel that it made no sense to turn around and head home after only a couple of days. Later, the railroads made it possible for people to pop up for a weekend to someone's country place and then be back in London by Monday. Even so, there remained the long excursions to the hinterlands, like the August or September visit to go grouse shooting at someone's castle in Scotland, and the long visit of the sort Alice makes to Lady Glencora.

The hostess with frequent visitors often sent them in advance a printed notice of the train schedule and an indication of the station at which to get off, together with instructions as to whether the traveler should expect to be met at the station or should hire a carriage. A visitor could bring a lady's maid or valet, but the *Habits of Good Society* pointed out that "children and horses . . . should never be taken without special mention." The thoughtful guest made an effort to arrive on time, usually in the late afternoon, recognizing that tardiness would interfere with the work of the servants as they prepared for dinner—the grand event of the day— or hold up the service of dinner for others while the new arrival "dressed for dinner." The hostess would offer the new guest tea while his luggage was taken up, then show him to his room, telling him the dinner hour and indicating the bell for the maid. He might be apprised of the "rules of the house"—if any—such as those prohibiting smoking or reading in bed, or setting limits on the amount to be bet at a game.

The subsequent daily routine was largely invariant. The day officially began with breakfast, an informal affair to which, Trollope tells us in *Can You Forgive Her?*, the ladies did not descend until ten thirty. In contrast to the elaborate dinner which took place at day's end, breakfast was relatively relaxed. There was no protocol—people came and went as they wished, sat where they pleased, helping themselves to food from the sideboard in the sunny and pleasant breakfast parlor or breakfast room where there would have been set out a hearty mixture of ham, eggs, pheasant, and other substantial fare necessary to fuel the guests for their day's activities out in the field. Indeed, although the ladies came down late, "some of the gentlemen would breakfast earlier, especially on hunting mornings, and on some occasions the ladies, when they came together, would find themselves altogether deserted by their husbands and brothers."

After breakfast the men headed out for the woods, fields, or stream, according to whether they planned to shoot, hunt, or fish. This could be problematic for "town" men like Mr. Bott, Trollope tells us. "Twice he went out shooting, but as on the first day he shot the keeper, and on the second very nearly shot the Duke, he gave that up. Hunting he declined, though much pressed to make an essay in that art by Jeffrey Palliser." One reason the ladies didn't hurry to get up is that there was so little for them to do. Most days after breakfast they typically went for a walk, strolled around the gardens, or wrote interminable letters on the mansion's stationery, to the periodic replenishment of which some servant would have been assigned. Sometimes, expeditions by horse and carriage to points of interest in the neighborhood might be arranged. At lunch the ladies would generally eat by themselves while the men picnicked somewhere out in the field. In the afternoon there might be a drive and a walk and then—beginning in the early 1870s—everyone would have gone upstairs to change into her tea gown and then present herself for five o'clock tea in the drawing room.

The great formal event of the day was dinner. A dressing bell was sounded about half an hour before dinner. Both ladies and gentlemen alike dressed formally for the great occasion, but it is worth noting in this connection what a production it had gotten to be by the end of the century for women to pack for a country weekend. You needed a breakfast outfit, something fancier for lunch, followed by the tea gown, and then the heavy artillery for dinner that night. And if you were just away for the weekend, you tried not to wear the same outfit twice, which meant that for a simple three days in the country you could go through about fifteen different outfits.

When the dinner bell sounded, everyone assembled in the drawing room, from which they eventually proceeded in to dine as they would at an ordinary dinner party. After dinner and the obligatory separation of the sexes had occurred—followed by their reunion for coffee or tea in the drawing room—there might be billiards, as in

Can You Forgive Her?, light talk, round card games, and whist, or, perhaps, as in *Jane Eyre*, a bizarre game of charades. The British habit of dressing up and acting out tableaux (it is in *Vanity Fair*, too) evidently died hard, for the *Etiquette of Good Society* in 1893 was still recommending charades for those long wintry nights in the country.

At a certain hour, a servant appeared with a tray bearing water, wine, and biscuits—the hostess might then discreetly suggest that it was time to turn in. The ladies then took their candles and retired, the gentlemen waiting a short interval before following them, or, sometimes, adjourning for a brief spell in the smoking room.

And so to bed—sometimes in ways not always called for in the official schedule of room assignments. The neutral ground of a great estate, after all, was one of the few mattress-filled places a woman could go in the days before "ladies" could visit restaurants and hotels. Assignations, therefore, were apparently not unknown, although negotiating one's way around a large mansion at night in order to carry them out was sometimes eventful. Lord Charles Beresford in the 1880s flung himself gleefully into a darkened room one night and jumped into bed, with a shout of "Cock-a-doodle-do"—only to find, when the lamps were lit, that the bishop of Chester was on one side of him and the bishop's wife on the other.

It should not be imagined that country house visits were any easier on the people who planned them than on the guests. (Lady Glencora openly pronounces her detestation of entertaining dreadful bores like the duchess of St. Bungay, though she stalwartly acknowledges the necessity of doing so if her husband is to further his political career.) The preparations required were certainly considerable. Rooms had to be found for everyone, a perplexing problem when there were thirty guests and only twenty chambers. When he invites his guests, Mr. Rochester sends directions to his housekeeper, Mrs. Fairfax: "for all the best bedrooms to be prepared; and the library and the drawing-rooms are to be cleaned out; and I am to get more kitchen hands from the George Inn, at Millcote, and from wherever else I can." The place is very clean as it is, Jane Eyre thinks, but nonetheless, "carpets were laid down, bed-hangings festooned, radiant white counterpanes spread, toilet tables arranged, furniture rubbed, flowers piled in vases; . . . The hall, too, was scoured; and the great carved clock, as well as the steps and bannisters of the staircase, were polished to the brightness of glass."

All this entertaining was not cheap, since to keep a house running in this fashion required not only lavish expenditures on food and entertainment for the guests but also maintaining servants to look after them. Plus room and board had to be provided for the valets and ladies' maids who often accompanied guests. The mistress of "Taplow" found upon reviewing her records for 1899 that to run the house for a year—guests came virtually each week—cost about £2,118.

The payoffs, however, could be numerous. Relaxation and gossip, of course, were always to be had, but, in addition, weddings might be engineered (or affairs facilitated), political and social intrigue carried forward or the friendships adjunct to such intrigue nurtured in a convivial and appealing setting. "Mr. Palliser remained three days at Monkshade, and cemented his political alliance with Sir Cosmo much in the same way as he had done before with the Duke of St. Bungay. There was little or nothing said about politics, and certainly not a word that could be taken as any definite party understanding between the men; but they sat down at dinner together at the same table, drank a glass of wine or two out of the same decanters, and dropped a chance word now and again about the next session of Parliament. I do not know that anything more had been expected either by Mr. Palliser or by Sir Cosmo; but it seemed to be understood when Mr. Palliser went away that Sir Cosmo was of opinion that that young scion of a ducal house ought to become the future Chancellor of the Exchequer in the Whig Government."

M O N E Y
Being Wealthy

*W*hat did it mean to be wealthy in the days before tax shelters, credit cards, junk bonds, and golden parachutes? No stocks and bonds, no money market funds—what did you put your money into?

First and foremost, it went into land. Land was socially prestigious and it also produced rent from tenant farmers that was probably the major source of income for most of the landed gentry and nobility during much of the 1800s. Good land, however, was not likely to be easily attainable. Much of it was tied up through entail in family estates, and it was an extremely complicated and expensive procedure to purchase it. A contemporary observer toward the end of the century said the legal fees involved were enormous and also pointed out that by then the 2 percent return on land made it a bad investment unless you didn't need a big income. In families, land always went to the men, while the women got things like government securities. Thus, in *The Warden*, the wealthy physician "Dr. Bold died, leaving his Barchester property to his son, and a certain sum in the Three per cents, to his daughter Mary."

Except for railway shares, no one would have had stocks or bonds from private companies until the second half of the century, for the excellent reason that even the smallest shareholders were 100 percent liable to the extent of all their goods and land for any debt incurred by the business of which they were part owners. Consequently, business transacted on the Stock Exchange, as a contemporary observer noted in 1832, "relates entirely to the purchase and sale of stock in the public funds, Exchequer bills, India bonds and similar securities." Gold and silver were popular forms of wealth, partly in the form of coins, of course, but also in the form of the "plate" (or silverware) which in great houses was locked up in a safe guarded by the butler at night and which accounts for the practice of those, who, like the well-off individuals in *Oliver Twist*, made a point when leaving London of "sending the plate, which had so excited Fagin's cupidity, to the banker's." Dickens wrote that in the 1830s. By 1867, things had evidently changed. "Everybody has these plated things now," says Mr. Musselboro in response to a neighbor's query about the lack of "real silver forks" at dinner in *The Last Chronicle of Barset*. "What's the use of a lot of capital lying dead?"

If you were a widow or single maiden lady or other soul without a grand establishment, at least until the middle of the century, you would have put your money into other things, notably, what Sam Weller's father in *Pickwick* describes as those "things as is always a goin' up and down, in the City." "Omnibuses?" says Sam. "Nonsense," replied Mr. Weller. "Them things as is alvays a fluctooatin' and gettin' theirselves involved somehow or another vith the national debt, and the chequered bills, and all that." "Oh! the funds," says Sam.

Indeed, the "funds."

The "funds" was simply another term for the national debt, since it was generally being paid off with the revenues from various accounts or funds. As the debt was backed up by the government and didn't involve the risks entailed in buying privately issued securities, the funds were a popular investment. In addition, they generally paid a perfectly respectable 5 percent. When Jane Eyre's uncle dies, leaving her the money that finally gives her independence, her cousin informs her that "your money is vested in the English funds," and in *Vanity Fair*, we are told that the selfish and disagreeable heiress Miss Crawley "preferred the security of the funds." "The great rich Miss Crawley," Becky Sharp calls her, "with seventy thousand pounds in the five per cents."

There was a particular kind of government security that was, perhaps, more popular with the slightly less affluent and, as a rule, paid only 3 percent a year. These were the famous "Consols" (or, as Sam Weller, Sr., an investor in them, calls them, "Counsels"). Consol was short for consolidated annuity, and the consols consisted of nine different annuities that had been consolidated into one before 1800. Annuities were very popular in the 1800s, no doubt because other securities didn't exist and people didn't always live that long. Mr. Rochester "settled an annuity on her for life," we are told of an old servant in *Jane Eyre*, and Henchard tells his daughter at one point in *The Mayor of Casterbridge*, "A small annuity is what I should like you to have—so as to be independent of me." The consols could *not* be cashed in like, say, a U.S. savings bond, but they paid you your annuity on a regular basis. These were the closest you could get to blue-chip widow and orphan investments in the days before there was much of a stock market. Sam Weller, Sr., gives some to his son as a wedding present at the end of *Pickwick*, and David Copperfield's aunt Betsey Trotwood sorrowfully recounts how she has been left destitute owing to the necessity of having to cash in her consols in order to help her improvident husband.

Having raised the specter of government finance, it may well be asked—what about taxes? When the young visitors are shown around Sotherton in *Mansfield Park*, Jane Austen comments at one point that they were not shown the chapel until after "having visited many more rooms than could be supposed to be of any other use than to contribute to the window tax." It is a passing remark, but one that gives a small glimpse of the remarkably extensive system of taxation that must have made the English one of the most taxed peoples in the world. During the nineteenth century, for example, there was a tax on land, income, the practice of law, newspaper advertisements, glass, candles, beer, malt, carriages, menservants, coats of arms, newspapers, paper, bricks, stone, coal, windows, corn, soap, horses, dogs, salt, sugar, raisins, tea, coffee, tobacco, playing cards, timber, silk and—but the extent of the taxation begins to become clear. There was even a tax on headgear, which, after Wordsworth was appointed as a collector of stamp duties, moved Byron to write: "I shall think of him often when I buy a new hat. There his works will appear."

The taxes were important not only because of the bite they put on people but because of their individual social consequences. Until repealed in 1861, for example, the tax on paper helped to keep books scarce and expensive. Soap was taxed until 1853 with the consequence of the poor personal hygiene which may have contributed to some of the epidemics of typhus and other diseases that periodically devastated elements of the population. (In fact, a black market sprang up in soap, and it was smuggled in from Ireland, where there was no tax, to the western shore of England.) The tax on windows mentioned in *Mansfield Park* was perhaps the most pernicious one, since even a hole cut in a wall for ventilation was counted as a window, making, among other things, for dark houses for the poor. The fact that a family was taxed £2 8s. for each male servant in 1812 (bachelors £4 8s.) helped to steer people toward womenservants— both this and the tax on carriages were based on the government's (correct) assumption that these were two of the leading ways to get revenues from the wealthy.

And these were only the national taxes. At a local parish level from the 1600s on, one could be required to pay a "rate" for the maintenance of the poor (one reason why people were always anxious to have the poor settle somewhere else besides their parish), to which, in due course, were added rates for highways and other local expenses. There was also a local church rate for the physical upkeep of the local Church of England house of worship until 1868. To the national taxes and this local tax must then be added the tithes which farmers and craftsmen had to pay the local clergyman in support of the Church of England. These amounted to one-tenth of the value of the year's annual produce and, until 1840, also had to be paid in kind, when it was "commuted" to payment in money. It is one of the happy attributes of the heartily democratic but well-born rector's wife Mrs. Cadwallader in *Middlemarch*, George Eliot tells us, that "such a lady gave a neighbourliness to both rank and religion, and mitigated the bitterness of uncommuted tithe."

Well (?) brought up.
First Juvenile: "May I have the pleasure of dancing with you, Miss
Alice?"
Second Juvenile: "A, no—thanks! I never dance with younger sons!"

Entail and Protecting the Estate

Jane and Elizabeth attempted to explain to her the nature of an entail. They had often attempted it before, but it was a subject on which Mrs. Bennet was beyond the reach of reason."

Nonetheless, as Jane Austen knew, entail was of vital importance.

The basis of wealth, status, and power in nineteenth-century

England was fundamentally land, as it had been for centuries. And the overriding concern of the great landed families who dominated English life was to maintain their influence and affluence down through the years by transmitting their enormous landed estates intact, generation after generation, to their descendants. A way to do this had, in fact, been found, and it had two elements. The first was the right of primogeniture, which meant that all the land in each generation was left to the eldest son instead of its being divided among all the children. The second was entail, which meant that sufficient restrictions were put on what could be *done* to the estate by that eldest son to ensure that when he died *his* eldest son in turn would inherit the estate intact, and not mortgaged or split up or— God forbid—not at all because, let us say, it had somehow been sold by his father.

Originally, primogeniture had to do with the king's need for warriors, not family continuity. The Crown in Norman times encouraged people to leave their land to just one child so that it would remain intact in each generation and therefore large enough to be economically capable of supporting a military force in the field that could aid the king.

By the nineteenth century the Crown had found other ways to defend itself, and primogeniture had become a means of protecting a family's greatness. The idea was for the estate (in the sense of land) to pass to one person so that it wouldn't be split up, with the great country house and the family name for which it was the material basis thereby becoming separated from each other. This, of course, necessitated that the land go to one child rather than being split among several. Also, a girl should not inherit because if she remained single the line could die out and if she married the estate would pass in possession to someone outside the family. Given the tradition of primogeniture already in existence, the logical heir, then, was the eldest son.

Primogeniture was an all but universal practice among English landed families. Typically, it was carefully provided for in their wills or deeds of settlement. So powerful was the hold of the idea that, until 1925, by law the land of someone dying without a will went to the eldest son, and middle-class efforts to change the law and have the land divided among all the children were consistently defeated by the old families. The plot of Trollope's *Can You Forgive Her?* turns in part on the fact that old Squire Vasavor cannot really countenance violating the principle of primogeniture by leaving his estate to his younger son, John (let alone John's daughter Alice) instead of to the worthless George Vasavor, the logical heir inasmuch as he is the son of the squire's deceased eldest boy. The estate, after all, "had come down from father to son for four hundred years," Trollope tells us. "I don't think I have a right to leave it away from him," the squire tells John. "It never has been left away from the heir." Trollope adds: "The right of primogeniture could not, in accordance with his theory, be abrogated by the fact that it was, in George Vasavor's case, protected by no law."

But, assuming that in a given instance the law of primogeniture was observed, what was to prevent the eldest son from selling the land, especially if he were a gambler or a wastrel?

Family pride, for one thing. "There was only a small part of his estate that Sir Walter could dispose of," we are told of the baronet Walter Elliot in *Persuasion*, "but had every acre been alienable, it would have made no difference. He had condescended to mortgage as far as he had the power, but he would never condescend to sell. No; he would never disgrace his name so far. The Kellynch estate should be transmitted whole and entire, as he had received it."

But suppose an heir lacked family pride, or was in such dire financial straits that, family pride or no, the temptation to start selling off the family acreage became almost irresistible?

This was where entail came in.

The restrictions of entail (usually formally embodied in a piece of paper called a deed of settlement or a "strict settlement") were a way of tying up the property so that the heir got only the *income* from the land—he couldn't sell or mortgage it. In fact, the settlement was usually a deed giving the land to the eldest son, but only for use during his lifetime, his rights to the property being thus restricted or "entailed" (from the French *tailler*, meaning "to cut off"). The idea was such a big hit that when entailing was first tried, people attempted to entail their estates more or less perpetually so that an estate could never be sold off or split up. However, the law refused to sanction entailing or tying up the estate for so long—in practice, it would only permit it to be entailed until the grandson of the man making the settlement turned twenty-one. Then, said the law, all the restrictions of the entail on the property had to be lifted, and the newly of age heir had to be given full ownership, i.e., he had to be able to sell it or give it away just like any other property.

So now the problem of keeping the estate intact in the first generation had been solved by leaving it all to the eldest son. And the problem of keeping it intact through the second generation had been solved by entailing it. Now the problem was, what happened when the *grandson* inherited Tipton Grange and all the rights to it? The law said he was free to sell or dispose of it all in the same way it had been feared his father might.

But an heir, of course, did not actually inherit anything until his father died, which, of course, might not be for years and years. Therefore, since few landed eldest grandsons (or sons) worked for a living, the father of this inheriting grandson then had merely to indulge in a little discreet coercion—sign a new deed of settlement tying up the estate until *your* grandson is twenty-one, he said in effect, or I cut off your allowance. This usually had the desired result of ensuring that the entail on the estate was carried on for two more generations. This technique was used in cases where family pride was not enough, and the result could be a continuing renewal of the entail which might then go on generation after generation.

That left only one mechanical—albeit serious—problem with the scheme: What if all the children were girls? This, it will be remembered, is the problem of poor Mr. Bennet in *Pride and Prejudice*. With daughters, as we have seen, the family name might disappear if they inherited the property, so what should be done in this situation? Quite often, the answer was that the deed of settlement or will entailing the property would provide for a lateral pass to another branch of the family that *did* have a young male. And this is what happens in *Pride and Prejudice*, where the obsequious Mr. Collins inherits Mr. Bennet's estate because "Mr. Bennet's property consisted almost entirely of an estate of two thousand a year, which, unfortunately for his daughters, was entailed in default of heirs male, on a distant relation," the "distant relation" being Mr. Collins. Likewise, Sir Walter Elliot in *Persuasion* has no sons; as a consequence the "heir presumptive" is a cousin, William Elliot.

Primogeniture and entail had indirect effects both on the families that engaged in these practices and the larger society.

Perhaps the most obvious of these was the production of eldest sons who were spoiled rotten, since they knew that they, and they alone, would inherit virtually all the family property. Young Tom Bertram, the heir to Mansfield Park, says Jane Austen apropos of how he treats his timid young cousin, had "all the liberal dispositions of an eldest son, who feels born only for expense and enjoyment. His kindness to his little cousin was consistent with his situation and rights; he made her some very pretty presents, and laughed at her."

Other children of wealthy families could expect little or nothing from the estate, which must have encouraged a certain amount of sibling resentment.

But at least the other boys had a chance to inherit if the eldest son dropped dead. The girls, however, could never inherit, yet the deep attachment to the family property fostered by the practice of transmitting it reverently from generation to generation obviously produced emotional scars when they had to leave. We can judge the strength of the attachment—and perhaps the poverty of single, genteel women—from the fact that Mr. Collins offers to marry various of the disinherited Bennet girls, and that Anne Elliot pursues her cousin when it is apparent that he will inherit the estate where she grew up. "She had, while a very young girl, as soon as she had known him to be, in the event of her having no brother, the future baronet, meant to marry him," says Jane Austen, "and her father had always meant that she should." Indeed, given the unquestioned propriety of cousins marrying for most of the 1800s, the girls may well have done better under this scenario than if a brother inherited the estate, a possibility that finds confirmation in *Wuthering Heights,* of all places, where the dying Edgar Linton tries to encourage his daughter Catherine's marriage to Heathcliff, her aunt's son—"though he had set aside, yearly, a portion of his income for my lady's fortune, he had a natural desire that she might retain—or at least return in a short time to—the house of her ancestors; and he considered that the only prospect of doing that was by a union with [the] heir."

Primogeniture and entail also apparently encouraged some intergenerational friction. "Take it as a rule," says a sardonic Mr. Eaves in *Vanity Fair,* "the fathers and elder sons of all great families hate each other. The crown Prince is always in opposition to the crown or hankering after it. . . . If you were heir to a dukedom and a thousand pounds a day, do you mean to say you would not wish for possession?"

Which brings us to the other area where all of this careful handing on of the estate had such an impact, namely, in what Trollope and others so delicately referred to as the "marriage market." In a society where the general rule among the wealthy is that the eldest son gets everything, then a population producing a roughly equal number of boys and girls (and England at mid-century was thought in overall population, at least, to suffer from a numerical *shortage* of marriage-age men) will witness a mad scramble among the girls—or their mothers—to try to land one of the relatively limited number of eldest sons. "Of course it was desirable," writes Trollope of Lady Baldock's match-making intent for her niece Violet Effingham in *Phineas Finn*, "that Violet should marry an eldest son, and a peer's heir." The flip side was that no one wanted a younger son. "Younger sons cannot marry where they like," says one of them, Colonel Fitzwilliam, to Elizabeth Bennet in *Pride and Prejudice*, and a real-life earl's younger son some years later spoke of how "he was repelled by the mothers whom he met in society as if he had the plague, lest he should fall in love with their daughters."

The social irony in all this was that if entail worked properly, it tied up the estate so magnificently that when debts were incurred there was then no way to get at the wealth, e.g., the family land, that might have been used to pay them off. In such an instance, as with Lord Fawn in *The Eustace Diamonds*, the only way to keep the proud old family name solvent and the ancestral estate intact was to marry a vulgar, parvenu heiress like Lizzie Eustace!

A debtor in prison.

Bankruptcy, Debt, and Moneylending

I rarely at this time had any money wherewith to pay my bills," wrote Anthony Trollope of his days as a young clerk in the Post Office. "In this state of things a certain tailor had taken from me an acceptance for, I think £12, which found its way into the hands of a money-lender. With that man, who lived in a little street near Mecklenburgh Square, I formed a most heart-rending but a most intimate acquaintance. In cash I once received from him £4. For that and for the original amount of the tailor's bill, which grew monstrously under repeated renewals, I paid ultimately something over £200. That is so common a story as to be hardly worth the telling."

It was, indeed.

To judge from the great novels, debt was widespread, galling, and often catastrophic in its effects in the nineteenth century. In *Dombey and Son* and *The Mayor of Casterbridge* the main characters are bankrupted; in *Middlemarch*, Mr. Bulstrode. In *Little Dorrit* the protagonist's father is imprisoned for years for debt; in *Vanity Fair* Mr. Sedley is ruined and Rawdon Crawley thrown into a "sponging house" for debt. And the pages of Trollope are replete with young men like the impecunious George Vasavor in *Can You Forgive Her?* who became the prey of bill brokers and moneylenders like the sinister Fledgeby of *Our Mutual Friend* and the persistent Mr. Clarkson, who hectors the eponymous hero of *Phineas Finn*. Then, of course, there is Mr. Micawber, whose travails and wanderings through the world of debtor's prisons and low finance are a capsule education in the subject of nineteenth-century debt.

The English of the nineteenth century looked on debt somewhat more harshly than we do now, which is, perhaps, one reason it was a subject of such interest to them. No doubt this is because personal savings rather than the use of credit cards were seen as the engine of economic growth. There is a good deal of not-so-subtle moralizing by Mr. Tulliver's relatives when he goes under financially in *The Mill on the Floss* to the effect that he need not have gotten himself into such a mess and that it betrays some flaws of personal character, not to say downright immorality, on his part. Mr. Tulliver's sister-in-law pointedly lectures her sister on "what disgrace your husband's brought on your own family," castigating family members who "have had the same chance as me, only they've been wicked and wasteful." One could also go to prison for debt.

It was also remarkably easy to get into debt or go bankrupt. Retailers, whether of beer or groceries, apparently encouraged their customers to go into debt by extending credit to them on a running basis—"there was a bar at the Jolly Bargemen," notes Pip in *Great Expectations,* "with some alarmingly long chalk scores in it on the wall at the side of the door, which seemed to me to be never paid off." Most such businesses, after all, were small, neighborhood enterprises, the customers local and generally known personally to the manager-owner. This made it sensible—and productive of client goodwill—to extend credit to regulars, especially when they knew they could be jailed for not paying their bills. Affluent households were encouraged to buy from their grocers and other suppliers on credit; one observer thought tradesmen saw it as a way to foster a sense of obligation on the part of their customers, and, of course, the novels are replete with wealthy young men like Pip running up huge debts at their tailors.

Which raises another point: for most of the century, standards of desirable behavior were set by the upper class, and an aristocratic life-style could not be maintained without spending a good deal of money. This did not worry a tradesman who extended credit to a young lord, however. On the contrary, a wealthy family's desire to keep the family name unsullied, to say nothing of the family wealth available to pay, meant the retailer would always receive his money in the end. It is, in fact, precisely this tendency on the part of tradesmen to deal liberally with "the quality" that makes the eminently practical and well-off Mrs. Greenow in *Can You Forgive Her?* regard the prospect of marrying a seedy ex-army captain with a certain degree of equanimity: "It is true Bellfield might have been a forger, or a thief, or a returned convict—but then his debts could not be large. Let him have done his best, he could not have obtained credit for a thousand pounds, whereas, no one could tell the liabilities of a gentleman of high standing."

Trollope's account of his own misfortunes when young points up the final trap for the would-be debtor. Once you got into debt, there were bill brokers and moneylenders like Fledgeby waiting to help keep you there by advancing you money—or extending the date of your repayment—in return for your signature on more or less extortionate bills of exchange and promissory notes. Given the lack of controls over what a moneylender could charge, this could rapidly transform a trifling debt into a substantial financial burden.

In novels like *The Mayor of Casterbridge* and *Dombey and Son*, however, there is a sense of misfortune greater than that we associate merely with getting into debt, and this is because personal economic difficulties have been joined to business reverses and, typically, they have simultaneously bankrupted a man's business and left him personally penniless. Today, it is our experience that the owner of a failed business declares it bankrupt and walks away from it, psychologically scarred, perhaps, but with his home and personal belongings intact. But, until the mid-1800s, virtually every owner of a business in England was personally liable to the extent of every last thing he owned—home and furnishings included—for any debt incurred in his business life. Thus, if he went bankrupt, he lost not only his business but, typically, all his personal property as well. This accounts for the utter and complete nature of the *personal* financial devastation that men like Henchard and Dombey suffered, and it is why such business reverses are invariably portrayed in the nineteenth-century novel as being so utterly catastrophic. Moreover, the legal liability of the owner in such an instance was reinforced by a powerful prevailing ethos of personal responsibility for business debts. When they go bankrupt we find Henchard, unasked for, offering a watch to his creditors, and Mr. Dombey proudly refusing to bargain for any personal advantage in the sale of his goods. "Mrs. Tulliver carried the proud integrity of the Dodsons in her blood," says Eliot in *The Mill on the Floss*, "and had been brought up to think that to wrong people of their money, which was another phrase for debt, was a sort of moral pillory: it would have been wickedness, to her mind, to have run counter to her husband's desire to 'do the right thing' and retrieve his name."

What happened when you got so far into debt that you obviously couldn't pay or creditors simply got tired of waiting? The answer depended on whether you owed money on a lease, a mortgage, a bill of sale, or on some kind of personal promise to pay like an IOU, a promissory note, or a bill of exchange. He is being watched over, writes Micawber to David Copperfield in a letter at one point, by a drunk "employed by a broker. That individual is in legal possession of these premises, under a distress for rent." If you owed money on a lease, the landlord could come in and get his back rent simply by seizing all the furniture in your apartment and, after five days, selling it to recover his money, a process whereby he was said to "distress" or "distrain" the items. Specially licensed secondhand-furniture dealers called brokers would often sell the furniture for the landlord, who was supposed to hand over any excess profits to the tenant. Owing money on a bill of sale or a mortgage was somewhat different. In those instances, you were promising the creditor to repay his money by a certain date or the document permitted him to seize, respectively, your personal property or your land. Lydgate is forced to give a bill of sale on his household goods when he and his new bride run up overly high household bills in *Middlemarch*, and Earnshaw gives a mortgage on Wuthering Heights to Heathcliff. When Earnshaw dies without paying it off, the farm, of course, goes to his wily nemesis.

When the debt you owed was for something other than rent or where it was not secured by a document like a bill of sale or a mortgage that expressly allowed the creditor to take your property you were declared to be either a "bankrupt" or a "debtor." If you were declared a bankrupt, your name was published in the official biweekly *London Gazette*. The bailiff came and took possession of your house and goods, and an arrangement was worked out with your creditors to liquidate your possessions to satisfy as much of the debt as possible. In *Dombey*, the contents of the family's house are auctioned off, "and herds of shabby vampires, Jew and Christian, over-run the house, sounding the plate-glass mirrors with their knuckles, striking discordant octaves on the Grand Piano, drawing wet forefingers over the pictures, breathing on the blades of the best dinner-knives, punching the squabs of chairs and sofas with their dirty fists, touzling the feather beds, opening and shutting all the drawers, balancing the silver spoons and forks, looking into the very threads of the drapery and linen, and disparaging everything." All is sold, the house is advertised for rent. "None of the invaders remain. The house is a ruin, and the rats fly from it."

However stark the consequences of bankruptcy might seem, neither Mr. Dombey nor his fellow bankrupts, Mr. Tulliver and Henchard, go to jail. They simply lost everything they owned.

If, however, for largely technical reasons having to do with whether you were a "tradesman" or not, you were defined by the law as a "debtor" rather than a "bankrupt," you were generally put in jail, and there was none of this business of working out an arrangement satisfactory to creditors.

Indeed, a recalcitrant or impoverished debtor could often be imprisoned twice for the same debt. You were jailed initially because the courts had long before decided that it was faster and more effective to get someone to show up in court to participate in a debt case by arresting him rather than by simply sending him a piece of paper telling him he was about to be a defendant. So your creditor or creditors paid a shilling for an arrest warrant, gave it to a sheriff's officer, and then he went off and arrested you and put you into a sponging house run by him and his wife. There you had a few days in which to make efforts to settle things or make up your mind to go to prison. "We're three of us—it's no use bolting," says one of the bailiff's men who nabs Rawdon Crawley in *Vanity Fair* in this manner one night. "It's you, Moss, is it?" says the colonel. "How much is it?" "Only a small thing," Moss whispers. "One hundred and sixty-six, six and eight-pence, at the suit of Mr. Nathan," and proceeds to take Rawdon home to the Moss family sponging house, where, as Mr. Moss assures him, "I've got a Doctor of Divinity upstairs, five gents in the coffee-room, and Mrs. Moss has a tably-dy-hoty at half-past five, and a little cards or music afterwards, when we shall be most happy to see you."

Notice, however, that in most cases involving debtors all this was just, so to speak, a way of getting your attention. (Unless you had already been found liable to pay someone money often there would as yet have been no legal finding one way or the other as to whether or not you were actually a debtor.) The arrest was simply a procedural device to ensure that you showed up in court for the trial to determine if you *were* a deadbeat.

If at trial you were found not to be a debtor or were found to be a debtor and paid up, you went home. If you were found to be a debtor and then didn't pay, you were thrown in jail again, but—no doubt a comforting thought—on a different theory. *Bankruptcy* law, it will be recalled, permitted creditors to seize and sell the bankrupt's belongings to satisfy the debt. The law regarding *debtors*, however, did not provide any such mechanism for a creditor to recover monies once the court had determined that he was owed them by a debtor. Therefore, if you refused to pay your creditor after a court found you to be a debtor, e.g., legally liable to do so, all the creditor could do was try to put the squeeze on you somehow so you *would* sell off your property or do something to pay him. Hence, the creditor typically got a writ to throw you back into prison until you paid—which is why Little Dorrit's father was rotting away in the Marshalsea all those years and why Micawber at one point winds up in King's Bench prison. After three months in prison, you could get out by agreeing to give up your goods to your creditors, and then something called the Court of Insolvent Debtors in Lincoln's Inn Fields—"a Temple dedicated to the Genius of Seediness," Dickens calls it in *Pickwick*—could set you free.

Such were the toils of debt and its attendant difficulties in the England of George and Victoria. One should bear in mind that all this was not confined merely to the first few decades of the 1800s. Imprisonment for debt was not abolished until 1869.

A division in the House of Commons: members passing the tellers.

POWER AND THE
ESTABLISHMENT
The Government

*W*ith respect to Mr. Gladstone," wrote Queen Victoria queru-
lously in 1885, "the Queen does feel that she is always kept in the
dark. In Lord Melbourne's time she knew everything that passed in
the cabinet and the different views that were entertained by the
different Ministries, and there was no concealment."

Her complaint was a measure of how much the cozy, clubby,
nature of English parliamentary government had changed since the
early 1800s. In Jane Austen's era, Parliament was a sleepy collection
of worthy peers in the House of Lords and landed gentlemen in the
Commons who sometimes fought off intermittently mad George
III's efforts to be another royal strongman but in general spent their
time haggling over minute questions of local government such as
whether or not a particular road should have a turnpike and whose
fields should be enclosed in tiny villages in the Midlands. There
were no hard and fast party lines, no mass party organizations, no
clear rules on when a government could stay in power (or when it
should resign), no truly popular elections. And there was very little
pressing business—other than to vote the army budget. George Eliot
could have been describing the entire country when she wrote of
Middlemarch during this period, "before Reform had done its notable part in developing the political consciousness, there was a
clearer distinction of ranks and a dimmer distinction of parties."

The House of Lords consisted of the peerage together with the
archbishops and bishops of the Church of England, who held their
seats, so to speak, ex officio rather than by election. Members of the
House of Commons had to get elected in their boroughs or counties,
not usually a difficult task since they were generally men of considerable standing in their home areas and probably the landlords of
many of the electors, as the voters were called. (There was no secret
ballot until 1872.) The candidate—if for some reason he actually had

to make a real speech—spoke from a platform called the husting after the alehouses had been opened for some hours to get everyone in a receptive frame of mind, There was then a public vote to determine who had won. The bias in favor of the wealthy and influential was reinforced by the fact that until 1838 M.P.'s were required by law to have a £600 a year annual income in the case of a county member and £300 a year in the case of a borough member. Property qualifications were not completely abolished until 1858, and members received no salary until the 1880s. Plus, Catholics could not sit in Parliament until 1829, nor Jews until the 1860s.

By law Parliament had to meet at least every three years, but in practice it met annually because the historic English antipathy to a standing army forbade Parliament to authorize any army budget that provided for more than a year's expenditure. Also, as the century wore on, there was simply too much business to be dealt with without an annual "session," as the period between January or February and August, when Parliament met, was called. Originally, Parliament was an assembly of notables collected by the monarch to advise him and perhaps to do his bidding, and its origins as an instrument of the monarch continued to be reflected in various practices long after the realities of the situation had changed dramatically. Thus, genial deference continued to be paid to the fiction of royal leadership by having the monarch open each session of the two houses with a speech explaining why they had been summoned. (This eventually became a summary of the government's legislative proposals.) Similarly, the members of the cabinet and other officials were formally "His Majesty's" ministers, and the foremost, or "prime," minister among them took office by visiting the monarch to "kiss hands" in a feudal gesture of fealty.

In fact, the monarch had long since ceased to play anything but an advisory role in the government, although Queen Victoria tried, once, to intervene early in her reign. Thus, though in theory the queen sent on her own initiative for a new prime minister to form a government when the old one fell, in practice, "the Queen will send for any one that the House of Commons may direct her to call upon," Mr. Bott points out in *Can You Forgive Her?* Trollope was writing in the mid-1860s, and his reference to the power of the House of Commons should be noted, for by then not only the monarch but the House of Lords as well was becoming irrelevant to the real exercise of power within the government. The growing tide of democratic sentiment in the nation meant that the nonelected

House of Lords could not credibly interfere with legislation proposed by a popularly elected body like the Commons. After the king threatened to pack the Lords by vastly enlarging the peerage when they refused assent to the Reform Act of 1832, the Lords backed off and became something of a rubber stamp to the Commons thereafter.

The House of Commons was divided between two main parties, which were known as the Whigs and Tories until the 1830s and, thereafter, respectively, as the Liberals and Conservatives. (There were also a small number of extreme democrats known as the Radicals.) The house organ for the Whigs was the *Edinburgh Review*, while the Tories had the *Quarterly Review*, which, we are told in *Mansfield Park*, was used to pass the time at Sotherton. New governments were formed when a cabinet in power resigned and was either replaced by a new one or dissolved Parliament so that new elections had to be held. In either event, the majority party then quickly selected their leader who became the new prime minister. The prime minister formed a cabinet consisting of some fifteen or so members, which always included the lord chancellor, the secretaries of state, respectively, for home and foreign affairs (also known as the home secretary and the foreign secretary), the Chancellor of the Exchequer and the first lord of the admiralty, plus, usually, the president of the Board of Trade, the lord privy seal, the postmaster general and the chancellor of the Duchy of Lancaster. Ordinary members of Parliament were styled "the Honourable"; members of the Privy Council, which also included all cabinet ministers, were "Right Honourables." The cabinet together with twenty-five or thirty-five other figures in the executive branch—such as the junior lords of the treasury and admiralty, the secretaries *to* the treasury, and the like—made up the "ministry."

The Treasury Department was the center of political power. The title of prime minister really denoted a position of collegial leadership (unlike, say, the post of the American president) rather than an actual executive position. However, the post of first lord of the treasury was always given to the prime minister along with the first lord's official residence, a house at 10 Downing Street next to the offices of the Treasury in Whitehall. (The front-row bench where the prime minister and other members sat in the House of Commons was known as the Treasury Bench.) Given the first lord's preoccupation with running the nation, it then devolved on the Chancellor of the Exchequer to actually run the department and the nation's financial affairs; in his hands, for example, lay the preparation of the budget. Chancellor of the Exchequer was an enormously influential post; it is Plantagenet Palliser's goal, of course, in *Can Your Forgive Her?* More important from the party's standpoint, there were always three junior lords of the treasury appointed from within the party. Nominally charged with supervising the nation's finances, they actually assisted the party's chief whip in Parliament—the parliamentary secretary to the treasury—in lining up members of the party for key votes. Phineas Finn, as befits a rising young political star, is happy to become one of the junior lords of the treasury in the novel that bears his name. The fact that these posts could have whacking good salaries when an M.P. received nothing is a consideration to Phineas, as it no doubt was to other ambitious young politicos. "Even as a junior lord he would have a thousand a year." As a barrister, Phineas thinks, it would have been years before he earned so much.

The departments of government tried to influence relevant matters in Parliament or respond to questions about their ministry by strategically placing their leaders in Parliament. Generally, each department therefore had a parliamentary secretary who was a political appointee, in addition to a permanent undersecretary who was a career official. As a rule, a parliamentary undersecretary would sit in one house while his boss sat in the other so they could keep both legislative bases covered. Lord Fawn in *The Eustace Diamonds*, who woos Lizzie Eustace, was a "Peer of Parliament and an Under-Secretary of State," we are told. He would thus have been used as a member of the Lords to counterbalance a department head who was a commoner.

All the important parliamentary ministers sat in the House of Commons on the Treasury Bench, which was placed at right angles to the Speaker's chair. Behind them sat the lesser members of the party, or "backbenchers." Opposite them—across the aisle—sat the Opposition, the members of the party out of power. Halfway down the benches was a passageway to the back called the gangway. Phineas Finn moves his seat "below the gangway" in what would have been seen as a move to register his dissent from a measure proposed by his party; to "cross the aisle," however, was a much more serious step.

The reader of nineteenth-century English novels is likely to come across two sorts of dramatic major parliamentary activity. The first is the questioning of ministers; they were expected to make them-

selves available several afternoons a week to defend government
policies to the Opposition. The second is the passage of legislation,
which required three readings of the proposed measure in each
House and approval by both Houses, formal votes in favor being
counted through a "division" in which the members of each party
walked out of their House of Parliament into one of the two adjoining lobbies to be counted for or against the measure. The "bill," as
it was called, if it then passed Parliament went to the monarch for
signature, whereupon it became an "act."

A ministry generally stayed in power until it was defeated on a
piece of legislation with which it was strongly identified or had
suffered an explicit vote of no confidence. The prime minister then
either resigned, in which case someone else would be requested to
become prime minister and form a cabinet, or else he dissolved
Parliament and called for new general elections. Dissolution was
obviously a more extreme measure than simple resignation, and it
was generally done only if the prime minister thought the popular
sentiment in the country favored him a good deal more than the vote
in the House of Commons had, or, sometimes, simply if he felt the
question was of such urgency that a direct popular vote on it should
be held. Resignation was more likely if an administration had suffered a number of reverses and was clearly unpopular. At the beginning of *Phineas Finn*, "Lord de Terrier, the Conservative Prime
Minister, who had now been in office for the almost unprecedent-
edly long period of fifteen months, had found that he could not face
continued majorities against him in the House of Commons, and had
dissolved the House. Rumour declared that he would have much
preferred to resign, and betake himself once again to the easy glories
of opposition; but his party had naturally been obdurate with him,
and he had resolved to appeal to the country." No one—including
one's opponents—particularly liked having to stand for election,
and, as Trollope suggests, a prime minister could therefore use the
threat of dissolution against an unruly opposition. In *Phineas Finn*,
he tells us that "the House of Commons had offended Mr. Gresham
by voting in a majority against him, and Mr. Gresham had punished
the House of Commons by subjecting it to the expense and nuisance
of a new election."

The conduct of parliamentary government could require endless
speech making, sometimes four or five hours worth from the prime
minister *alone* when a major issue was at stake. Plantagenet Palliser,
we are told in *The Eustace Diamonds*, speaks for three and three-

quarter hours on decimal coinage. This loquacity was no doubt facilitated by the fact that until 1888, the Commons met at 3:45 on Monday, Tuesday, Thursday, and Friday with no cutoff time. Debates therefore often went on until well after midnight. Several hours after the afternoon session began members would begin drifting away for dinner. Then around ten o'clock they would wander in wearing evening dress, ready to go again and sometimes not adjourning til two or three in the morning. Conducting late-night business was also possible because quorums for conducting business were quite small. "The mystic forty," as Trollope puts it in *Phineas Finn*, were needed in the Commons—a mere "three" in the Lords.

A line-of-battle ship, and a merchant brig alongside.

Britannia Rules the Waves

*I*n the days when Fanny Price's brother went off to join the Royal Navy as a midshipman in *Mansfield Park*, the fleet was composed of great three-masted square-rigged sailing "ships-of-the-line" carrying crews of hundreds that sailed into battle launching broadsides from their several decks of cannon against the enemy, hoping to pound them into submission. A line of battle consisted of three squadrons of ships, 100 yards apart, each squadron commanded by "flag officers" (that was how they communicated), a vice-admiral in a leading ship (with a white flag), the commanding admiral in the center (a red flag), and a rear admiral in the ship at the back (his flag was blue). During Jane Austen's era, ships were officially rated according to the number of guns they carried. A first-rate and second-rate ship carried 90 guns or more, each capable of firing every three minutes two 18-pound cannonballs a distance of about 2,000 yards. Typically, each ship had a crew of about 900 men, cost about £120,000 to build, and required an average of 3,500 oak trees (which took a century to mature)—the equivalent of about 900 acres of forest—for their construction. They were commanded by a captain assisted by a commander, with lieutenants and young midshipmen like Fanny's brother beneath him, after which there were warrant (noncommissioned) officers like the boatswain and master, and then the ordinary seamen to do the actual heavy work. Under full sail, the vessels went about ten knots an hour.

Once the British defeated Napoleon, they had no other major naval engagements to fight (except in the Crimean War) until World War I and spent a good deal of their time patroling the periphery of the empire, cracking down on the slave trade and sending people off on jaunts like the ill-fated Franklin expedition to explore the more obscure parts of the globe.

This was just as well, because the navy was extraordinarily unpopular among those who fought in it, at least among the ordinary sailors, and, in addition, Parliament kept cutting it to tatters and then being surprised when it was unable to fight effectively.

Recruitment techniques were a major source of unhappiness. The navy recruited its ordinary sailors through the "press-gang." This meant that whenever it needed crews the navy just grabbed civilian seamen off the streets, sometimes nabbing them as they returned from a long voyage in the regular commercial fleet, and then slapped them aboard men-of-war. Given the technological similarity between warships and regular vessels and the relatively simple nature of armaments, this was a perfectly feasible method of obtaining personnel, however unpopular. There was no career security. Until the 1850s, after each voyage you were dumped on the dock—now suddenly an *ex*-navy man—and there were no pensions.

Officers had other gripes. For many years the system worked on the basis of "interest," that is to say, connections. "Interest" got you your initial berth as a midshipman when you were in your early teens, aboard, say, the vessel of a captain with whom your family had connections or to whom he owed a favor. After six years you were entitled to take the test for lieutenant, and thereafter you could become a captain. The problem, however, was that—pensions being what they were—no one ever retired. At one point after the Napoleonic Wars, for example, there were some 5,339 commissioned officers in the Royal Navy and only 550 of them were working; since you could not advance to captain without the requisite number of years at sea, you could literally get stuck as a lieutenant for decades. And the determination of who did get a shot at the available positions was usually made on the basis of "interest." Admiral Croft chides Captain Wentworth in *Persuasion* for what he imagines is the man's complaint about the sloop he commanded: "He knows there must have been twenty better men than himself applying for her at the same time. Lucky fellow to get any thing so soon, with no more interest than his." (Once you hit captain the rules changed—you were promoted to rear, vice, and full admiral in strict order of seniority as those ahead of you died.)

Unlike the army, however, you did not have to purchase a commission, which meant that for poorer boys or younger sons, like William Price, the navy could be a more viable career than the army, or, as Sir Walter Elliot remarks, again in *Persuasion*, "a man is in greater danger in the navy of being insulted by the rise of one whose father, his father might have disdained to speak to, and of being prematurely an object of disgust himself, than in any other line."

Cavalry and artillery reinforcements, l. to r.: 8th Hussars, 17th Lancers, Royal Horse Artillery, 5th Dragoon Guards, 4th Dragoon Guards, 1st Royal Dragoons, 14th Hussars.

The Army

*I*n the 1800s the army was built around the regiment, a unit nominally commanded by a colonel, in reality usually by a lieutenant colonel. In the case of the infantry, a regiment usually consisted of some 750 or more men, divided into eight to ten companies of 60 to 100 men each. These were in turn each commanded by a captain who was assisted by a commissioned officer like a lieutenant and by an ensign, as well as by a "ranker," or noncommissioned officer, like a sergeant. In battle several regiments might be slapped together to form a brigade. Thus, the "Charge of the Light Brigade" was composed of the 8th Light Dragoons, the 11th Hussars, the 13th Light Dragoons and the 17th Lancers. Units such as brigades were never more than temporary forms of organization, however, for the spirit and identity of the British army, perhaps uniquely among European armies, lay always in its regiments.

Partly this was owing to the system of officers' having to purchase their commissions, a practice that was not abolished until 1871. The hapless Richard Carstone, we are told in *Bleak House,* decides at one point on a military career, and accordingly "his name was entered at the Horse Guards as an applicant for an ensign's commission; the purchase-money was deposited at an agent's." This purchase system meant that an officer literally had an investment in his regiment. When he left the service the only way he could make some money, especially in prepension days, was to sell the commission to somebody else. In *Can You Forgive Her?* Trollope tells us that Captain Bellfield "had been obliged to sell out of the army, because he was unable to live on his pay as a lieutenant. The price of his commission had gone to pay his debts." This is why being "cashiered" was so feared—in addition to the dishonor, being discharged from the army in that manner meant that you were barred from selling your commission.

Commissions were not cheap either: in 1821 it cost £1,200 or more to buy a commission in the Household Foot Guards or Cavalry, £800 for a regular cavalry post, and £450–£500 for the infantry. (Artillery and engineer ranks were not for sale.) This, of course, meant that the army was characteristically officered by the well-to-do—especially, perhaps, the younger sons, like Rawdon Crawley in *Vanity Fair,* who would not inherit the family estate.

The oldest and most prestigious regiments were the Household Troops or Guards that guarded the royal family, which were composed of the Foot Guards (infantry), made up of the Scots, Grenadier, and Coldstream Guards, and the Household Cavalry, which was made up of regiments of the Life Guards and the Horse Guards (the so-called Blues). Rawdon Crawley, being well connected and able to afford an expensive commission, has, Thackeray tells us, his "commission in the Life Guards Green." These were the "tony," aristocratic units, headquartered, of course, in London. (The Horse Guards building in Whitehall became the army headquarters, and the term "Horse Guards," like the term "Pentagon" in the United States, a synedochal appellation for the military high command.) Below them ranked the other cavalry, which included the dragoons (originally mounted cavalry who dismounted and fought on foot), the lancers (so named for their weapons), and the hussars (known for their colorful uniforms). The regular "line" infantry came last, numbering among its regiments the fusiliers, so named from the light muskets they carried at one time, and the grenadiers, the grenade throwers who were supposed to be taller than the average, in order to lob their explosives a long distance. "Ensign Spooney," says Thackeray, contrasting him with a short soldier in another regiment, "was a tall youth, and belonged to [Captain Dobbin's] the Grenadier Company." Because of the costs associated with the obligatory entertaining of fellow officers in the mess and the like, the cheapest place to be an officer was India—this was where the more impecunious of the younger sons who entered the army generally went.

To the population at large, the cavalry were the glamorous branch of the army. Like the aristocracy, they rode horseback and their costumes could be elaborate and colorful, since they did not, like the infantry, have to wade through mud and dirt. There was also an aura of recklessness about them, born perhaps of their dashing charges, and their prowess in the legendary "sword exercise" which taught them the use of their primary battle weapon (guns were too difficult to aim charging on horseback). It is thus almost invariably the cavalry who really set feminine pulses racing in nineteenth-century English fiction. "I saw an officer of the Hussars ride down the street at Budmouth," Eustacia Vye tells Clem Yeobright passionately in *The Return of the Native,* "and though he was a total stranger and never spoke to me, I loved him till I thought I should really die of love." In *Far from the Madding Crowd,* the dashing Sergeant Troy, we learn, is of the 11th Dragoon Guards, and Bathsheba Everdene is bedazzled by his virtuoso display of the sword exercise's finer points. In *Vanity Fair,* we are not surprised that the virtuous but plodding Captain Dobbin is in the infantry—and the stupid but swaggering Rawdon Crawley in the Life Guards.

The army as a whole was treated miserably by the English for most of the 1800s. They were quartered in the Tower of London and in local alehouses until Pitt got them barracks to live in, and they were fed only two meals a day for many years (beef—and only three quarters of a pound of it at that—plus bread) with the consequence that they were often sick and hungry and drank heavily to compensate for it. In his observations on Brompton, Stroud, Rochester, and Chatham, Mr. Pickwick records that "the streets present a lively and animated appearance, occasioned chiefly by the conviviality of the military. It is truly delightful to a philanthropic mind, to see these gallant men staggering along under the influence of an overflow, both of animal and ardent spirits." Until 1847 enlistment was for life, and men were typically sent overseas with their regiment for periods of up to sixteen years to places like the West Indies, where death rates from tropical diseases could be appallingly high. In *Vanity Fair*, Napoleon's escape from Elba occasions rejoicing in the regiment of Dobbin and George Osborne, we are told, because it allows them "to show their comrades in arms that they could fight as well as the Peninsular veterans, and that all the pluck and valour of the ———th had not been killed by the West Indies and yellow fever." Until the 1890s, many citizens regarded soldiers as little better than unsavory felons and made meager provision for their relief in old age beyond providing in-patient care for a few doddering veterans at the army's Chelsea Hospital. But then England cherished a long-standing distrust of standing armies that required Parliament to authorize the army's existence and size anew every year through the passage of the famous Mutiny Acts.

Indeed, when it came to defending England itself against attack the tendency was to rely on amateurs rather than beef up the real army. Hence the presence of the militia to which the wicked Wickham in *Pride and Prejudice* belongs, a novel that takes place during the era of worries about a trans-Channel invasion by Napoleon. The militia was an institution dating back to Saxon times, but in the early 1800s, when Napoleonic invasion seemed likely, Parliament mandated that men be selected from each parish by lottery to serve for five years in a local anti-invasion force with twenty-eight days' annual training, uniforms courtesy of His Majesty. There was never an invasion, of course, and the militia languished—to be revived briefly during the Crimean War when they garrisoned Gibraltar and Malta—and their place was taken in the late 1850s by the Volunteers, when a new Napoleon, Napoleon III, seemed menacing. The Volunteers were basically middle-class gentlemen who liked parading around with—or shooting—rifles on the weekend. At their peak there were about 200,000 of them; George Vasavor, so Trollope tells us in *Can You Forgive Her?*, was one.

The Church of England

*I*n 1800 the Church of England enjoyed a position of extraordinary influence in English society. It was the official state church, it had its own court system, with virtually exclusive jurisdiction over wills,

The Church, Somerford Keynes.

marriages, and divorces, it was entitled to one tenth of the nation's farm produce each year through the tithing system, and its members alone were eligible to attend (and teach at) Oxford and Cambridge and to hold public office. Significantly, its leader, the archbishop of Canterbury, took precedence over everyone in the kingdom except the royal family and, along with the archbishop of York, sat in the House of Lords along with the church's twenty-four bishops. It was, of course, the Protestant church that Henry VIII created when he broke with Rome. The monarch thereafter was "supreme governor" of the church, and by law the Book of Common Prayer was required to be used in all church services so as to ensure the uniformity of liturgical practices and worship. The "prayer book," as it was some-times called, contained among other things the text for the service of the two sacraments of the church—baptism and communion—and a rubric, or set of directions printed in red for the conduct of services. The prayer book also contained a catechism, a series of questions and answers concerning the faith to be mastered by those seeking to undergo confirmation, along with the Thirty-nine Arti-cles, the elements of belief to which a clergyman or lay member of the church had to subscribe. The articles contained a number of relatively straightforward statements of Christian faith, together with some deliberately anti-Catholic dicta such as a requirement that services be conducted only in English. Parents customarily took their newborns to church to be christened, or made a member of the church, by being dipped in water while friends or relatives of the family called godparents forswore the devil for the child on its behalf. When the child reached its teens and had mastered the catechism, it ratified or "confirmed" those same promises independently—now that it had come of age—at a confirmation ceremony, in order to demonstrate that it now appreciated the full import of the promises its godparents had made on its behalf. This involved a laying on of hands by the bishop to make the confirmation candidate an adult member of the church.

As befitted a large and powerful institution, the Church of England had an elaborate hierarchy of governance. At the top, just below the monarch, were the archbishop of Canterbury, who lived in Lambeth Palace, just across the Thames from Westminster; and the archbishop of York, each with responsibility for the "province" covering his part of England. The archbishops were chosen, generally from among the bishops, by the prime minister. The Canterbury prelate, by long custom, had precedence over his counterpart in the north of England. In addition to exercising a general supervision over the church, the archbishops are of most interest to the novel reader because of their ability to grant special marriage licenses enabling one to get married anywhere at any time.

The bishops, priests (i.e., the local rectors and vicars), and deacons made up the three "orders" of church. Laypeople becoming ordained thus spoke of "taking orders." Historically, bishops were chosen by the monarch, but by the 1800s Parliament—as it had with so many other royal functions—had largely usurped this one, too. Casaubon "is a tiptop man and may be a bishop—that kind of thing, you know, if Peel gets in," says Mr. Brooke to Dorothea in *Middlemarch*. When a bishop died, as we see at the beginning of *Barchester Towers*, the prime minister consulted with the two archbishops on what was supposed to be a list of at least three candidates. When one had been agreed upon, a written *congé d'élire* ("permission to elect") was sent to the dean and chapter of the bishop's see authorizing them to select a new bishop, as was their nominal right. But this was merely a courtesy. The *congé d'élire* always included a Letter Missive—which designated the person whom the chapter was actually required to elect.

The bishop's special responsibilities were to ordain new clergy, to confirm the faithful who wanted to become full members of the church, and to supervise the diocese, the administrative unit of the church over which he had authority. If he were lucky, he would eventually get to sit in the House of Lords. Historically, both arch-bishops and the nation's twenty-four bishops all had had seats there, but when the population grew and the church created additional bishops in the 1800s, no additional parliamentary seats were created for the additional clergy. In consequence, except for the bishops of London, Durham, and Winchester, the twenty-four episcopal seats in the House of Lords had to be parceled out on the basis of senior-ity, and some clerics just got left out until the older bishops died off. Dr. Proudie in *Barchester Towers* is lucky. "He was selected for the vacant bishopric, and on the next vacancy which might occur in a diocese would take his place in the House of Lords." Nonetheless, in the House of Lords or not, the post of bishop was a grand one. The bishop was customarily addressed as "My Lord," and his primary residence was always known as a "palace." As garb emblematic of the office, he wore an apron and sleeves made of lawn, one of the finest varieties of linen.

The archdeacon was the bishop's subordinate and assisted him in governing the diocese, in part through the making of "visitations," or inspection tours throughout the parishes in the diocese. He was often assisted by one or more rural deans, who kept tabs on parish operations in the diocese. In the immediate vicinity of the bishop's cathedral there was invariably a chapter house, a meeting place for the dean, and canons who composed the chapter. They were in charge of seeing to the physical maintenance of the cathedral and the conduct of its services. The canons were sometimes referred to as prebendaries, since they were generally paid by a prebend, or a share of the endowment that had at one time been given to the cathdedral. (Cathedrals often had attached to them as well a pre-centor or a minor canon who helped with the choral services; the minor canon was *not* a member of the chapter.)

The local representative of the church was the parish "priest," as the vicar, rector, or perpetual curate of a parish was known. He conducted the services in the local parish church, tended to the sick, officiated at baptisms, christenings, funerals, and so on. His post was officially known as a "benefice" or a "living" and it could be used to maintain a handsome life-style. The minister was entitled to all or part of the local tithes, the mandatory annual payments by parishio-ners to sustain the church, which, until they were commuted to a monetary payment in 1840, consisted of one tenth of the farm pro-duce in the area. In addition, he was often able to obtain some revenue from the glebe, that is, the farmlands that went along with the parsonage itself. The glebe could be quite a help to a clergyman with a large family, like Jane Austen's father, who used the glebe at Steventon to grow wheat and raise sheep, cows, and pigs to help feed his eight children. In *The Warden*, we learn that the living of Septimus Harding, Crabtree Parva, "was only worth some eighty pounds a year, and a small house and glebe," but that there were also sizable livings like Crabtree Canonicorum, where "there are four hundred acres of glebe; and the great and small tithes, which both go to the rector, are worth four hundred pounds a year more."

Naturally, as we learn in *Pride and Prejudice* and *Mansfield Park*, these were sought-after positions, especially since the only formal obligation was to preach one Sunday sermon each week. Some livings were "within the gift" of the bishop. Such a living, called a "collation," could be bestowed by him unilaterally, and its incumbents were called "rectors" and received all the tithes. Other parishes, however, were administered by "vicars," who were entitled to only part of the produce, the so-called "small tithes," because these clergy were actually the representatives ("vicar" has the same root as "vicarious") of the *real* rectors. These latter reserved for themselves the "great tithes" of corn, wood, and hay. Typically, such a parish was one in which a monastic order centuries before had purchased the living and in so doing become the de facto rector and received all the tithes. In such instances, the order appointed a deputy or vicar (or sometimes a "perpetual curate" like the accused Mr. Crawley in *The Last Chronicle of Barset;* the Brontës' father was the real-life perpetual curate at Haworth) to perform the clerical duties of the parish. In later years, such livings generally passed into the hands of large landowners, like Lady Catherine de Bourgh, who is the "patron" of the obsequious Mr. Collins in *Pride and Prejudice*, and then people might curry favor with the patron to get the post, since the church would not usually ordain someone a full priest unless he had a living to go to.

In 1830, some 7,268 of the 11,342 livings in England and Wales were in the control of private parties. Lady Catherine bestowed her living gratis on the unctuous Mr. Collins, and Sir Thomas Bertram in *Mansfield Park*, likewise, gave a living at Mansfield free to the Rev. Mr. Norris, who has "scarcely any private fortune" and who is both his friend and the new husband of his sister-in-law. Since they carried a nice steady income with them, however, such livings were much sought after, and, in fact, they were widely bought and sold—

just like annuities—as well as simply given away. In fact, when the Rev. Mr. Norris dies, Sir Thomas winds up selling the Mansfield living to a Dr. Grant in order to pay for his son Tom's "extravagance." Indeed, as late as the 1880s, perhaps one third of the 6,000 livings in private hands were still bought and sold in this manner. They were even advertised for sale in the *Times*. "Often the notice mentions that the incumbent is old," wrote a contemporary observer, "and the property is so much the more valuable, for the succession will be speedier."

Told in *Sense and Sensibility* of a living worth "about two hundred a year," John Dashwood finds it all but incredible that it should have been given away: "For the next presentation to a living of that value—supposing the late incumbent to have been old and sickly and likely to vacate it soon—he might have got I dare say—fourteen hundred pounds." In a well-to-do family, the alternative to giving away the living or selling it was to give it to one of the younger sons in the family who would not, like the eldest, be inheriting the estate. This, in fact, is what Sir Thomas proposes to do with two livings at his disposal in *Mansfield Park*, i.e., to give them to his younger son Edmund. The problem here was always that of ensuring that the living would somehow become vacant at precisely the time that the son fulfilled the requirements for ordination and was actually eligible to become the incumbent. Typically, a family with a younger son in this situation would keep such a living "warm" for him—as Sir Thomas Bertram tries to do for Edmund—by appointing a friend and/or curate to fill the post on a temporary basis until the son was ordained. This was the plan with one of the livings destined for Edmund, which, had his brother's extravagance not necessitated selling it, "would have been duly given to some friend to hold till he were old enough for orders." John Dashwood infers a similar scheme in *Sense and Sensibility* upon hearing that Colonel Brandon has offered a free living to Edward Ferrars: "Edward is only to hold the living till the person to whom the Colonel has really sold the presentation is old enough to take it."

If you *did* get a living, there was a certain ritual to be observed in assuming the office. Once you had been appointed (or "presented") to the living by your patron, if the living was not a collation, the bishop was then more or less obligated to "institute" you, or perform the tasks necessary to make you the true spiritual incumbent of the priest's office in the parish. In addition, you also had to be "inducted," that is, placed in possession of the physical church property itself, which might involve being led up to the church door and having your hands placed on it, ringing the bells, and so on. Chapter 23 of *Barchester Towers* is entitled "Mr. Arabin reads himself in at St. Ewold's"—this additional step called for the reading aloud of the Thirty-nine Articles to the congregation from the pulpit of the parish church.

Below the bishop and the parish priest came the third and lowest of the three orders of the church, the deacon. He was a parson in training who assisted the parish priest in conducting the services, especially communion, helped the children with their catechism and visited the sick. After a year he could become a rector or vicar himself.

Altogether different from the dean was the curate, a full-fledged clergyman—but one without a benefice or living of his own. He assisted the rector or vicar in a parish. The curate was not the same as the perpetual curate, who was basically the same as a vicar, i.e., a permanent incumbent of a living which belonged to some lay rector. The real curate was, in fact, the "poor relation" of the Church of England, a source of cheap labor who very often made life cushy for clergymen who held livings but didn't really want to do the parish work associated with them. In *Middlemarch*, for example, Edward Casaubon is the rector at Lowick, but his absorption in his studies leads him to abjure all duties except giving the Sunday sermon; he leaves the rest to his curate.

The situation in another nearby town is somewhat different, as we learn when Eliot tells us of the rector, Mr. Cadwallader, "being resident in Freshitt and keeping a curate in Tipton." That is, the rector held more than one living simultaneously, not an unusual circumstance in the early part of the century. "Her father was a clergyman," we learn of Catherine Morland in the first paragraph of *Northanger Abbey*. "He had a considerable independence besides two good livings." Jane Austen's father himself was rector of both Deane and Steventon in Hampshire, and the incumbents of no fewer than 6,120 out of the 10,533 livings in England in 1827 were nonresidents. Where the rector was a nonresident, the spiritual care of the parish would generally be entrusted to a curate. It was also not unusual for a clergyman to hold an incumbency and a nonparochial post like a deanery. Sometimes, as in the case of the Reverend Vesey Stanhope, whose family's return wreaks such havoc in the Barchester Close in *Barchester Towers*, the rector did not even have to live in England. "He held a prebendal stall in the diocese; one of the best residences in the close; and the two large rectories of Crabtree Canonicorum, and Stogpingum. Indeed," says Trollope, "he had the cure of three parishes, for that of Eiderdown was joined to Stogpingum. He had resided in Italy for twelve years." However, in the wake of the reform spirit that swept through England in the fourth and fifth decades of the century, this practice of pluralism, as it was called, became the target of increasing criticism, and the Pluralities Act of 1838 officially abolished it.

In fact, this criticism was part of a larger wave of reaction against laxity in the church, a reaction born in part of the preachings of John Wesley, a member of the Church of England who had begun preaching a new, back-to-the-Bible, born-again gospel of the heart at open-air services attended by craftsmen, poor people, and laborers in the early 1700s. His followers separated from the church of England and formed the Methodist Church. Its grim emphasis on hellfire and damnation made the term "methodist" a by-word for dour, uncharitable churchgoing fanaticism. The term is applied to the misanthropic farm servant Joseph in *Wuthering Heights* and to Dorothea Brooke in *Middlemarch* by Mrs. Cadwallader when she describes Dorothea as having "a great deal of nonsense in her—a flighty sort of Methodistical stuff." None of the Victorian novelists seem to have liked the sect; in *Tess of the d'Urbervilles* the villainous Alec d'Urberville becomes a preacher for the "Ranters," or Primitive Methodists, without any discernible change except to make his sordid passion more hypocritical.

Wesley's message was really for the poor and the working class. When it filtered upward to the middle class, it took the form of the Evangelical movement, whose members, like the Brontës' father, remained inside the Church of England. Not that the Evangelicals pleased Dickens and Trollope any more than the Methodists. Murdstone and Obadiah Slope are classic portraits of the baneful influence of the new movement. "Low Church" in their tendencies, they preached the desperately sinful nature of man and abhorred ceremony and ritual. As other influences from within the Church of England grew, they transformed it from the relatively relaxed latitudinarian institution that we encounter in *Middlemarch* or *Silas Marner* ("there was no reason, then, why the rector's dancing should not be received as part of the fitness of things quite as much as the Squire's") into the austere, disapproving bastion of grimness that Bishop Proudie and his wife represent in *Barchester Towers*. "I can remember," says one observer in *The Last Chronicle of*

Barset, recalling the earlier era, "when the clergymen did more dancing in Barchester than all the young men in the city put together."

Barchester Towers centers on the conflict between the Low Church tendencies of this new Evangelical faction and the old-fashioned High Church tendencies represented by Archdeacon Grantly. But in fact, the "High Church" group split within itself. Originally, High Church designated no more than the old, comfortably Tory group within the Church of England, the element characterized by men like the Grantlys in *Barchester Towers* and the morally relaxed, hunting and fishing clergy in *Middlemarch*. However, a group at Oxford University centered around John Keble and E. B. Pusey, a professor of Hebrew, began publishing in the 1830s a series of tracts (the group was sometimes known as the Tractarians) opining that the church was *too* close to the people. They suggested reconsidering some of the practices that had gone out when the church had divorced itself from Rome, such as chanting, the wearing of colored vestments, and so forth. But this High Church predilection for ritual and semi-Catholic doctrine, as Trollope points out, was no more to the liking of the old-fashioned Grantly faction than the Low Church tendencies of the Proudies. "They all preached in their black gowns as their fathers had done before them; they wore ordinary black cloth waistcoats; they had no candles on their altars, either lighted or unlighted; they made no private genuflexions. . . . The services were decently and demurely read in their parish churches, chanting was confined to the cathedral, and the science of intoning was unknown. One young man who had come direct from Oxford as a curate to Plumstead had, after the lapse of two or three Sundays, made a faint attempt, much to the bewilderment of the poorer part of the congregation." The conflict is dramatized in the dispute between Obadiah Slope and Mr. Arabin, the former declaring that "the main part of the consecration of a clergyman was the self-devotion of the inner man to the duties of the ministry. Mr. Arabin contended that a man was not consecrated at all, had, indeed, no single attribute of a clergyman, unless he became so through the imposition of some bishop's hands, who had become a bishop through the imposition of other hands, and so on in a direct line to one of the apostles." The battles between these groups went on for years, with the addition of still another, "Broad Church," faction, which tried to provide for a moderate, common ground among the other groups. As late as 1874, however, feeling was still running sufficiently high on the matter to lead to the passage of the Public Worship Act, under whose provisions a number of Anglican churchmen actually went to jail for allegedly introducing "Catholic" practices into their worship.

Oxford and Cambridge

*Y*es, 'tis a serious-minded place. Not but there's wenches in the streets o' nights," says a carter to Jude Fawley in *Jude the Obscure* about Christminster, which Thomas Hardy meant to stand in for Oxford. "You know, I suppose, that they raise pa'sons there like radishes in a bed? And though it do take—how many years, Bob?— five years to turn a lirruping hobble-de-hoy chap into a solemn preaching man, with no corrupt passions, they'll do it, if it can be done, and polish un off like the workmen they be, and turn un out wi' a long face, and a black coat and waistcoat, and a religious collar and hat."

And so they did—just as Oxford and Cambridge also turned out future prime ministers, distinguished physicians, would-be barristers, and countless numbers of perfectly ordinary aristocrats and country squires.

Each some fifty or so miles north of London, both Oxford and Cambridge dated back to the 1200s when Oxford was founded along the Thames by a "university" or collective organization of scholars and their masters, and Cambridge by a splinter group from Oxford a few years later.

The two universities were organized around colleges, which were some twenty or more units of residency and instruction. Each college had a head (known variously as a president, dean, warden, provost, or master), a governing body of "fellows," some of them tutors of the undergraduates, and a number of undergraduate students. All Souls, Balliol, Christ Church, Jesus, Magdalen, Merton, Oriel, and Trinity were among the more famous of the colleges at Oxford; Corpus (Christi), Emmanuel, Jesus, King's, Magdalene, Queen's, St. John's, and Trinity among the more celebrated at Cambridge. Collectively, the heads of the colleges ran the university. Although administration was nominally in the charge of a chancellor

(Prince Albert for a while at Cambridge), a vice-chancellor selected by the colleges really ran things. Instruction—such as there was—took place within the colleges, since for much of the century the university made only perfunctory attempts to provide university-wide instruction. The tutors who took charge of this instruction within a college were fellows, that is, undergraduates who had been elected to permanent membership in the college's governing body as a consequence of doing well on undergraduate exams. Fellowship brought with it not only influence within the college but a permanent stipend, frequently without any duties attached to it, so that a fellowship, if you wanted to be nonresident, as some were, was really a kind of permanent subsidy to start you—or keep you—going in a career. Angel Clare apostrophizes Tess Durbeyfield, calling her "the great prize of my life—my Fellowship, I call you. My brother's fellowship was won at his college, mine at Talbothays Dairy."

What was college life like? Students attended chapel at eight o'clock, then they had meetings with their tutors in the morning and lectures—if there were any—in the afternoon. They dined "in Hall" at five and were required to be back in their college by nine. If they were not, they were fined. Discipline for the colleges was enforced by two proctors assisted by men known as "bull-dogs." An American visitor to Oxford in the 1870s noted that they wandered in search of rule-breaking undergraduates through "the streets day and night and are obliged to look into billiard rooms, hotels, and bars, and have the right to search any house in town with only ten minutes' notice, by virtue of an old provision in the charter of Oxford." Infractions of the rules could result in confinement within the college boundaries (being "gated"), suspension (being "rusticated"), or expulsion (being "sent down"). (To be "plucked" was to fail an exam.) The undergraduate curriculum took three years to complete, the university terms being Michaelmas, Hilary, Easter, and Trinity at Oxford; Michaelmas, Lent, and Easter at Cambridge.

Class distinctions were rife. In some colleges the nobility wore distinctive clothing and sat at special tables. Their caps sometimes carried special tassels or "tufts"; "tuft-hunting" passed into the language as a synonym for sucking up to the aristocracy. Scholarship students ("sizars" at Cambridge; "servitors" at Oxford) were publicly distinguished from their fellow students, who were called "commoners" at Oxford and "pensioners" at Cambridge. Scholarships could provide great opportunity, though; we are told in *Bar-*

chester Towers that Obadiah Slope has progressed from sizar to M.A. to preacher.

For many years, an inordinate percentage of Oxford and Cambridge graduates became Church of England clergy. At Oxford, for example, 18 of the 19 heads of colleges were clergymen as late as 1851, as were 349 out of the 542 fellows, and 215 undergraduates were ordained that year. The university offered several routes into the church. On the one hand, you could graduate as a simple B.A. and become a rector or vicar, as Fred Vincy considers doing in *Middlemarch*. On the other, as in the case of Mr. Arabin in *Barchester Towers*, if there was no living immediately available, you could become a fellow and teach—Mr. Arabin is a professor of poetry— while waiting for a parish position to open up.

Partly because of this clerical tradition, fellows had to be unmarried until the 1880s (even though clergy outside the universities were almost always married). And until 1871 you could not hold the post of fellow or any other faculty or administrative position in the universities without being a member of the Church of England, nor could you matriculate in either of the universities without church membership until 1854. It is this deep intertwining of the church and academic life that suggests why the most important movement within the nineteenth-century Church of England—the aptly named Oxford Movement—originated at one of the two universities. Mr. Arabin—sent to Barchester to do battle with the Low Church Obadiah Slope—is, of course, an Oxford man, but then Oxford was always the more Tory and High Church of the two universities, even before Newman and Keble. The liberal-leaning Mr. Brooke, the adherent of Wilberforce and of "Thought," tells us in *Middlemarch* how he "was at Cambridge when Wordsworth was there." Indeed, Cambridge had a reputation for rationalism and mathematics exemplified in the career of her most famous scholar, Isaac Newton. In reviewing a prospective teacher's qualifications for a young Tulliver in *The Mill on the Floss*, Mr. Riley thinks that, after all, the man in question "was an Oxford man, and the Oxford men were always— no, no, it was the Cambridge men who were always good mathematicians."

There were, of course, those undergraduates who did not become clerics, who kept horses, led dissolute lives, caroused, got into debt, and did all the other things that were the essence of a solid liberal arts education for many in the upper classes. Each college at

Oxford, for example, had its own crew of eight oarsmen. At the end of *Jude the Obscure*, the boat racing, or "bumping," provides an ironic counterpoint to the description of Jude's death.

At the same time, however, there was a gradual effort during the 1800s to introduce higher academic standards in the colleges. In the early part of the century, Cambridge created its tripos exams, so called from the three-legged wooden stools on which the examiners usually sat. These were honors exams in classics and math. The best math honors students were called wranglers and the best of these wranglers was called the senior wrangler. At Oxford, the top distinction in a subject was a "first"—starting in 1808 the man who did best in both math and classics there got a "double first"—an award given to both William Gladstone and Sir Robert Peel. (But not—we are clearly told—to Mr. Arabin, who "had occupied himself too much with High Church matters . . . to devote himself with sufficient vigour to the acquisition of a double first.")

The pace of educational reform, however, was slow, and in the middle of the century Parliament unleashed a commission on the universities to inquire if they couldn't—like everything else retrograde in the country—be reformed. The commission recommended that the university side of things be built up, the colleges' power reduced, the antiquated provisions for scholarships and the like be ended, and various other reforms be introduced to nudge the universities quietly into the nineteenth century. This was done, and, in addition, the Test Acts were abolished, fellows were allowed to marry, and the universities expanded in size—by 1900, Oxford was some 2,500 strong; Cambridge had grown to almost 2,800.

Schools

*T*he picture of educators in the nineteenth-century novel is fairly grim—tormented governesses like Jane Eyre, evil schoolmasters like Wackford Squeers or Eugene Hexam, fatuous headmistresses like the pompous Miss Pinkerton, the obnoxious Mr. McChoakumchild, and the unhappy would-be instructress Sue Bridehead, who runs away from her teacher's college—the dreary catalogue goes on and on.

The reality most children encountered was perhaps not as bad as this list would suggest. At the top of the ladder came the great "public" schools, so called because originally they were open to all. The public schools were nonprofit institutions founded with money left by generous donors to teach the local lads in the town of Eton or Harrow or wherever Latin and Greek grammar. (Hence, "grammar schools.") It was not until later that they began to take rich children, and, in so doing, to become more like what we would consider private schools. The public schools were of great social importance but little literary consequence; not even Dickens, perhaps the novelist most concerned with education, deals with them other than by a passing reference.

However, they at least provided some form of education. Much of what passed for elementary and secondary education in England in 1800 was—to put it kindly—catch as catch can, as witness the kind of dame or evening school that Pip attends in *Great Expectations*, "taught" by an old woman "of unlimited means and unlimited infirmity, who used to go to sleep from six to seven each every evening, in the society of youth who paid twopence per week each, for the improving opportunity of seeing her do it," or her real-life counterpart who was appointed parish schoolmaster because "he was past minding the pigs."

There was no national school system at the beginning of the era, and no one cared. The poor were apprenticed at an early age or went to work in the fields, and the rich had a governess for their daughter and a clergyman tutor for their son until he went away to Eton or Oxford. (Women, of course, generally did not learn Latin and Greek, "those provinces of masculine knowledge," as Eliot calls them in *Middlemarch*, whose mastery, Dorothea Brooke initially believes, would allow her a vantage point from "which all truth could be seen more clearly." In 1869, an etiquette manual observed that "gentlemen should not make use of classical quotations in the presence of ladies, without apologizing for, or translating them.")

It was not until members of the Church of England became appalled at the thought of lower-class children growing up in godlessness because they could not read the Bible that things changed. In 1811 those who were worried formed the National Society for Promoting the Education of the Poor in the Principles of the Established Church throughout England and Wales to spread the Word of God by teaching people to read the Bible.

At first the institutions they created were Sunday schools only, but gradually they became weekday elementary schools. They were such a hit that by 1839 Parliament was supporting these "national" schools, as they were called, with an annual grant of £30,000, a public subsidy of religious education that is not quite so surprising if we recall that the Church of England was the official state church. Most national schools were run on the monitorial, or mutual, system, which was advertised as permitting the remarkably cost-saving and efficient pupil-teacher ratio of 500 to 1. The teacher taught the monitors, who were students themselves, and then the monitors went and taught the bulk of the children while the teacher taught still more monitors. After a special Privy Council committee report, this evolved into the pupil-teacher system, that is, pupils were formally apprenticed to a teacher for a period of time during which they were trained in teaching techniques, at the end of which time they could take an exam for "training college" (a teacher's college). If they completed the training college curriculum they would theoretically be in excellent shape to obtain the certificate that allowed them to teach.

It was a noble idea and a chance—the only chance—for a "poor" person to get any higher education in Britain for much of the nineteenth century. The training school, however, often emphasized mastery of a killingly heavy dose of facts. Mr. McChoakumchild, the schoolmaster in the ghastly opening scenes of *Hard Times*, is a product of just such a course: "He and some one hundred and forty other schoolmasters had been lately turned at the same time, in the same factory, on the same principles, like so many pianoforte legs . . . he had worked his stony way into Her Majesty's most Honourable Privy Council's Schedule B, and had taken the bloom off the higher branches of mathematics and physical science, French, German, Latin and Greek. He knew all about the watersheds of all the world (whatever they are), and all the histories of all the peoples, and all the names of all the rivers and mountains. . . . If he had only learnt a little less, how infinitely better he might have taught much more!"

Sue Bridehead in *Jude the Obscure* attends such a college near the end of the century, a grim place from the sound of it, as Hardy points out while telling us the population from which its students were drawn: "The seventy young women, of ages varying in the main from nineteen to one-and-twenty, though several were older, who at this date filled the species of nunnery known as the Training School at Melchester, formed a very mixed community, which included the daughters of mechanics, curates, surgeons, shop-keepers, farmers, dairymen, soldiers, sailors and villagers."

In 1862 the government took another halting step toward uniform national education (elementary education was not made compulsory until 1880) by requiring children in subsidized schools to meet a series of standards—the boys and girls being required by the end of the sixth standard to read and write simple passages and to do arithmetic, and the girls to be capable in needlework, too. As late as 1871 more than 19 percent of the men and 26 percent of the women getting married could only make an "X" next to their name in the parish register. By 1891 these percentages dropped to about 7 each.

But it was not a matter of simply learning to read or write when one attended these schools, for the children were exposed to the world outside their own local area, sometimes in ways that set them apart from the older generation. "Mrs. Durbeyfield habitually spoke the dialect," Hardy tells us of Tess's mother, "her daughter, who had passed the Sixth Standard in the National School under a London-trained mistress, spoke two languages; the dialect at home, more or less, ordinary English abroad and to persons of quality." It was a dramatic change in the old ways—one can scarcely conceive of the intellectually egalitarian romance between Angel Clare and a cottager's daughter like Tess taking place half a century earlier.

"The Law Is a Ass"

*I*n the early 1800s there were three kinds of law in England: common law, equity, and church, or canon, law. Common law was the ancient, everyday law of the land, the law built up century after century through the accretion of custom, countless decisions by judges, and the practices and understandings of the commercial, criminal, and rural worlds as they went about their routine or nefarious business. As a rule it was common law to which people turned to determine if a contract was good, if someone were guilty of murder, or if the land that they disputed ownership of with their neighbor was theirs or his. Three great London courts heard common-law cases—King's Bench, the Exchequer, and Common

Pleas. King's Bench usually heard criminal matters, the Exchequer—so called from the checked cloth that originally adorned the table when the court sat—disputes over monies like customs and fines owed the Crown, and Common Pleas heard cases involving disputes between two citizens. (It is in Common Pleas, for example, that Mrs. Bardell sues Mr. Pickwick for breach of promise.) The judges of these courts—called lord chief justices in Common Pleas and King's Bench, barons in the Exchequer—held court during the four "terms," or sessions, of Michaelmas, Lent, Easter, and Hilary. Their decisions could be appealed to the Court of the Exchequer Chamber, which consisted of the judges of the two common-law courts not being appealed from listening to an appeal from the other, and from there appeal lay to the House of Lords, which, in one of its roles, acted as the country's Supreme Court. In London the common-law judges heard cases generally at Westminster Hall in the Houses of Parliament. When they were not sitting in London, some of the judges went circuit-riding to the hinterlands, where, adorned in magnificent scarlet robes, they held the assizes. These were the periodic itinerant sessions at which the London judges heard civil and criminal cases that were too difficult or too grave for local magistrates.

The law of equity was dispensed in the Chancery Court by the lord chancellor, his mace and bag containing the great seal on the table before him, along with a bouquet of flowers, assisted by various vice-chancellors and the master of the rolls. Chancery was where you got relief from decisions at common law that were too strict or inflexible, and originated when the king's chancellor—who was originally his secretary—got petitions from people who felt the results they had obtained in one of the common-law courts were unfair. They sought "equity," or fairness, from the representative of the ultimate authority—the monarch—by way of redress.

In practical terms, the difference between common law and equity meant that the common-law courts would typically uphold a contract to repay a moneylender £5 at 5,000 percent interest that you had taken out to buy a last meal for your dying mother as long as it was properly signed and drafted. Chancery, however, at least in theory, would look to see whether your circumstances when you signed had put you at such a colossal disadvantage that the contract should be voided. As this suggests, Chancery looked after those who could not look after themselves, like the wards in Chancery we find in *Bleak House,* children whose interests Chancery was supposed to safeguard when they had no other guardians. It also looked after lunatics and oversaw the estates of those who died intestate, and it oversaw the administration of trusts, the devices typically used by fathers concerned about protecting their daughters' money from bullying or wastrel husbands. The Chancery Court generally met in Westminster Hall during "term-time" and otherwise—as the first page of *Bleak House* tells us—in Lincoln's Inn.

There were four church courts, referred to collectively (along with the admiralty courts) as Doctors' Commons. The Court of Arches was the court of the archbishop of Canterbury, and he also had a Court of Faculties, which was in charge of giving special permission to do things, like hold plural livings. The Consistory Court was the court of the local bishop of London, and it handled divorces and wills. The Prerogative Court handled the wills of bishops and of people who died in one bishop's diocese but left property worth more than £5 in another bishop's diocese.

This court system did not survive the century unchanged. Chancery, for example, had become a bad joke by the mid-century. Indeed, a boxing hold in England had arisen called "to get in Chancery," and it consisted of your opponent getting your head locked under one of his arms while he pounded it with his other fist. It also says something about the Chancery Court that the suit which helped inspire *Bleak House,* the Jennings case, began with an old man who left £1.5 million when he died in 1798 and had still not been settled in *1915,* by which time the costs in the case had risen to £250,000. No evidence could actually be introduced in a Chancery suit—it was all done by questioning people. Nor could the parties or their lawyers participate in the questioning. If additional facts were needed to clarify a point, you were required to file a phony suit in one of the common-law courts; for example, if you were trying to determine, say, whether a house mentioned in the case belonged to John Jones, you had to start a lawsuit in another court with one party alleging that John Jones owned the house and the other alleging that he didn't. You could *not*, God forbid, just produce a deed. At least one of the lord chancellors took what can be charitably described as an inordinately long time to render some of his opinions. "Having had doubts upon this will for twenty years," he began one decision, "there can be no use in taking more time to consider it." Antiquated, time consuming, absurd, Chancery had become just as bad as Dickens said in *Bleak House*. Common-law courts were not much better. In a not atypical instance, one plaintiff spent fourten years patiently working his way through the system, getting all the way to the Lords in his appeal, only to be told he was seeking the wrong remedy. And in an increasingly secular—and denominationally diverse—society it became absurd for the Church of England to decide matters relating to wills and divorces.

In 1857 Parliament therefore took divorce and probate matters away from the church courts and gave them, respectively, to new civil courts of divorce and probate. Then the Supreme Court Judicature Act of 1873 combined the three common-law courts and Chancery under one roof into what was called the Supreme Court.

Lawyers

*L*awyers enjoyed a somewhat ambiguous status in nineteenth-century England. On the one hand—"I wouldn't make a downright lawyer of the lad," says Mr. Tulliver in *The Mill on the Floss*, "I should be sorry for him to be a raskill." On the other hand—Phineas Finn, a perfectly respectable young man, could become a barrister, and with such a status almost any desirable goal not requiring noble birth could be open to him.

The Court of Chancery.

English lawyers were of two kinds—those who argued in court, and those who prepared the cases for these courtroom lawyers and hired them after themselves being retained by clients. The barristers pled in the equity court (Chancery), the serjeants in the common-law courts (King's Bench, Common Pleas, and the Exchequer), and the advocates pled in the admiralty and church courts (Consistory Court, Court of Arches, Prerogative Court, Faculty Court, and Admiralty Court). The lawyers, respectively, who hired them and back-stopped them, were the attorneys, the solicitors, and the proctors.

The courtroom lawyers had the prestige and, among them, the barrister—in social standing (and often in fees)—headed the list. The barrister was often well born, and if not, becoming a barrister could make one an important figure, possibly putting one in line for a government post. As Trollope says of John Vasavor in *Can You Forgive Her?*, who signs accounts for nine hours each week for eight hundred a year, "a practising barrister is always supposed to be capable of filling any situation which may come his way." The wife of a barrister was eligible for presentation at court, while that of a solicitor was not, and barristers had their own special law school/offices/apartments in the four Inns of Court located near St. Paul's Cathedral.

The inns—the Inner Temple, the Middle Temple, Lincoln's Inn, and Gray's Inn—were ancient lodging houses, which by the 1800s housed attorneys, the offices of senior lawyers, and, in the case of Lincoln's Inn, at times the Court of Chancery as well, in a collegial fashion not unlike that which prevailed at Oxford and Cambridge. Each inn was run by senior barristers called benchers, who were generally King's Counsel (K.C.) or Queen's Counsel (Q.C.). Together with the law students and younger practicing barristers, they regularly ate "in Hall." Until the latter part of the century, no exams were required of those who wished to become barristers. The sole requirement was to "eat your terms," that is, to show up for dinner a certain number of times for at least three years so the older lawyers could meet you informally and see if they approved of you. If, after the requisite period of time, they found your work and character satisfactory, you were "called to the bar," i.e., a small barrier, presumably in the Hall, that separated the area where the senior lawyers, or benchers, sat from where those who had not yet been called were. You were thereafter entitled to appear before the courts as a barrister.

Some did so at once. Others might work for a while with a

"special pleader," an inn member not admitted to the bar who drafted court papers, or "pleadings," as they were called. Others would try to obtain "chambers"—office space that could also serve as an apartment—in or near their inn. Here they would sit alone— barristers could not have partners—and wait for a solicitor to bring them a "brief," or case. Or they might follow a circuit of the assizes judges if they were just starting out. The young Eugene Wrayburn fantasizes in *Our Mutual Friend* about taking over a lighthouse with a solicitor friend: "And there would be no Circuit to go. But that's a selfish consideration." The twenty-nine-year-old Frank Greystock, beloved of Lucy Morris in *The Eustace Diamonds*, Trollope tells us, "had been called to the Bar, and had gone—and was still going—the circuit in which lies the cathedral town of Bobsborough. Bobs- borough is not much of a town, and was honoured with the judges' visits only every other circuit. Frank began pretty well, getting some little work in London, and perhaps nearly enough to pay the cost of the circuit out of the county in which the cathedral was located."

If you distinguished yourself in practice over a number of years, you might be entitled to trade the ordinary "stuff" gown you wore for one of silk, that is, you could become a King's or Queen's Coun- sel. That was an honor that entitled you to write the appropriate initials after your name, and in his chapter on "Mr. Abel Wharton, Q.C." in *The Prime Minister*, Trollope tells us Mr. Wharton thought "he would take the silk as an honour for his declining years, so that he might become a bencher at his inn."

Prior to the 1800s the serjeants, or serjeants-at-law, of which, perhaps, Serjeant Buzz-Fuzz in *Pickwick* is the most memorable example, enjoyed more prestige than the barristers. Indeed, so pres- tigious had the serjeants been that for a long time one could not become a common-law judge without first being a serjeant. They had their own Serjeants' Inn, and it was not until the mid-century that the order of serjeants was abolished.

One could not engage the services of a barrister or serjeant directly; one had to hire a solicitor or attorney to do this. We note in *Pickwick* that Pickwick's counsel Serjeant Snubbin is not hired by Mr. Pickwick directly but by Mr. Perker, Pickwick's solicitor. And when one had to pay for the courtroom services rendered by the barrister, the payment was always made to the solicitor. Thus, "Messrs. Dodson and Fogg, two of his Majesty's Attorneys of the Court of King's Bench and Common Pleas at Westminster, and solicitors of the High Court of Chancery" would have paid Serjeant

Buzz-Fuzz for his work on behalf of Mrs. Bardell. Indeed, legally the fee paid to the barrister was considered a gift rather than wages, so that he could not even sue for his money if he were not paid.

This peculiar setup enabled the barristers and serjeants to pretend they were not "in trade," since it removed from them the necessity of taking money directly in payment for their services. On the other hand, it made the barristers dependent on the goodwill of solicitors for their livelihood. Consequently, the barristers often hung around courtrooms looking busy and in demand in an effort to impress solicitors from whom they hoped to get business. The eponymous barrister hero of *Phineas Finn*, rejoicing at the prospect of a lucrative government post, thinks by contrast of "how long he might have sat in chambers, and have wandered about Lincoln's Inn, and have loitered in the courts striving to look as though he had business, before he would have earned a thousand a year!" As the barristers gather in the courtroom before the Pickwick trial, Dickens notes that "such of the gentlemen as had a brief to carry, carried it in as conspicuous a manner as possible, and occasionally scratched their noses therewith, to impress the fact more strongly on the observation of the spectators. Other gentlemen, who had no briefs to show, carried under their arms goodly octavos, with a red label behind, and that underdone-pie-crust-coloured cover, which is technically known as 'law calf.' Others, who had neither briefs nor books, thrust their hands into their pockets, and looked as wise as they conveniently could." Solicitors were not, however, of the same status as barristers. They had no collegial institutions equivalent to the Inns of Court, and they were not self-regulating, as the barristers were. Instead, they were subject to the control of Parliament and the courts, who decreed that no one should become a solicitor without "articling" or apprenticing himself for five years to a practicing lawyer, which is how the "articled clerk" came into being.

We have spoken thus far of the equity and common-law lawyers, who, of course, handled the bulk of legal matters, but, in fact, fiction's most famous articled clerk—David Copperfield—served his apprenticeship in law amid the advocates and proctors who practiced in the church and admiralty courts at Doctors' Commons. David, it will be remembered, is articled as a clerk to Mr. Spenlow so that he may learn to become a proctor himself. Advocates in Doctors' Commons, the courtroom lawyers, were sometimes spoken of as "civilians," because one needed a doctorate in civil laws from Oxford or Cambridge to appear in court there. Unhappily for them, when Parliament transferred jurisdiction over probate and marriage from the ecclesiastical courts to common law courts in 1857, the civilians began to lose out, and they were abolished altogether in 1873, when the entire upper court system was reorganized. Simultaneously, the "attorneys" who had fulfilled the role in the common-law courts played by solicitors in Chancery were also abolished, and their status merged into that of the solicitors, leaving thereafter only the two classes of barristers and solicitors.

Crime and Punishment

In England in 1800 one could be hanged for sheep stealing, sodomy, murder, impersonating an army veteran, stealing something worth more than five shillings from a shop, treason, doing damage to Westminster Bridge, and about two hundred other offenses. (Killing a man in a duel, although murder, was considered socially okay for people of quality, so juries generally didn't convict until the

The treadmill at Brixton.

1840s. Thereafter it became advisable to duel on the Continent, as Phineas Finn does.)

Following execution the criminal's body would either be given to a surgeon for use in an anatomy class or else, until 1832, it would be hung in chains—preferably at a crossroads (Jude Fawley's ancestor "was gibbetted just on the brow of the hill")—from a gibbet, a crosspiece set about twenty feet off the ground, of which Pip sees a specimen at the beginning of *Great Expectations* "with some chains hanging to it which had once held a pirate."

It has been argued that this harshness was necessary because there was no real police force to deter crime. In the country parishes there existed only an unpaid constabulary made up of locals with no real police training. In London there was only "the watch." Sometimes known as "charleys" because they originated in Charles II's reign, the watch tramped through the streets at night armed with cutlass, lantern, clacker (to summon aid), and truncheon, shouting out the time and weather—"One o'clock on a rainy night and all's well"—before returning to sit in their little sentry boxes and keep an eye on the immediate street area.

These individuals were not powerful deterrents to the criminal element. In 1750 John Fielding and his brother Henry, the novelist, accordingly founded the Bow Street Runners in London. A step in the direction of a real police force, they were in part really detectives. Few in number, they worked on a fee and reward basis, which ultimately laid them open to charges of corruption. We meet them in *Oliver Twist* interrogating the hero after he is caught in a London burglary. They were also empowered to go outside London, and we find them turning up in the marsh areas of Pip's boyhood to try to solve Mrs. Joe Gargery's murder in *Great Expectations*. In 1792 more "police offices" like the one at Bow Street were set up, staffed by justices of the peace or police magistrates who both directed the constables who worked out of the office and heard criminal cases there.

But they were not enough either. The citizens of the capital were accordingly quite pleased when Sir Robert Peel managed to create a Metropolitan Police Force in London in 1829. Its men were promptly dubbed "peelers" or "bobbies" in his honor. Essentially, they were the old parish constables, only now on a full-time, salaried basis, and they still bore the title of constable. Each constable reported to a sergeant, who reported to an inspector, who in turn reported to a superintendent, whose boss was the home secretary.

There were about 3,000 bobbies to begin with, and they originally wore tall hats made stiff enough to stand on so they could peer over walls; they were headquartered at Scotland Yard. They were viewed as such a success that in 1856 Parliament decided that rural areas should have them, too, and the genial, bumbling village constable who bicycles past the vicarage and into the pages of so many contemporary British murder mysteries put in his first appearance.

The number of capital crimes was cut back over the years so that by mid-century one was hanged only for murder, piracy, treason, or setting fire to a dockyard or arsenal. How was a finding of criminality made? If a death had occurred under suspicious circumstances, a coroner was required to empanel a jury and look into the circumstances of the death—as we find the coroner doing when Mr. Krook autocombusts under mysterious circumstances in *Bleak House*. If the coroner then concluded that a murder had occurred and could point the finger at the person who did it, his finger pointing in and of itself had the legal force of an indictment. Other cases of treason and felony required formal indictment, however, which would have to be brought by a jury based on a prosecution by the police or an informer. "And you might be in for it now," says Caleb Garth to the farm laborers in *Middlemarch* when they try to attack the railroad surveyors, "if anybody informed against you." "Informing" in this context was the same process that went in other circumstances by the name of "laying an information." The chilling memory of the Star Chamber abuses never altogether ceased to haunt the corridors of the English legal mind, with the consequence that England never established a post of public prosecutor, such as a district attorney, fearing the effect of such prosecutorial power in state hands. Instead, the Crown relied on private individuals—including, but not limited to, victims—to bring a prosecution or lay an information against someone before a magistrate. Thus, when Oliver Twist is brought before the magistrate on charges of stealing a handkerchief from Mr. Brownlow as he stood before a bookstall, Brownlow brings the charges; "the prosecutor was reading, was he?" asks the magistrate when told of Mr. Brownlow's stance at the time of the theft.

To encourage citizens to point the finger, especially when they themselves were not the victims, the law even provided incentives such as a share in any fines collected from an offender if the prosecutor were successful in his endeavors. The slimy Noah Claypole, we learn at the end of *Oliver Twist*, knowing the penalty for taverns illegally open on Sunday, "went into business as an Informer, in which calling he realizes a genteel subsistence. His plan is, to walk out once a week during church time attended by Charlotte in respectable attire. The lady faints away at the doors of charitable publicans, and the gentleman being accommodated with threepennyworth of brandy to restore her, lays an information next day, and pockets half the penalty."

This does not mean that the police had to wait for a private individual to conduct an investigation and bring charges, but it did mean that the fiction was maintained that when the police acted to bring charges they were doing so only in their individual capacities as private citizens just like everyone else. And when it came time to conduct the prosecution's case in a courtroom, lawyers in private practice had to be hired on an ad hoc basis. "Who is conducting the prosecution?" asks Mr. Toogood in *The Last Chronicle of Barset*. "Walker, Walker, Walker? oh—yes; Walker and Winthrop, isn't it?," while in *The Eustace Diamonds* the fact that Lizzie Eustace will not come to testify at the great trial ensures that "the attorneys engaged for the prosecution were almost beside themselves." " 'That won't do at all,' said an old gentleman at the head of the firm. 'She has been very leniently treated and she must come.' "

When a supposed malefactor was actually brought to court, if the offense were relatively trivial the justice of the peace or his London equivalent, the police magistrate, would hear the charges and mete out punishment on the spot with no jury trial. If the matter were more serious, the criminal would be tried at the quarter sessions when all the justices in the county met together or, if graver still, by the assize judges (the Common Pleas, King's Bench, and Exchequer court judges riding circuit from London). In London, the quarter sessions and assizes were combined and held at the Central Criminal Court at the Old Bailey. It is where the trial of Mr. Benjamin and Mr. Smiler takes place in *The Eustace Diamonds*. Fagin is tried here, too; the Old Bailey was right next to Newgate Prison, which made it convenient both for purposes of incarceration and execution.

Whatever our notions of the great Anglo-Saxon heritage of impartial justice, we should not imagine that nineteenth-century England went out of its way to protect the rights of accused criminals. Until 1848, for example, the police magistrate was not charged with evenhandedly weighing the evidence brought before him in a prosecution. On the contrary, the law presumed that a crime had been committed and that it was the magistrate's job to ferret out the evidence that would prove it—a fact that accounts in part for the adversarial stance Mr. Fang so rapidly assumes when Oliver Twist is brought in on suspicion of trying to steal from an old gentleman at a bookstall. Until 1898 the accused was not permitted to testify at all, even on his own behalf. A lawyer for the accused in felony cases was permitted no chance to question or cross-examine witnesses nor could he make any speeches to the jury in most cases until 1837, nor could you see the "written record of evidence" against you before trial until 1839.

You were not even guaranteed a prompt trial. In London things might happen fairly rapidly, but since in the country serious crimes had to go before an assize judge there could be a substantial delay between the time of commitment to jail and the time of trial. In the six counties in the north of England, for example, the assize judges showed up only once a year, in the summer, until well into the 1800s—which meant that if you got hauled in just after their annual trip you could stay in jail eleven months just awaiting trial.

Trials, however, were undeniably swift. In fact, the first English criminal trial ever to run for more than a day did not take place until 1794. Moreover, executions by law were to take place within two days of sentencing, in order to drive home to people that the Crown was serious about law and order. In *Oliver Twist*, Fagin is found guilty on Friday; he is then imprisoned in Newgate Prison and hanged the following Monday. This was not atypical. In 1812 a man named Bellingham shot Prime Minister Perceval on May 11, was tried and convicted on May 15, and was executed on May 18.

If the accused were found guilty and the sentence were death, London executions occurred on a scaffold erected outside Newgate, and enormous crowds would attend. We catch glimpses of them in *Oliver Twist*, waiting for the chance to witness Fagin's end in the dawn before he is to be hanged. A husband and wife team of murderers were executed together in 1849 before a crowd of 30,000. A railroad rented excursion trains for the execution of a mass murderer during the same period, and a man from Madame Tussaud's showed up to try to get the criminal's clothes. Public executions were not confined to the city; as a boy, Thomas Hardy witnessed the execution of a woman at the Dorchester jail through a telescope that perhaps influenced his depiction of the death of Tess Durbeyfield. Public executions were not halted until 1868.

For many years, the Crown's pursuit of felons did not end with their death. Treason until 1870 was punishable by the loss of one's land, and any other felony by the loss of everything else the guilty party owned. "Lay hold of his personal property," Wemmick warns Pip when Magwitch—illegally—returns to England in *Great Expectations*. "You don't know what may happen to him. Don't let anything happen to the portable property." Pip is not mindful of this practical advice, and when Magwitch is seized, the convict himself is not aware that his capture has now ensured Pip's financial ruin. "I've seen my boy," the injured convict says, "and he can be a gentleman without me." "No. I had thought about that," Pip tells the reader. "No. Apart from any inclinations of my own, I understood Wemmick's hint now. I foresaw that, being convicted, his possessions would be forfeited to the Crown."

Trials did not always end in death, of course. The real innovation in the correctional system during this period was undoubtedly transportation. That is, if one were found guilty of something—send him to another continent. Originally this led to dumping convicts in the American colonies—a custom which grew more difficult with the outbreak of the American Revolution. Temporary holding pens consisting of old prison ships—the "hulks" described at the beginning of *Great Expectations*—were accordingly pressed into service beginning in 1776, the convicts being sentenced to hard labor gathering ballast for shipping on the Thames.

Then someone got the bright idea of shipping all the criminals to Australia. This should have put an end to the hulks, but it did not, since they continued until 1858. In the meantime, however, transportation proved quite popular—between 1810 and 1852 some 140,000 convicts were sent "down under." Eventually, however, the Australians began complaining about being a dumping ground for criminals, too, and so it became necessary to imprison people in England again.

There were several varieties of English prisons. Dickens shows us the grimness of Newgate, but we also catch a glimpse in *Little Dorrit* of the rather cheap-hotellike Debtor's Prison in the Marshalsea. But the Marshalsea and Newgate were characteristic of a cruder, more haphazard approach to punishment that sought only to confine and not to "correct" or "reform." It was left to the reformers of the early 1800s to take steps toward the more systematic persecution of the criminal element.

"The Treadmill and the Poorhouse," says Scrooge when benevolent philanthropists visit him for a Christmas donation on behalf of the poor, "are in full vigour then?" Of course—his visitors reply—and indeed they were. Invented in 1818, the treadmill was a nasty device typical of the new "reform" era that consisted of a great metal cylinder with steps built on it so far apart that one had to step way up to catch the next one before the cylinder revolved around from under one's feet. Convicts were required to walk on the treadmill six hours at a time, a practice that certainly did nothing for the health of the weak or sickly and merely drew the convicts' attention to how boring, pointless, and repetitive their lot was. "Lucy is Threatened with the Treadmill" Trollope called one of his chapters in *The Eustace Diamonds*. The device was finally abolished in 1898.

A prisoner too young or ill for the treadmill would in all likelihood be set to picking oakum, the rope which when unwound by hand through long and tedious work was made to yield strands that could be used for caulking ships. Or so the theory ran. Prisoners were kept at the work even after ships no longer used oakum, and in some of the new model prisons the work was required to be carried out in absolute silence. Indeed, the so-called silent system forbade any conversation with guards, visitors, and other inmates on the logically unassailable principle of penological reform that bad associations bred bad (criminal) people—cut out any chance for association and you eventually cut out the criminal behavior. The idea was a hit for some time in criminological circles; its logical analogue—that prisoners should be kept isolated from one another in individual cells rather than sojourn in large communal areas as in the sprawling prisons of the 1700s—is with us to this day. Cells and hard labor became the hallmark of the new nineteenth-century prisons that replaced the old, ramshackle confinement of places like the Marshalsea or the King's Bench.

Transition

THE HORSE

*B*efore the railroad, the horse was the way you got somewhere if you weren't going on foot, whether you went on its back or by "waggon" or coach. After the railroad, though, the horse was just as important until cars came along. In the country, there were plenty of places railroads didn't go, so the horse had to instead. Even in the city, it still supplied the motive power for cabs and buses, and there were hansoms in London up through 1900.

Horses were specialized in what they could do. The hack was the ordinary everyday horse you used for just clip-clopping along. In addition, there was the sleek, nervous racehorse. Also the hunter—a horse bred specifically for fox hunting, who was not even used in its chosen sport until several years old. You used the hack to get to a "meet," and the hunter you would use to hunt with once you got there was brought along separately. For fat people, there were cobs—short, sturdy draft horses suitable for carrying or pulling heavy loads. For riding, stallions were usually too frisky, geldings best, and mares were in between, but women and children favored ponies; small children rode along beside their parents on horseback in Hyde Park on their little ponies, and at the end of *Great Expectations* the "sad" ending Dickens originally wrote finds Pip meeting Estella driving a pony carriage in Piccadilly. As well she might— ponies were smaller and easier to handle than horses, and, if women did drive horses, they usually drove a one-horse carriage. Only men would venture to try controlling the three additional horses required in a "four-in-hand." On horseback, ladies rode side saddle, alternating sides each day so as not to develop an overly enhanced buttock on one side. Riding astride seems to have been looked on as risque, if Hardy's description of Bathsheba Everdene when "she had no sidesaddle" is anything to go by. "Satisfying herself that nobody was in sight, she seated herself in the manner demanded by the saddle, but hardly expected of the woman."

Except for a racehorse, an animal generally hit his prime around six. This is not to say that some horses didn't wear out sooner than others. A horse pulling a fast carriage would typically have a "working life" of only four years. Its top speeds under these circumstances, judging from the prodigious accomplishments of the mail coaches, was an average eleven miles an hour. Generally, a horse could go twenty-five to fifty miles a day, but not for any long period. On a dirt road pulling a load a team could generally haul about a ton; a major factor in the building of canals was that they enabled a horse to pull fifty tons instead.

Horses were expensive both to buy and maintain, so it is not surprising that in 1848 out of a population in excess of 18 million only 100,000 had their own carriage or riding horses. In the 1820s, a good carriage horse or hunter could run £100 and even an ordinary hack could cost £25 to £40. Plus horses, unlike cars, had to be fed, sheltered, and cared for daily, which meant that if you got a horse you were also entering into a subsidy of the horse transportation business. You were buying the services of a corn dealer (fast horses ate 72 pounds of straw, 56 pounds of hay, 2 bushels of oats, and 2 bushels of chaff a week), a blacksmith, a saddler, a coach maker (if you had a carriage), a harness maker, and—if you were fancy—a coachman and a groom as well. Some people simply opted out and went to livery stables, where you could rent horses. In addition, the rich and the nobility in England by the latter part of the century, at least in London, almost invariably went to a "jobber" or rent-a-horse man for their horses, presumably leaving their own good ones back at the country estate where they could rest up for the summer and fall during the London season. This "jobbing" cost about £85 a year in the 1880s but freed one from all the worry about the lameness, illness, and death of the horses.

The poor couldn't afford horses, and, if, like the costermongers, they needed a beast of burden, they resorted to donkeys. They were cheap; at mid-century you could get one in London for five shillings and a deluxe donkey was only three pounds. They were easily managed little beasts who had the additional merit of being willing to eat almost anything. Some of them were almost like pets to the "costers" whose carts they pulled, but they were, sadly, more likely to succumb to the cold than their sturdier equine cousins.

Horses died, too, of course, and when they did, it was off to the "knacker"—the slaughteryard. Here, in death as in life, the horse served mankind. He was sliced, diced, and chopped into an amazing variety of products—his hair for horsehair sofas and mattresses (and the ghastly crinolines, *crin* being French for "horsehair"), his hooves for glue, his skin for tanning, his bones for manure, his bone fat for harness and cartwheel grease, and his approximately 350 remaining pounds of horseflesh for dog food and cat food.

PLEASE, JAMES, THE COACH

*T*he oldest form of wheeled transportation in nineteenth-century Britain was the waggon, a long, heavy vehicle like the American covered wagon, except bigger and clumsier, pulled by up to ten horses with drovers plodding patiently alongside. When David Copperfield is deemed to have overeaten along the coach route he is taking, he is "the subject of jokes between the coachman and guard as to the coach drawing heavy behind, on account of my sitting there, and as to the greater expediency of my travelling by waggon." The waggon made its way through the English countryside carrying heavy goods and people who didn't have the money to travel fast or were not pressed for time, averaging three to four miles an hour. For moderately faster and/or shorter-distance travel there was the van, a smaller vehicle which servants might use to get themselves back and forth between London and their master's country estate and which really served as the local bus in the countryside. To get to her ersatz cousins, the "d'Urbervilles," Tess "walked to the hill-town called Shaston, and there took advantage of a van which twice in the week ran from Shaston eastward to Chaseborough."

Next up the scale in speed and prestige came the coaches—stage or mail. Coaches were enclosed, four-wheel vehicles that were not terribly fast until the roads were improved in the late 1700s. The invention of springs in the latter part of the 1700s and early 1800s made it possible to suspend the body of the coach instead of fastening it onto a stiff "perch"—which also made for a more comfortable ride, notwithstanding that a mail coach measured only forty inches from seat cushion to roof.

In nineteenth-century England carriages carried people, while waggons carried goods. (Stagecoaches and humble vehicles like pony chaises might carry people, too, but they did not incarnate the grandness and gentility that a vehicle graced by the name carriage did. To call a pony chaise a carriage smacked of absurd social pretensions.) Barouches, landaus, victorias, curricles, and broughams were all carriages—they varied in their body shape, the number of horses that pulled them, the number of passengers they took, and the number of wheels they had, but they all embodied a certain social dignity. Carts, drays, vans, and waggons, on the other hand, were generally used for carrying goods. They could also be used to carry people as well, but, if so, they were generally people of the lower orders.

As a rule, coaches were used for long-distance travel. For shorter distances in the country, there were two sorts of vehicle—the gig and the curricle in the two-wheel department and the waggonette and the cart in the four-wheel. The gig was the basic two-wheel, all-purpose, everyday work-pleasure vehicle, especially in the country, the vehicle that Farmer Boldwood uses in *Far from the Madding Crowd* and the one people often drive in Jane Austen when they are not trying to impress anyone or are not carrying a large group. It was a one-horse, two-person vehicle, of which the stanhope and the tilbury were two varieties. The curricle, popular in the first half of the century, was the same idea, except—alone of the two-wheel vehicles—it was built for two horses, which made it more of a rich man's toy, especially given the difficulty of finding a well-matched, high-quality pair. Catherine Morland finds in *Northanger Abbey* "that a curricle was the prettiest equipage in the world" and, by comparison, "the chaise and four wheeled off with some grandeur, to be sure, but it was a heavy and troublesome business." The curricle is very fast on her journey: "so nimbly were the light horses disposed to move, that, had not the general chosen to have his own carriage lead the way, they would have passed it with ease in half a minute." It was probably really a young man's carriage, like a sports car; it was one of the first things the young Dickens bought when he made money with his writing.

Carriages were, in fact, the cars of the nineteenth century—part status symbol, part self-expression, part necessary means of transport. They were often lavished with care when first built to make sure, for example, that the coat acquired just the right sheen—the coachman in *Mansfield Park* is furious when a carriage is taken through the woods and the veneer on the side is scratched, since part of a coachman's task was to maintain as well as drive the household carriages. It was important to have the right kind of carriage. Closed carriages seem to have been the fanciest, no doubt because they were associated with the chariot and private coach used by the rich. There were other distinctions, however. In the 1830s, a contemporary recorded that in the countryside the "close carriage" set looked down on the people with barouches or phaetons, and the barouche and phaeton people in turn looked down on those who drove gigs. Even the rules of the road seemed to reflect acknowledgment of a hierarchy. "Carriages painted with a coat of arms take precedence over all others," wrote a foreign observer in the 1840s, "middle-class carriages with four horses have precedence over those with only two, the latter over cabriolets and tilburys, hired landaus over coaches, coaches over omnibuses, omnibuses over cabs, and so forth down to the trap, and even it has right of way over the cart."

One cannot appreciate many of the fine points of nineteenth-century life and fiction, however, without understanding that some carriage was absolutely crucial to any pretense of social standing. "Evil-doing will be spoken of with bated breath and soft words even by policemen, when the evil-doer comes in a carriage, and has a title," says Trollope apropos of Lizzie Eustace in *The Eustace Diamonds*. Prime Minister Pitt taxed carriages during the Napoleonic War on the understanding that it was really a disguised income tax on the rich, while at the beginning of *Pride and Prejudice* Mrs. Lucas expresses some understanding of why Mr. Darcy did not talk to Mrs. Long at the ball, given his exalted social status: "I dare say he had heard somehow that Mrs. Long does not keep a carriage, and had come to the ball in a hack," a remark that might have seemed silly or exaggerated to a nineteenth-century audience, but one that they would have understood. Fictional examples could be multiplied at length. In *Vanity Fair*, the young William Dobbin at one point mocks George Osborne for being a merchant's son: "My father's a gentleman, and keeps his carriage," retorts Osborne.

Barouches and landaus were the fancy family vehicles of the gentry and the nobility in the early part of the century. Then came the brougham, the idea, not surprisingly, of Lord Brougham. It was an effort to produce a two-wheel vehicle like the gig or curricle, except—unlike them—one with a "closed" or hard top. Why not? The new French cabriolets of the 1820s demonstrated that you could have a small, light vehicle enclosed just like a coach. The brougham was very successful, so successful that it gave way to a four-wheel variety as well, which was like the old coaches except sleeker and built lower to the ground. It became the "in" family vehicle for the *latter* part of the 1800s, playing perhaps the same role as that played by the barouche in the first half of the century, and, since it is always best to be a two-car family, you supplemented it where possible with a victoria. These little numbers were also low built—like the brougham—but, in addition, were open and thus suitable for summer or daytime driving. Primarily, they were regarded as ladies' carriages.

The carriage did *not* die with the coming of the railroad. The railroads did nothing, for example, to eliminate the private vehicles that took you from the station to your front door. Nor did they really interfere with the flourishing horse-drawn public transportation system that London enjoyed right up to the turn of the century. In 1800 the market for cabs in the great city was dominated by hackney coaches—basically, old noblemen's coaches that someone hitched up and drove around for hire. Pip hires one of these magnificent, if fatigued, specimens when he first arrives in London to see Mr. Jaggers; "it was a wonderful equipage, with six great coronets outside, and ragged things behind for I don't know how many footmen to hold on by, and a harrow below them, to prevent amateur footmen from yielding to the temptation." They could be hired at stands where they were attended by "watermen" who watered the horses.

Cabriolets were a big innovation in the 1820s. These hackney cabriolets, or cabs, as they came to be called, thus giving birth to a whole new generic term, were the inspiration for Lord Brougham's brougham. They were, in turn, succeeded by cumbersome four-wheel coaches called growlers. *Their* competition for the last half of the century were the famous hansom cabs, which first appeared in the late 1830s, and which were marvelous two-wheel vehicles that perched the driver way up in back behind the passengers so they could get an unobstructed view of the city streets ahead. The speedy hansom was a big item for years and years, but it was tippier than the four-wheelers, which drew the patronage of the timid and the elderly, and it lacked room for luggage.

Engine, tender, and carriage.

THE RAILROAD

*T*he railroad, like many technological innovations, was not immediately seen as radically different from its predecessor modes of transportation, with the consequence that just about everything about it was initially modeled on the stagecoach.

The nomenclature and design, first of all. The engineers were called "drivers" and the conductors "guards." The railway cars were called "carriages," and the first-class carriages were made up of three "coaches," each with room for six passengers, as in a stagecoach, with semicircular stagecoachlike windows next to them and coach-bodylike curves reproduced on the outside of the car. Until 1891, there were no common passageways or corridors, so there was no way to get from one compartment to another.

There were originally just two classes of passenger, first and second class, corresponding to the inside and outside of the coach. It was not until later that a third class was added and, when it was, it consisted initially simply of cattle cars with no covering from the elements or, as the board of directors of one railway casually described them in the minutes of an 1838 meeting, "open boxes—no roofs." Thomas Hardy described what a ride was like for the poor in those days: "The seats for the humbler class of travellers in these early experiments were open trucks, without any protection whatever from the wind and rain . . . the unfortunate occupants were found to be in a pitiable condition from their long journey; blue-faced, stiff-necked, sneezing, rain-beaten, chilled to the marrow."

There was no illumination on many trains—people often brought candles for night reading. Until 1874, when steam heating came in, keeping warm during a winter journey meant having the porter bring you a metal foot warmer filled with hot water. Dining cars did not exist for any class of passenger until 1879, so people brought prepacked lunches or made a mad dash for the station eatery when the train stopped. They also made a mad dash for the lavatories, since there were no toilets on trains until 1892. Ladies might travel together in compartments separate from the gentlemen, for long journeys bringing chamber pots concealed in discreet baskets, while for gentlemen long tubes that could be strapped along the leg under a trouser were advertised.

On the other hand speeds were (relatively) fast and fares undeniably cheap. Trains in the 1850s averaged more than twenty miles per hour, the expresses almost forty, although the engines were initially not all that powerful. Sometimes they were brought to a halt along the coast of North Wales by a high wind. By the end of the century the *Flying Scotsman* that ran from London to Edinburgh, supposedly the speediest train anywhere, averaged fifty-five miles per hour. Fares were cheaper than stagecoach fares, and, then, in 1844, Parliament required every railroad to run at least one train a day along its entire route, making all stops and charging no more than a penny a mile. These "parliamentary" trains, as they were called, were even cheaper than third class, and for the first time whole categories of people who never dreamed of travel before could get around England, as Mrs. Bounderby in *Hard Times* eagerly relates when asked how she got down to Coketown to see her somewhat less than grateful son. "By parliamentary, this morning. I came forty mile by parliamentary this morning, and I'm going back the same forty mile this afternoon." By the 1870s third-class passengers—perhaps as a consequence—outnumbered first and second class almost two to one.

The social and economic effects of the railroad were, of course, many. Stagecoaches vanished, great herds of sheep and cattle no longer had to be driven to market along the roads, and new industries that needed overnight access to large markets because of their perishable products sprang up to take their place. "Londoners will drink it at their breakfast tomorrow, won't they?" Tess shyly asks Angel Clare when they drive the milk cans from the dairy to the train one day during their courtship, and, indeed, a farm given over wholly to producing milk like the one where Tess and Angel meet would have been impossible in prerailroad days.

THE MAIL

$\mathcal{L}$etters!
Letters told you whether or not you had inherited the estate—
whether someone had agreed to marry you—whether cousin Frank
was lost at sea—whether a long-lost heir was actually alive and in
New Zealand and was now returning to claim his fortune—

The mail was expensive, except to M.P.s, who, until 1840, could
"frank" it, i.e., send it free. Postage was billed on the basis of the
number of miles the letter traveled in England, fourpence for the
first fifteen miles, eightpence for eighty, and so on up to seventeen-
pence for a letter going seven hundred miles. In addition, if you put
any enclosures in the letter (even a second sheet of notepaper) the
charge was double. And the recipient always paid, not the sender.
We learn how beloved Amelia Sedley was of her classmates at Miss
Pinkerton's at the start of *Vanity Fair* when a classmate who is
"generous and affectionate" cries out at her departure, "never mind
the postage, but write every day, you dear darling."

Naturally people tried to avoid paying these charges. One obvious technique, employed by Edmund Bertram in *Mansfield Park* to
help his homesick cousin Fanny Price send a letter to her brother,
was to get a friend or relative who was an M.P. to send the letter
for you. "As your uncle will frank it," he says, knowing of the Prices'
poverty, "it will cost William nothing." Or, perhaps, you could find
a friendly—or mercenary—coachman to take the letter some miles
farther toward its destination before mailing it. The poor used a
simpler device. Coming one day upon a postman disputing with an
old lady about a shilling charge for a letter from her son, Coleridge
was sufficiently moved by her poverty to pay the charge for her. As
it turned out, the letter was empty—by simply writing her name on
the outside in his handwriting, her son was able to let his mother
know when she saw it that he was still alive and well. More genteel
ways to save postage included using lots of abbreviations in one's
letters and also "crossing," or turning the letter at right angles after
one had written a page and writing over it. In general, says Miss
Bates of a correspondent to the heroine in *Emma*, "she fills the

whole paper and crosses half. My mother often wonders that I can
make it out so well. She often says when the letter is first opened,
'Well, Hetty, now I think you will be put to it to make out all that
checker-work.' "

Local mail was not as expensive, at least in big cities like London.
Within the city and the surrounding area, there was a "two-penny
post" that was organized and run separately from the General Post
Office that handled national mail. The two-penny post delivered
letters left at designated local shops or with its carriers for the price
indicated by the service's name. It was fast—a letter dropped off
before ten went out on a noon route, and, if the carrier waited for
a quick reply, the response could be back in the first sender's hands
by about seven that evening. A sort of proto zip code was developed
for London, too, that permitted letters to be "directed" or addressed
in accordance with a letter code that marked letters *E* for the East
End, *W* for the West End, *EC* for the City, *WC* for Holborn, *N* and
NW for north of the old City, and *S* and *SW* for the south bank and
the like.

In 1840 the postal system changed. A "penny-post" was created
that permitted one to send letters anywhere in England for a uniform rate of one penny per half ounce. At about the same time the
railroads began to take over the job of transporting the mail from the
horse-drawn mail coaches, which vastly increased the speed and
ease with which letters could be sent, although before the coming of
the railroads, the mail consistently traveled faster than almost anyone or anything else in England. Starting in 1784, the mail was
carried in special stagecoaches carrying only a few or no outside
passengers at an average speed of eleven miles an hour, which made
them a good bit faster than ordinary stagecoaches. Turnpike keepers
had to open the gates when they saw the mail coach coming or heard
the sound of the guard's warning bugle, innkeepers could lose their
licenses for delaying one, and anyone else was subject to a five-
pound fine if they interfered with a mail coach in transit.

Until the 1840s envelopes were not in widespread use so you
wrote your letter on a sheet of paper, folded it up and then sealed
it and that was your de facto envelope. In Jane Austen, we find the
characters using a wafer to seal their missives. This was a small disk
made of gum and flour which you licked and then stuck on to the
letter to close it. Alternatively, there were seals—gentlemen sometimes carried them on a chain hanging from their waistcoat—which
were dipped in beeswax or a similar compound that was melted with

the aid of a little desk taper and then applied to the letter. Red sealing wax was for business, other colors for social correspondence, and black for mourning. "In those days there was an art in folding and sealing," wrote Jane Austen's nephew in a memoir of his aunt in 1870. "No adhesive envelopes made all easy. Some people's letters always looked loose and untidy; but her paper was sure to take the right folds, and her sealing-wax to drop into the right place." We are forcibly reminded of the dangers of sloppy letter sealing when Mrs. Henchard's letter about her daughter's past falls prey to her husband's snooping eyes in *The Mayor of Casterbridge*, with the usual dire Hardy consequences: "In sealing up the sheet, which was folded and tucked in without an envelope, in the old-fashioned way, she had overlaid the junction with a large mass of wax without the requisite undertouch of the same. The seal had cracked, and the letter was open."

The day came, of course, when letters were not the only means of communication across long distances in the country. By 1857 most of the large towns in England were linked by telegraph, and in 1879 the first telephone exchange in the country appeared in London.

The
Country

L IFE ON THE F ARM

*T*he English countryside dominates many of the great nineteenth-century novels. Hardy, of course, writes at length of farming customs and practices, notably in *Far from the Madding Crowd* and *Tess*, but its rhythms are in the background of his other novels, too. We also find Mr. Rochester talking with Jane Eyre in the drowsy orchard as "a splendid Midsummer shone over England . . . the hay was all got in"; Heathcliff concerned with the safety of his flock during a winter storm; and the rural laborers in *Middlemarch* rising in protest to denounce the incursion of the railroad into their countryside as Mr. Garth plots ways to improve farming in the area. There were, after all, only nine English towns in 1801 with a population over 50,000. We may therefore have a better understanding of many of the novels if we know the rhythms and practices of everyday farm life in nineteenth-century England.

The three great products of English farming in the 1800s were corn, sheep, and cattle. "Corn" as the English used the term was not the American corn of corn on the cob, i.e., maize, but rather referred to grains such as wheat, barley, and oats. Wheat was grown to make bread, barley to make beer and ale (and sometimes bread), and oats to make oatcakes and other food as well as feed for horses. Sheep were raised for wool and for mutton, and, secondarily, as a portable source of manure. Cattle provided meat, butter, and milk and pulled ploughs and farm waggons. (Turnips, Swedes (Swedish turnips), and mangel-wurzels were grown to rest fields and as fodder for the animals during the winter.)

Wheat harvest.

There was some specialization, but generally sheep, cattle, and corn were all raised on the same farm. Bathsheba Everdene, for example, though she concentrates on growing corn, also keeps sheep, as readers of the sheep-washing and -shearing scenes in *Far from the Madding Crowd* will recall. Raising corn, sheep, and cattle simultaneously was good insurance against a bad year with any one or more of them. In addition, sheep and cattle needed the hay from arable fields to sustain them, and cornfields benefited from sheep manure and plowing by cattle.

Together with her neighbor, Farmer Boldwood, Hardy tells us, Bathsheba farms about two thousand acres. This was not an inordinately large farm. A contemporary study found that the typical Dorset farm had about 660 acres. On it there worked twenty-nine men and boys, who were helped by fifteen more men and women at harvest time, the work force being made up mostly of carters to deal with the horses and waggons, shepherds, and ordinary farm laborers and ploughboys to do the basic work of ploughing, sowing, and weeding.

Farming practices varied from farm to farm, and local wisdom dictated when various activities were to be carried out, along with the farmer's own inclinations and the climate of the regions; planting and sowing took place somewhat earlier in the warmer, southern parts of the country. Nonetheless, all farms followed a basic seasonal calendar for the cultivation of crops and the raising of livestock. The year's work often began with plowing in late fall or early winter for a spring wheat crop. This involved driving a plough in long straight lines through the earth to break up the ground, a boring task usually allocated to the adolescent ploughboys. The fields were then harrowed, which meant that the remaining clumps of earth were further broken up by dragging a toothed instrument called a harrower across them. Lambs were born in the winter, and shepherds stayed up day and night, as Gabriel Oak does at the beginning of *Far from the Madding Crowd* before his flock is killed, ensuring that they got enough milk and care if their mothers were unable or reluctant to provide it. The only other significant winter work was threshing the corn harvested during the preceding summer and fall. Before the advent of the mechanical threshing machine, this involved walking around in a circle in the barn with wooden instruments called flails, literally "flailing away" at the corn until the grain separated from the stalk. The grain was then sifted, or "winnowed," to separate the wheat, or other desirable end product, from the chaff, after which the former would be put into bags for market.

In spring, barley was sown, and in May the sheep were driven out into the fields after being marked with a substance to identify them, like the "raddle" (red earth) purveyed by raddlemen like Diggory Venn of *The Return of the Native*. On farms where corn was grown the sheep munched their way through the meadows of grass down near the riverbeds during the day. At night they were penned up in the cornfields in portable pens called "hurdles"— moved to a different spot each night—so that they could fertilize the corn in an era before artificial fertilizer was widely available. During these weeks, the cattle were also brought out of the barns to graze.

The wool that had kept the sheep warm during the winter was becoming hot (and salable) by the end of May, and so the sheep were washed clean of dirt and raddle by swimming them through a pond or stream, a process described in *Far from the Madding Crowd,* and then sheared of their wool a week later when it had dried. The sheep were also moved out of the hayfields so the grass could grow back long enough to be harvested to provide winter food for the animals. This took place while the cornfields were being tended and weeded to safeguard their crop.

By June, "haymaking" occurred, that is, the hayfields were cut. Extra laborers were hired, and then the men and women began moving through the fields, reaping the hay with a scythe while gatherers followed behind them, collecting the hay into bushels. These were bound together either by the gatherers or by tiers coming behind them. The hay then had to be gotten quickly into stacks, or ricks, so it could be dried, since hay packed together that was moist was capable of generating enough heat to actually ignite. Even in the urbane world of Jane Austen, the necessity of such activity is conceded, when Miss Crawford complains in *Mansfield Park* that she can find no waggon or cart to transport her harp because it is "in the middle of a very late hay harvest."

"When you *do* think of it," says Edmund Bertram not unkindly, "you must see the importance of getting in the grass."

Mrs. Crawford's use of the term "harvest" to describe getting in the hay is, perhaps, one mark of her distance from the rural landscape that environs the orderly world of Mansfield Park. For the actual "harvest," the climax of the farmer's year, which took place in late July or August, referred to the gathering in of corn, not hay. The hay, after all, was merely to feed the animals; corn was the cash crop, and it was vital to get it in before the rains came and ruined it. Thomas Hardy tells us in *Far from the Madding Crowd* that Bathsheba Everdene's harvest has produced eight ricks, worth £750, and half the produce of the farm for the entire year. The fact that her lover, Sergeant Troy, unthinkingly gets the laborers drunk before they can cover the corn from the rain vividly shows us how dangerously irresponsible he is.

The actual harvesting was long, slow, tedious work, and generally involved use of a small sickle rather than the great sweeping scythe used in haymaking. A team of five men working well together might hope to harvest about two acres of fields a day. On the "average" 660-acre Dorset farm (not all arable, of course) this obviously could mean several weeks of back-breaking labor. And when that was done, the corn, like hay, had to be brought to the farm and put up in great ricks raised up off the ground by staddles to prevent damage by moisture and rats. The ricks would then be covered with cloths or actually thatched to keep the elements out.

The farmer by custom then gave a "harvest home" that involved feasting the laborers in celebration of the successful conclusion of the harvest, and the agricultural year was at an end. In the days before the railroads began hauling freight, the end of the farm year was also the signal for the drovers to drive their extra cattle and sheep to the big markets and sell them off before winter set in. This was one of the world's less exciting jobs, sheep in flocks tending to move at an average of about a mile an hour. Sheep, however, could at least feed as they went along; cows required a complete stop after they began chewing in order to digest their cud.

THE MIDLANDS, WESSEX, AND YORKSHIRE

*T*here are three great rural landscapes in the nineteenth-century English novel: the Midlands, Hardy's Wessex (really Dorset and other nearby counties in the southwest of England), and the Yorkshire moors of Emily Brontë's *Wuthering Heights*.

The Midlands were central England—Salopshire, Worcestershire, Warwickshire, Leicestershire, Northamptonshire, Bedfordshire, Staffordshire, and parts of Oxfordshire, Buckinghamshire, Berkshire, Derbyshire, Nottinghamshire, and Herefordshire. Much of it was rolling hills and good farmland, which was often planted with hedgerows, which blossomed so beautifully in the spring with the hawthorn's white blossoms and the red flowers of the dog roses. The Midlands, in short, bore a tamed and domesticated aspect to an extent greater than many other regions of the country. Indeed, the long rows of fields with trimmed hedges helped turn the "shires," as they were called, in the Midlands into the center of fox hunting during the 1800s as well.

Wessex was described by Hardy as the "province bounded on the north by the Thames, on the south by the English Channel, on the east by a line running from Hayling Island to Windsor Forest, and on the west by the Cornish coast." This is southwest England, once the scene of the ancient Saxon kingdom from which Hardy borrowed the name Wessex, and it was a relatively poor region of England for much of the 1800s. Unlike the middle or northern parts of England, Wessex had little industry, which kept farm wages low

Village of Whit Hurch, Dorset.

since there was no competition for the labor of farm workers from factories, as there was elsewhere.

Then there was Yorkshire, specifically the brooding, desolate west riding in which the scene of *Wuthering Heights* is laid. Exposed to the icy northern gales of the Pennine mountains, the region was hilly and rocky—hard to farm and running wild to gorse and heath where it was not cultivated (oats were the corn crop). The steepness of the hills was probably one reason Wuthering Heights raised sheep, which did better than cattle in such an environment. The village, that tight social clustering of diverse humans characteristic of the Midlands landscape of Eliot, never took hold to the same degree in the north.

In the north, the typical pattern of settlement was often the solitary farmstead—like Wuthering Heights—sheltering against the side of the hill miles from its neighbor. Rural isolation was reinforced by the tendency, longest lived in the north, for farm servants to actually live in the farmstead with the family—as do Joseph and Zillah at Wuthering Heights—rather than in their own cottages away from the farm where they worked, as Bathsheba Everdene's laborers in Casterbridge did or as the farmers did in the Midlands.

On the other hand, there was an abundance of coal in the region, which meant that the standard of living benefited twice over, first because of the relatively low cost of fuel for heat and cooking, and second because the growth of industry meant that nearby farmers were competing with factories for labor and consequently had to pay higher wages than farmers paid to their laborers elsewhere.

Perhaps the most comfortable, familiar landscape of the three was that of the Midlands countryside described by Eliot. The prickly borders of shrubs and trees along the edges of the carefully cultivated fields, however, in reality often were emblematic of the unhappy and turbulent displacement of the area's recent inhabitants. Until the enclosures began, men worked and farmed great unbounded areas in which arable land, pasture, and wastes were intermingled.

The time came when individual farmers and large landowners wanted some of this land for themselves, and they won the legal right to remove the other users. They then planted hedges as boundary markers and to keep others off, a purpose admirably served by the hedgerows woven together of holly, hawthorn, and dog rose that blossomed so beautifully in the brilliant May sunshine. Before long, the hedgerows were a prominent feature of the Midlands landscape. They also served to keep cattle from wandering. They were planted out of hawthorn (also called Maythorn or whitethorn) because it grew fast and was virtually impenetrable. (Its "haws," or red berries, provided food for the birds and set off the white blossoms it sent forth in spring, as did the "hips" of the dog rose or briar rose that often grew among the hedge trees.) Because of its prickliness holly was also used as a hedge tree, although it was not as hardy as hawthorn. Blackthorn had the merit of flourishing in harsh soil; its black berries—the sloe that were cousins to the domesticated greengages and damsons and plums—also provided jam and sloe gin, and the tree could be made into a walking stick or, in Ireland, a shillelagh.

The landscapes of the far north and south were, of course, quite different. But in the place of gently rolling hills and carefully delimited fertile fields with sleepy villages, the landscapes of *Wuthering Heights* and the Hardy novels alike engendered a feeling of desolation and helplessness in the face of an indifferent but enduring nature. Wuthering Heights, we are told, is surrounded by acres and acres of boggy moor over which the unwary traveler goes at his peril, as Mr. Lockwood finds when he tries ill-advisedly to venture forth in the snow on one occasion; while *The Return of the Native* revolves obsessively around Egdon Heath, the vast, desolate, fictional expanse of heath and furze that Hardy imaginatively distilled out of a number of actual heaths.

In fact, heath and moor are different names for a similar terrain, namely, a desolate, sandy-soiled place, where dead vegetation piles up and accumulates into peat. The difference between a heath and a moor is the greater amount of rainfall on the moor, which, unlike the heath, is characteristically boggy and marshy. Hardy remarks both on the similarity of and transition from the one to the other in a passage from *The Return of the Native* where "they wandered onward till they reached the nether end of the margin of the heath, where it became marshy, and merged in moorland."

The landscapes of the far north and south shared the same plants. The furze Clem Yeobright cuts to his wife's horror when his eyes give out in *The Return of the Native* was a yellow-flowered shrub growing up to eight feet in height that could be used as fuel. In the middle of England it was called "gorse," and in the north it was called "whin," under which name it appears in *Wuthering Heights*. This was not the only shrubbery the two terrains had in common. In her ultimately fatal journey across Egdon Heath, Mrs. Yeobright comes across a "little boy gathering whortleberries in a hollow." Sometimes they were called huckleberries, blackberries, or blueberries, but they turn up on the wild moors of *Wuthering Heights* as bilberries, a small plant growing no more than two feet in height, with delicious bluish-black berries. In a hungry moment, the exhausted heroine of *Jane Eyre* makes her way across a moor: "I saw ripe bilberries gleaming here and there, like jet beads in the heath; I gathered a handful, and ate them with my bread."

But it is the heath plant itself, the very shrub that gave its name to the characteristic landscape called a heath, that was perhaps the most typical plant of all. "Heath," as it was called in the south of England—"ling" in the Midlands and "heather" in the north—was a shrub not more than a few feet high that produced light purple or sometimes white flowers. In the blaze of summer, according to Hardy in *The Return of the Native*, it conferred a transitory glory on the heath when "the July fire shone over Egdon and fired its crimson heather to scarlet. It was the one season of the year, and the one weather of the season, in which the heath was gorgeous." It was what the sheep grazed on in the northern moors with their sparse vegetation, a source of fuel (and brooms), and it could even be used for thatching a house. It was also a stuffing for beds and a source of honey; Catherine Linton confides to Nelly Dean how Linton "said the pleasantest manner of spending a hot July day was lying from morning till evening on a bank of heath in the middle of the moors, with the bees humming dreamingly about among the bloom." The harebell (or heathbell)—Scotland's famous bluebell—grew here, too. It was a small, purplish flower capable of producing a distinct whispering murmur when the autumn had come, "a worn whisper, dry and papery," "the united products of infinitesimal vegetable causes . . . the mummied heath-bells of the past summer, originally tender and purple, now washed colourless by Michaelmas rains, and dried to dead skins by October suns."

The British yeoman.

WHO'S WHO IN THE COUNTRY

*R*ural England was governed by a strict hierarchy. At the very top were the landed aristocracy, the old, powerful families with hereditary titles and large estates. Typically, such families were of the peerage and had lived at their "seat," or estate, for generations and owned thousands upon thousands of acres of land. The duke of Ancaster in 1888, for example, controlled more than 163,000 acres of British countryside. Altogether perhaps some one fifth of England was tied up in these great estates, which on the average consisted of 10,000 acres or more. As the earl of Derby noted in 1881, this kind of landownership yielded many rewards: political power, social influence, the pleasure of managing a great estate, rental income from tenant farmers, and the fun of shooting and hunting. The estates were typically rented out to farmers who rented homes on the land and worked it with rural laborers under the supervision of the lord's land agent and bailiffs. Because of their exalted station, the estate owners typically spent only August through December on their estates, and their involvement in day-to-day county affairs was generally minimal. Typically, such a magnate might serve as lord lieutenant and select the local justices of the peace, but his attention would have been largely centered on London, Parliament, and national affairs.

Next in rank came the gentry, the people who had less land than the landed aristocracy, perhaps on the average some one thousand to three thousand acres. It was the gentry who constituted the real local leadership in county matters and on whose affairs the great novels like *Middlemarch* or *Pride and Prejudice* generally turn. The gentry were not peers, but their upper ranks would have included knights and baronets. They owned their own land and often rented it out for farming like the great aristocrats above them. The lower tiers of the gentry included those with long ties in the region who would be designated "squire." Either to him or another member of the gentry, perhaps the local clergyman, would fall the post of justice of the peace. Squire Ullathorne in *Barchester Towers* in the latter part of the century fits this mold; in an earlier era we find the rough-riding Squire Cass of *Silas Marner,* "the greatest man in Raveloe," whom Eliot depicts in a manner that recalls Fielding's Squire Western. Dorothea Brooke's uncle and the senior Mr. Linton in *Wuthering Heights* were nontitled members of the gentry, although they were not squires, and both served as justices of the peace. It is the gentry from whom Jane Austen draws most of her characters—educated, comfortably well-off—they do not work themselves but oversee the work of others and spend their time plotting how to marry off their children, paying calls or seeking to elevate their social standing. Where the great aristocrats spent time in London and, perhaps, even abroad, men like Mr. Rochester and Sir Thomas Bertram or Sir Pitt Crawley would venture only occasionally to the capital on "law business," or to have a daughter presented, but would otherwise concern themselves with local "county" matters—hunting, the militia, the petty sessions and quarter sessions, and so on.

Below the gentry were the yeomen, or gentlemen farmers. Some of the gentry had not much more land than their farmer neighbors, but the farmer often would have to dirty his hands working the land himself. Nonetheless, many gentlemen farmers were prosperous enough to maintain a life-style like that of the gentry, which meant that the farmer was always trying to elbow his way into their society. In *Can You Forgive Her?* Mrs. Lookaloft seeks to make her way into the company of the gentry at Squire Ullathorne's big fete. "To seat the bishop on a arm-chair on the lawn and place Farmer Greenacre at the end of a long table in the paddock is easy enough; but where will you put Mrs. Lookaloft, whose husband, though a tenant on the estate, hunts in a red coat, whose daughters go to a fashionable seminary in Barchester, who calls her farmhouse Rosebank, and who has a pianoforte in her drawing-room?" This same tension is present in *Wuthering Heights* between the gentry of Thrushcross Grange and the farmers at Wuthering Heights, a house with no park but only a mean, stunted garden. It is always referred to as a "farmhouse" and, even after she marries Edgar Linton, Cathy jokes: "Set two tables here, Ellen: one for your master and Miss Isabella, being gentry; the other for Heathcliff and myself, being of the lower orders."

Traditionally, the yeoman was the small landholder who was the mainstay of the countryside—sturdy, loyal to his king, independent, and ready to stand shoulder to shoulder with his mates, as the "yeomen archers" did at Agincourt, in defense of English freedoms. As the century wore on, however, yeomen became a dying breed. Owing to nineteenth-century economic realities, the yeomen either lost their land and descended to the status of rural laborers or became tenant farmers of the big estate holders. Indeed, by the end of the century, the term "yeoman" had passed from use, as virtually every farmer of wealth and position usually rented from a large landowner. In *Far from the Madding Crowd* both Bathsheba Everdene and Farmer Boldwood are such farmers (who, between them, rent some two thousand acres), and both live extremely well. In fact, as Hardy says of Boldwood, "his person was the nearest approach to aristocracy that this remoter quarter of the parish could boast of." This was not uncommon. Though some farmers worked only what they owned, many others rented land from the aristocracy and gentry and then hired laborers who would do the actual farming work.

Together with the local tradesmen like the carpenter and the blacksmith, these laborers made up the cottagers, the people at the very bottom of the rural social world who inhabited the small one-, two- or four-room thatched or slate dwellings in the local village or on one of the estates. Typically, their cottages and the few acres that might go with them were owned outright by the local squire or aristocrat. Where this was not the case, a cottager may have owned only the house itself and a few tiny acres nearby, enough, perhaps, for a small garden and a place to keep a pig, if he were lucky. These are the people, it will be recalled, whose lot Sir James Chettam, at the ardent behest of Dorothea Brooke, wishes to improve in *Middlemarch*. Improving landlords were always full of schemes to build better cottages and sometimes better lives for the cottagers, too, as the century wore on, and their ladies bountiful were sometimes keen to assist by helping with the local school, distributing goods among the poor, and so on.

But the changes wrought in the cottagers' lives in the nineteenth century were seldom happy. Before 1800, a cottager could often count on his family staying on the land generation after generation, either because the cottager owned the land (which was called a freehold), had a lease (leasehold), or had a long lease, of which a copy was on the lord of the manor's rent roll (copyhold). With the acceleration of the enclosure movement, however, and the trend toward large-scale commercial farming, the cottagers often lost their rights to the common land in the village where they were once able to graze their animals or to the waste areas where they could gather fuel, important resources for families living close to the margin. More and more frequently the large landowners kicked the lease-holding cottagers out of their cottages when their leases expired instead of renewing them as they previously had for generation upon generation—which is what happens to Tess's family in *Tess of the d'Urbervilles*. The cottages were then often torn down or given up to the short-term agricultural workers who were becoming a more and more common feature of the rural landscape. Unlike cottagers, short-term workers could be easily fired without the land-lord having any of the traditional sense of responsibility for them that he might have had for the local, rooted poor. "When Tess's mother was a child the majority of the field-folk about Marlot had remained all their lives on one farm, which had been the home also of their fathers and grandfathers," Hardy tells us in *Tess of the d'Urbervilles*, "but latterly the desire for yearly removal had risen to a high pitch," and Tess, of course, spends her brief life as an itinerant farm laborer, working here for a dairy farm, there cutting turnips—but always moving on when the season is over and the task is done. We are made witness in the tale of her life to the story of an itinerant laborer whose own destruction is meant to mirror the disappearance of the traditional English countryside.

SHIRE AND SHIRE ALIKE: LOCAL GOVERNMENT IN BRITAIN

The full title of *Oliver Twist* was *Oliver Twist, or, The Parish Boy's Progress*. The term "parish" referred not to an ecclesiastical unit of jurisdiction but rather to the fundamental form of local government in England. Virtually all of England was divided into parishes (some 15,000 in the 1830s), units presumably modeled after or derived

from the parishes of the Church of England but with whose boundaries they had often long since ceased to coincide. Created in Elizabethan times, the parish was organized to serve the purposes of poor
relief, keeping the peace, and maintaining the highways and church
property. Parishes ranged in size from a tiny cluster of rural cottages
to areas in London full of vast numbers of tenement houses.

The parishes were overseen by a churchwarden (there were
often two), a constable, an overseer of the poor, and a surveyor of
highways. The term of office was one year, and all local members of
the parish were required to take their turn at these posts, except
august folk like the nobility, clergy, and M.P.'s. Being churchwarden
was a position of some prestige. (In *The Mayor of Casterbridge*
Henchard held the post in addition to being mayor.) The churchwarden was charged with responsibility for the upkeep of the church
and churchyard, and also, at least in early times, with monitoring the
moral conduct of local parishioners. Constable and surveyor of the
highways, on the other hand, were jobs to be avoided. Constables
were required to keep the peace, something which might not endear
you to your neighbors when you tried quieting them down after a
rowdy evening at the alehouse; a surveyor of the highways had to
supervise the work done on the local highway once a year by the
able-bodied men of the parish. Overseers of the poor were charged
with maintaining the workhouse and providing for any necessary
"outdoor relief" to those not living under its roof, and they would
presumably see to it that the "settlement" laws were vigorously
enforced. These laws generally required that one be born in the
parish, have lived there a year, or have been apprenticed there at
least forty days in order to find shelter in the local workhouse. The
overseers were replaced by elected boards of guardians under the
New Poor Law of 1834; Oliver Twist is brought before the "board"
when he is taken from the children's "farm" by Mr. Bumble, the
beadle, and told by them that "you have come here to be educated,
and taught a useful trade . . . so you'll begin to pick oakum tomorrow
morning at six o'clock."

Beadles were very minor parish officials, which makes their immense self-importance in the various works of Dickens that much
the more comical. For the most part, this often ridiculous figure with
his old-fashioned cocked hat and his staff, whom Dickens caricatures
in *Oliver Twist* in the pompous person of Mr. Bumble, assisted the
parish officers, helping the constable to keep the peace, the overseers to deal with the poor, and any other parish official to do his

duties, which sometimes meant that the beadle was no more than a glorified messenger boy. He was sometimes charged with keeping order in church. David Copperfield recalls "once, when Steerforth laughed in church, and the beadle thought it was Traddles, and took him out."

As all this suggests, the parish was not so much an organ of self-government as it was a handy unit of administration through which services could be exacted from the locals and order maintained. The same may be said of the county. In the gray old days before the Normans conquered England, the island was divided into shires, each of them commanded by a shire-reeve (sheriff) and an earl. When the Normans took over, they kept the shires but renamed them "counties." (The Anglo-Saxon earl for each county was deemed equivalent to the Norman "count." An earl's wife in England was therefore called a countess.) There were fifty-two counties in England and Wales in the 1800s, and many of them—Hampshire, Worcestershire, etc.—retained the "-shire" in their names despite their new, formal political status. The high sheriff was at one time the most important royal administrator in the county. However, his power dwindled after his term of office was limited in the twelfth century to only a year, and by the late 1800s he had become a somewhat marginal figure who hired the bailiffs to serve process, executed court judgments, and ceremonially welcomed the king's judges on their circuit at the assizes.

The lord lieutenant was another county official who had in large measure become a figurehead by 1800, although he still retained considerable power over the militia. The post of lord lieutenant was created in the 1600s during the tumult accompanying the civil war; it was his task to summon the county militia to arms against invasion. By the 1800s, however the post was a largely ceremonial distinction bestowed on one of the great landed magnates in the county. Plantagenet Palliser, Trollope tells us in *The Prime Minister*, by then duke of Omnium, felt a modest pride when he "saw the flag waving over the Castle, indicating that he, the Lord Lieutenant of the County, was present there on his own soil." It is a post held also by the odious marquis of Steyne in *Vanity Fair*. As Sir Pitt Crawley—wrongly—observes of him: "The Lord Lieutenant of a County, my dear, is a respectable man." Acting on behalf of the monarch, the lord lieutenant formally designated the justices of the peace.

These justices, or magistrates, as they were called, were picked from among the gentry and were often squires or clergymen; by law, the post could go only to a man with an income of at least £100 or more a year. Dorothea Brooke's uncle in *Middlemarch;* Edgar Linton and his father in *Wuthering Heights;* Sir Pitt Crawley and his son, young Pitt, in *Vanity Fair*—all of them, held "commissions of the peace." They appointed the overseers of the poor, the constable and the surveyor of highways, and they were responsible in their area of the county for maintaining the peace, summarily trying petty offenses, keeping the local government running smoothly, and, in general, running local affairs, a not terribly difficult task when we consider that the justice of the peace was often the landlord of all the other parishioners. "I've been robbed!" shouts Silas Marner, stumbling into the local tavern when he discovers the theft of his hoard. "I want the constable—and the Justice—and Squire Cass—and Mr. Crackenthorp." The local magistrate dispensed justice on his own when necessary, sometimes with another justice in the county at the petty sessions, and at least four times a year he met with all the other justices to hold the quarter sessions, where countywide administrative matters were dealt with and criminals were tried whose cases were too tricky for a local hearing but not so grave that they had to be passed on to the assize courts. The justices were the people really responsible for local law, order, and administration in England, and a statistic may suggest something of the extent of their authority; in 1883, a year when English juries convicted only 12,000 people, magistrates sent 80,000 people to jail, all without a trial.

The remaining unit of local English government was the borough, generally a town that had been granted a charter of local self-government by the king. Some, indeed, had their own officials, called recorders, instead of justices of the peace, and were therefore not part of the county justice system. Boroughs were generally ruled by a corporation consisting of councillors who designated an aldermen and a mayor. Casterbridge is a borough, and the eponymous hero of *The Mayor of Casterbridge* is pointed out to his wife as she comes seeking him after many years: "That's Mr. Henchard, the Mayor, at the end of the table," says an onlooker, "and that's the Council men right and left." These governing bodies were not necessarily very representative in nature. In Plymouth, for example, at one time only 292 out of the town's 75,000 residents could vote for its leadership. After 1835, however, the borough ratepayers got to elect their councillors.

In the early 1800s, most of the counties had the right to send two members of the local gentry to the House of Commons as members of Parliament (M.P.s). The boroughs could often send representatives to Parliament, too, but over the years many boroughs lost most—or almost all—of their electorate as the local population died out or emigrated, with the consequence that often a member of Parliament was representing only a handful of people. These virtually depopulated, or "rotten," boroughs were in some cases scarcely different from that of the borough of Queen's Crawley that Thackeray describes in *Vanity Fair*, in a village of which Sir Pitt Crawley's former servant Horrocks leases an inn. "The ex-butler had obtained a small freehold there likewise, which gave him a vote for the borough. The Rector had another of these votes, and these and four others formed the representative body which returned the two members for Queen's Crawley." In fact, shortly before 1800, it was found that fewer than 50 voters elected the members of Parliament in 51 of the parliamentary constituencies, and in 130 of the boroughs there were less than 300 votes cast. Thus, a distinction developed between a parliamentary borough that could send someone to Parliament and a municipal borough that was a self-governing municipality. Middlemarch is evidently a borough of both varieties, however. In its municipal capacity it was governed by Mr. Vincy as mayor, while as a parliamentary constituency, it was the object of a campaign by Mr. Brooke, "and his estate was inherited by Dorothea's son, who might have represented Middlemarch, but declined, thinking that his opinions had less chance of being stifled if he remained out of doors."

This system of local government creaked along for some years into the nineteenth century. Communications were poor, the desire to interfere from London in local affairs (excepting enclosure) virtually nonexistent, and the local adherents of change were generally both outnumbered and outargued. With the coming of the railroads and mass communications, however, much of this insularity was broken down, and legislative changes drastically reshaped the local political landscape. In 1834 the New Poor Law took away from the parish the exclusive authority for dealing with poverty—a major function. In 1856 London required localities to replace the old part-time constabulary with full-time bobbies, and the Municipal Corporation Act of 1835 began opening up boroughs to real self-government by the electorate. Finally, increasing demands for more sophisticated local health care, education, and the like gradually reduced the principal features of the old local self-government to a shell or eliminated them.

"THE THEORY AND SYSTEM OF FOX HUNTING"

*a*re we hunting a fox now?" asks Lizzie Greystock of Lord George Carruthers in *The Eustace Diamonds*, at a point, Trollope tells us, when "they were trotting across a field or two, through a run of gates up to the first covert."

"Not quite yet," replies Lord George. "The hounds haven't been put in yet. You see that wood there? I suppose they'll draw that."

"What is drawing, Lord George? I want to know all about it, and I am so ignorant. Nobody else will tell me."

"Then Lord George gave his lesson," says Trollope, "and explained the theory and system of fox-hunting."

Originally, hunting foxes wasn't a sport at all. Foxes were officially regarded as livestock-destroying vermin, and a statute passed in Elizabethan days required churchwardens to pay bounties for their heads. Robin Hood, Henry VIII, and everybody else in those days meant deer, not foxes, when they talked about hunting.

But deer became scarce. Trees were felled for fuel or to make ships for the king's navy, and at the same time more and more land was put into cultivation, and, as a consequence, the forest the deer needed vanished. And so the deer vanished, too.

Why not, then, hunt foxes instead, thought someone.

Foxes, however, are fast as well as tricky. New, improved hounds were therefore needed to track foxes for sport, since hounds bred for the chase had traditionally been used to chase hares, a type of game that was clever rather than fast. Lo and behold, however, in the mid-1700s, Hugo Meynell began breeding dogs at Quorn Hall in north Leicestershire that were fast enough to keep up with foxes, and suddenly everyone was off and running.

The sport worked like this: in the early morning people were sent out to stop up the holes of foxes in the hunt area. This was done to prevent the foxes—nocturnal animals—from returning to their dens. About eleven o'clock all the mounted sportsmen (the "field"), plus the yapping hounds (usually forty or fifty to a pack), gathered together at the "meet" under the overall supervision of the master of the foxhounds, who was the local worthy in nominal charge of the whole proceeding. The physical work was actually the responsibility of the huntsman, often a local working-class man who had bred the hounds, could frequently identify each one individually by bark, and was in charge of putting them through their paces on the day of a hunt.

Once assembled, the field followed the huntsman and his hounds out to a covert (pronounced "cover"), a gorse patch or thicket of some kind in which a fox was thought to have sought refuge when it found its front door locked. The hounds were sent in at one end of the covert, the idea being that they would sniff their way through it until they flushed the fox out into the open. (This was the "drawing" about which Lizzie asks George Carruthers.) Once the fox was spotted, the observer shouted "Tally-ho!"—or just shouted—and the huntsman and his hounds took off after the fox, with the field following at a discreet distance.

From then on, the idea was simply to gallop across country at top speed and have a whale of a good time splashing through rivers and dashing across fields in pursuit of the hounds and the fox without breaking your neck. The fun was in the gallop plus the sport of watching the hounds chase down the fox.

When the fox was finally cornered, the hounds killed him. They customarily devoured him except for his "brush" (tail) and "mask" (head) and "pads" (paws), which could be cut off and awarded as trophies. Squire Cass, the rough-edged member of the gentry in *Silas Marner*, has a brush on his parlor wall. A child riding in his first hunt might be "blooded" by being smeared with the blood of the dead fox.

That was it.

Traditionally, fox hunting began on the first Monday in November, although September often witnessed "cub hunting," a sort of training for inexperienced foxes and riders. The best fox hunting was in the middle of the country in the Midlands areas that fox hunting men called "the shires," especially Rutland, Northamptonshire, and Leicestershire. Fox hunting was felt to be manly, patriotic, and good training for war as well as fun. Numerous regiments gave their men leave during the hunting season to go dashing around the countryside, and perhaps it wasn't too different from everyday workouts for the cavalry. In addition, it was probably the only exercise many country gentlemen ever got, and for the young, it had the added advantage of being dangerous if done recklessly enough. And, of course, it was very social. There were sometimes "lawn meets," when people from all over gathered on the grounds of a great estate and were regaled with food and drink as the hunters prepared for their "run." There were hunt balls, too, sponsored by the hunt clubs that had originally grown up to provide stables and quarters for hunters in the days when hunts covered wide areas of country. Also—if you did it right—the activity was expensive. The Quorn's annual operating expenses in 1821, though admittedly above the average, were £4,000. A good hunter of moderate ability might cost 100 guineas (Lizzie Greystock pays 160 pounds for each of hers), and then there was always hay and stabling to be paid for as well.

As a rule, people did not go in for great soaring leaps over fences—such feats were very risky and required a good deal of skill. "No hunting man ever wants to jump if he can help it," wrote Trollope flatly in *Can You Forgive Her?*

Not everyone had a benign view of the sport. Oscar Wilde called fox hunting "the pursuit of the uneatable by the unspeakable." The farmers whose crops were trampled by hunters or whose lambs were eaten by foxes imported when the indigenous supply ran low sometimes became clandestine midnight fox killers.

VERMIN, POACHERS, AND KEEPERS

Game was defined legally as hare, partridge, pheasant, black game (black grouse), red grouse, and bustard. A law was passed in 1671 restricting the right to hunt game to people with a freehold of at least £1,000 a year or a leasehold of at least £150—in other words, the aristocracy and the gentry. This was the law until 1831. No one else could hunt game. Period.

This meant that the only way for anyone else to get game was to poach it, for which you were fined five pounds or put in jail for three months. It was also illegal to sell game or to possess dead game if you did not meet the law's property qualification, and if you were poaching at night with at least two other people and one of you had a weapon, you could be sent to Australia for seven to fourteen years or sentenced to hard labor in England. And these laws were enforced—perhaps not surprisingly since the local justices of the peace were often the same landowners on whose land the poachers—if they were caught—would be caught trespassing. In fact, the laws were enforced so strictly that during the three years ending in 1830 one out of every seven people found guilty of a crime was convicted for violating the game laws.

These laws became a most bitter source of class friction in rural England. As industrialization spread and the enclosures diminished the supply of public land available for grazing and gathering fuel, the poor tried to supplement their income by trapping game, either for their own use as food or for sale on the black market in London. Game was considered a great delicacy and a thoughtful gift, partly because, like alcohol during Prohibition, it was hard to come by. (Poached game was preferred by the discriminating, because it had to be trapped with wires or nets—not shot—due to the need to trap silently to avoid discovery.) Thackeray talks in *Vanity Fair* of how one must butter up a rich relative who comes to visit: "What good dinners you have—game every day." Local poachers who had the touch would hand their game over to coachmen who would smuggle it to London, where it would be sold by poulterers who presumably didn't ask too many questions.

Many landowners put their gamekeepers to watching the woods at night for poachers, and they set spring guns with wires attached to the triggers running off into the woods to blow the head off whoever sneaked in to get a pheasant at night. Man-traps were also popular. These were like traps for animals except bigger; a substantial one weighed eighty-eight pounds and had teeth one and a half inches long that snapped shut on the leg and could do serious damage. Both devices, however, were completely legal until 1827, although they were unable to discriminate between the lawbreaker and the casual stroller. But, as Lord Ellenborough serenely observed: "The object of setting spring-guns was not personal injury to any one, but to deter from the commission of theft; and that object was as completely obtained by hitting an innocent man as a guilty one."

At the same time poaching was becoming a nuisance to landed gentlemen, "shooting" was becoming more and more of a systematic, large-scale enterprise. For the first time, people began stocking and breeding pheasant for their coverts (wooded areas) in large numbers. Breeding pheasant was not cheap; it could run £500 to £700 a year on a large estate. It was therefore the task of the gamekeeper to keep the poachers away from the pheasant, protect and nurture the young game, and destroy any vermin. There were always plenty of vermin. "Vermin" included weasels, stoats, badgers, otters, foxes, hawks and owls and any other creatures who ate the eggs of young game or preyed on mature specimens. But raising all this wonderfully healthy game was a nightmare for farmers on the estate where they were raised because the pheasant ate their corn. "Squire Cass had a tenant or two," George Eliot tells us in *Silas Marner*, "who complained of the game to him quite as much as if he had been a lord." It is a measure of the rural landowners' power that it was not legal for a tenant farmer to kill any game that attacked his crops until 1881.

Sometimes some of the locals—and friends, too—could be mollified by letting them come shoot with you. If, as was often the case, they didn't meet the property qualifications for shooting specified by the law of 1671, you "deputized" them to shoot by virtue of your own right to do so. When Admiral Croft talks of trying to rent a house from Sir Walter Elliot in *Persuasion*, Sir Walter's lawyer friend assures the reluctant baronet that Admiral Croft will not be a demanding tenant and "would be glad of the deputation, certainly, but made no great point of it;—said he sometimes took out a gun, but never killed—." This allowed friends to be invited in early fall to come shooting grouse at a country place in the north. (Grouse shooting ran from August 12 through November, the partridge season from September to January, and the pheasant season from October to January.)

Game began to be hunted as well as raised more systematically in the 1800s. In the old days Squire Ralph set off with his favorite dog, and they tramped through the woods all day until he found a pheasant, whereupon the pheasant—startled—rose up toward freedom and the good squire blasted—or tried to blast—the daylights out of him. In the nineteenth century, however, this solitary pursuit of rather inconsequential amounts of game by individual hunters was increasingly replaced by mass animal hunts that became a staple feature of late Victorian weekends at country houses. Instead of the solitary hunter there were now shooting "parties" or groups that went on "battues," where nets were raised up to keep the game from flying away from the shooters as "beaters" walked through the fields in front of the sportsmen and drove the game up into the air. It therefore became possible to shoot birds in large numbers. In 1876, the Maharajah Duleep Singh slaughtered 2,530 partridge in two weeks; in 1864, at Lord Stamford's park over the three days from January 4 to January 7, hunters killed 4,045 pheasant, 3,902 rabbits, 860 hares, 59 woodcocks, and 28 creatures described as "various." A certain Lord Ripon alone between 1867 and 1900 killed 142,343 pheasant, 97,759 partridge, 56,460 grouse, 29,858 rabbits, and 27,686 hares. A major theme of *Tess of the d'Urbervilles* is, of course, the destruction of the traditional English countryside, and Hardy describes Tess awakening after a night in the woods to find pheasants lying about her, "their rich plumage dabbled with blood; some were dead, some feebly twitching a wing, some staring up at the sky, some pulsating quickly, some contorted." They are, she realizes, victims of a shooting party that have dragged themselves away after being hit but not killed.

"Tess's first thought was to put the still living birds out of their torture, and to this end with her own hands she broke the necks of as many as she could find, leaving them to lie where she had found them till the gamekeepers should come—as they probably would come—to look for them a second time."

Fairs and Markets

*F*airs and markets were among the major events and diversions for country people during the period before 1800 and for a long time afterward. Markets dating back hundreds of years were often weekly affairs in rural areas, places where people came to sell their cheese, grain, milk, cattle, and the like and also to buy things they needed such as hats, shoes, farm implements, and so on. For many villages with few or no shops, the weekly market day was the sole chance to get these items.

Fairs were grander events, held usually once a year and often, unlike the markets, not in the town itself but in the countryside nearby, frequently in the late spring or after the autumn harvest so as not to conflict with farm work. The annual Weydon Fair at which

Henchard sells his wife in *The Mayor of Casterbridge*, for example, takes place on September 15. Around then, farm laborers would have received their harvest wages, servants their Michaelmas pay if that was when their term of service ended, and everybody would be ready for one last good time before the winter set in.

Some fairs were very grand. The great Goose Fair in October at Nottingham opened with a formal procession of the mayor and aldermen in their scarlet robes, a trumpet blowing, and beadles marching along with their staves. Six acres of marketplace, said a contemporary observer, were "jammed full of stalls, shows, bazaars, and people." In the morning farmers' daughters would sit by their family's cheeses as the cheese dealers made their purchases, while horse buyers haggled and swapped talk with the horse traders. ("Many hundreds of horses and sheep had been exhibited and sold in the forenoon," Hardy says of the Weydon Fair.) By noontime at Nottingham, business would be winding down, and from then till eleven or midnight there was dancing, flirting, and entertainment— traveling shows (like the one in which Sergeant Troy appears in *Far from the Madding Crowd*), cockfights, smockraces in which women competed, wrestling, magic shows, and rope dancers. Fairs were a magnet for the young and single, and the relaxed, exhilarating atmosphere meant that single servants who were generally denied any opportunities for courting by their masters often produced a number of pregnancies in the ensuing months. At Nottingham, in fact, the "quality" let the lower orders have the fair all to themselves on the first day and did not come to enjoy things themselves until the second.

There were also what were called "statute" or "hiring" fairs or "mops." Held generally around Michaelmas, or sometimes at Martinmas or Christmas, or in May, these were pre-employment-bureau gatherings at which a farmer or the master of a household could hire agricultural workers or household servants for the upcoming farm season or year. These fairs persisted until well into the nineteenth century—in *Tess* we are told of "the Candlemas Fair. It was at this fair that new engagements were entered into for the twelve months following the ensuing Lady-Day, and those of the farming population who thought of changing their places duly attended at the county-town where the fair was held." Gabriel Oak is driven to seek work at such a fair at the beginning of *Far from the Madding Crowd* after he loses his sheep. Typically, each worker wore a distinctive article of clothing to identify the position he was seeking to fill.

"Carters and waggoners were distinguished by having a piece of whip-cord twisted round their hats; thatchers wore a fragment of woven straw; shepherds held their sheep-crooks in their hands," Hardy tells us, "and thus the situation required was known to the hirers at a glance." Bargains were sealed at these fairs with a handshake and a payment of "earnest money" (sometimes called a "fastening penny"), a token sum designed to show the employer's good faith. In the afternoon, with the bargaining out of the way, the servants and laborers danced and had fun.

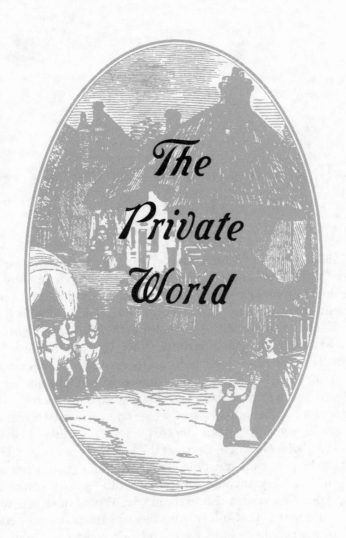

The
Private
World

"READER, I MARRIED HIM"

*U*ntil 1823, a man or woman under the age of twenty-one could not marry without parental permission. This is one reason why *Pride and Prejudice* involves a clandestine elopement in the face of parental opposition, and why the nineteen-year-old Isabella Linton dashes off into the night with Heathcliff in *Wuthering Heights* to be married without telling her parents. Note that the action of both these novels takes place long before Queen Victoria ascended the throne. After 1823, this particular source of melodrama was not available to a novelist; a boy was legally able to marry without consent at age fourteen and a girl when she turned twelve.

You could not marry your deceased wife's sister—"she is my sister-in-law," objects Angel Clare at the end of *Tess of the d'Urbervilles* when, knowing she must die, Tess tells him to marry her sister. On the other hand, you could—and many did—marry your cousin, including your first cousin. Emma and Mr. Woodhouse scheme for her to do just that, Mr. Collins proposes to various Bennet cousins in *Pride and Prejudice*, Jane Eyre and her cousin St. John River consider marriage, first cousins Cathy Linton and Hareton Earnshaw marry in *Wuthering Heights*. This attitude did not change until the end of the century, when we find Jude Fawley thinking apropos of his feelings for his own cousin Sue Bridehead that they are not quite right.

Courtship was a very serious matter indeed. *Can You Forgive*

Her? asks Trollope of his readers when they learn that Alice Vasavor has changed her mind several times about marrying. Echoing an apparently not uncommon Victorian sentiment, she agonizingly asks herself, "Am I a jilt?" There was, perhaps, a sound economic as well as emotional reason for this impatience with female uncertainty. Since for many years, by law virtually all of a woman's property became her husband's upon marriage, his courtship was in some measure a career move as well as a search for a life partner. Thus, to lead him on would be to ask him to make a bad investment of his time. Indeed, when rich or upper-class people got married, a wife generally brought a generous dowry with her as an inducement to marriage. "Once a woman has accepted an offer of marriage," advised *The What-Not, or Ladies' Handbook* in 1859, "all she has or expects to have becomes virtually the property of the man she has accepted as husband and no gift or deed executed by her is held to be valid; for were she permitted to give away or otherwise settle her property between the period of acceptance and the marriage he might be disappointed in the wealth he looked to in making an offer."

There was little false delicacy about this sort of economic maneuvering. Indeed the financial aspects of an impending marriage were considered quite openly. A contemporary courtship etiquette manual says very straightforwardly that once you propose, "your course is to acquaint the parents or guardians of the lady with your intentions, at the same time stating your circumstances and what settlement you would make upon your future wife; and, on their side, they must state what will be her fortune as near as they can estimate to the best of their knowledge at the time you make the enquiry."

If this sounds like the preliminary negotiations to a corporate merger rather than the joyous coming together of two lovesick young people, that is because in a society where power, money, and prestige were still often tied to the possession of great estates and a name, an economic transaction is really what it was. A husband often had to have a rich wife in order to keep up the ancestral family name in style. And since *her* fortune by law became her husband's property at marriage, the bride's family had to worry about making sure she and her children had something to live on if her husband died or were a wastrel. Women had a right of dower—or the income from approximately one third of their husbands' land—when their husbands died, but this was all but abolished by the Dower Act of 1833. Typically, then, the bride's family would have their lawyers negotiate with the husband's lawyers to get the husband to agree to guarantee her "pin money," which was a small personal annual allowance, while he lived, a "jointure," a hefty chunk of property or money to support her after he died, and "portions" of money for their children. All this would be written up into a "marriage settlement" by the lawyers before anyone walked down any aisles. (One of the final chapters of *Oliver Twist*, in which the impoverished Henry Maylie proposes to Rose, is headed, in part, ". . . comprehending a Proposal of Marriage with no Word of Settlement or Pin Money"). In addition, family lawyers set up what was called "separate property" and/or a "separate estate" for brides, especially if they were heiresses. This was basically a trust overseen by the Chancery Court which gave the woman access to all her property and money upon application to a trustee but kept it out of her control so her husband couldn't "kiss or kick it" out of her, nor his creditors take it to pay his bills. Edgar Linton sends for the attorney Mr. Green to draw up a will creating just such a trust when he finds out about the marriage Heathcliff proposes between Catherine Linton and young Heathcliff, but dies—too late to prevent it.

If an engaged person decided to terminate the engagement he or she faced the possibility of legal action from the former heartthrob. Such a "breach of promise" suit, as Mr. Pickwick learns to his cost in *Bardell* v. *Pickwick*, could result in a judgment against the party alleged to have broken off the engagement for a sum equal to any actual damages—such as the cost of a wedding dress—plus an amount equal to whatever the jury thought adequate to teach the offending party a lesson. In *The Eustace Diamonds* Lord Greystock at one point is forced to consider the likelihood of such a suit if he breaks off his engagement to Lizzie Greystock. George Osborne tells Dobbin his worries about Joseph Sedley leading Becky Sharp on at the beginning of *Vanity Fair:* "That's why I told him to look out, lest she brought an action against him." At least one contemporary manual of courtship advised its readers not to put anything into a love letter that they would not wish to see appear in a courtroom during a breach of promise suit should the engagement sour.

Assuming you did follow through, however, there were four routes to go. Assuming you were marrying within the Church of England, you could have the banns "published," that is, ask that the impending wedding be announced three Sundays in a row from the parish pulpit. Any marriage thereafter within three months was valid unless someone spoke out against the proposed marriage dur-

ing one of the announcements. The advantage of the procedure was
that it was cheap: "Banns will do?" Jude Fawley asks Sue Bridehead
when they consider marriage. "We shall save a pound or two." The
publicity, of course, was the drawback. Tess Durbeyfield is pleased
when Angel Clare tells her of his decision to be married by license
rather than banns, having "feared that somebody would stand up
and forbid the banns on the ground of her history." Mistress Yeobright does just this in *The Return of the Native.* "I forbid the banns,"
she says, standing up during the service.

There were other ways to get married. "Marriage by banns is
confined to the poorest classes," sniffed one mid-century etiquette
manual, "and a license is generally obtained by those who aspire to
the 'habits of good society.' " Ordinarily, for a few pounds you could
obtain a license either from a local clergyman or at Doctors' Commons in London, which would let you get married in a parish where
one of the parties had lived for at least fifteen days. Outside of very
poor and rural areas, this would have been the usual way to get
married for most of the century and it avoided publication of the
banns.

The most expensive procedure was to get a special license that
enabled you to get married any place at any time. This could only
be obtained from the archbishop of Canterbury and cost a whacking
great sum—twenty-eight guineas in the middle of the century—and
would probably only be available to the well connected, since it was
granted at the archbishop's discretion. "A special license," exclaims
Mrs. Bennet in *Pride and Prejudice* when she discovers that at long
last Elizabeth is to marry the great and wealthy Mr. Darcy. "You
must and shall be married by a special license."

Finally, there was the civil license, which could be obtained after
1836 from the superintendent-registrar, a sort of clerk of records.
This was the marriage license you got if you were Catholic, Jewish,
or a Dissenter. It permitted you to be married either in a church
ceremony or in the registrar's office. Jude Fawley and Sue Bridehead, as befits their ultramodern approach to marriage, seriously
consider going this route in *Jude the Obscure.*

In the early years of the century, people who wanted to evade
these requirements skipped across the border into Scotland to a little
town called Gretna Green—as the wicked Wickham and Elizabeth
Bennet's sister Lydia are presumed to have done in *Pride and Prejudice* when they elope. Here you could be married under the looser
regulations of the Scotch Presbyterian church. You simply showed

up in town and pledged yourself to your partner in the presence of another person—often the local blacksmith—until a twenty-one-day residency requirement imposed in 1856 slowed things down a bit.

Weddings were required by law to be morning affairs until the late 1880s, when permissible hours were extended to 3 P.M. This is why marriages were customarily celebrated with a "wedding break-fast" and, of course, accounts for the peculiar hour and minute in *Great Expectations* in Miss Havisham's house "at which she after-wards stopped all the clocks." As Herbert Pocket tells Pip, she received a letter breaking off her marriage the day of her wedding. "When she was dressing for her marriage?" Pip asks. "At twenty minutes to nine," Herbert assents.

The wedding ceremony itself invariably saw both the clergyman and the parish clerk in attendance. When it was over, the couple had to sign their names—the bride her maiden name—in the parish register in the vestry. Then they returned—or went out—for the traditional wedding breakfast followed by departure on their honey-moon. It was the custom to throw shoes after the departing couple, and, at least in the early part of the century, the bride sometimes took a female companion along on her honeymoon. "I still regret your sister is not to accompany us," Casaubon says to Dorothea Brooke sorrowfully in *Middlemarch* of their honeymoon trip abroad.

When the husband and wife exchanged vows, they became one person, and, in the words of the jurist William Blackstone, "the husband is that person." The wife, as noted earlier, upon marriage lost virtually all powers over any property that she possessed. All her *personal property* automatically became her husband's property to do with as he saw fit, which is why Heathcliff locks up Cathy Linton until she will marry his son—his objective being, as Edgar Linton divines, to "secure the personal property [of the Lintons], as well as the estate, to his son, or rather himself"—that is, to transfer owner-ship of the money Edgar Linton has left to Cathy to young Heathcliff via a coerced marriage. Since Heathcliff Senior, controls his son, Heathcliff *père* will thereby gain effective control over the Lintons' personal property. A wife's *land* was in a somewhat different cate-gory; her husband could neither sell nor mortgage it, but he owned any income from it such as rent.

Once married, a wife could not sue or make a contract on her own nor make a will without her husband's consent. If he wished to confine her against his will, as Mr. Rochester does his wife at Thorn-field Hall, until 1891 he was well within his rights in doing so. He could "correct" her if he wished, too, a right which was supposed to mean only verbal chastisement but in practice often meant physical punishment.

This presumptive legal unity of husband and wife could cut the other way, too. The husband was considered legally liable for the debts and civil wrongs of his wife. If she committed a crime she was presumed to be acting under his influence (although the presumption did not run the other way) as Dickens makes clear in Mr. Bumble's famous reaction upon being told that because his wife made off with the trinkets from Oliver Twist's dying mother that "the law supposes that your wife acts under your direction." Bumble, of course, rejoins in exasperation, "the law is a ass—a idiot. If that's the eye of the law, the law is a bachelor."

Happy or unhappy, a marriage was difficult to dissolve. Divorces until 1857 were the exclusive concern of the Church of England, at the Consistory Courts in Doctors' Commons in London. Three types of divorce were possible. Divorce *a vinculo matrimonii* meant that the marriage was a nullity from the beginning due to an improperly close blood relationship, insanity, impotence, or a similar impediment. It permitted you to remarry but made your children illegitimate. Divorce *a mensa et a thoro* did not let you remarry but permitted you to separate and was available in cases of adultery, sodomy, or cruelty, which last was usually understood to mean actual violence. Parliamentary divorce (usually for men) offered a third alternative; you got a divorce *a mensa et a thoro* and then sued your wife (successfully) for adultery and then Parliament granted you a real divorce that did not make your children illegitimate.

If you did have legal grounds for a divorce, the proceedings were enormously expensive, especially—God forbid—if you went the route of parliamentary petition as well. "Why, you'd have to go to Doctors' Commons with a suit, and you'd have to go to a court of Common Law with a suit, and you'd have to go to the House of Lords with a suit, and you'd have to get an Act of Parliament to enable you to marry again," Mr. Bounderby remorselessly explains to Stephen Blackpool in *Hard Times* when he inquires about getting free of his destructive wife, "and it would cost you (if it was a case of very plain sailing), I suppose from a thousand to fifteen hundred pound . . . Perhaps twice the money." His estimates were fairly accurate. Women, of course, were less likely to have access to this sort of money than men; of the ninety parliamentary divorces granted before 1857, women obtained only four.

Faced with this situation, some of the poor did just what Henchard does in *The Mayor of Casterbridge*—they auctioned off their
wives. This was not a startling bit of fictional business Hardy invented for the sake of his novel. "She was by no means the first or
last peasant woman who had religiously adhered to her purchaser,"
Hardy says of Susan Henchard after she's sold, "as too many rural
records show." Between 1750 and 1850, in fact, there were some 380
of these do-it-yourself divorces effected in rural England. The general procedure was even crasser than Hardy suggests, for you typically put a halter around your wife's head and shoulders and led her
to the auction place like a cow, the only checks on the practice being
occasional ostracism and not very stringent legal penalties.

Legislation ultimately changed a good deal of the most archaic
laws regulating marriage and divorce. The Divorce Act of 1857 took
jurisdiction over divorces away from the church courts and gave it
to a new civil divorce court instead. The law also changed the
grounds needed for divorce by permitting men to divorce on the
grounds of adultery; women on the grounds of adultery *and* either
incest, rape, sodomy, bestiality, bigamy, physical cruelty, or two
years' desertion. The Married Women's Property Act of 1870 allowed women to treat as their own the money they were willed by
others, or got from various investments, and the Married Women's
Property Act of 1882 made basically all property that a woman
acquired on her own hers to do with as she pleased, in addition to
giving her the right to sue and be sued with respect to the property,
and make contracts about it.

S E X

*T*he majority of women (happily for them)," wrote the eminent Dr.
William Acton in the mid-1860s, "are not very much troubled with
sexual feelings of any kind. . . . No nervous or feeble young man
need, therefore, be deterred from marriage by an exaggerated notion of the duties required from him." Indeed. "The married
woman," continued the good doctor, "has no wish to be treated on
the footing of a mistress."

Dr. Acton's books were very popular, and they suggest how

much truth there was in our stereotypes of the constrained character of nineteenth-century English sexual behavior. In proper middle- and upper-class circles, for example, women were supposed to have no sexual contact before marriage—a hand around the waist, a kiss, and a fervent pressing of the hand was probably the accepted limit in most cases.

It was only marriage that licensed proper women to inquire into "improper" subjects at all. ". . . get Dorothea to read you light things, Smollett—Roderick Random, Humphry Clinker," Mr. Brooke suggests to the doubtlessly unreceptive Edward Casaubon in *Middlemarch*, "they are a little broad, but she may read anything now she's married you know." An end-of-the-century *Punch* cartoon showed a new bride of three hours in a railway station begging her husband to buy *Tom Jones* for her: "Papa told me I wasn't to read it till I was married! The day has come . . . at last! Buy it for me, Edward, dear."

The consequence of this prudery was that women often came to their wedding nights ignorant and terrified. If they survived it with sexual feelings intact, the absence of effective birth control, other than coitus interruptus or breast-feeding, meant that sex equated to constant pregnancy (Dickens's wife had ten children in thirteen years), which—in addition to the fatigues of pregnancy itself— meant all those children to care for. Plus the risk of dying in child-birth was about 1 in 200 in 1870. The fact that the law for many years basically guaranteed a man access to his wife's body whether she desired it or not—a right that induced Harriet Taylor to flee in disgust from her bewildered husband to the sympathetic embrace of John Stuart Mill—cannot have made women feel more comfortable about this. Yet Dr. Acton's reassuring murmurings about the absence of sexual feeling among nineteenth-century Englishwomen were contradicted even by contemporary scientific evidence. A Scottish gynecologist with sufficient prestige to address the Royal College of Physicians wrote in the 1890s that of the approximately 190 women out of 504 who had responded to his questions, 152 said, yes, they did have sexual desires, and 134 reported that they had orgasms.

The dreary asexuality of the Victorian era was not characteristic of the early years of the century. In Jane Austen's era, Evangelicalism had not yet cast its blight over everyday middle-class and upper-class life, and clothes were still gaily colored and tight fitting—in women's cases sometimes damped down with water to hug the body—and unmarried men and women could sometimes socialize or go for carriage rides together, unchaperoned, as do Catherine Morland and Mr. Tilney in *Northanger Abbey*, without damage to reputations or anyone fearing that the country had succumbed to immorality.

The same would not have been true thirty years later. Layers upon layers of shape-concealing petticoats and crinolines had been imposed on the female body, and men adopted heavy materials and shapeless trousers in lieu of the previously form-fitting tights. An anaphrodisiac black became the basic color of all male garments, and Evangelicalism had helped to make sexual pleasure and activity seem wicked and base.

There were varying responses to this new prudery. In some cases it undoubtedly froze sexual relations to the level Dr. Acton imagined, perhaps partly sublimated in Murdstonian talk of a higher piety. In cases like that of the Reverend Charles Kingsley (author of the children's book *The Water Babies*) the sexuality and the morbid religiosity born of Evangelicalism were fused in a passionate mixture that produced letters to his fiancée in the 1840s that spoke of how "my hands are perfumed with her delicious limbs, and I cannot wash off the scent. And every moment the thought comes across me of those mysterious recesses of beauty where my hands have been wandering." Together, he and his fiancée shared drawings he had made of them having sex while floating across the ocean tied on a cross.

In some cases the emotional warping was complete. Lewis Carroll—his father a prominent clergyman—never married and acquired a passion for soliciting the friendship of little girls whose nude photographs he sometimes took, generally dropping all acquaintance with them when they reached puberty. The critic John Ruskin was unable to consummate his marriage and was divorced by his wife, only to fall in love with a ten-year-old girl when he was forty. Perhaps because of the growing inhibitions against mature sexuality, we should not be surprised that not until 1885 did Parliament raise the age of consent for girls from thirteen to sixteen. "Oh, my husband and father" says the infinitely younger Annie Strong to her husband in *David Copperfield*, a much-older man whom she marries who was "the friend of my dead father." The May-December marriage of a Casaubon and Dorothea Brooke was surely more likely among the English in the 1800s than it is today.

For those who weren't sexually dysfunctional, there was still the problem of what to do for a sexual outlet before marriage. Among the working classes in London this was not much of a difficulty, it seems—many costermongers lived with their girlfriends starting in their early teens. Elsewhere in the working class premarital sex was generally winked at as long as the couple got married. Indeed, in 1800, about a third of the brides were pregnant on their wedding day.

For middle- and upper-class men, premarital sex would have been with servants and prostitutes since, of course, "nice girls" didn't engage in sex before marriage. Despite the legend of the master seducing the parlormaid, such evidence as exists suggests this may have been somewhat more rare than popular legend would lead one to believe. Only 659 out of a survey of 16,000 "fallen women" said that a "gentleman" had first seduced them, and, in their usage of the term, they included clerks and shop assistants. Perhaps more common was the Jane Eyre master-and-governess syndrome. George Eliot, for example, boarded awhile in the house of her employer, the editor of the *Westminster Review*, who carried on a ménage à trois with his wife and his children's governess. Governesses were sometimes kept by dashing young men in secluded apartments around London. Nor was it only the gentlemen who dallied with their servants. "I often heard the name of a duchess, not now living," wrote an American diplomat in the 1880s formerly at the Court of St. James's "connected with that of her groom of the chambers, and a countess who waited at Windsor was discovered caressing her footman in her own drawing-room."

It is hard to know how widespread prostitution was. The count frequently given of 80,000 prostitutes in London seems high, but "gay" women with their "fancy men" (pimps) were not uncommon in the city. They congregated near Covent Garden and in the theater district, skirts partly tucked up as a badge of their calling, sometimes wandering into theater lobbies during intermission to solicit customers. Hippolyte Taine reported shortly after the middle of the century that it was impossible to walk down the Strand or Haymarket in the evening without being solicited by prostitutes, asking for gin or for rent money. They were unusually alluring to soldiers, most of whom were forbidden to marry. Venereal disease was sufficiently widespread in the army that, starting in 1864, Parliament passed a series of Contagious Diseases Acts, which provided for the examination of prostitutes in military towns, and, if they proved to be infected, their detention for a cure.

By the end of the century things began to change. Once again the country had an heir apparent whose attentions to the ladies were well known. Oscar Wilde was able to publish his *Picture of Dorian Gray*, with its fairly clear suggestions of homosexuality, and Thomas Hardy published a frank account of a woman's adultery, seduction, and bodily charms in *Tess of the d'Urbervilles*, boldly subtitling it the story of "a pure woman."

On the other hand, homosexuality was still punishable as a criminal act. (Since 1563 the act of sodomy had been punishable by death, and the last executions for such an offense were in the 1830s.) In 1885, a new law was passed—the one under which Oscar Wilde was convicted—making the solicitation or commission of any homosexual act in public or private punishable by up to two years in prison.

AN ENGLISHMAN'S
HOME

*T*he dwelling of the rural poor was generally a thatch- (or slate-) roofed cottage, with one big room if the family were very poor, or a kitchen and then a separate bedroom if the family were a bit better off, and up to four rooms (in a substantial cottage, maybe even a second story) in a really good dwelling. In places like the East End or St. Giles, the very poor in London made do with a single room, where they were all jammed in one on top of another, eating, sleeping, and preparing food in the same room, where they cooked over a small fireplace with a grate. Those too poor to afford a room slept on the stairways or landings. Workers with some income could do better, and a clerk like Bob Cratchit, at the bottom of the middle class, characteristically might enjoy a small four-room house in a London suburb like Camdentown with one room for the kitchen, one for a dining room–parlor, and the other two for bedrooms.

For those with more money, the object was to have a house like the nobility or gentry. Where space and expense were less of a concern, the house was divided into an area for public entertaining and an area for the family's private use. As the century wore on, these areas were in turn subdivided so that the children's rooms were separated from those of the parents, and the rooms of servants were increasingly separated from those used by the dwelling's owners.

Fundamentally, a wealthy family's private quarters consisted of chambers, workrooms, and sitting rooms. "Chambers" were the bedrooms, sometimes with smaller rooms—dressing closets—where the master and the mistress of the house could dress. The children would sleep in a nursery until they were old enough to have their own bedrooms, all of which would typically be over the bedrooms of their parents. There would also be a schoolroom in the upper area of the house, where the older children had their lessons. The mistress of the house would have a boudoir for her correspondence and the handling of the household affairs; for an equivalent purpose a man would have a library or study (typically, a country gentleman would receive his tenants or keeper here) .

In grander houses, the large public rooms might be referred to as salons. In a house that lacked a great hall, the most imposing of the reception rooms was always the drawing room, a room purely for public purposes. It was in the drawing room that a hostess received people paying calls on her and in the drawing room that guests assembled before dinner and to which they retired thereafter, when the gentlemen had been permitted a short interval in the dining room to fill up on port.

In addition to the obligatory dining room, a well-off family might have a separate breakfast room for the informal morning meal. There might also be a morning room, which was really an informal room for family gatherings, or a "sitting room." In general, a sitting room seems to have been what we would call the living room today, an area for members of the family to sit in and chat informally or read. People renting apartments or chambers—even old Mrs. Wopsle in *Great Expectations*—customarily had a bedroom and a sitting room, the latter serving in small dwellings as a place to receive callers as well. The "parlor," a more formal space, was the poor man's drawing room, it appears. In *Great Expectations* the Gargerys, for example, have a "state parlor" where everything is kept under wraps and cloth except on great occasions. Shops, moreover, were customarily divided into a shop area in front and a parlor behind where the owner could eat his meals and relax. "Come into the parlour," says the rag-and-bone man in *A Christmas Carol* to the ghoulish beneficiaries of Scrooge's death. "You were made free of it long ago," the mock "parlor" in this case being "the space behind the screen of rags."

In London the density of population, and consequent scarcity of land, meant that the great town houses of the nobility and gentry had to be organized around a vertical rather than a horizontal division of space. That is, the town houses even of the grandest aristocrats were generally buildings jammed into a space so narrow compared to that of the country that functional areas had to be stacked on top of one another rather than connected horizontally. The kitchen was always located in the basement and looked out onto a small courtyard, called the "area," from which a set of steps led up to the street, surrounded by the "area" railing. (The newly reformed Scrooge strolled through London on Christmas Day "and looked down into the kitchens of the houses, and up to the windows.") The dining room was always on the "ground" floor (street level), and the drawing room was always on the "first" floor above it. In spacious country houses the dining and drawing rooms were both on the ground floor—when the time came for dinner the gentlemen simply led the ladies across the hall to dine, so that in *Can You Forgive Her?* Lady Glencora Palliser instructs her husband's cousin at Matching Priory, "You must take my cousin, Alice Vasavor, in to dinner." In London, however, the gentlemen would customarily take the ladies "down" to dine. A guest awaiting the commencement of a London dinner party in the Veneering drawing room in *Our Mutual Friend* is told "Dinner is on the table!" and, "having no lady assigned him, goes down in the rear, with his hand to his forehead." And when visitors came calling, the proper London hostess receiving them in her drawing room always asked the help to "Show him up." Parental bedrooms in the town house were usually above the drawing room on the second floor, with nursery and children's bedrooms on the third floor, and servants' sleeping quarters above that.

As the century wore on, the desire to separate servants from the family increased, and so did the felt necessity of maintaining a proper separation of the sexes. Hence large country houses sometimes had one wing for male servants and male unmarried guests and one wing for female servants and female unmarried guests. Sometimes each group's sleeping quarters had their own set of stairs, and there would be an additional set of back stairs for the servants to use for work. In addition, there might also be a grand

staircase for use only by family and guests, running from the bedrooms on the first floor down to the great front hall.

There were also—as wealth and taste permitted—billiard and/
or smoking rooms (for men only, of course), a library, conservatories
to bring a touch of warmth and greenery to otherwise grim winters,
and sometimes a gallery. Galleries were long rooms for indoor walking (some consequently dead-ended into a wall), which had first
become popular in the 1600s and were then often rededicated to the
housing of ancestral portraits.

Outbuildings, sometimes called "offices," for any respectable
country mansion would also be approriately grand. A dairy, a brewery, stables—Wuthering Heights has a washhouse to which the
young Cathy Earnshaw and Heathcliff are banished for "a light
offence"—would not have been unusual. Within the house itself
there would be a servants hall where the servants ate together, a
special pantry where the butler kept the plate and fine china and
from which he directed the male servants, a room for the housekeeper where she bottled preserves, kept the household accounts
and saw to the direction of the housemaids, plus a larder for un-
cooked perishables like meat, a stillroom for making spirits or storing
coffee, a wine cellar, a laundry, and so on.

Even the grandest house was not terribly warm. The problem
was the absence of any genuinely effective central heating. The
great country houses had it only on the ground floor and then usually
only in the main hall until the 1880s. In their individual rooms guests
or family members made do with a coal fire religiously maintained
by a housemaid or maid-of-all-work. (A thirty-bedroom mansion in
the north of England went through a ton of coal a *day*.) To clean
themselves guests generally washed in the hip baths and basins of
water dragged up the stairs by these same maids or—in a few
grander country houses—by the stolid watermen who made their
rounds with great buckets of water on their shoulders. As for the
taps, "a call on the hot water . . . did not meet with an effusive or
even warm response," wrote one memoirist of country-house life.
"A succession of sepulchral rumblings was succeeded by the appearance of a small geyser of rust-coloured water, heavily charged with
dead earwigs and bluebottles. This continued for a couple of minutes and then . . . ceased. The only perceptible difference between
the hot water and the cold lay in its colour and the cargo of defunct
life which the former bore on its bosom. Both were stone cold." The

widespread availability of heat awaited the coming of the twentieth century. The great nineteenth-century country houses were, indeed, great—but they were not warm.

H O U S E S   W I T H   N A M E S

*M*any of the great English novels take place or develop in houses with grand-sounding names—Thrushcross Grange, Thornfield Hall, Ullathorne Court, to name a few. In some cases, a particularly grand residence gave its name to one of the novels, notably Mansfield Park, Bleak House, and, of course, there are Northanger Abbey and Wildfell Hall as well. Examination suggests that some of the generic residence names reveal something about the nature of the dwelling, those that live there, or both.

Court—A residence constructed around some kind of courtyard. So, at any rate, Trollope tells us in his description in *Barchester Towers* of Ullathorne Court, which was, he says, "properly so called; for the house itself formed two sides of a quadrangle, which was completed on the other two sides by a wall about

Salmeston Grange, Margate.

twenty feet high." Originally, such buildings were constructed for defensive purposes, with windows facing inward, so life within the dwelling could proceed in the courtyard even in the midst of an armed attack.

Grange—A residence like Thrushcross Grange of the Lintons in *Wuthering Heights* or Mr. Brooke's Tipton Grange in *Middlemarch* was so named because it was a grain storehouse or granary, sometimes attached to a large monastery. By the 1800s the term designated isolated farmsteads, too, a description that would fit Thrushcross Grange and also Moor House, the "sequestered home" St. John Rivers terms "this crumbling grange," where Jane Eyre stumbles upon her cousins.

Hall—As in Mr. Rochester's Thornfield Hall in *Jane Eyre* or Sir James Chettam's Freshitt Hall in *Middlemarch*. The word "hall" in the name of a dwelling meant that the house had centered on a great hall for entertainment, dining, and ceremonial living on a grand scale, as in feudal times. The term thus connoted both a certain grandeur ("a small, humble place," a servant describes her cousin's ancestral home to Jane Eyre, "naught to compare wi' Mr. Oliver's grand hall down i' Morton Vale") and the sort of ancient architecture likely to be associated with an old, august family. Vasavor Hall in *Can You Forgive Her?* belongs to "a family so old that no one knew which had first taken the ancient titular name of some old Saxon landowner— the parish or the man."

House—There is, of course, Bleak House and Netherfield House, which Mr. Bingley rents at the outset of *Pride and Prejudice* and which occasions all the events that follow. The coming into use of the term "house" reflects a period when residential comfort was increasingly of concern, and the period of naming things "castle," "abbey," or "manor" was long past. Moreover, it is interesting that neither Bingley nor Mr. Jarndyce are titled.

Manor—The dwelling to which Mr. Rochester withdraws when Jane Eyre leaves him and Thornfield Hall burns is Ferndean Manor. The term "manor" implied a dwelling inhabited by a lord of the manor whose tenants lived on and worked the surrounding land. Obviously suggestive of a rather grand social status as well as a lineage dating back to Norman times, when the manorial system originated. In *Tess* the country home of her ersatz d'Urberville relatives "was not a manorial home in the ordinary sense, with fields, and pastures, and a grumbling farmer, out of whom the owner had to squeeze an income for himself and his family by hook or by crook." Thornfield Hall was in fact probably more of a manor than the isolated Ferndean Manor; Jane Eyre describes it as "a gentleman's manor-house" at one point. Characteristically, a manor house was often the dominant architectural feature of the local village, which was evidently the case at Thornfield. "A little hamlet, whose roofs were blent with trees, straggled up the side of one of these hills: the church of the district stood nearer Thornfield; its old tower-top looked over a knoll between the house and gates."

Park—As in Mansfield Park. Originally, a park was an area which the king permitted a large landowner to enclose for the sake of chasing deer. Park came to mean a closed-in area, often landscaped with trees and lawn to present a pleasing and aesthetically appropriate picture. Both Mansfield Park and the park belonging to Sir Leicester Dedlock in *Bleak House* are the property of baronets, and having a park certainly connoted gentlemanly status; a large one is attached to Thrushcross Grange. It advertised that you had both the means to withdraw otherwise productive land from cultivation for purely esthetic appreciation and the leisure time to enjoy it.

One should not conclude that every park had at one time been the result of a special grant from the king or that each manor was the remnant of a feudal estate. Buying land and blending in with the landed gentry, after all, was the chief means of advancing into the upper echelons of English society in the 1800s. There were no doubt innumerable parks, halls, and manors whose existence dated from no earlier than the time the contractor's men had first begun laying the foundations for some new magnate's country estate. Also, as the case of Thornfield Hall suggests, one dwelling could combine the features of several different types of residence. Mr. Bingley's residence in *Pride and Prejudice*, for example, is referred to at different times both as Netherfield House and Netherfield Park. Partly this was because an estate or house might have multiple architectural and social features, and it was also because, depending on one's point of view, the same dwelling was notable either for its social-political function, i.e., a manor house that embodied social and political dominion, or for an architectural characteristic, such as a large hall or a big central court.

F U R N I T U R E

$\mathscr{S}$he had been educated at a time when easy-chairs were considered vicious, and among people who regarded all easy postures as being so; and she could still boast, at seventy-six, that she never leaned back." So Trollope describes Lady Macleod in *Can You Forgive Her?*

Perhaps this distaste for comfortable furniture was making a virtue out of a necessity, for furniture at the beginning of the 1800s was stiff and unwelcoming. For one thing, there were no springs until 1828, which meant that when one sat on a chair or sofa, it did not "give" at all. The nearest approach to a sofa was the ottoman, a long, flat board with no back or sides (although it was considered too luxurious for any except the elderly or the ill).

Making chairs more yielding by adding springs led to a corresponding movement to make them deeper, that is, deeper back to front. With suitable stuffing, you could now sit back in a chair comfortably instead of having to sit on a narrow ledge of board. But social progress always creates new problems—the fact that gentlemen with their new macassar-oiled hair could now sit back in chairs meant that ladies had to knit antimacassars to protect the headrests on their chairs.

The growing cult of domesticity as the century wore on was no doubt a factor in the tendency to accumulate houses full of useless furniture and bric-a-brac, and an emerging upwardly mobile middle class used the proliferation and elaboration of furniture as a way to show off their newly attained wealth. The clutter and confusion were worsened by the fact that rooms were kept dark with heavy curtains to keep carpets from fading and to protect ladies' skins against the wrinkles, freckles, and darkening of skin for which exposure to sunlight was held responsible.

Two articles of more humble furniture—usually found in a tavern or farm home—lent themselves particularly well to the novelist's use, since they could conceal unseen listeners. The settle was a high-backed bench that could be pulled up to the fire so that the cold drafts in the rest of the room would be kept away. "It is, to the hearths of old-fashioned cavernous fireplaces, what the east belt of trees is to the exposed country estate, or the north wall to the garden," says Hardy in *The Return of the Native*. "Outside the settle the candles gutter, locks of hair wave, young women shiver, and old men sneeze. Inside is Paradise. Not a symptom of a draught disturbs the air." Precisely because of its ability to shield everyone and everything, the settle acts as a convenient means of letting Heathcliff overhear the fateful conversation in *Wuthering Heights* in which Cathy Earnshaw is heard to say that "it would degrade her to marry him, and then he staid no further. My companion," says the narrator of Cathy Earnshaw, "was prevented by the back of the settle from remarking his presence or departure," with fateful consequences.

The chimney corner, the large recess inside old-fashioned fireplaces where a person could sit to get warm, served the same purpose. "A person might sit there absolutely unobserved, provided there was no fire to light him up, as was the case now and throughout the summer," says Hardy of the chimney corner in the Quiet Woman inn in *The Return of the Native*. It is there that Diggory Venn eavesdrops unnoticed on Wildeve's activities, again with important consequences.

LIGHTING

*I*n *Great Expectations* Pip wearily seeks refuge at a small hotel after finding that Estella is engaged to marry a brute and that the authorities are hot on the trail of his benefactor, Abel Magwitch. He requests a "night-light"—and so is brought "the good old constitutional rush-light of those virtuous days—an object like the ghost of a walking-cane, which instantly broke its back if it were touched, which nothing could ever be lighted at, and which was placed in solitary confinement at the bottom of a high tin tower, perforated with round holes that made a staringly wide-awake pattern on the walls."

Rushlights were simply rushes dipped in drippings or other greasy substances and then set alight. They made ideal nightlights not only because they were cheap but because—unlike candles—

when the wick burned down it simply crumbled into ash. They were probably the most widely used form of illumination in England before the coming of gas. The poor could make them for free, and, besides, there was a tax on all candles, tallow ones 1*d.* a pound, wax candles 3½*d.* a pound. Besides, in the country the sheep fat needed to make tallow candles could be saved and kept for soap or cooking instead. In addition, the cotton or linen from which candle wicks were made cost money.

Those who were better off used tallow candles, since they did not need to pinch pennies so much, but the really rich preferred real beeswax candles, no doubt in part because tallow could sometimes give off a faint odor, presumably sheeplike in nature, when it burned. In addition, tallow candles did not burn that well, and the wicks, unlike those of wax candles, had to be regularly "snuffed," that is, the snuff, or wick, had to be cut off with special scissorslike instruments periodically or the candle would cease to burn properly. "There was no sound through the house but the moaning wind which shook the windows now and then," says Isabella Linton in *Wuthering Heights,* recounting to Mrs. Dean how she sat at Wuthering Heights one night, "the faint crackling of the coals, and the click of my snuffers as I removed at intervals the long wick of the candle." We can thus see in *Emma* when it is said admiringly of someone that "she moved in the first circle. Wax candles in the schoolroom," that a good deal of gentility is being imputed to the party spoken of. It also would have said much to a nineteenth-century reader that when Pip first visits Miss Havisham during the daytime he finds her "in a pretty large room, well lighted with wax candles." It suggested considerable wealth—as well as madness—to keep all those *wax* candles burning day and night for so many long, long years.

In addition to candles there were always lamps, for which kerosene and paraffin were the favored fuel. These lamps, however, required constant refilling, and they got very dirty. Between lamps and candles, lighting a house could be quite a chore. At the duke of Rutland's Belvoir in the 1890s there were three or more men who worked all day cutting wicks, removing wax from the candelabra, filling lamps, cleaning black off lamp chimneys, and pouring paraffin oil. At night they snuffed the candles, adjusted wicks, and removed wax from the extinguishers that were used to put out candles. This was not a small task; even a modest home might have some twenty or so lamps.

But what everyone associates with nineteenth-century England, particularly London, is gas light, and gas lamps came into use quite early. Before the advent of gas, London streetlamps were lit with whale oil, but it did not provide very good light. Then gas—made, like almost every other product for fuel or heating in the 1800s, from coal—appeared. Textile manufacturers used it first in order to keep their factories going all night and cut their insurance premiums; by 1814 gas light was spreading through London, and the first theaters were lit by gas in 1817. By 1834, London had over 600 miles of gas lines for street lighting. The coal gas, derived from the heating of coal (the by-product was coke), was water cooled, purified, and then driven underground through a network of cast-iron pipes to the lamps from which it issued. At dusk the lamplighter made his rounds, carrying a pole with a fixture in the end which, when inserted into the bottom of the lamppost, turned the gas on for that streetlight. He then released a small burst of flame with the pole—how, no one seemed to know exactly—which ignited the flame in the lamp.

Gas light did not, however, in its first incarnation, produce the mysterious, softly lit city of swirling fogs that we associate with the Sherlock Holmes stories. For one thing, outdoor gas lighting was not evenly distributed throughout the city. In the 1860s, for example, a visitor to London would have found gas lamps concentrated in the larger thoroughfares, with fewer on the sidestreets, and none at all in some poorer areas. Secondly, as sources of indoor illumination, the early gas lamps had definite drawbacks. They were smelly and they could leave terrible black marks on ceilings.

In rural areas there was no outdoor illumination at all. Private drivers carried lanterns on their coaches so as to be seen by other on-coming riders or vehicles. There were no lanterns powerful enough to illuminate the road. For this reason, balls and dinner parties in the countryside were planned to coincide with the full moon. Sir John Middleton apologizes in *Sense and Sensibility* for not having more people for the Dashwood ladies to meet when they come to stay with him. However, "he had been to several families that morning in hopes of procuring some addition to their number, but it was moonlight and everybody was full of engagements."

Domestic sanitary regulations.

HOW THE ENGLISH KEPT CLEAN

*I*n the early part of the nineteenth century you would have been well advised to stand up wind of anyone with whom you were having a conversation.

Only the hands, neck, and arms were frequently washed. By mid-century, however, houses were beginning to install special rooms for baths, and a vicar's daughter from Hertfordshire reported in her memoirs that as a child during this period she bathed every day. This seems to have been the rule among the well-to-do. An 1869 etiquette manual also recommended daily baths for young ladies, two in summer, in fact, although it cautioned against prolonged immersion in baths over 100 degrees in temperature "as it exhausts the physical powers." Wholesale ablution could not have been all that uncommon, for in *Can You Forgive Her?*, written in 1864, Trollope advises that "it is better to pull the string at once when you are in the shower-bath, and not to stand shivering, thinking of the inevitable shock which you can only postpone for a few minutes."

However, the poor must have bathed infrequently, at best. The middle class, although they apparently washed their hands and feet daily, usually made do in the 1860s with one big bath on Saturday night in which the entire household took part, perhaps because it was such a nuisance to boil all that water. And at Mrs. Browning's Academy in Blackheath for young ladies a weekly hot bath was charged as an extra.

Partly this was due to a lack of readily available water. In the countryside water came from streams, rivers, wells, or—though presumably only in villages—pumps. Typically, the great country houses had no piped water at all above the ground floor. Guests wishing to wash or bathe were dependent on the hordes of housemaids (or watermen) who carried buckets of water up and down the stairs all day long with which the guests could wash their hands and bathe.

Many houses had rain barrels, or water butts, that caught the rain coming off the roof. The water was then poured from a tap. When Pip is to visit Miss Havisham in *Great Expectations,* he tells us, "my head was put under taps of water-butts" in the process of cleaning him. London had a water supply conducted into various houses by old elm pipes. This system lasted until the 1840s, although the pipes broke often and had to be replaced every two to four years, could not withstand much pressure, and were small of diameter. If they were well off, residents might also obtain water from water carriers who brought their casks around with a horse and wagon.

In London the introduction of metal pipes made the supply of water more accessible, but it did not magically transform conditions overnight. The water supply was not a public service provided to all but was instead a system controlled by private companies—and they turned on the water for only a few hours a day until 1871.

The intermittent character of this water supply was one reason for the unsanitary conditions that prevailed with respect to toilets. A primitive kind of toilet was in use in many London houses fairly early in the century, but there was no way to prevent fumes from backing up into the house. Some houses had "earth closets" in which a supply of fine earth in an attic area was periodically discharged down through the pipes to carry away waste. Some dwellings, especially those of the poor, where a backyard privy substituted for a water closet, emptied their waste into cesspools. With luck, "nightmen" would come around periodically to empty them. Sewage pipes in other parts of the city conducted waste away from homes directly into the Thames, where it helped fuel the periodic epidemics of cholera that swept the city until efforts were made in the 1840s to filter and empty the waste farther down the river from the water intake and at high—rather than low—tide. At the great country houses cesspits were used. There were some fifty-three of them, overflowing, discovered at Windsor Park at mid-century, and a carriage simply disappeared partway into an old one at a mansion in the northern part of the country one day.

Washing clothes was not easy in the early part of the 1800s. The poor fared worst. Few of their houses in the city had piped-in water until late in the century. This meant standing in line at pumps and wells to get water for washing or cooking. In the countryside some did their work in a river or stream and beat the clothes with a paddle until they were clean. Soap—until it became widely and cheaply available—had to be made from tallow, which, in the countryman's view, was better saved for food or other purposes.

Also, like most useful articles in the early part of the century, soap that was not homemade was taxed. In certain respects, too, soap was rather a mixed blessing, since, unlike the other methods of washing, it required hot water. This made laundry day such a chore that many better-off households hired a washerwoman to do it, since immense amounts of water had to be boiled, the clothes blued and starched by hand, ironed, and then put through a mangle, a tablelike contraption with two rollers through which you rolled the clothing until it was pressed.

"Please, Sir, I Want Some More."

*S*o goes the most famous request for seconds in history—and it was for workhouse gruel. But then, gruel was made from oats or barley—the "corn" which, in the form of bread, was the basic building block of the English workingman's diet.

The poor man lived on bread. " 'There's nothing like bread,' say the men," recounted a mid-century observer of working-class life. " 'It's not all poor people can get meat; but they must get bread.' " Bread and onion if the poor man were lucky, or bread "and—," the "and" consisting of potatoes or bacon, while his wife and children often had only bread—the breadwinner being the one who needed to keep up his strength. He ate cheese rather than butter, fish rather than meat—because they were cheaper. He also ate oysters, no doubt because they could be pickled to keep several weeks and salted so as to taste reasonably fresh. "Poverty and oysters always seem to go together," Sam Weller observes in *Pickwick*, ". . . the poorer a place is, the greater call there seems to be for oysters," he remarks of Whitechapel, a fact reflected in the virtual depletion of natural oyster beds by the 1850s. In 1864 a student of the matter found the average farm laborer had one hot meal a week; fuel was often expensive, and those who cooked had to do so over an open fire, since few of the poor had ovens. On Sunday and Christmas, the poor therefore generally took their geese or other meals to the local bakehouse or baker's to get them cooked. Scrooge and the Ghost of Christmas Present witness "innumerable people, carrying their dinners to the bakers' shops," which Scrooge soberly reflects are "their means of dining every seventh day, often the only day on which they can be said to dine at all."

The middle-class diet was built around mutton, well-cooked vegetables, and potatoes. Salads were out—no one knew about vitamins, and it was thought that eating raw foods was tough on the digestion. Cheese was a lower-class favorite, as was bacon (pigs, unlike cattle, could be kept on a small plot of land—sometimes even in the city). Pigs were a sign of decent rural lower-class food. "Everybody was well off in Lowick," the curate tells Dorothea Brooke in *Middlemarch* of the village where she had hoped to exercise her altruistic impulses; "not a cottager in those double cottages at a low rent but kept a pig, and the strips of garden at the back were well tended." Pigs could be converted into a number of dishes, including black pudding, brawn, bacon, and ham. In addition, they were fecund, fast growing, able to forage in wooded areas, and replete with fat, as well as being easy to preserve through smoking and salting. Its lower-class connotations kept bacon away from upper-class menus, however.

Apart from the limited diet, perhaps the major problem with food was keeping things fresh. In poor households when the pig was killed in autumn, the sides, or "flitches," were hung up in the chimney to be smoked and preserved. On first arriving at Wuthering Heights, Lockwood notices that the ceiling of the "family sitting-room" is concealed by "clusters of legs of beef, mutton, and ham." Due to the lack of refrigeration, housekeepers were forever bottling things and making preserves. In general, where perishables like meat and vegetables were obtained in advance, a good deal of kitchen time was spent curing, bottling, or otherwise preserving them.

No one drank water because it was feared, often rightly, to be unsafe and impure. The preferred drinks were beer and ale—later in the century, coffee and tea. It might be thought that at least children would have been given a somewhat healthier diet but they were not. In infancy, babies whose mothers did not want to breast-feed them found wet nurses instead, like Mrs. Toodle, little Paul Dombey's wet nurse in *Dombey and Son*. (Failing that, donkey's milk was often pressed into service in the upper classes.) After infancy, though, it was all down hill. The child was fed on mutton, potatoes, and bread (both preferably some days old because new food was viewed with disfavor), milk, suet or rice pudding, and oatmeal. Anything more adventurous was strictly avoided until about the age of seventeen—children's stomachs were thought to be more delicate and more incapable of digestion than adult digestive systems. Fresh milk, especially in towns, was too expensive for the poor and was often contaminated and germ laden before the advent of widespread pasteurization in the 1890s. It was also not appreciated that growing children need great amounts of food—one reason, besides neglect and cruelty, that there were the sometimes appallingly niggardly portions of bread and potatoes meted out at workhouses like the one in which Oliver Twist finds himself. Even at the great public schools, where money was certainly no object to the parents of most of the students, the children often went hungry.

There was a thriving confectionery trade, but the process of selling sugar in caked sugarloafs made the preparation of cakes and desserts in the home difficult, perhaps a factor in the popularity of pastry cooks and of treacle (which was nothing more than molasses). Unfortunately, too, colored food additives were in their infancy: to get gold and silver colors, copper and zinc were added; for blues, iron; and lead was used for reds. Occasionally, arsenic seems to have been used to achieve greens with fatal results in at least one case.

It was a standing complaint in a good many better-off households that the cooks hired to prepare all this food drank. And no wonder. Typically, they worked in a hot kitchen, often in the basement—probably badly ventilated—since holes for ventilation were taxed as windows. And once a roaring fire in the coal stove was built to cook something it heated up the whole kitchen; it couldn't just be turned off like a gas or electric range. Not surprisingly, the cook could develop a thirst, which was aggravated by the constant tasting of food and perhaps by the addition of spirits to certain dishes now and then as well.

Taking up the Christmas pudding.

P U D D I N G !

*H*allo! A great deal of steam! The pudding was out of the copper. A smell like a washing-day! That was the cloth. A smell like an eating-house, and a pastry cook's next door to each other, with a laundress's next door to that! That was the pudding. In half a minute Mrs. Cratchit entered: flushed, but smiling proudly: with the pudding, like a speckled cannon-ball, so hard and firm, blazing in half of half-a-quartern of ignited brandy, and bedight with Christmas holly stuck into the top."

This was Christmas plum pudding, but there was also batter pudding, black pudding, kidney pudding, marrow pudding (*Bleak House*), bread and butter pudding (*Little Dorrit*), blood pudding, suet pudding, roly-poly pudding, and so on and on. Pudding was one of the favorite lower-class English dishes.

Pudding was a favorite of the Romans, who evidently brought with them when they conquered England the *ur*pudding, sausage. Into a skin of animal's intestines they poured meat or blood, spices, and other ingredients. Sometimes this package was then smoked. Pepper and the smoke kept microorganisms from forming in the food and hid the taste if it started to go bad, and spices made the food tastier when it was finally eaten. This was the origin of the blood, or black, pudding (sometimes called blackpot in Hardy), a sausage whose name was derived from the blood that was brushed on it when it was stuffed. When Jude Fawley first meets Arabella Donn, the daughter of a pig breeder, in *Jude the Observer*, she explains that her companions "are helping me wash the innerds for black-puddings and such like." In *Tess*, similarly, we are told Angel Clare looks around when he returns home for the food he has brought with him from the dairy where he worked, "black pudding, which he had directed to be nicely grilled."

After the Romans had had their day, some clever person invented pudding cloth, thereby eliminating the need for an animal-skin container. This was a great improvement, since animal intestines were messy and available only at animal-killing time. Moreover, with the new cloth packaging, the pudding could be wrapped up in a ball and dropped in the cooking pot along with whatever else was cooking over the poor man's fire—thus saving costly fuel by cooking two courses at once. Pudding also had the great merit of not needing to be cooked in an oven, something most lower-class homes didn't have. Then people began adding things like dried fruit and sugar to puddings, with the consequence that dessertlike items such as the Christmas plum pudding evolved. True to its origins, however, the plum pudding was still made with meat in some parts of the British Isles as late as the early 1800s, and, especially at Christmastime, the so-called plums from which it drew its name were always raisins, not the plump, juicy fruits that the name suggests today.

Pudding was an excellent dish for the poor, in part because you didn't need as much fat for a pudding as you needed for other kinds of pastry, and you could get away with less filling than a meat pie required. Batter pudding, of which Yorkshire pudding was a variant, for example, was made principally from dough and "drippings." This is the dish the greedy waiter consumes from David Copperfield's dinner when the young boy stops, unescorted, while traveling, at a hostelry for a meal. In London, while working for Mr. Murdstone's firm, the perpetually hungry David alternates between two pudding shops, depending on how much money he has, one with a pudding "made of currants," the other—cheaper—with "a stout pale pudding, heavy and flabby, and with great flat raisins in it." Street vendors sometimes sold puddings that were really no more than dumplings to hungry street children. On the whole, however, puddings were a sensible and economical bundle of food values for the relatively less well off. The carbohydrates and the fat kept you from getting too cold, while the sugar and the fruit kept you from running out of energy.

TEA

*T*ea caught on long before the nineteenth century. By the 1800s, it rivaled beer in popularity even among the lower classes—it was, after all, a hot item to liven up the otherwise cold meals of the poor, and the fact that the water was boiled made it safe to drink, unlike beverages made with water right out of the ground.

Originally, tea was imported from China by the East India Company under a virtual monopoly, and for a long time it was so expensive that it was sometimes kept in locked boxes called tea caddies. The tea was not very strong, and the monopoly was broken in 1833, but until the early 1870s 85 percent of British tea came from China. Subsequently, imports of the substance began to pour in from India and Ceylon (gunpowder-green being a favorite type), but in the meantime a flourishing market in ersatz and secondhand tea had grown up, so great was the demand. Enterprising "tea" merchants busied themselves converting things like blackthorn leaves into reasonable facsimiles of tea leaves by the addition of artistic coloring here and there, a business so successful that the government estimated that for every seven pounds of authentic East India tea being sold under the monopoly, there were four phony pounds being sold to unsuspecting buyers. Even when the import monopoly ended, import duties kept the price very high. So people recycled—sometimes for profit. Indeed, by the 1840s there were eight factories in London busily recycling used tea leaves, often dyeing them and then mixing them with new tea for resale. At one point it was estimated that about 80,000 pounds of tea were gathered annually and rejuvenated in this manner.

We think of afternoon tea as being an English practice of long standing, but in fact the habit began in the 1840s. Before that, tea was frequently offered after dinner, when the ladies and gentlemen had gathered together in the drawing room. By the 1860s or so, five o'clock tea was a recognized social ritual, company sometimes being formally invited to partake, and by 1877 there was even a special costume—the tea gown—with which ladies could grace the occasion. Tea was customarily served in the drawing room, although, at a country estate, if the weather were good, it might be served outdoors on the lawn à la *Portrait of a Lady*.

DRINK AND THE EVILS
THEREOF

*T*he Englishman liked his alcohol. It seems you cannot turn a page of Dickens or Eliot or Hardy without someone reaching for his gin or port or wine or beer or rum. This was true to life. Throughout the century, the English consumed annually about thirty gallons of beer per capita.

In part this was because alcohol was generally safer than untreated water, which, at least in urban areas, gave rise to the cholera epidemics of the century. Alcohol and boiled beverages like tea or coffee were the only sure ways of getting a drink that would not endanger your health. But tea was expensive owing to high import duties and the East India Company's virtual monopoly on its importation until 1833. On the other hand, the materials for brewing or distilling liquor lay ready to hand. England's agriculture was based on corn—oats, wheat, and barley—and the barley was grown for malt and ale. Indeed, there was something of an "alcoholic-industrial complex," given the volume of malt consumed in the country and the countless farm workers for whom it provided a living. "What'll we do about the barley?" angry farm workers shouted at temperance lecturers, pointing out that drinking produced jobs as well as drunkards.

Brewers, in fact, were respected figures in the countryside. Many made their fortunes by acquiring local alehouses through which they distributed their product. They owned some 14,200 of the country's 48,000 licensed alehouses in 1816, and controlled many more whose owners owed them money for advances on their stock. Brewers were sufficiently respectable for their daughters to be suitable marriage partners for the landed quality. Pip explores with interest the old brewery on the grounds of Miss Havisham's house in *Great Expectations*. "Well! Mr. Havisham was very rich and very proud. So was his daughter," Herbert Pocket tells Pip of the ancient would-be bride, pointing out that her father was a brewer. Indeed, the wealthy Miss Crawley laments of her young relative Rawdon in

Vanity Fair, "What a pity that young man has taken such an irretrievable step in the world!," adding, "with his rank and distinction he might have married a brewer's daughter with a quarter of a million."

There were inns for the traveler to drink in and taverns for the casual drinker (these were the public houses, or "pubs"). The former were natural gathering places because they were where the mail and newspapers were delivered—what could be more natural than to stop for a glass as you came to claim your letter from Aunt Fanny? And the bone-shaken traveler always wanted a glass or two when he clambered down tired, cold, and hungry from his jolting, long-distance stagecoach ride. Less exalted was the village alehouse, which generally sold no spirits. In *Far from the Madding Crowd* Sergeant Troy forces the rustic laborers to drink brandy at the harvest home, imperiling the hay crop since, as Hardy points out, they had "from their youth up been entirely unaccustomed to any liquor stronger than cider or mild ale." Beerhouses appeared in the 1830s, places where any ratepayer could sell beer for an annual two-guinea fee, the government having become concerned about the rising consumption of spirits among the lower orders. "Gin palaces" were a product of the same era, flourishing in urban areas when for a brief period the absence of import duties made gin as cheap as beer.

The class distinctions of English life were reflected in where and what the different classes drank. In *Silas Marner,* for example, we learn that the Rainbow tavern was divided into the "bright bar or kitchen on the right hand, where the less lofty customers of the house were in the habit of assembling, the parlour on the left being reserved for the select society in which Squire Cass frequently enjoyed the double pleasure of conviviality and condescension." Such parlors were frequently furnished with pictures on the wall, decent chairs, and so on, while what would be called the "tap room" in a grander establishment than the Rainbow would have been set aside for the humbler customers and perhaps furnished with settles and wooden tables around a large fire. In *The Return of the Native* "the large common room of the inn" boasts "seats divided by wooden elbows like those of crude cathedral stalls . . . [a] long table before the sitters," and a fireplace with a chimney corner large enough to conceal Diggory Venn. The customers were served by a barmaid or potboy who brought drinks to their seats. Notwithstanding the case of the Rainbow, the bar in the early 1800s was neither a room for customers to gather in nor a counter to drink at, the notion of stand-up drinking being an innovation borrowed from the counter takeout or stand-up-and-drink "dram shops." Rather, the bar was generally a small room near the entrance to the pub with a table and, perhaps, fireplace, where the landlord could greet customers as they entered and keep an eye on things. "Miss Potterson, sole proprietor and manager of the Fellowship-Porters, reigned supreme on her throne, the bar," in *Our Mutual Friend*, which seems to have been halfway between the old and new model bar. "The available space in it was not much larger than a hackney coach; but no one could have wished the bar bigger, that space was so girt in by corpulent little casks, and by cordial-bottles radiant with fictitious grapes in bunches, and by lemons in nets, and by biscuits in baskets, and by the polite beer-pulls that made low bows when customers were served with beer, and by the cheese in a snug corner, and by the landlady's own small table in a snugger corner near the fire, with the cloth everlastingly laid. This haven was divided from the rough world by a glass partition and a half-door with a leaden sill upon it for the convenience of resting your liquor."

Except for the gin, brandy, and rum favored by the urban poor and lower middle class, only the rich drank spirits and wines, port being the favorite drink for after dinner. James Crawley is knocked out of the running for his rich relative's wealth in *Vanity Fair* when she discovers he's been drinking gin with the riffraff at a local establishment. "Had he drunk a dozen bottles of claret, the old spinster could have pardoned him. Mr. Fox and Mr. Sheridan drank claret. Gentlemen drank claret. But eighteen glasses of gin consumed among boxers in an ignoble pot-house—it was an odious crime." By mid-century, there was a whole variety of wines that were supposed to be set out for a proper dinner party—"sherry with soup and fish; hock and claret with roast meat; punch with turtle; champagne with whitebait; port with venison; port or burgundy with game; sparkling wines between the roast and the confectionery; madeira with sweets; port with cheese, and for dessert, port, tokay, madeira, sherry and claret."

The crinoline and its covering.

WOMEN'S CLOTHING

*I*t was filmy, gauzy, and virtually transparent at the beginning of the century. "Mrs. Powlett was at once expensively and nakedly dress'd," wrote Jane Austen with her customary acidulousness of a dinner companion to her sister in 1801. The lady in question wore a dress of the then-fashionable variety: thin muslin with only light stays, if that, and a chemise underneath. The dresses were frocks— that is, they buttoned down the back. They were cinched up high just under the breasts to suggest a high waist. They had no pockets, and personal items had to be carried in a small bag or "reticule." The more daring damped down their chemises underneath for a more revealing effect—the idea being to capture the "natural look" that had come out of France with the revolution. At the same time everyone looked innocent and girlish, in part because most frocks were white. Sometimes a sleeveless top called a pelisse was worn over the dress, going about halfway down the thigh or to the knee, and sometimes a shortish, waist-length jacket called a spencer was also worn. Headgear was always worn—caps could be worn indoors; bonnets invariably when outside. When it rained women walked on pattens, which were metal rings on small stilts that they strapped to their shoes that kept them an inch or so off the ground.

There was a gradual movement during the succeeding era to a more bell-shaped figure. The line of the waist on dresses descended to something approximating its anatomical location, and dresses became much fuller as petticoats were added underneath. Dress material became heavier and richer as velvets and silks became popular, and camisoles were worn between the dress and the corset to protect the dress as the loose, gauzy look vanished and the dress became tighter and tighter. A good deal of ornament was worn— feathers, jewelry, and the like. The richness of the fabric and the bluish hue of many of the colors may seem extreme unless it is borne in mind that until the 1890s lighting—whether by candle or gas— was dimmer and also yellower than it is now. Blue was needed to counteract this yellow light, and some of the accessories whose colors seem to us a bit too much would have looked a good bit softer under a subdued, nonelectric light.

The 1850s and 1860s saw the rise of one of the great gifts to the century's cartoonists—the crinoline—as women abandoned the five or six layers of petticoats in favor of this stiff horsehair material that could support the new heavier dress fabrics. Alas, the crinoline was bulky and unsatisfactory, too. In the 1850s the answer seemed to have arrived—the "cage crinoline," an apparatus that looked like an inverted, cone-shaped trellis designed for a rather large creeping plant. The cage dispensed with layers of petticoats but created other difficulties and inspired more jokes than perhaps any other women's fashion except the miniskirt. It was difficult to fit through doorways in the crinoline, hell to sit down in, embarrassing on windy days if the wind caught it underneath, and you could fall down steps in it if you weren't careful. When maids insisted on wearing it, they had an unfortunate tendency to sweep all the bric-a-brac off the tables they were supposed to be dusting, and it bobbed up and down like a large, swinging birdcage when you walked unless you took short, careful, mincing steps. It could get also cold outside in the winter now that you were wearing only a big birdcage and a light petticoat and chemise underneath, so a fashion for red flannel petticoats developed. (These were also protection against the consequences of a crinoline wearer's overturning in a public area, perhaps a reason why the new undergarments, drawers, became standard equipment.)

And then the crinoline and the big round skirt along with it promptly began to dwindle away, leaving only the back of the big round skirt—the bustle. In addition, except among the poor, the bonnet gave way to the hat, and indoor caps shrank away. The bustle vanished in the 1870s, only to reappear again in the 1880s. In the meantime, the tea gown had been introduced, serving notice of a new elaboration of dress, and sporting costumes for activities like archery and bicycling and tennis were beginning to put in an appearance for the new, more active young woman. Things could get quite complicated. The *Habits of Good Society* noted that its female readers would need at least a walking dress, a country dress, a carriage or visiting dress, an ordinary evening dress, a dinner dress, and a ball dress.

For most of the century, ladies always wore gloves outside (so did gentlemen). In addition, they wore them for the most part indoors as well (always at balls, for instance). Coming down to breakfast (though they were removed for the meal), ladies wore gloves, too, and in the schoolrooms in the sixties and seventies proper little girls wore them doing their lessons.

Special circumstances demanded special attire—weddings, for example, where white was *not* a universal color. Colors were sometimes favored, and a twenty-three-year-old wore gray silk in 1871 because she was "too old to wear white." For mourning, on the other hand, elaborate black costumes were required of women, with precisely prescribed periods during which they were to be worn.

MEN'S CLOTHING

*L*ike women, men revolted at the end of the eighteenth century against the artificiality of the mannered clothing associated with the royal court. Instead, the new style of dress was to be natural, unartificial—it was modeled after the riding costume. This consisted of a linen shirt, a stiff neckband (a stock) or a cloth square that had been folded into a triangle and was tied around the neck (a cravat). The pants were tights, with tall boots worn over them, and for the upper body there was a vest (a waistcoat), standard with all suits until the end of the century, and a "dress" riding coat, cut high up and double-breasted with large lapels in the front over the waist and long-tailed in back.

This was the costume that would have been favored by Jane Austen's heroes. In the 1820s the dandies modified it. Cinched-in waists, sometimes achievable only with a corset, became fashionable, and breeches basically disappeared. We hear of gaiters being worn with tights shortly thereafter. Pickwick, being a would-be sportsman, wears gaiters to keep his legs free from mud and dirt, and Dickens tells us that Marley's ghost wears tights. So tight were the tights, in fact, that a purse had to be carried separately to put money in; there was no room for it in the skintight pants. Also, the new fashion dictated a change in material; ordinary material was insufficiently "pliable" and body molding for the new pants so buckskin began to be used instead.

By the 1830s colors grew darker, at least for men's coats: thirty years later, the standard color would be black. It would remain so for the rest of the century. As a sort of last sartorial gasp, however, splendidly colored silk cravats and ornamented waistcoats of dizzying hues put in a brief appearance.

Meanwhile, the dress coat was less and less the uniform of everyday wear. It was relegated to the evening, where it turned black and became the standard "white tie and tails" outfit that is worn formally to this day. During the day, meanwhile, men now wore the frock coat, a long, almost-to-the knee garment of black that was cut to a uniform length all around and in which prime ministers and other sober folk appeared until the end of the century.

By mid-century men in society wore gloves (preferably not cotton or worsted, but often colored) in the street, and they wore white gloves for dinner parties—they could be removed for the actual eating—and for balls. Except for buckskins, all outer garments were generally made of wool, which meant that they wrinkled terribly without extraordinary care. There were no pants presses until the 1890s, and Beatrix Potter recorded of Prime Minister Gladstone that he looked "as if he had been put in a clothes-bag and sat upon. I never saw a person so creased."

Shirts and underwear were of linen. It was cool, long wearing, and easily washed; in fact, for shirts it had snob appeal because it dirtied so quickly that if you could wear clean linen all the time you obviously had enough money to be a gentleman. The upper classes wore linens made to a thin consistency, like lawn or muslin; the poor wore garments of thicker varieties. All men customarily wore boots. Shoes were considered somewhat less than formal, and in the first part of the century a gentleman was never without his top boots (boots turned down—or made to look as if they were—at the top), Hessians (with a tassel in front), or Wellingtons (they came up to a uniform height all around). Given the condition of roads and streets and the need to ride horseback frequently, boots were quite practical. Ornamental strings of seals and small gewgaws were often worn attached to a watch chain, as we are reminded when the ghouls are haggling over Scrooge's personal effects in the rag-and-bone shop in the grim future that the Spirit of Christmas to Come foreshadows for him.

As to whiskers, men were usually clean-shaven until the 1850s, when the soldiers returned from the Crimean War with beards. Do not "sneer at modern literature to a man with a beard, for if he is not a Crimean officer, he is sure to be" a literary man, wrote the author of a somewhat lighthearted contemporary etiquette book. Soon, however, every respectable man sprouted one. Which meant that thirty or forty years later aesthetes like Aubrey Beardsley (we find his contemporaries Yeats and Wilde also lacked whiskers) adopted a clean-shaven look as a specific mark of protest against the middle-class Philistines.

And the cane, of course. No gentleman was ever without one or its doppelgänger, the tightly furled umbrella. These were the descendants of the sword, which any eighteenth-century gentleman of consequence habitually carried about with him as a sign of gentle birth. The sword, along with knee breeches, was part of the required male dress at court well into the 1800s.

SERVANTS

*H*e must be respectable—he keeps a man-servant," says a nervous lady apropos of Mr. Pickwick when he is found in dubious circumstances.

But, of course.

If you could afford one in the 1800s, you had one. Or more. Sometimes, indeed, you had more than you needed just to show off—and to keep ahead of other people who might be catching up to you socially.

Aside from land, carriages and servants were the two sure signs of wealth in nineteenth-century England—so much so, that they were taxed, along with fancy carriages, during the Napoleonic Wars to ensure that the rich paid their share.

Quite apart from reasons of status, you had to have servants unless you wanted to do housework yourself. There were no electric lights for most of the century, nor vacuum cleaners, nor floor polishers, nor dishwashers, nor driers—if you wanted to do something, you did it by hand. And even transportation required horses that someone had to groom, water, and feed every day of the year. If you wanted a hot bath, you generally had to heat the water over a fire and then transport it upstairs in buckets and pour it into a hip bath. Plates and dishes all had to be scrubbed by hand after each meal or dinner party. Carpets had to be beaten and cleaned manually, and halls and floors and stone stoops had to be scrubbed on hands and knees. It all took manpower or womanpower—there were no technological shortcuts.

Plus there was always a lot to be done, given the lavish scale on which the nineteenth-century middle and upper classes lived. A ten-course meal was not uncommon for a fancy dinner, and an eighteen-guest dinner party might generate as many as five hundred items to be washed when it was over. Even a normal, everyday meal in a large household might have to be served in the nursery (for infants), schoolroom (the older children), dining room (the adults), steward's room (the upper servants), and servants' hall (the lower servants). By mid-century women's clothes came in multiple layers of petticoats and skirts, and they would be changed several times during the day at, say, a house party, as a woman went from morning gown to walking dress to archery dress to tea gown to formal evening dress—and they all had to be washed and cleaned by hand. Homes were cluttered with intricately carved and designed furniture and bric-a-brac well suited for catching dust. Heavy carpets, mirrors, old china figurines, Uncle Albert's malacca walking cane, the stuffed cockatoo from Australia, the chimneypiece ornamentation, the epergne and so forth—all these had to be kept clean and dusted, and the more of them there were the more servants were needed to keep them clean. Plus there were always guests coming to stay, and a servant would need to attend to their rooms at least four times a day. In the morning, she—it was usually a housemaid—would draw the blinds and curtains, remove soiled boots and clothes, and bring hot water for bathing or washing before breakfast. She would bring fresh water at noon and seven o'clock for washing before meals, and then before bedtime she would prepare the bed, close the windows, and bring fresh towels and clean water.

It would certainly not have occurred to nineteenth-century English gentlemen to do any of this, nor could Victorian ladies undertake housework either. That was, after all, the whole point of being a lady—you didn't *do* anything, except tell the servants what to do, receive your callers, and work on your embroidery or perhaps paint decorative flowers on the fire screen for the hearth. Manual labor of any kind would have cast serious doubts on your eligibility to be received in polite society. Explaining why she needed a lady's maid, Trollope says of Lizzie Eustace in *The Eustace Diamonds* that "it was necessarily part of the religion of such a woman as Lizzie Eustace that she could not go to bed, or change her clothes, or get up in the morning, without the assistance of her own young woman. She would not like to have it thought that she could stick a pin into her own belongings without such assistance."

To do the work that the master and mistress did not do, then, required "help." A small household would be able to afford only a maid-of-all-work, a girl who cooked, cleaned, scrubbed, mended, looked after the children, and got to stay home at night by herself in the dank, empty kitchen while the family went out or enjoyed themselves reading the latest installment of Dickens aloud to one another in the front parlor. She was paid perhaps something on the order of two shillings a week. A grander household, say that of a professional man, like a doctor or a banker, would perhaps have had a cook, a housemaid, and a nurse. In the still grander households, there would be male servants as well, at which point an elaborate hierarchy of upper (and under) male and female household servants would be organized.

The servants in a great house could amount to a small army. The duke of Westminster had fifty indoor servants at his Eaton Hall. Indeed, servants made up 16 percent of the national work force in 1891. Each large household had a male staff presided over by a butler and a female staff presided over by a housekeeper. (In an unusually grand household a steward would preside over the entire staff.) The butler and housekeeper were each typically in charge of hiring, firing, and supervising the servants under them. As a mark of respect, the butler was addressed by the family by his surname (and called "Mr." by the under servants); the housekeeper was "Mrs.," whether she were married or not. Besides supervising the footmen (including their waiting at dinner), the butler was in charge of the wine cellar (the word "butler" comes from *bouteille*), taking care of the "plate," or family silverware, announcing visitors when the occasion called for it, and, due to the fact that the ink on nineteenth-century newspapers was generally still tacky when they were delivered, ironing the master's newspaper each morning. The butler's command post was a special pantry where the plate and fine china were kept when not in use, the plate sometimes in a safe which he slept nearby to guard. His job often called for an ability to intuit social distinctions; when his mistress was "at home," he was to lead a gentleman or lady directly into the drawing room while ensuring that all other callers, e.g., tradesmen, waited in the hall. The house-keeper had a special room to work out of as well, and, in addition to supervising the maids' housework, she made preserves, saw to the tea and coffee, ordered and kept the household accounts, and was responsible for the household linen. Her mark of office was the great ring of keys she carried wherever she went.

The male staff reporting to the butler might consist of one or more footmen and a boy or page. The footmen had duties both outside and inside the home—in the residence they trimmed lamps, carried coal, sometimes cleaned silverware, announced visitors, and stood around looking imposing. In their public capacity they waited at dinner and attended the mistress when she went calling—leaving the visiting cards at the front door while she waited in the carriage. They also attended family members to the opera, riding on the back of the coach or carriage—partly to keep street boys from jumping up and getting a free ride—in their "livery," or household uniform of fancy coat, knee breeches, stockings, and powdered hair, a costume that endured to the end of the 1800s. Because of their appearance at dinner and in public with the family, footmen were supposed to be the most "presentable" of the male servants. They were evaluated on the basis of the appearance of their calves in silk stockings, and they often gave their height when advertising for positions in the paper—it was considered absurd to have a pair of footmen who didn't match in height. Ideally, they were supposed to be quite imposing. Lizzie Eustace's "footman was six feet high, was not bad looking, and was called Thomas," we are told. Popular writings joked incessantly about their humorless self-importance.

There was generally some kind of "outdoor" staff as well, typically consisting of a coachman (who maintained as well as drove the coach), a groom (who looked after the horses), and, in the country, a gardener and a gamekeeper, the latter with the responsibility for raising and protecting the game on the property and taking the master and guests shooting. The bailiff or land agent who collected the rent from tenants and oversaw the argricultural management of a large estate was typically a local tenant farmer, or, in the case of an agent, an "independent contractor."

On the female side, below the housekeeper came the housemaids. They were in charge of keeping the house spic and span and supplying bedrooms with water for washing and bathing and with keeping the fires going so no one got cold. Below them came the kitchenmaid, who helped the cook prepare meals, and then the scullerymaids, who washed the dishes and the pots and pans.

Being in service was not a glamorous life. The hours were long and hard—a maid-of-all-work might begin work at six in the morning and often not go to bed until eleven at night. Servants were paid poorly—some mid-century housemaids got only £11 to £14 a year. Standard vacations were two weeks off a year plus a half day off on Sunday, one evening out a week, and a day off each month. The servants slept in tiny, overheated or freezing-cold attic rooms and worked in dank, dark basement areas that were too hot or too cold, making sure to keep out of the way of the master and the rest of the household (unless they were a lady's maid or butler or footman) in keeping with the Victorian dictum that servants generally be neither seen nor heard. Married help was not usually wanted, and maids with young male "followers" were told to discourage them—if found pregnant, even by members of the household, women servants were liable to summary dismissal. They were ordered around, sometimes insulted, and frequently treated with minimal respect for the long, hard back-breaking hours of work they put in.

Why, then, did they do it? Many did not. By the end of the century, admittedly when the bloom of domestic service was off the rose, the average length of service in a home was not even a year and a half. Those who did stay with it, however, liked the security of the job, the chance, perhaps, to be eligible for some sort of pension at the end of years of service, or the possibility of travel (even going up to the London town house from the country estate would have been something, especially in the days when London was the most important and exciting city in the world). And what were the alternatives? Not always very good; for a woman, say, without education, primarily shopwork or the factories. Besides, in a great household, there was the opportunity to attain a higher status.

Status was taken very seriously by those in service. A butler might have spent years working his way up to his post of responsibility from a boy or a footman, and a housekeeper might have worked years as a housemaid before being entrusted with the keys to the household storerooms. The butler and the housekeeper, together with the lady's maid and valet—if any—were the upper servants. (The coachman and head gardener from the outdoor staff also had senior status.) As such, they were entitled to respect and deference from the under staff. "i had to wait on the butler & the town housekeeper & clean their sitting room," wrote one young kitchenmaid of the upper staff; in the servants' hall, the upper staff sat in the head places at dinner, in a caricature of the middle-class Victorian dinner party, with the other servants ranged along the side of the long table; visiting servants were seated according to the ranks of their master or mistress. Sometimes upper servants even ate separately in the steward's or housekeeper's room, while the other servants had to eat in the servants' hall. Mr. Rochester's housekeeper tells Jane Eyre what a relief it is to have a nice, intelligent girl like herself at Thornfield after all this time, the others being "only servants, and one can't converse with them on terms of equality; one must keep them at due distance for fear of losing one's authority."

Perquisites were accorded some servants. A lady's maid was generally entitled to her mistress's cast-off clothes and could also keep a rag bag of linen that she was free to sell, presumably to a rag-and-bone shop. The cook was permitted to sell the household's "drippings," if she wished, once the household was done with them. All servants who were materially helpful to visitors at a great house expected tips, or "vails," when a guest left; the Sedleys' groom refuses to hand down Becky Sharp's trunks from the carriage when she departs "as she had given nothing to the servants on coming away." As a rule of thumb, it was suggested by one aid to the perplexed that lady visitors tip their housemaid five shillings for a stay of three or four days, ten shillings for a week or more. Gentlemen were to tip the valet if they didn't bring one of their own, and also give the coachman a half-crown if that servant drove him to the railroad station. He was also to give five to ten shillings to the groom if he went riding, and the gamekeeper was to get at least ten shillings for every day's good shooting. "I never bring a man with me," announces the experienced Mr. Rather to the eponymous hero of *Phineas Finn* as they are traveling to visit Mr. Kennedy. "The servants of the house like it much better, because they get fee'd." By century's end, it appears, the tips expected were often so high that some people were deterred from visiting friends in the country not by the costs of the railroad ticket but by the anticipated cost of tipping all the staff.

At the beginning of the century, there was very little to distinguish servants by dress from their masters. This changed, the general rule thereafter being that the costume, or livery, of servants was the dress of their betters or masters—only of a generation or so before. Thus the formal knee breeches and stockings of the footman—perfectly fine for a gentleman's formal wear in 1800 but rather anachronistic by 1840 (butlers wore them until 1870), while the streamers and cap of the parlormaid of the 1890s reflected the attire of a well-dressed middle-class miss of some thirty years before. Dress was not necessarily simple either. Maids were expected by century's end to wear print dresses in the morning and then change into black (with a white apron) for the afternoon work. Grooms and coachmen wore the crest, if any, of the family on their buttons, and close students of old photographs of waistcoated male staff will note that coachman and groom wear vertically striped waistcoats—those of indoor staff like the butler are invariably *horizontally* striped.

THE GOVERNESS

a young lady accustomed to tuition' (had I not been a teacher two years?) 'is desirous of meeting with a situation in a private home where the children are under fourteen.' (I thought that as I was barely eighteen, it would not do to undertake the guidance of pupils nearer my own age.) 'She is qualified to teach the usual branches of a good English education, together with French, Drawing, and Music.' "

Thus, Jane Eyre preparing the fateful newspaper ad that will land her at Thornfield Hall. In 1850, there were 21,000 governesses registered in England, and probably many of them were well-educated but impoverished, just like her. Some, apparently, were massively cultured. Miss Pinkerton in *Vanity Fair* holds out her young ladies as being "perfectly qualified to instruct in Greek, Latin; and the rudiments of Hebrew; in mathematics and history; in Spanish, French, Italian and geography; in music, vocal and instrumental; in dancing, without the aid of a master; and in the elements of natural sciences. In the use of the globes both are proficients." (The globes consisted of a celestial and a terrestrial globe, used, respectively, to teach heavenly and earth-bound geography.)

A governess taught the children of middle- and upper-class households until they were old enough to go away to school, college, or to a private tutor, or, as was sometimes the case with girls, "come out." She was probably often not as well educated as the ladies from Miss Pinkerton's. Many, no doubt, were like Mrs. Garth in *Middlemarch*, who "had been a teacher before her marriage" and therefore presumably had "an intimacy with Lindley Murray and Mangnall's *Questions*," the latter (Miss Mangnall's *Historical and Miscellaneous Questions for the Use of Young People*) being a widely known rote question-and-answer book for the desperate governess in over her head. Being a governess was one of the few occupations considered suitable for middle-class girls who needed to earn their own living, but although the governess was expected to have the education and mien of a "lady," she was treated as a servant. "I can be treated as one of the family, except on company days, when the young ladies and I are to dine upstairs," writes Becky Sharp to her friend Amelia, and we can be sorry—even for Becky Sharp—for the neither-an-outsider-nor-insider status of the post that made the task lonely and difficult. (At the same time, this in-between position made it a marvelous, relatively detached standpoint from which the novelist could describe at close quarters the workings of a household.)

Many women hated the work. Jane Fairfax, anticipating in *Emma* that she will become a governess, avers that she is in no rush to go to town and visit "offices, where inquiry would soon procure something—offices for the sale not quite of human flesh, but of human intellect." Similarly, the independent Mary Garth, as Rosamond Vincy observes in *Middlemarch*, is resigned to looking after the querulous Peter Featherstone "because she likes that better than being a governess." The help hated governesses because "they give themselves the hairs and hupstarts of ladies," as Mrs. Blenkinsop says in *Vanity Fair*, "and their wages is no better than you nor me," while people of their employers' class found them too "low." George Osborne is horrified to find Joe Sedley contemplating an alliance with Becky Sharp while he's thinking of marrying Amy: "Who's this little schoolgirl that is ogling and making love to him? Hang it, the family's low enough already, without her. A governess is all very well, but I'd rather have a lady for my sister-in-law." The extraordinarily genteel Mrs. General agrees graciously to undertake the instruction of the Dorrit female children in the finer ways of society but when Mr. Dorritt timidly inquires "what remune—" "Why, indeed," the old battleaxe interrupts, she is too delicate to talk of cash. "I am not, as I hope you are aware, a governess—" "O dear no!" says Mr. Dorrit. "Pray, madam, do not imagine for a moment that I think so."

Being neither family nor servant could lead to a terrible isolation in the very midst of a bustling household life. One real-life governess made a point of spending five hours writing each letter that she sent: ". . . it has been a great amusement . . . during many a solitary hour when I had no other employ." Perhaps it was worse, because, if the examples of Jane Eyre, Becky Sharp, and Lucy Morris in *The Eustace Diamonds* are anything to go by, many were orphans.

However, as the cases of the three fictional governesses suggest, governesses *did* sometimes have a way of catching the masculine eye in a family. Alone, genteel, perhaps in "reduced" or "distressed" circumstances—and well-educated with all the character and refinements of a lady—can it be wondered at that younger sons or even the head of a household under the same roofs with such creatures found them appealing? Especially in a culture that emphasized the sacred obligation of the gentleman to come to the aid of all distressed members of the weaker sex? The case of Jane Eyre—romance-novel prototype though it may seem—was evidently not altogether atypical. Becky snags Rawdon Crawley, and David Copperfield's mother (also an orphan) explains in a rather wistful portrait of the governess's life how "I was nursery-governess in a family when Mr. Copperfield came to visit. Mr. Copperfield was very kind to me, and took a great deal of notice of me, and paid me a good deal of attention, and at last proposed to me." For every fictional Jane Eyre, who knows how many real-life counterparts there were, like the governess in the household of the editor of the *Westminster Review,* on which George Eliot worked, who carried on an affair with him while they lived together with his family. The visiting Hippolyte Taine maintained that a good many well-off men in London kept governesses as their mistresses. If Thackeray is correct, the susceptibility of males in a household to a governess's charms was well understood. And he suggests how the canny employer may have solved the problem. In *Vanity Fair*, Miss Pinkerton writes to Mrs. Bute Crawley to recommend two candidates for a post as governess, noting that both are well qualified, though one, in fact, is slightly more so than the other. "But as she is only eighteen years of age, and of exceedingly pleasing personal appearance, perhaps this young lady may be objectionable in Sir Huddleston Fuddleston's family. Miss Letitia Hawley, on the other hand, is not personally well-favored. She is twenty-nine; her face is much pitted with the small-pox. She has a halt in her gait, red hair, and a trifling obliquity of vision."

A TAXONOMY OF MAIDS

*N*ursemaids, housemaids, parlormaids, scullerymaids, chambermaids, dairymaids, lady's maids—a bewildering array of servants was necessary to keep the large nineteenth-century English household running smoothly.

The most exalted was the lady's maid, the only maid always considered one of the upper servants. She was free of the housekeeper's control, unlike the other maids, and attended the lady of the house, personally dressing and undressing her, arranging her hair, reading to her if need be, and using her needlework skills to do repairs on items of personal dress. If possible, she was French, although, of course, it was sometimes felt that her consequent liveliness might be compromised by a deficiency of character. (Mrs. Greenow seems to deal with this problem in *Can You Forgive Her?* by referring to her unrelentingly English maid Jenny, who seems to be in part, at least, a lady's maid, as "Jeannette.") Less desirable was an English girl, but in all events a lady's maid was supposed to be youthful and more personable than the housemaids who drudged away all day long doing the household's heavy manual labor. "They told me I was pretty," a woman told a mid-century inquirer, "and as I had not been accustomed to do anything laborious, they thought I would make a good lady's maid." The lady's maid had the privilege of being given her mistress's cast-off clothes.

The housemaids were the people who really kept the household running. They were the ones who made the fires, brought up clean water for bathing and washing, and took away the dirty water (the former sometimes four times a day—before breakfast, at noon, before dinner, and at bedtime), emptied and cleaned the chamber pots, drew the curtains and turned down the beds at night, and cleaned the bedrooms and the public rooms and areas in the house. Their work was time consuming and back breaking. Floors had to be scrubbed on hands and knees, and the grates had to be emptied each day and then cleaned and polished with black lead as they filled up with coal ashes; since virtually all town houses lacked running water and the working area was in the basement, maids often had to lug the hot water up past the ground floor (where the dining room was) on past the first floor (the drawing room) and up to the second floor—the American third floor—where the bedrooms were. And this not once but several times a day in order to make sure that everyone got hot water for their bath and a clean water basin in which to wash their face and hands before each meal. Sometimes there was more than one housemaid. An *upper* housemaid might then undertake the light work of arranging decorations, getting flowers, and the like, while the *under* housemaid scrubbed and polished and cleaned.

Next down the scale were the kitchenmaids. They worked in the sometimes miserable basement kitchens lighting fires in the stoves and helping the cooks prepare the food. Below them came the scullerymaids, the girls in charge of cleaning the pots and pans and dishes after breakfast and lunch and tea and dinner and supper and evening tea. They slaved away, at the bottom of the ladder in terms of respect and status, with the upper servants patronizing or mocking them and the household, of course, taking no notice of them whatsoever. Archdeacon Grantly's son Samuel, we are told in *The Warden*, to demonstrate his mildness, was "courteous to all, he was affable to the lowly, and meek even to the very scullery maid." "Poor little devils," recalled the butler at Cliveden, "washing up and scrubbing away at the dozens of pots, pans, saucepans and plates, up to their elbows in suds and grease, their hands red raw with the soda which was the only form of detergent in those days, I've seen them crying with exhaustion and pain, the degradation, too, I shouldn't wonder."

In the country there were sometimes dairymaids, too. Butter was much in demand at country estates and the dairymaid might well be the sort of strapping, robust creature she was made out to be by popular stereotypes—indeed, she would generally have to be in order to churn butter and carry around great pails of milk all day.

The nursemaid was, of course, necessary in a household with children. Her job was to dress and care for the smaller children and take them for walks. Nursemaids were often singled out by soldiers and policemen on the make in London's parks, no doubt because they were virtually the only female servants required—or able—to get out of the house on any regular basis and because they were usually quite young. Many were less than twenty—the loving and protective Susan Nipper in *Dombey and Son* is no more than "a short, brown, womanly girl of fourteen" when she scraps pluckily with her employer on behalf of her little charge Floy. "A nursery maid is perhaps more exposed to danger than any other class of servant," darkly warned *The Nursery Maid*. "She walks out a good deal with no other companions but children who are not old enough to understand what is said and whose presence affords a pretence and an excuse for addressing her."

Parlormaids were not very common until later in the century. They were evidently employed chiefly in households that wanted the status of having a special servant to open the door but couldn't afford a butler. (One snob refused to visit a household that had "only a parlour-maid" and not a male servant.) Male servants, after all, had to be paid higher wages, and until 1937 there was a special tax on them of fifteen shillings a year, plus they were often more difficult for the mistress of the household to handle with authority than a female servant. Parlormaids answered the door and announced visitors and sometimes served at dinner, doing, in short, all the things that a footman and butler were supposed to do. Just as a footman was supposed to be handsome and imposing, so a parlormaid was expected generally to be prettier than the housemaids who did their work "behind the scenes." Perhaps as a consequence there was a belief that parlormaids were often the object of advances from male members of the family.

Finally, in less affluent households, there was the poor maid-of-all-work, the young girl or teenager hired to do all the things for a household that a wealthier family would have divided up among a cook, housemaid, nursemaid, lady's maid, and so on—washing, scrubbing, cooking, cleaning, taking care of the children—with nothing to look forward to at the end of the day except falling asleep or sitting alone in the kitchen while the family enjoyed their evening together in the upstairs room. In *Pickwick*, the maid-of-all-work at the lodging house in Southwark, which Pickwick visits for Bob Sawyer's supper party, washes the glasses, answers the door, and does God knows what else. When they ring for her to make supper, there is no answer—"it was necessary to awaken the girl, who had fallen asleep with her face on the kitchen table." They were ubiquitous—perhaps some three fifths of all maids in the England of Queen Victoria were maids-of-all-work.

A London dustyard.

VICTORIAN RECYCLING

*O*ur *Mutual Friend* opens with Lizzie Hexam and her father dragging the Thames for bodies from which to retrieve money and other wealth. And from there the story progresses to the tale of Mr. Boffin, heir to the dustman who has made a fortune collecting dust and then sifting it for valuable and selling it. At a school frequented by naïve philanthropists, we are told of the mudlarks, who also survived off what they can scrounge from the river's bottom, and after a while we have the sense of a novel dominated by a society that lives by scavenging.

It began Dickens made none of this up, including the mudlarks, who scavenged for salable bits of coal and iron on the beaches of the Thames. Indeed, the nineteenth century poured an extraordinary amount of energy into the reuse of its households' discards and leavings.

It began at the top. When a lady finished with her gowns, it was very often the prerogative of her lady's maid to take them and wear them next. Household servants were sometimes allowed to keep "ragbags" for the collection of stray bits of used cloth. (In David Copperfield's household sheets are stolen from him and his wife in the ragbag.) From there the rags might well go to a street buyer or a rag-and-bone or rag-and-bottle shop like that run by the sinister Mr. Krook in *Bleak House*. If the rags were of linen they were bought for eventual shipment to a paper manufacturer, since paper was made of linen and rag until well into the century. A more sinister variation on the clothes-recycling theme turns up in the person of the "child-stripper" "Good Mrs. Brown" in *Dombey and Son*. "Don't vex me," she warns Florence Dombey when she manages to separate the child from her companions in the streets. "If you do, I'll kill you. . . . I want that pretty frock, Miss Dombey," she continues, "and that little bonnet, and a petticoat or two and anything else you can spare. Come! Take 'em off." Mrs. Brown belonged to a category of criminal that, again, Dickens did not invent; it was not uncommon for certain thieves to lure well-dressed children into dark alleys and remove their good clothes to be subsequently sold "secondhand."

In private homes, used tea leaves were employed to clean carpets and sometimes given to charwomen, who sold them to dealers who eventually recycled them illicitly—with some artificial colors—as tea. Drippings—the fat from roasted animals—were sometimes the prerogative of the cook or housekeeper; they were used as substitute butter by the poor. Bones were sold to the rag-and-bone man for fertilizer, and the household ashes, or "dust," that were emptied into the dustbin were sold for bricks and manure by men like Mr. Boffin's employer after they were sifted for objects of value by his workers. (In addition to searching for inadvertently discarded pieces of silverware, sifters salvaged old tin kettles for trunk fastenings, brick chips and oyster shells for construction material, and old boots and shoes for makers of Prussian blue.) Even the soot swept out of the chimneys by chimney sweeps was turned into manure and insect killer.

Public areas were picked clean, as the example of the draggers in the Thames suggests. The streets were scavenged for cigar butts, and some of the poor collected dog mess—or "pure" as it was called—and then sold it to tanyards who used it in processing the morocco and leather for the "kid" gloves worn by the upper crust at fancy operas and balls.

There were a number of reasons for this immense amount of scavenging. The people scrounging through sewers and picking up dog excrement were desperately poor, and hence not likely to overlook any possible means by which to sustain themselves when the only alternative was the workhouse. (There were even those who scavenged in the sewers.) Also, technologies were different—unlike today when there are no longer coal ashes to recycle because gas and electricity provide heat and illumination. Then, too, the acceptance of social hierarchy in England seems to have made it easier for servants to take worn-out clothes of their masters and the poor to accept worn-out clothes—or drippings—from the household of their "betters." Lack of concern about transmitting germs obviously helped here, as did the fact that much of the material was organic, and could be easily reused without complicated chemical processing—there were no synthetic fibers and no Styrofoam cups, and there was also a ready chain of buyers and sellers.

And, finally, perhaps, the nineteenth century worshiped thrift.

The Grim World

THE ORPHAN

*B*ecky Sharp of *Vanity Fair*, Jude Fawley of *Jude the Obscure*, Hareton Earnshaw of *Wuthering Heights*, Bathsheba Everdene of *Far from the Madding Crowd*, Jane Fairfax of *Emma*, Pip of *Great Expectations*, Dorothy and Celia Brook (and Mr. Bulstrode, too) of *Middlemarch* and Oliver Twist and David Copperfield of the novels that bear their names—all were orphans. Why so many parentless protagonists?

There was a tradition of literary foundlings that influenced the nineteenth-century novel—Tom Jones comes to mind—and there was a contemporary "romantic" predilection for the abandoned protagonist who must make his or her way, unaided, alone through the world. This is presumably the sort of romantic fiction that Jane Austen mocks at the outset of *Northanger Abbey*, where she notes dryly of the mother of Catherine Morland, "instead of dying in bringing the latter into the world, as anybody might expect, she still lived on—lived to have six children more." But there were real-life reasons why there were so many orphans in nineteenth-century English novels—there were, in fact, many orphans.

In 1870 the rate of death in childbirth was 1 in 204. Given the Victorian penchant for large families, the chance of a mother dying in childbirth sooner or later was therefore fairly good. Fathers could be carried off at an early age, too, given the rather poor state of medicine and sanitation. In 1839 the average age at death was twenty-six and a half years in rural counties like Rutland, and in cities like Leeds or Manchester or Liverpool it was only nineteen. In mid-century working-class areas it appears that 8 percent of the children lost both parents by the time they were fifteen and almost a third had lost at least one.

Once you became an orphan there was no official apparatus to take care of you except the workhouse. Oliver Twist was probably lucky to wind up there; at least, he had something to eat and some clothing. Before 1834, an effort was sometimes made to get orphans to board with their relatives, sometimes with a small payment to help out. In *David Copperfield*, we are told when David visits Mr. Peggotty that "Ham and Em'ly were an orphan nephew and niece, whom my host had at different times adopted in their childhood." But Em'ly is seduced and ruined by the heedless Steerforth. It is perhaps significant in this connection that, uniformly, nineteenth-century sources found that only a third of the prostitutes they surveyed had both parents still living.

OCCUPATIONS

a host of nineteenth-century occupations have passed into oblivion, owing to changes in taste, scientific advances, social customs, and the like. Their practitioners still remain, however, alive and well in the pages of the nineteenth-century novel to mystify and intrigue the contemporary reader who cannot quite figure out just exactly what it was they did.

Herewith, then, a short guide to some of the more striking occupations of the last century:

Articled clerks—These were young men who had been apprenticed or "articled" to practicing lawyers, generally for a period of five years, so that they could learn the profession. Boys were not articled to courtroom lawyers like barristers but rather to solicitors and other nonlitigating practitioners. David Copperfield speaks of himself and his fellow "articled clerks, as germs of the patrician order of proctors." In *Pickwick* Dickens alludes to "the Articled Clerk, who has paid a premium, and is an attorney in perspective, who runs a tailor's bill, receives invitations to parties, knows a family in Gower Street, and another in

A ratcatcher with his terriers.

Tavistock Square: who goes out of town every Long Vacation to see his father, who keeps live horses innumerable; and who is, in short, the very aristocrat of clerks."

Chandler—Originally, a chandler was a dealer in candles. By the nineteenth century, however, a chandler was the man who ran the neighborhood store on the corner. He sold many of the basics needed by the poor such as cheese, bacon, and other groceries.

Cheap-jack—A familiar figure at fairs, the cheap-jack sold inexpensive metal objects and hardware like watch chains, carving knifes, and the like and was a "patterer"—his spiel was a key to his success.

Coal porters—The men who unloaded coal from ships at wharf-side or from the lighters into which coal had been unloaded by coal whippers from the colliers. In addition, coal porters often delivered the coal to residential customers.

Coal whippers—So called because they "whipped" the coal out of the colliers that brought it down the coast and into the Thames into the lighters and barges from which it was then unloaded by coal porters. The whipping was done with a rope and pulley arrangement. As Pip makes his way down the Thames to try to spirit Abel Magwitch out of England in *Great Expectations,* he passes "colliers by the score and score, with the coal-whippers plunging off stages on deck, as counterweights to measures of coal swinging up, which were then rattled over the side into barges."

Costermonger—In theory a fruit and vegetable seller (the "costard" of "costermonger" was a kind of big apple), but he also sold fish, sometimes at a stall, sometimes walking street to street crying his wares. In London, costermongers bought their merchandise at Covent Garden or Billingsgate, sometimes traveling ten miles a day on foot to hawk it. Among the elite of street sellers, they probably numbered around 12,000 in mid-century London.

Crossing sweeper—There was a crossing sweeper like *Bleak House*'s little Jo at every major street intersection in London. Dodging in and out of passing waggons and carriages, they brushed away the mud and dust that collected on the streets—they did their best business in wet weather—so that the genteel could cross the street without getting their feet dirty. It was not very remunerative, seven shillings a week being a decent average wage, but with luck a sweeper who stayed at the same spot might get to know the "regulars," who might send him on small errands.

Dustman—Most city houses had dustbins into which the dust—the refuse from the ashes and cinders of coal fires and similar household matter—was regularly dumped. The dustman would periodically come around to collect the dust, whence it would be hauled away to be used ultimately for bricks and manure after being carefully sifted for inadvertently discarded valuables and other salable items. The most famous fictional member of this occupation is, of course, Mr. Boffin, the "Golden Dustman" in *Our Mutual Friend.*

Mudlarks—Because the Thames is a tidal river, at low tide it was possible to walk out into the mud and scrounge for coal, rope, bones, and copper nails as the mudlarks did, praying that they would not cut their bare feet on the glass or nails; many of them were six-to-twelve-year-old children. One observer wrote of a boy who stood in the waste stream of hot water from a steam factory to keep his feet unfrozen in winter while trying to earn the threepence a day he could make doing this if he were lucky. In *Our Mutual Friend* Dickens mocks a school run for prostitutes, "unwieldy young dredgers and hulking mudlarks" on the "grimly ludicrous pretence that every pupil was childish and innocent."

Orange girl—Selling oranges or bootlaces and staylaces was among the most viable street occupations if you were very poor because the start-up costs were so low. By comparison, most costermongers needed a barrow or a stall; if you sold hot fish or puddings you needed a warmer, too, for coffee. For oranges you just needed the 15*d.* to 18*d.* necessary to buy fifty oranges. The next step down economically were match girls, who often went door to door with their infants on their arm, all but begging.

Packman—A traveling peddler who carried his wares of cotton or linen goods for ladies about in his pack. The occupation ultimately adopted by Bob Jakin in *The Mill on the Floss.*

Pieman—A seller of pies whose ingredients could run the gamut from apple, currant and gooseberry to beef, mutton, or eel. There were recurrent suspicions as to the *kind* of meat that found its way into pies. Quite apart from the story of Sweeney Todd, there were many who would have believed Sam Weller's account of a conversation with a pieman who kept a lot of cats. " 'You must be wery fond o' cats,' says I. 'Other people is,' says he, a winkin' at me; 'they an't in season till the winter though,' says he. 'Not in season!' says I. 'No,' says he, 'fruits is in, cats is out.' " A real-life pieman complained indignantly to an observer in the mid-1800s that when he went into some areas, people began "crying 'Mee-yow,' or 'Bow-wow-wow' at me." On the other hand, sometimes the customer at least got the food for free. In *Dombey and Son* Dickens recounts how Rob the Grinder accepts a half-crown, "ran sniggering off to get change, and tossed it away with a pieman." This was a common practice that involved flipping a coin with the pieman when you were going to buy from him. If the pieman guessed right, he got your penny and you went hungry; if he guessed wrong, you got the pie free.

Ratcatcher—A good occupation for a lower-class boy who liked some excitement, animals, and had no education, like Bob Jakin in *The Mill on the Floss,* who tells Tom Tulliver of his desire to be a ratcatcher. Rats were all over, due to inadequate sewage, granaries, and the ubiquitous stables filled with oats for horses. The ratcatcher operated with arsenic, with which he poisoned the rats, or else used a ferret ("Lors! you mun ha' ferrets," says Bob) to chase them out of their holes whereupon his terrier would kill them. The going rate for deratting a London house at mid-century ranged from two shillings to a pound.

Sweep—"I wants a 'prentis," says Mr. Gamfield, the chimney sweeper, at the beginning of *Oliver Twist,* explaining to the workhouse board that lighting fires under the "chimney-boys" while they're cleaning the chimney is "humane" because it "makes 'em struggle to hextricate theirselves." Before Parliament outlawed the use of climbing boys in 1832 children as young as four or five were sent crawling up the 12-by-14-inch chimneys (some were only 7 inches square) of nice middle-class homes to clean out some of the five bushels of soot that coal fires deposited there on the average each year. Since the chimney surfaces were generally smooth inside, only the pressure of their elbows and knees got—or kept—the small boys up, and older boys often stood below them holding lighted straws to their feet or sticking them with pins to "encourage" them. Or they were simply beaten. Country children were warned that "the sweeps will get you" to keep them from wandering; in fact, small children in rural areas were sometimes kidnapped for the trade.

Waterman—The name was applied to two different kinds of London workers. First, to the men who rowed people across the Thames or out to vessels on the river they were trying to reach. To be a waterman required a seven years' apprenticeship. "Waterman" was also the name given to the men who watered the horses at cab stands.

APPRENTICES

*I*n the nineteenth century, the road to success and fortune often lay along the road of apprenticeship. Surgeons, lawyers, milliners, teachers, shoemakers—all underwent a process of training with a master of some kind in order to get experience necessary both practically and legally to practice a craft.

The legal requirement was theoretically in force for a good part of the century. Under the Statute of Apprenticeship passed in 1563 it was made unlawful "to exercise any craft, mystery or occupation" then practiced in England without having served an apprenticeship of seven years or more, and the law was not fully repealed until 1875.

In essence, apprenticeship was a preindustrial means to ensure that people in skilled occupations learned their business thoroughly and that the established members of the field weren't overwhelmed by competition from cheap upstarts who hadn't worked their way up through the system.

Not everyone was apprenticed, of course. According to the law an apprenticeship was required only for a "craft" or "mystery" in existence in 1562. An occupation like coach making, therefore, did not require apprenticing, because there were no real coaches until the 1680s. Other occupations the courts declared too simple to require any training, i.e., they were presumably not really crafts or mysteries. By the early 1800s, surgeons, shoemakers, silk weavers, milliners, soap makers, and cooks were on the list of those required to be apprenticed to learn their trade; butchers, collar makers, costermongers, rope makers, and merchants were not.

To become apprenticed the youth or his parents or guardians found a master willing to take him on and then signed a contract, called an indenture, binding, or "articling," him to the master. (Apprentice solicitors, for example, were known as articled clerks.) In law the agreement was actually between the apprentice and the master. In *Great Expectations*, "The Justices were sitting in the Town Hall near at hand, and we at once went over to have me bound apprentice to Joe in the magisterial presence. . . . Here, in a corner, my indentures were duly signed and attested, and I was 'bound.' " In his undertaking to accept Pip as an apprentice, Joe Gargery, as usual, is very generous. When he and Pip give the indentures to Miss Havisham to read, she notes that he has waived payment of the customary "premium," which the parents of the child being apprenticed paid to the master as compensation for training him.

The master was allowed to beat the child in his keep, but was not supposed to grossly mistreat him. Short of that, generally only a few major catastrophes like the master's death or bankruptcy could cancel the contract until the seven statutory years were up, unless he and the master agreed to cancel their contract first, which, again, Joe generously agrees to do so Pip can go away to London to become a gentleman. ("You would not object to cancel his indentures, at his request and for his good?" says Mr. Jaggers, to which, of course, Joe replies, "Lord forbid. . . .")

For the very poor, things were grimmer. If you were a pauper like Oliver Twist, the overseers of the poor could apprentice you—without your consent—once you turned nine until such time as you turned twenty-one. This is what happens to Oliver when he makes his famous request for "more"—"Oliver was ordered into instant confinement and a bill was next morning pasted on the outside of the gate, offering a reward of five pounds to anybody who would take Oliver Twist off the hands of the parish. In other words, five pounds and Oliver Twist were offered to any man or woman who wanted an apprentice to any trade, business, or calling." By not having to meet the requirement that the child consent, parishes could more easily sneak him into the hands of a thug like the brutal chimney sweep Gamfield. As Dickens suggests, if the master lived in a parish other than the pauper's, there was a financial incentive for the pauper's parish authorities to place him with the master, for after the child spent forty days in another parish, he was no longer the financial responsibility of the parish that had bound him out. (*Oliver Twist; or, the Parish Boy's Progress* was the book's original title.) Fortunately, there was also a requirement that indentures be approved by two magistrates. Until 1834, during which time the magistrates chose the overseers of the poor, this was probably often no safeguard at all. However, it saves Oliver when he falls to his knees begging the magistrates not to be sent away with the sweep. "We refuse to sanction these indentures," one of them then says to the representative of the local Poor Law authorities. "Take the boy back to the workhouse, and treat him kindly. He seems to want it."

In real life, however, things were not always so pleasant. Until 1816, parish workhouses in London shipped batches of apprentices to mill owners in Lancashire, the requisite signatures of approval by two magistrates sometimes being affixed to blank indentures that bound the children from the age of eight until they were twenty-one to employers and working conditions of which nothing was known. In general, it seems likely that a parish apprentice's lot was not an enviable one.

At the end of his seven years the apprentice became a journeyman (from the French *jour*, for "day") that is, a man entitled to work on his own. He was now free to hire himself out to whoever wanted him. Hardy tells us in *The Mayor of Casterbridge* that after his bankruptcy Henchard is forced to hire himself out for "journeyman work," but what the craftsman really wanted was to accumulate enough money and experience to set up a shop on his own and be his own boss. By so doing he himself became a master who could then take on apprentices, and thus the whole cycle of apprenticeship began all over again.

Ultimately, the system could not survive the century. Adam Smith attacked it early on for locking people up in dying occupations—made obsolete by the new industrial revolution—while new kinds of work were opening up that suffered from a shortage of people that could have used some of those who were imprisoned by their indentures.

The Workhouse

*W*e seem to be in the fictional world of Dickens except that the words in this instance come from the actual correspondence of a workhouse inspector in Kent in 1839. "A short time back," he wrote, "it was circulated in this county that the children in the workhouses were killed to make pies with, while the old when dead were employed to manure the guardians' fields, in order to save the expense of coffins."

A workhouse interior.

The workhouse, or, as it was sometimes called, the "house," the "poorhouse," or the "union" (entering the workhouse was sometimes called "going on the parish")—why did people hate and fear it so?

Noah Claypole in *Oliver Twist* attends a charity school, and he is ridiculed by one and all for being a "charity-boy." Whom does he pick on? Oliver Twist—because Oliver is "Work 'us," or, as Dickens says, "Noah was a charity-boy but not a workhouse orphan." Through the pages of *Our Mutual Friend* wanders Betty Higden, pleading again and again to be allowed to die safe from the clutches of the parish authorities, and it is to the workhouse that poor, desperate, dying Fanny Robin is driven in *Far from the Madding Crowd*, her subsequent funeral a bungled, miserable, rain-sodden affair without even the customary death knell being rung on the parish church bells because the workhouse won't pay for it. "Please, sir, I want some more," says Oliver in the workhouse—a quote rendered so pathetic by its setting as to have achieved immortality.

The workhouse system came into existence in 1834. Until then, relief of the poor, though required by statute, had been exclusively a local parish obligation. Each year poor rates were established to defray the cost of maintaining the indigent in the local workhouse, and the local overseer of the poor then did what was necessary to see that the funds were properly utilized and the poor adequately provided for.

The system was fine as far as it went, but it was meant to deal with isolated instances of local poverty and not with systematic economic impoverishment on a large scale, which is what took place in England in the late 1700s as the poor farmer or laborer was forced off his land by enclosures or denied the use of hitherto public land for fuel gathering or pasture.

Some parishes in desperation tried to pay farm laborers who were still working but not earning enough to keep body and soul together a supplement to bring them up to a minimal living standard so they wouldn't have to go into the workhouse and seek relief there. This so-called "outdoor relief" was based on the notion that it was more desirable to keep people out of the workhouse, but it ran into bitter opposition. The incentive to work was being destroyed, cried opponents, and the supplements being paid in this way were said to be an unfair subsidy to local farmers, so the old system was reformed out of existence in 1834 and replaced with the New Poor Law, an act that set up a national board of three Poor Law commissioners in London who supervised the new boards of guardians elected by the local ratepayers that now replaced the overseers of the poor. The guardians were to run the local workhouses on the union system, that is, the programs for the poor in a group of parishes were to be run together—if possible, all out of one large central workhouse. (There were some 650 such unions in the country.)

The major problem for the reformers was now to make sure that people got adequate food and clothing without at the same time making the workhouse so attractive that the not-so-idle and idle poor would all flock there at the ratepayers' expense.

There were, in fact, already restrictions on who could get help in a local area. "Settlement" laws dating back to Elizabethan times required that you demonstrate a connection of some kind with the local parish in order to be eligible for workhouse relief. Though the regulations were somewhat complex, for the most part being born in the parish was a sufficient qualification—which is no doubt one reason, quite apart from sentiment, why desperate homeless people like Fanny Robin in *Far from the Madding Crowd* always returned home, i.e., to their place of birth, when in trouble. Being apprenticed in the parish for forty days also did the trick; the parish in which Oliver Twist asks for "more" deliberately binds him out to a master in another parish to get him off their rolls in just this way. One year's domestic service in a parish also qualified you for assistance until 1834, a regulation which led some parishes to encourage or require employers of servants to hire them for periods no longer than eleven months and three weeks. At a convivial gathering at the malthouse in *Far from the Madding Crowd*, the old maltster recalls how "Old Twills wouldn't hire me for more than eleven months at a time, to keep me from being chargeable to the parish if so be I was disabled." Paying rates or marrying a man from the parish also got you a settlement there.

But how to keep even these eligible poor from flooding the workhouses? The solution adopted was to make the workplaces as grim and grinding as possible so that a recipient of workhouse charity would avoid going on relief if at all possible. The food was often insubstantial, amounting to less than what prisoners were fed, noted a prison steward in 1843 who had previously been master of a workhouse. No razors, no tobacco, no alcohol. You got issued a standard workhouse uniform and yielded up your regular clothes, and you had to abandon your personal possessions. Children were routinely separated from their parents, and husbands and wives were generally separated from one another within the workhouse walls, too. As Dickens mordantly put it in *Oliver Twist*, the board of guardians "kindly undertook to divorce poor married people, in consequence of the great expense of a suit in Doctors' Commons; and, instead of compelling a man to support his family, as they had theretofore done, took his family away from him, and made him a bachelor!" There was no going out to Sunday service; a chaplain was imported to say the service instead within the workhouse walls, and the work you were given to help the workhouse live up to its name was picking oakum or breaking stones—the same work you would have been given in contemporary prisons.

Indeed, many of the new workhouses were deliberately built to look as grim and forbidding as possible. "Their prison-like appearance," wrote an assistant commissioner with relish, "inspires a salutary dread."

DISEASE

*a*mong the things that have faded—if not vanished—with the passing of the nineteenth century are a host of physical complaints and illnesses. Gout, apoplexy, dropsy, ague, quinsy—these are all terms we associate with the age but may be hard put to define exactly now.

Ague—Another name for malaria, or the stage of malaria characterized by chills and shivering, hence, any such chill or fever. We think of it as primarily a tropical disease and, of course, people caught it in the West Indies, but it existed on its own in England at least up through the middle of the nineteenth century, spread by the same *Anopheles* mosquito that carried the disease elsewhere. When Pip brings Magwitch the food he has stolen from the Gargerys in *Great Expectations*, he finds the convict shivering along the river and says, "I think you have got the ague. . . . It's bad about here. . . . You've been lying out on the meshes, and they're dreadful aguish." Their conversation, of course, takes place in the marshes and those in the area of Cambridgeshire and Lincolnshire were known for their malaria. Local chemists did a brisk business in quinine in the 1800s until drainage helped to eradicate the disease.

Apoplexy—A stroke. The victim was struck down suddenly and rendered unconscious, the result sometimes being death. In some cases, recovery was accompanied by paralysis. Apoplexy was—is—associated with violent emotional outbursts, too much exertion, high blood pressure and the like. In *The Mill on the Floss* Eliot talks of the "sort of remote pity with which a spare long-necked man hears that his plethoric short-necked neighbour is stricken with apoplexy." At the end of *Mansfield Park*, Jane Austen tells us of a Dr. Grant, who "had brought on apoplexy and death, by three great institutionary dinners in one week."

Cholera—Caused by a bacillus that lives in the intestine and is excreted in human waste. In the days when London sewers ran untreated into the Thames, which was London's water supply, the disease was caught through drinking water. Cholera came from Asia originally and did not affect Europe until the 1830s, when it struck in recurrent epidemics that spread throughout the world, including the United States and South America. The symptoms included nausea, dizziness, vomiting, and diarrhea, followed by cramps and a desperate, burning feeling in the stomach with an overwhelming thirst—followed by death, often within twenty-four hours of the first appearance of any of the symptoms. It hit the poorer areas worst—some saw it as an Establishment plot to kill them off.

Consumption—A tuberculosis of the lungs. (There are other varieties.) It was spread through the air or by spitting or by a break in the skin. It could incubate for long periods of time and then erupt into weakness, fatigue, and the "wasting away" that characterized true consumption. The latter stages of the disease were often accompanied by a sudden burst of energy, glittering eyes, and a mania that sometimes produced a frenzied outpouring of creative work and so lent currency to the belief that the disease was somehow associated with artistic productivity or genius. Jane Eyre's best friend, Helen Burns, dies of the disease at the Lowood School. The illness killed 60,000 people in Britain during the period of 1838–43 alone and ultimately wiped out more Britons in the 1800s than did smallpox, measles, typhus, whooping cough, and scarlet fever all combined.

Croup—A name originally applied to several different kinds of diseases, including diphtheria, with which it was often confused in the early 1800s. It mainly hit children. Croup led to trouble breathing and hoarseness when talking. In *Pickwick* the medical man Jack Hopkins tells of a child who swallowed enough beads to make him rattle when his father shook him; "he's got the croup in the wrong place!" exclaims the parent. In severe cases there could be convulsions and death.

Diphtheria—The disease of which Eugene Lydgate ultimately dies at the end of *Middlemarch*. Not diagnosed accurately and named until the 1820s, it was often confused with croup. It affected children the worst, inflaming the mucous membranes to the point where breathing became extremely difficult and often impossible, causing death. It was transmitted by sneezing.

Dropsy—A symptom of something wrong and not a disease in itself. The root word means "water," and dropsy meant a swelling of some part of the body with fluid, due to poor circulation, hardening of the arteries or kidney problems, such as, for example, might accompany diabetes or emphysema. "Dropsy!" says Lady Chettam in *Middlemarch*, of "poor Mrs. Renfrew." "There is no swelling yet—it is inward. I should say she ought to take drying medicines, shouldn't you?—or a dry hot-air bath."

Dyspepsia—Indigestion, with symptoms taking various forms. Perhaps more common in an age of bad teeth that made thorough chewing impossible and that often featured considerable overeating, to say nothing of food that was not refrigerated or otherwise well preserved.

Gout—A disease that can be hereditary and was common among the upper-class because of the superabundance of meats and wine they consumed. The basic problem was an excess of uric acid, which caused a swelling in the joints, especially in the foot and the big toes, of considerable painfulness. In *Northanger Abbey* "Mr. Allen . . . was ordered to Bath for the benefit of a gouty constitution," where he would have drank or bathed in the waters there, while family and friends socialized—not that "the waters" in themselves were likely to do any good. We are presumably to measure the failure of Lydgate's idealistic dreams of reforming the medical profession at the end of *Middlemarch* by the fact that he finished his career treating gout patients.

Palsy—Paralysis. There were various kinds: Parkinson's disease (shaking palsy), sciatica, muscular dystrophy, the partial paralysis caused by apoplexy, paraplegia, and so forth.

Pleurisy—An inflammation of the pleura, which are two sacs in the chest. Dry pleurisy just produced coughing. In the other kind, gunk seeped into the pleura and you could get a sharp pain in your side or chest. If chronic, the swelling might compress the lungs or other internal machinery and the sufferer could wind up hunched over with spinal curvature and internal organs somewhat rearranged.

Quinsy—The old word for bad tonsillitis. Your throat swelled up and you could get chilled and run a temperature.

Typhoid fever—Often confused with typhus due to somewhat similar symptoms and the difficulty of accurately differentiating it without laboratory tests, the disease was first recognized as different from typhus in the 1820s. Drinking water or eating food contaminated by human waste either directly or by flies or by a human carrier (the infamous "Typhoid Mary" was a cook) brought it on. The disease killed one in four if untreated and could cause delirium and a rash like that caused by typhus. Prince Albert is thought to have died of it.

Typhus—The disease, so Jane Eyre tells us, that laid low forty-five of the eighty girls at the horrible Lowood School. This is not surprising. The illness was spread by body lice and consequently developed in dirty conditions; Napoleon's army lost thousands upon thousands of men to the disease in the retreat from Russia in 1812. Symptoms included delirium, headaches, a rash and high fever, which usually cleared up unless the disease—in about two weeks' time—proved fatal. (In 10 to 40 percent of the cases it did.) Mr. Willoughby tells her sister at one point in *Sense and Sensibility* that he heard "Marianne Dashwood was dying of a putrid fever," this being another name for the disease.

Yellow fever—A disease of tropical Africa and America that is spread by mosquitoes and was generally of local incidence, e.g., in a port city or ship or jail. The name was derived from the jaundice that accompanied severe cases (mild ones were like flu), which were often accompanied by kidney and liver failure and then death. "Mine a yellow face?" says George Osborne in *Vanity Fair*. "Stop till you see Dobbin. Why, he had the yellow fever three times, twice at Nassau, and once at St. Kitts." In *Dombey and Son,* Joey Bagstock describes how "his elder brother died of yellow Jack in the West Indies." The disease gained the nickname Joey gives it because of the yellow flag required to be flown by ships that had infected persons on board.

DOCTORS

*T*he next thing I remember is waking up with a feeling as if I had a frightful nightmare, and seeing before me a terrible red glare, crossed with thick black bars . . . someone was handling me, lifting me up and supporting me in a sitting position," says Jane Eyre, recalling a horrible experience of her childhood. "I scrutinized the face of the gentleman; I knew him; it was Mr. Lloyd, an apothecary, sometimes called in by Mrs. Reed when the servants were ailing; for herself and the children she employed a physician."

It is a neat little vignette that sums up a good deal about early nineteenth-century English medicine and tells the reader familiar with the social standing of various English medical men what Mrs. Reed thought of Jane Eyre. The rich got the physician, the poor got the apothecary, and—though such a figure was not in the Reeds' sphere, apparently—both of them might call for, as Mr. Rochester does later on in the novel, a surgeon.

Physicians had the most prestige in 1800. They were called physicians because they only administered drugs, or "physic." They did not deal with external injuries or perform surgery or set bones or do physical exams, other than of the patient's pulse and urine. They took detailed case histories and then wrote out a prescription to be filled by an apothecary. "Professional practice," as George Eliot dryly observes in *Middlemarch*, "chiefly consisted in giving a great many drugs."

Physicians made up only a tiny handful of the doctors practicing in early nineteenth-century England, but they were concentrated in London, where it was perhaps easier to find a substantial patient population of wealth and social standing. To practice as a physician in London you had to be licensed by the Royal College of Physicians. If, in addition, you had gone to Oxford or Cambridge, you could become a Fellow of the College (F.R.C.P.) too, which meant a good deal more status, exemption from unpleasant things like jury duty, and the right to a say in the internal governance of the college. There was no system of medical school training and only a handful of hospitals (in 1851 there were only some 7,500 hospital patients in the United Kingdom out of a population of 18 million). No doubt if there had been any medical schools, many of the physicians would not have been interested in them anyway, because they believed quite firmly that medicine was to be taught largely out of books, and antique ones at that. As late as 1819, the licensing exam given by the Royal College could require the applicant to construe passages from first-century and seventeenth-century medical texts; the fellowship exam took place entirely in Latin.

For to be a physician was to be rather a gentleman (their wives could be presented at court, while those of surgeons could not), and anything that smacked of manual labor—like, for example, cutting people open or doing serious physical exams, was not gentlemanly. Tapping on the chest and the use of the stethoscope were apparently slow to be adopted in British medicine for just that reason.

Next below the physicians in the medical hierarchy were the

surgeons. They were the men who cut people open, dealt with fractures, skin diseases, V.D., eye problems—anything, in short, for which a physician could not simply give a prescription. "John is gone for a surgeon," says the housemaid at Thornfield when Mr. Rochester tumbles from his horse. When Mr. Dombey also falls from a horse, the surgeon is likewise sent for; indeed, accidents involving horses apparently made up a good deal of surgical practice.

From a social point of view the problem with being a surgeon was that the actual work involved was like manual labor; you did, after all, use your hands to treat people and did something with them—unlike the physician—besides just write on a piece of paper. In addition, it had not been so long—1745, in fact—since surgeons had been formally linked with barbers, and what's more, until 1833 surgeons got the bodies on which they learned their anatomy from graveyards—sometimes by rather unscrupulous means.

Perhaps because of this difference in status the physician was usually addressed as "Dr.," while the surgeon made do with plain "Mr." On the other hand, you did not need a license to practice surgery, and it cost less to train as a surgeon than as a physician. The cost of the usual necessary preliminary education at Oxford and Cambridge put physic out of reach for most poor boys. Instead, surgery was learned, like other manual skills, largely by being apprenticed. If you *really* wanted to find out what was going on in the surgical world, you went to Edinburgh and Paris, as does the reforming Lydgate in *Middlemarch*.

However, the boundaries between physician and surgeon began to blur as the century wore on. The surgeons tried to make themselves more prestigious by allowing the Royal College of Surgeons in London to create Fellows like the ones the physicians had. At the same time, with scientific discoveries coming thick and fast it was becoming apparent even to the physicians that you now had to study germs and bodies the same way a surgeon did. Hence, the rise of the "general practitioner"—the man who, like Lydgate, "resolved to resist the irrational severance between medical and surgical knowledge," as Eliot puts it. Such a man, knowledgeable in both physic and surgery, became an increasingly influential figure in the English medical world.

And then there was the apothecary—the man for whom Mrs. Reed sent to attend to Jane Eyre while her own children were cared for by a physician. The apothecary was the lowest man on the medical totem pole. He was originally only supposed to make up prescriptions for the physicians, but in many areas there were no physicians so the apothecary began giving advice, too. This was officially permitted in the eighteenth century—but with the stipulation that he could not charge for the advice, only for the drugs. Like the surgeon, he learned his trade by apprenticing himself to a man with experience. He was selling things over the counter and, hence, "in trade," which made him hopelessly lacking in social status.

Death and Other Grave Matters

*D*eath—early death—was no stranger to the nineteenth-century English family, and perhaps that is why they loved to weep over the lingering demises of Dickens's small heroes and heroines. Certainly, they made a big production out of it in every other respect.

In some rural communities the ritual began even before one died, with the ringing of a "passing bell" in the parish church to signal that a member of the community lay on his or her death bed. Characteristically, the bell tolled six times to indicate the passing of a woman, nine (the famous "nine tailors") to indicate the passing of a man, followed by a peal for each year of the dying person's life.

When a person died a large funeral was held with everyone dressed in black (unless the deceased were a child or a young, unmarried girl, when the costume was white); mourners received black gloves and black scarfs. Sometimes special mourners carried staves wrapped in black; when he returns for Mrs. Gargery's funeral, Pip finds at the house "two dismally absurd persons, each ostentatiously exhibiting a crutch done up in a black bandage." The not atypical hearse used to convey the body of little Paul Dombey in *Dombey and Son* is described in terms of there appearing at Mr. Dombey's "four black horses at his door, with feathers on their heads; and feathers tremble on the carriage that they draw."

In most communities funerals were an important social event, and propriety and due regard for the family's social standing necessitated that they be done right. "Funerals were always conducted with peculiar propriety in the Dodson family," George Eliot tells us in *The Mill on the Floss.* "The hatbands were never of a blue shade, the gloves never split at the thumb, everybody was a mourner who ought to be, and there were always scarfs for the bearers." Characteristically, the undertaker would provide professional mourners or "mutes" dressed in black to stand about and lend dignity to the affair. "There's an expression of melancholy in his face, my dear," says Mr. Sowerberry, the undertaker, to his wife when he takes on Oliver Twist as an apprentice, "which is very interesting. He would make a delightful mute, my love . . . I don't mean a regular mute to attend grown-up people, my dear, but only for children's practice. It would be very new to have a mute in proportion." When the body was actually brought to the gravesite for burial, there was often an additional tolling of the bells—the death knell—to let the parish know of the final laying to rest of the deceased. From the standpoint of the workhouse authorities, this was often considered a luxury; when Fanny Robin is buried in *Far from the Madding Crowd,* the "Union" refuses to pay the shilling demanded for performing this office.

There were exceptions to the rules governing these matters. "Correctly," scowls Heathcliff when Hindley Earnshaw dies of drink, "that fool's body should be buried at the cross-roads, without ceremony of any kind . . . he has spent the night in drinking himself to death deliberately." Heathcliff's allusion is to the contemporary statute dealing with self-destruction. If you were a suicide, until 1823 you were required to be buried by law at a crossroads with a stake through your heart, a ceremony actually witnessed by Thomas Hardy's mother. The stake was to prevent the ghost from walking, and the burial at a crossroads was believed to dilute the evil influence of the deceased by spreading it in four separate directions. Until 1870, all your personal property was forfeit to the Crown, too, and, once the stake business was ended, you were, until 1832, required by law to be buried at night only, between the hours of nine and midnight. And, although suicides were thereafter permitted to be buried in a Church of England graveyard, no service could be said over the body.

Once a corpse was buried, there was for many years a decent possibility of premature resurrection. This was because there was no way for surgeons to get cadavers to dissect except by using the bodies of executed criminals and—despite the contemporary enthusiasm for capital punishment—there were never a sufficient number for the purposes of anatomical study. Accordingly, surgeons retained "resurrection men" to obtain suitable material for them at two guineas a cadaver. Decedents' families were, of course, not enthralled with this practice, and it became the custom for some of them to set watchers or even traps at graveyards to ensure that no one made off with the remains of Uncle Edward in the wee morning hours. The cagy body snatchers struck back—they would hire a superannuated prostitute, who, suitably attired in black, would arrive at the gravesite just after the service concluded, pretending to be a tardy mourner. She would then mentally photograph the layout—including traps, if any—and report to the body men who would then set to work with the information that night to retrieve the corpse. The actual exhumation took only a short time if the resurrection men knew their job. You dug down to where the head was, opened the top part of the casket and drew the body out, thereby causing minimal disruption to the site, and then you removed any graveclothes. Strangely enough the law was not harsh on people having bodies, unexplained, in their possession, but if the bodies had graveclothes on them, the punishment was seven years' transportation.

The departed were always to be mourned for specifically prescribed periods of time, which, in practice, affected mostly the clothes the survivors were permitted to wear and whether they could have fun or not. Men had it easy; they needed only to wear black armbands, a custom adopted from the military in the early years of the century. Women, however, were supposed to dress all in black. "My dear Celia," says Lady Catherine Chettam of Dorothy Casaubon after her husband's death, "a widow must wear mourning at least a year." This meant an all-black wardrobe (the so-called widow's weeds), frequently of bombazine, a material especially favored because it did not gleam in light, and no jewelry or ornaments except for beads made of jet, a kind of coal. When she first sees her cousins Mary and Diana Rivers, Jane Eyre tells us they "both wore deep mourning of crape and bombazine" because their father had just died. A widow was expected to mourn her husband for two years, but she could moderate her funereal clothing a bit after a while to "half-mourning," which consisted of pinstripe black. Parents and children were to be mourned for a year, a brother, sister or grandparent for six months, an uncle or aunt for three months, and a first cousin got six weeks. (In-laws were mourned too, but for lesser periods of time.) Some women remained in their mourning garb for the rest of their lives. "Forty years at least had elapsed since the Peruvian mines had been the death of Mr. Pipchin," we are told in *Dombey*, "but his relict still wore black bombazeen, of such a lustreless, deep, dead, sombre shade, that gas itself couldn't light her up after dark, and her presence was a quencher to any number of candles." Of course, the lead in this fashionable mourning was set in part by the queen. After the death of her beloved Albert in 1861 until her own death in 1901 portraits generally show Victoria in the somber black and white attire suitable for honoring the memory of a late departed.

PART TWO

Glossary

abigail—A lady's maid.

acceptance—The act of putting one's name on a bill of exchange and writing "accepted" across it, which then made one liable to pay it.

The bill of exchange being accepted.

accommodation note or bill—A bill of exchange that one "accepted" for someone else so he could, in effect, borrow money based on one's credit-worthiness.

act—A piece of legislation that had passed both Houses of Parliament, been signed by the monarch and become law; before that, it was called a "bill."

adder—A snake, especially one that struck out.

advocate—The name given to the lawyers (counterparts of the serjeants in the common law courts and barristers in the Court of Chancery) who argued cases in the old courts of ecclesiastical law and admiralty law in Doctors' Commons. The proctors, corresponding to solicitors in the other courts, assisted the advocates.

advowson—The right to appoint someone to a benefice.

agent—In rural areas a land agent was the manager of a large estate for one of the great landowners. Sometimes assisted by bailiffs, he oversaw the farming of the property by tenants, a role performed in the previous century by a steward. George Eliot's father was an agent. In cities a house agent was a person who rented apartments and houses. There were also parliamentary agents who could be hired to help you win an election.

ague—Basically, malaria and the chills that went with it. Later generalized to include any similar fever or chills.

aldermen—In a municipal borough, the aldermen were the members of the government, often elected by the council, who were supposed to assist the mayor in governing.

ale—What was the difference between ale and beer? Sometimes the term "beer" included ale. Sometimes it didn't. Sometimes ale was supposed to be stronger than beer, other times not.

almshouse—Lodgings for the poor supported by private rather than public charity. Publicly funded lodgings were called poorhouses or workhouses.

ankle jacks—Jackboots that came up above the ankles.

antimacassar—The Victorian gentleman often applied macassar oil to his hair. To prevent it coming off all over their nice furniture, Victorian ladies pinned antimacassars—little white doilies—on their armchairs and sofas where a gentleman's head would be. Considering the other hair-control substances that might have come in contact with the nine-teenth-century English sofa, macassar oil might not have been so bad— *David Copperfield* also instances beef suet and bear's grease.

St. Pancras Almshouses, Kentish-Town.

apoplexy—A stroke. Sometimes fatal, sometimes resulting in recovery with partial paralysis but generally accompanied when it struck by paralysis and coma. In *Mansfield Park* a minister is described as a "short-neck'd, apoplectic sort of fellow and, plied with good things, would soon pop off."

apothecary—Among medical men, the lowest ranking socially. They sold drugs and were probably distinguished in their own minds from druggists and chemists by virtue of the fact that they sometimes made house calls and gave advice. There was no way they could become really respectable—selling things over a counter made you a tradesman.

apprentice—The practice of apprenticing people to a trade lasted well into the 1800s. As a rule, one had to consent to being apprenticed unless one was a workhouse child. The term of apprenticeship was generally seven years and the master who took one on was paid a fee for so doing called a premium. When one finished, one was a journeyman and able to hire oneself out to others for wages.

apron—Part of a bishop's characteristic formal garb, the other recognizable element being lawn sleeves.

appropriated—When tithes from a local parish went to a religious entity other than the incumbent, rather than to a layman, when tithes were said to be impropriated.

aquatint—A type of etching that looked as if it were done in India ink or watercolor and involved the use of nitric acid.

arabs, street—Street children, perhaps so called because they had no homes, like the nomadic arab tribes.

archbishop—There were two archbishops in the Church of England. The archbishop of Canterbury ran the southern part of England and had precedence over the archbishop of York, who ran the northern part. The archbishop of Canterbury took precedence over everyone except the royal family, and was addressed as "Most Reverend." Perhaps his most important function from the standpoint of many nineteenth-century novels was his ability to grant a "special license," which permitted you to be married anywhere and at any time, as opposed to the restrictions required by a regular license or by having the banns published.

archdeacon—The clergyman who assisted the bishop in running the diocese through the inspection tours known as "visitations." His subordinates were the rural deans. Addressed as "Venerable." The post held by Dr. Grantly, son-in-law to Septimus Harding, in *The Warden.*

area—In London town houses, there was customarily a basement courtyard some six to eight feet below street level that could be reached by a flight of steps from the street. This was the area. It was protected by a railing and sometimes had a water butt in it.

aristocracy—An imprecise term, but probably most frequently used to designate the peerage.

armoire—A big clothes cupboard that was either freestanding or set into the wall.

army list—A list of every commissioned army officer.

arrowroot—A type of plant, originally from the West Indies, that could be made into a variety of starchy food.

articled—Legal documents then (and now) are often divided into sections marked "Article 1," "Article 2," etc. (They are parts of the document that join together—the root is the same as that of "articulation" in the sense of joining together bones.) When a child was apprenticed to a master, he signed an indenture that was often broken up into such articles so that "to article" someone came to mean binding him to be an apprentice.

assemblies—Assemblies were large-scale evening gatherings for the quality popular in the early part of the century, the most famous being Almack's in London. For a ten-guinea subscription, one got twelve weeks of a ball and supper each week, a highly prestigious event initially, with top members of the aristocracy attending and tickets almost impossible to get.

assizes (pronounced with emphasis on the second syllable)—In areas outside London, justice was generally dispensed by justices of the peace at the petty or quarter sessions. Civil and criminal cases that were too tricky for them or—like capital cases—too serious, were handled by circuit-riding judges from the superior common law courts in London of Common Pleas, King's Bench and the Exchequer after they had finished their regular terms. These sessions, supposed to be held twice a year, were the assizes. They were occasions of considerable ceremony. The judges upon arriving in an assizes town were met by the high sheriff, a special assizes sermon was preached and a great banquet was given for the local notables, the actual work of judging beginning on the succeeding day.

attorney—The term came to be used loosely for any kind of lawyer. Originally, however, it referred only to those lawyers who assisted the serjeants in the common law courts. Attorneys were eliminated when the old court system was abolished in 1873, and their functions were taken over by solicitors.

backboards—Stiff, straight boards that girls wore against their backs in order to improve their posture. Sometimes they were apparently strapped on.

back parlor—Many residences, especially small shops, often had a front parlor or shop used for customers or transacting business. The small, modest space at the back of the building for household affairs was the back parlor.

bagatelle board—Somewhat like billiards. A table with nine holes in it at one end was the playing surface; one tried to knock balls into it with a cue. It turns up in *Little Dorrit*—Dickens himself played it while barricaded into an inn across the street from a violent election campaign he was covering as a reporter that was probably the model for the Eatanswill goings-on in *Pickwick*.

bagman—A commercial traveler, that is, a traveling salesman.

bailey—The outside wall of a fortress or castle; also the space enclosed by such an outside wall. Old Bailey, the site of the main criminal court in London, was formerly within the confines of the ancient bailey between Ludgate and Newgate, which gave rise to the name.

bailiff—The term formerly had two principal meanings. On the one hand, it referred to a sheriff's officer who carried out court orders and, in particular, seized goods or people for debt. In *Far from the Madding Crowd* Gabriel Oak tries to hire himself out as another kind of bailiff before he goes to work for Bathsheba Everdene; this was the man who managed a large farm for its owner (or assisted an agent in so doing), collecting rents, responding to complaints from tenant farmers, and so on.

baize—A coarse woolen material used mainly for lining and covering things.

bakehouse—A structure with an oven in it for baking bread. Bakehouses (or bakeries) would let the poor use these premises to heat their Sunday meals for a small charge since most of the poor lacked ovens and could cook only over an open fire.

ball—A dance usually of some size and grandeur. Private balls became fashionable as the century wore on. There were also public balls—notably those given by hunt clubs and the like, to which tickets of admission were required.

ballast lighter—A boat that carried ballast to colliers in the Thames that had unloaded their cargo of coal from the north and needed to take on additional weight in order to sail home safely.

ballet—Not just sylphs and tutus but a kind of silent cross between vaudeville and commedia dell'arte, often performed in taverns, with slapstick routines and clowns. "They are all comic, like pantomimes," said one mid-century observer. "They're like the story of a pantomime, and nothing else."

bandbox—A box used for storing or carrying hats and bonnets, etc.

bands—Part of the customary costume of the clergy when officiating at a service during the early part of the century. The bands were two pieces of cambric, each some four to nine inches long and a few inches wide, connected by a piece that went under the chin, and were generally worn with a black gown and a wig.

the Bank—a/k/a the Bank of England—a/k/a the "Old Lady of Threadneedle Street" from its location in the City in London. Founded in the late 1600s by a group of merchants as a private institution, it was the main lender to the British government on numerous occasions and became so intertwined with the fiscal affairs of the Treasury as to eventually become semipublic in nature. The Bank Charter Act of 1844 gave it the exclusive right to issue the bank notes which became the universal paper currency in England.

bank notes—Promissory notes of a bank, that is, a promise by a bank to pay. They were the only form of paper currency in England. They were circulated by numerous banks in England in the early part of the century before the Bank acquired a monopoly on their issue.

banns—It was the cheapest—but most public—way to get permission to marry. To "publish the banns" required the parish rector or vicar to announce an impending wedding during the service on three consecutive Sunday mornings. If no one arose to "forbid the banns" in the course of the reading—as Clem Yeobright's mother does in *The Return of the Native*—the couple could get married within the succeeding three months.

baptism—Usually incident to a christening, it referred to the practice of dipping a child in water at the font in church by the appropriate Church of England clergyman as the child was brought ceremonially within the fold of the church.

Bar—Collectively, the barristers of England. To be "called to the bar" meant one had become eligible to practice as a barrister. The "bar" in question was a barrier separating the senior members of an Inn of Court from the junior ones. When the senior members (or benchers) felt a youngster was ready to begin the practice of law he was called forward to join them. In a courtroom, the term "bar" referred to the barrier separating the judge from everyone else, as in "the prisoner at the bar." It was sometimes erroneously believed that it was this "bar" to which the practice of "calling to the bar" referred.

bargeman—The owner of or worker on a barge.

bark—A three-masted sailing ship, the foremost two masts usually being square rigged, the sternmost mast fore-and-aft rigged.

baron—The term conjures up someone rich and grand—steaming flagons of Rhenish and the hounds scrounging for bones under the table in the great hall. Actually in the 1800s the baron was the lowest of the five ranks of the peerage. He was addressed as "Lord_____," the "_____" frequently being a surname (Alfred, Lord Tennyson), rather than the territorial designation (the duke of Windsor) favored by the higher peerage. The deceased father of the Blanche Ingram in whom Mr. Rochester interests himself at one point in *Jane Eyre* was a baron. The judges in the Court of Exchequer were also called barons.

baronet—Not, in fact, a very small baron, but the title of the first rank below the peerage. A baronet ranked just below a baron and just above a knight and was considered a member of the gentry, not the nobility. He was addressed as "Sir" (he could have "Bt." or "Bart." after his name), and his title was hereditary. Fictional baronets include Sir Pitt Crawley in *Vanity Fair*, Sir James Chettam in *Middlemarch*, Sir Leicester Dedlock in *Bleak House*, and Sir Walter Elliot in *Persuasion*.

barouche—A four-wheel fancy carriage with a fold-up hood at the back and with two inside seats facing each other. It was *the* fancy carriage of the first half of the century.

barrister—The lawyers in the Court of Chancery who actually argued in court, as opposed to the solicitors, who were not allowed to speak but who met with clients and drew up wills and the like. The Bar enjoyed a good deal of status and was considered a means of gaining entry to political or governmental office. It was suitable for a gentleman, because there was no money grubbing involved—the clients paid the solicitors, who in turn hired and paid the barristers. You could become a barrister only by attending one of the four Inns of Court in London and then being "called to the bar."

barrow—A small hill or a mound of earth, used as a burial place.

barton—A farmyard.

Bath—During the late 1700s the city became popular for the healing properties supposedly to be derived from imbibing or bathing in its mineral water—much recommended in particular for bibulous or gourmandizing gentlemen suffering from gout. Since gout was not exactly a disease likely to afflict the poor, before long Bath became a fashionable gathering spot for the gentry as family members came along to solace the invalid in his nontreatment hours and ladies came along in the hopes of finding someone well-to-do—ill or assisting an invalid—with whom they could arrange an alliance. It spawned the fashionable assemblies and flirtations which Jane Austen describes in *Northanger Abbey* and has been characterized as the first place in which the gentry were able to assemble and socialize with one another in the way that the nobility had long been able to do in London.

Bathchair—A big wheelchair used for the propelling of the aged or infirm.

bathing machine—If one wanted to swim in the sea one climbed into one of these things, which were basically large covered wagons attached to a horse who towed one out into several feet of water. There one was assisted down the steps and into the sea by a frequently unsober female attendant. This was after undressing inside the machines, which were small, uncomfortable, badly ventilated, and poorly lit, the only light coming from tiny openings placed high up to deter voyeurs. In the water one either swam or hung onto the rope attached to the machine while the waves washed over one. Men and women swam many yards apart— partly because men swam nude until the 1870s.

battalion—A subdivision of a regiment.

batter pudding—A floury concoction made with grease or drippings, of which Yorkshire pudding was one variety.

battery—A gun emplacement.

battledore and shuttlecock—A game like badminton, played on the lawn with a shuttlecock (the feathered thing you hit) and the battledore (the thing you whacked it with).

battue—A French term to describe the large outings for shooting that became popular with sportsmen in the 1820s and then again toward the

Bathing machines.

middle of the century. Characteristically, battues involved having beaters drive huge numbers of game in front of the sportsmen.

bazaar—An institution apparently originating after the Napoleonic Wars, in which distressed widows and orphans of veterans were given free stalls in which to sell things in an open-air marketplace in London, fashionable ladies thereafter evidently taking it upon themselves to patronize bazaars as a charitable endeavor.

beadle—The parish officer whom Dickens caricatures so memorably in the person of Mr. Bumble in *Oliver Twist*. The beadle was basically the general assistant to the parish beadle, the man deputed to assist the constable in keeping order, or to help the overseer of the poor look after the poverty stricken. Sometimes he turns up with his hand out for a gratuity in the aftermath of a wedding; it was also his task to "Sssh!" people in church. Some parishes hired them to help run the workhouse after the New Poor Law was passed in 1834. His uniform included an impressive staff and a cocked hat trimmed in gold lace—an old-fashioned form of dress which suggests that the office was becoming an anachronism. A beadle must have done something to outrage Dickens at some point; it is hard to find one of his major novels in which he does not take a poke at them.

beck—A stream or a brook.

bedesmen—People who said their "beads," that is, poor people who prayed for someone who had endowed a chapel or almshouse for their support. Hence, the inmates of a privately financed or endowed charitable institution.

Bazaar in the Shire-Hall, Worcester.

Bedlam—A contraction for the Hospital of St. Mary of Bethlehem, an insane asylum that was run by the City of London, eventually from a location in Lambeth.

beerhouse—A place where one could sell beer for payment of an annual fee of two guineas, promoted by the government in the 1830s to divert the poor from gin and make beer easier to sell than it was through the alehouses.

beeswax—Just what it says it is. Produced by bees as they go about constructing their hives, it was the favorite material for making the best quality candles (tallow, by comparison, had to be snuffed constantly). Also sometimes recommended for application to floors before balls.

beggar my neighbor—The card game played by Pip, appropriately, the first time he meets Estella at Miss Havisham's old house. Two players divided the deck between them and then they took turns, turning over their top cards. When one of them turned up an ace, king, queen or jack, the other had to give him, respectively, four, three, two or one of his own cards, the winner being the person who ended up with all the cards as they played out their hands. However, if the person who had to give up his cards to the player with the ace or face cards himself turned up a court card, then the other had to play to that card, and so on.

Belgrave Square—A ritzy area of London, in the West End, but south of Hyde Park, newer and slightly less fashionable than Mayfair.

Belgrave Square.

bench—Upper case, the "Bench" collectively were the judges of England. Lower case, the term in parliamentary circles referred to the long benches on which the members of the House of Commons sat, the party in power sitting on the benches at the right hand of the Speaker, facing the Opposition, who sat on the other side of the aisle. Members with prominent positions in the ministry sat on the frontmost bench, which was called the Treasury Bench (the prime minister being invariably also first lord of the treasury). The rank and file behind them were the "backbenchers."

bencher—A senior, governing member of an Inn of Court.

bender—A sixpence.

benefice—A "living," that is, a post as a parish vicar or rector in the Church of England.

benefit of clergy—A rapidly disappearing privilege in the 1800s. In the old, old days, the lay courts turned clergy suspected of various crimes over to ecclesiastical courts for trial instead of subjecting them to secular punishment. Hence the term. It was assumed thereafter in a society where literacy was largely confined to clerics that anyone who could read must be of the clergy. As a consequence, convicted thieves and murderers who could read got "benefit of clergy" and could thus get their thumbs branded instead of being executed. The government then systematically began making various crimes not "clergyable" and in 1827 the privilege vanished altogether. As late as 1822, however, manslaughter, no matter how horrible the circumstances, was clergyable.

bergamot—A citrus tree or a fancy pear.

berlin—A kind of big four-wheel carriage with a hood. Also the name of a certain kind of fancy wool used for knitting and for making a kind of glove.

besom—Twigs of various trees or shrubs gathered together and made into a broom.

bespeak—To order something, like a dinner. Also, to ask a favor—as in, to "bespeak a dance."

bilberry—A shrub found in moors and other waste places that produced a small bluish berry and a pretty flower. In *Wuthering Heights* Catherine is buried in a churchyard corner where "the wall is so low that heath and bilberry plants have climbed over it." Also called a whortleberry or a blueberry, it was edible. Jane Eyre munches on them at one point on a heath when she runs short of money.

billet—A lodging for a soldier. Also a brief note.

Billingsgate—The name of the big fish market in London. Tempers were at one time so short and the language so strong there that the term became a synonym for wildly abusive language.

bill—The term for a piece of legislation in Parliament before it became law. (After which it was called an "act.") Also, the legal document with which someone initiated a lawsuit in the Chancery Court. Finally, "bill" was short for a bill of exchange.

bill broker—A man who bought and sold bills of exchange.

bill of exchange—Originally used only by merchants, it was not unlike a check. Merchant A out in the country instructed Merchant B in London to whom he had sent goods to pay C an amount equal to the value of the goods on such and such a date. B agreed by writing "accepted" across this written instruction from Merchant A; the result was a bill of exchange. From being a technique used by merchants, however, the use of bills broadened into a way for private individuals short of cash to raise money. Either you wrote the bill out instructing yourself to pay or, if your credit was lousy, you wrote out instructions to a friend with *good* credit to play the part of Merchant B and pay a C to whom you owed money or from whom you were borrowing. This second arrangement was called an "accommodation bill." Where you agreed to pay, say, £500 to the moneylender to whom you made out the bill but only received £300 from him, the bill was said to be "discounted."

bill of sale—A document giving rights in household furniture and other similar personal property. It worked like a mortgage; one gave a bill of sale on one's household goods to the person from whom one borrowed cash and if one didn't repay him in time he took the goods.

bills of mortality—A district of London, so called because within its boundaries bills, or lists, of the dead were published during a great plague in the late 1500s.

bishop—A member of the highest of the three orders in the Church of England, a bishop ranked right under the two archbishops who ran the church. There were some thirty bishops in England by the end of the 1800s. Most of them sat in the House of Lords and exercised jurisdiction over a diocese from their seat in a cathedral town. One addressed them as "Right Reverend" or "My Lord." "Bishop" was also the name of an alcoholic beverage, composed of hot red wine poured over bitter oranges with sugar and spices added. "I'll raise your salary and endeavour to assist your struggling family," says the reformed Scrooge to a bewildered Bob Cratchit at the end of *A Christmas Carol*, "and we will discuss your affairs this very afternoon, over a Christmas bowl of smoking bishop, Bob!"

bitters—Various kinds of alcoholic concoctions of supposedly medicinal benefit in which things like orange peels or wormwood had been steeped.

blackbird—An English songbird that was a thrush and not the same as the American bird by that name.

Blackfriars—The area between Ludgate Hill and the Thames.

blacking—The substance used to black shoes. Dickens was put to work in a factory putting labels on bottles of blacking when he was about twelve and never forgot the misery of the experience. Apparently blacking came off in the rain, too. It was sometimes sold in the form of cakes wrapped in paper.

blacklead—A type of graphite—not lead at all—used for polishing grates.

black pudding—A sausage made with blood and various other ingredients, the blood spread on the outside giving it its name. Sometimes called "blood pudding" or, in Hardy, "blackpot."

blood pudding—The same as black pudding.

blucher—A half boot.

blue—The color had a number of quite specific associations in nineteenth-century Britain, being, notably, the color associated with the Tories and, subsequently, the Conservatives. (Yellow was the Whigs' color.) It was also the varsity color at Oxford, Cambridge, Eton and Harrow, and it was the color of the ribbon worn by members of the Order of the Garter.

bluebag—The bag carried by barristers.

blue books—The books of parliamentary commissions of inquiry (so called from the color of their covers) that investigated and reformed every conceivable institution in nineteenth-century England including Oxford and Cambridge.

bluebottle—A big fly with a bluish body.

blue pill—A pill supposed to counteract bile, made up of glycerin, honey, and mercury.

Blues—Nickname of the Royal Horse Guards, one of the three regiments of Household Cavalry that guarded the sovereign and were among the most prestigious in the country.

blunderbuss—A short gun with a wide barrel that blew shot in all directions when it was fired.

board—As used in *Oliver Twist,* it is short for board of guardians, i.e., the local officials charged in a given district with responsibility for the poor, including running the workhouse, by the Poor Law of 1834. Their functions were previously performed by the overseers of the poor.

boarding school—Very popular in the nineteenth century. Boys boarded at Eton and Rugby, but the term was also used with reference to academies for young ladies, like Miss Pinkerton's *(Vanity Fair),* where girls were often sent after they had been taught everything that a governess could think of. There were also "for profit" boarding schools like the ghastly Dotheboys Hall in Yorkshire described in *Nicholas Nickleby.* In contrast to Rugby and Eton, these were profit-making places, often started by men who had failed in some other line of work. Places way in the north of England like Dotheboys Hall were particularly attractive to wealthy parents whose child might be illegitimate; Yorkshire was far from London and it was cheap.

Board of Trade—A government department (formally a committee of the Privy Council) whose chief was called a president and who generally sat in the cabinet. The board looked after railroads and the merchant marine.

boatswain—Pronounced bo'sun. A warrant officer, that is, neither an ordinary seaman nor a commissioned officer but in between. He was in charge of the sails and rigging and blew a whistle to call the sailors to their tasks.

bob—Slang for a shilling. "Bob had but fifteen 'Bob' a week himself," says Dickens of Bob Cratchit; "he pocketed on Saturdays but fifteen copies of his Christian name."

bodkin—To sit bodkin was to sit in between two people on a seat meant to hold only two.

bolus—A round tablet of medicine meant for swallowing that was bigger than a pill.

bombazine—A favorite black material for ladies' mourning clothes. It absorbed light instead of reflecting it and was generally made out of worsted or worsted plus some other fabric. It was considered somewhat old-fashioned during the latter part of the century.

Bond Street—A fashionable shopping street in the West End of London, located in the Mayfair district.

bonne—A nursemaid.

bonnet—An obligatory outdoor head covering for all women in the first part of the century. It was evidently often worn with a shawl, and came in innumerable varieties, including the poke bonnet, the coal scuttle, the tilt bonnet (apparently resembling the tilt on a waggon) and the kiss-me-quickly, popular in the 1860s. By the latter part of the century fashionable women were wearing hats instead, and the garment survived only among the poor.

Book of Common Prayer—Declared the official prayer book for the Church of England by act of Parliament in the 1500s. It was called "common" because it replaced a variety of prayer books that had been used in different parts of the country. It contained the text for various services, such as marriage and the burial of the dead, plus the catechism and the psalms. It is written in a rich Elizabethan English and aspects of the services have passed into the language. "Give peace in our time" and "to love, cherish, and obey" come from the Prayer Book, as it was called.

boot—A place in a coach where luggage was put.

bootjack—A device used to remove boots.

boots—A servant at an inn or hotel whose job was to clean the guests' boots. In *Pickwick* we find him bringing in the luggage.

borough—A town that had been granted certain rights of self-government by the Crown, so that, typically, it had a mayor, aldermen, and council, elected by the freemen or burgesses. References to *the* borough in con-nection with London, e.g., in Dickens, refer to Southwark. Thomas Hardy's "Casterbridge" was a borough. Some boroughs were so inde-pendent that they virtually opted out of the county government and had their own quarter sessions run by an official called a recorder instead of by justices of the peace. Thackeray provides a fanciful origin for one such grant of municipal rights in *Vanity Fair*: "It is related, with regard to the borough of Queen's Crawley, that Queen Elizabeth in one of her pro-gresses, stopping at Crawley to breakfast, was so delighted with some remarkably fine Hampshire beer which was then presented to her by the Crawley of the day (a handsome gentleman with a trim beard and a good leg), that she forthwith erected Crawley into a borough to send two members to parliament." Which brings up the matter of parliamentary representation. Some boroughs could send members to Parliament, as the counties all did. However, by the 1800s, the parliamentary boroughs and the municipal boroughs were often no longer the same. A large urban area might have one mayor but be divided into several parliamen-tary boroughs, while some once populous boroughs that still sent repre-sentatives to Parliament might have become so depopulated as to be virtually representing villages.

bottom—Of a dance—the opposite of the top.

bound over—To "bind over" was to prevent two quarrelsome people from injuring one another by requiring each to post a sum with the local court that would be forfeit if he caused any trouble.

boudoir—Today, the term carries some suggestion of an intimate bedroom area. However, in the 1800s, the term designated a room set aside for a lady to write her letters, conduct household business, and do such other things as were necessary to the running of the household and the public side of her life.

bowler—The hat that is called a derby in the United States. It was a big hit when it was introduced in Britain in 1868 because it was better ventilated and lighter than the top hats men wore until then.

Bow Street Runners (also known as the **Robin Redbreasts** because of their scarlet waistcoats)—The predecessors of the London bobbies. Created by the novelist Henry Fielding and his brother John in 1750, the Runners did detective work. Since they worked for fees and rewards, there were occasionally hints of corruption about their activities. They investigate Oliver Twist's break-in and descend on the countryside of Pip's child-hood to investigate the murder of Mrs. Joe Gargery. (Their operations were not restricted to London.) They went out of existence in 1839.

box, Christmas—It was customary for people to fill up small boxes with money before Christmas. On the first weekday after Christmas they would then give them to those, like servants, who had helped them during the year, or to the poor. The day the box was given was called Boxing Day. "I remembered," says Nelly Dean in *Wuthering Heights*, "how old Earnshaw used to come in when all was tidied, and call me a cant lass, and slip a shilling into my hand as a Christmas box."

Boxing Day—*See* box, Christmas.

boxseat—The large boxlike seat on which the coachman sat while driving a carriage. In the early days of coaching, young bucks used to bribe the coachman so they could sit up on the seat and "take the wheel," a practice that was discouraged in view of their invariable tendency to speed. "Keep the box for me, Leader," says Sir Pitt Crawley to the coachman on his way back to the ancestral home, to which the coachman replies, " 'Yes, Sir Pitt,' with a touch of his hat, and rage in his soul (for he had promised the box to a young gentleman from Cambridge, who would have given a crown to a certainty)."

brace—A brace of something meant two of them, usually with a suggestion of a matching pair if it was something like a brace of pistols, although one could also have a brace of (presumably unmatched) pheasants.

braces—Suspenders.

bracken—A fern, sometimes a group of ferns. Sometimes used as bedding, and sheep ate young bracken.

Bradshaw—*The* schedule for trains in England, first issued in 1839.

brake—It was either a fern or a little bunch of bushes.

brawn—A food word. Brawn was the flesh of a hog or a boar, especially after it had had spice added to it, been pickled, etc.

brazier—A man who made things out of brass.

breach of promise—In the old days, if either party broke off an engagement, the other could sue just as if any other kind of contract to do something had been broken. The plaintiff was entitled to his or her actual damages sustained in anticipation of the promised event, e.g., the cost of a wedding dress, plus any award the jury might want to make to compensate the aggrieved party for anguish and suffering.

breakfast room—A room likely to be found in somewhat grander homes, which was used for the morning meal instead of the dining room, which was saved for the more formal dinners. Lunch, perhaps because only the ladies usually dined at home, had no room of its own.

breeches—A word used during the first part of the century to mean pants that descended only to the knee and were worn with stockings. It retained this meaning thereafter when applied to footmen, whose livery was deliberately anachronistic until the end of the century. In other contexts, it came to mean simply a pair of trousers.

brevet—A brevet commission entitled one to be called by the military rank next higher than that which one actually held. Thus, a brevet captain would actually be a lieutenant. A brevet rank did not entitle one to the additional pay that normally accompanied the higher rank.

brier rose—The dog rose.

bridewell—A contraction from St. Bridget's Well in London, the site of a house of correction (torn down in 1863) that gave its name generically to houses of correction.

brief—A summary of a client's case prepared by a solicitor before he hired a barrister to take it to trial. To be a "briefless barrister" meant you had no work. In *Vanity Fair* Thackeray alludes to "Mrs. Briefless, the barrister's wife, who is of a good family certainly, but, as we all know, is as poor as poor can be."

brig—Generally, a square-rigged ship with two masts.

brigade—An army unit, usually composed of at least two regiments.

Brighton—A seaside resort that became fashionable in the early 1800s, owing to an emphasis on the health benefits said to be derived from regular immersion in salt water. Perhaps chiefly notable for the construction of a monstrous imitation Near Eastern villa by the prince regent. In *Mansfield Park* we are told the resort was "almost as gay in winter as it is in summer." It was about forty-five miles south of London.

Broad Church—An element within the Church of England that favored tolerance of both High and Low Church tendencies.

broadcloth—A fancy kind of woolen that was made from yarns of fine merino.

brocade—A material that had elaborate designs of raised gold and silver or something similar on it.

broker—Sometimes used to mean a stockbroker or pawnbroker. The term was also applied to a secondhand furniture dealer licensed to appraise household goods or sell them when someone fell behind on the rent. In one of his frequent epistolary communications of disaster, Micawber writes to David Copperfield that he is being watched over by a drunk "employed by a broker. That individual is in legal possession of these premises, under a distress for rent." Less often, perhaps, the term "broker" might have been used to refer to the bill brokers who bought and sold bills of exchange.

broomstick, over the—One way of getting married in some rural areas of England was for the couple to jump over a broomstick together.

brougham—The all-purpose everyday vehicle for the quality in the latter part of the century. It was originally a two-wheel vehicle designed in imitation of the cabriolet, the point being to combine the features of the two-wheel open vehicles like gigs and curricles with the closed character of the cabriolet. However, in the latter part of the century broughams were probably most often four-wheel carriages.

Brummagem—From Birmingham, meaning in some instances, cheap, shoddy goods.

brush—In fox hunting, the term for the fox's tail. Sometimes cut off at the end of the hunt and given as a trophy. In *Silas Marner* Squire Cass's parlor has "walls decorated with guns, whips, and foxes' brushes."

buckram—A linen or other cloth that has been made stiff with glue, paste or gum.

buckskins—Made originally from deerskin and very fashionable in the early part of the century. Later made out of sheepskin as well.

buff—Short for buffalohide. In color, light or yellowish.

buggy—A one- or two-passenger carriage pulled by one horse.

bull—Slang for a crown or a five-shilling piece.

bulldog—One of the men who helped the proctors at Oxford and Cambridge to discipline rule-breaking undergraduates. Trollope tells us in *Phineas Finn* that Lord Chiltern "had taken by the throat a proctor's bull-dog when he had been drunk at Oxford, had nearly strangled the man, and had been expelled."

bull's-eye—A kind of lantern, so called because the swelling in the glass looked like the eye of a bull.

bumper—A glass of liquor that had been filled to the very top.

burdock—A weedlike plant, found in unpromising, desolate areas, whose flower was a burr.

burgess—An inhabitant of a borough who was entitled—at least in theory—to enjoy the privileges thereof.

burk—The verb means to kill somebody by strangling or similar means in order to sell the body for dissection to a surgeon or anatomist, as did Mr. Burke of the infamous team of Burke and Hare in the early 1800s.

bushel—A measurement of volume equal to four pecks or eight gallons.

bustard—The largest bird ever found in England, it resembled a turkey and is now extinct there.

bustle—The dress style they couldn't kill. Dresses in the 1850s and 1860s were so voluminous that the dress spread out on all sides of the woman wearing it. It was cut back, therefore—in front. The extrusion remaining behind was the bustle, which disappeared in the 1870s and then returned in the 1880s.

butler—The servant in charge of the wines (the name comes from the French *bouteille* for "bottle") and of officiating at dinner. He also looked after the family "plate" (silverware), sometimes sleeping in a room next to the safe in which it was locked at night. In the absence of a steward, he was the senior member of the male household staff, with power to fire the footmen. He also sometimes warmed and ironed the newspapers before the master's breakfast.

butterfly kiss—One brushes one's eyelashes along somebody's cheek. "Celia, dear, come and kiss me," says Dorothea Brooke as her sister is about to go to bed in *Middlemarch*, whereupon, we are told, "Celia knelt down to get the right level and gave her little butterfly kiss, while Dorothea encircled her with gentle arms and pressed her lips gravely on each cheek in turn."

cab—The term was a contraction of cabriolet, the name of a light two-wheel carriage introduced into England from France at the end of the 1820s. There were already hackney (for hire) coaches operating as cabs on the streets of London. Cabriolets displaced many of them and were, in turn, superseded by the hansom.

cabinet—The core group of some fifteen or so ministers within a government. Headed by the prime minister, the cabinet was composed generally of the lord chancellor, the Chancellor of the Exchequer, the home secretary, the foreign secretary, and the first lord of the admiralty, along, often, with the lord privy seal, the postmaster general, and others. It was thus made up on the one hand of executive department heads such as the Chancellor of the Exchequer and the secretaries of state and on the other hand of people such as the lord privy seal who had only nominal official responsibilities but gave advice or assisted in keeping the affairs of the majority party running smoothly.

cabinet piano—A kind of upright piano made in the early 1800s that was about five and a half feet high.

cabriolet—*See* cab. The derivation of the word— possibly of interest to those who have taken taxi cabs in large American cities—is from the French for leap, which comes in turn from the word for a he-goat.

cad—A term used in the mid-1800s to refer to an omnibus conductor in London.

cadet—The younger or youngest son or branch of a family.

calash—A large hooded hat for women that could be folded back, so named from the similar hood on a French carriage of the era.

Calendar—*See* Newgate Calendar.

calfskin—In the early 1800s books in England were generally bound in calfskin, although the "calf" could well turn out to be a goat. The narrator of *Wuthering Heights* dozes off in reading and, on awaking, "discovered my candle wick reclining on one of the antique volumnes and perfuming the place with an odor of roasted calf-skin."

calico—A cotton cloth first imported from Calicut in India, hence the name. Originally a colored cloth in England and then white.

called to the bar—Authorized to practice law as a barrister. This occurred when the benchers in one of the Inns of Court called the eligible law students to the barrier or "bar" which separated the two groups. It did *not* refer to the bar in a court of law (as in the "prisoner at the bar").

calomel—A tasteless, gray medicine, sometimes powdered, that was made of mercury and chlorine.

cambric—A type of linen cloth, quite fine, or an imitation of it. Often popping up in handkerchief form as an emblem of gentility.

Camdentown—A part of London, slightly north of the City, where Bob Cratchit lived in a four-room house with his six children on about thirty-seven pounds a year, so Dickens says in *A Christmas Carol*. In 1822, Dickens's father, John, an impecunious clerk in the naval pay office, moved into a four-room house with basement and garret at No. 16 Bayham Street, Camdentown (rent, twenty-two pounds a year).

camel leopard—A giraffe.

cameo—The opposite of intaglio. A precious stone is cut so that a head or other figure is raised on it in relief.

camisole—A kind of woman's undershirt worn between the dress and the corset to protect the former from the latter.

canals—England had a good many canals, some 3,000 miles' worth in the 1820s, because in the early 1800s it was realized that horses could pull a great deal more along a body of water than they could on their backs or behind them on a road. Built by the workers called "navvies," most canals were in the north and the Midlands and were for freight rather than passengers.

candles—How, we wonder, did they avoid fires? They didn't. In the period from 1833 to 1849, out of some 660 fires a year in London, about 170 were caused by accidents with candles, a cause far in excess of any other.

Candlemas—A church festival held on February 2 which celebrates the purification of the Virgin Mary and the presentation of Jesus in the Temple.

canons—Members of the chapter attached to a cathedral who assisted the dean in running the physical plant and conducting the services. Minor canons, who helped with the choir, were not members of the chapter.

captain—In the army a captain commanded a company if he were in the infantry; if he were in the cavalry, a captain commanded a troop. He ranked above a lieutenant, below a major. In the navy a captain was a man in charge of a warship and ranked under a rear admiral or commodore, and above a commander. In the early part of the century, real captains were called post-captains to distinguish them from officers like commanders who might be given a temporary captaincy of a vessel.

caravansery—A fancy word for an inn.

carking—Having the ability to worry someone or make them careworn.

carman—The driver of a cart or waggon or a carrier.

carpetbag—A bag for traveling that was usually made out of a carpet.

carriage—Generally, a generic term for a vehicle that carried people rather than goods, with the additional connotation of a vehicle used by the well-to-do. A pony cart, for example, would probably not have been called a carriage; a barouche or a victoria would have.

carrier—The carrier and his cart or van were the usual way of getting from one place to another in rural areas. He carried goods and people, usually on a regular route. Barkis in *David Copperfield* is a carrier.

A Phaeton carriage.

carter—The driver of a cart or waggon, including a farm waggon.

casement—A window hinged on the side.

cashiered—To be discharged from the army in disgrace, usually after a court-martial. Officers who had been simply dismissed from the army could be reinstated; officers who had been cashiered could not. It was a particularly heavy blow before the purchase of commissions was abolished in 1871 because it meant the man cashiered could not sell his commission to someone else, as was normal practice upon leaving the army.

casino (or *cassino*)—A card game for two to four people. The idea is to take whatever card is face up by matching it at once, e.g., taking a 4 with a 4, or by building on it, e.g., putting down a 3 on the 4, and then matching the combination in the next round, taking the 4 with the 3 atop it with a 7.

cassock—A long garment worn by Church of England clergy under the surplice.

castors—Little dinner-table things like salt and pepper shakers and cruets. *Castor* is also Latin for "beaver"; the term was sometimes applied to hats made from the animal.

catarrh—The head, nose, and throat fill up with mucus due to an inflammation. Basically like a cold or mild flu.

catch—A round for three or more singers, often humorous, in which each player had to "catch" the melody as it came turn for him to sing it. "Three Blind Mice" is a catch.

catechism—The questions and answers about the Church of England set forth in the Book of Common Prayer that were to be mastered by a child before he or she could be confirmed.

cathedral—*Cathedra* is the Latin word for the throne in which a bishop sat. The church accommodating this throne—and hence, usually, the main church in the diocese—was the cathedral.

Catholic question—Should Catholics be allowed to hold public office? This was a question which became prominent in English politics after the union of England and Ireland occurred in 1801. The Tories by and large fought Catholic office-holding and then the duke of Wellington—Tory prime minster—turned around and engineered the passage of the acts in 1828 that permitted it.

caul—A membrane covering a child's head at birth, which could be purchased to bring good luck. It was supposed to be especially good at preventing drowning. "I was born with a caul," David Copperfield tells us, "which was advertised for sale, in the newspapers, at the low price of fifteen guineas. Whether sea-going people were short of money about that time, or were short of faith and preferred cork jackets, I don't know; all I know is, that there was but one solitary bidding." "And I was born wi' a caul," says Christian in *The Return of the Native*, "and perhaps can be no more ruined than drowned?"

causeway—A highway raised up to prevent water from getting on it or sometimes merely a paved highway.

cellaret—A cabinet for storing liquor.

certificate—One needed to get a certificate after 1846 if one wanted to teach in a national school. (Normally, one did this by attending a training college, as Sue Bridehead does in *Jude the Obscure*.)

chaffinch—A pert little songbird, favored as a pet, and deriving his name from the fact that he frequented barns, pecking up the loose chaff.

chaise—A hard term to pin down the precise meaning of, but it seems to have been used to refer generally to a two- to four-wheel vehicle that carried a maximum of two and had a top, if any, that was convertible.

chaise cart—A kind of small cart that could be used for driving.

chamber—In a dwelling, it was a private room, generally a bedroom, as opposed to the public rooms like the dining room or drawing room. In a place like the Inns of Court, "chambers" in the plural referred to a barrister's office, which sometimes doubled as his living quarters.

chambermaid—A woman who cleaned the rooms in a hotel or inn.

chancel—The portion of a church extending east beyond the nave, where the choir sat and where the altar was.

chancellor—Chancellor was a title that designated various dignitaries. It generally referred to the various lesser judges of the Courts of Chancery or the Chancellor of the Exchequer or the lord chancellor himself. It also referred to a church official subordinate to the dean of a cathedral chapter and, in addition, to the ecclesiastical judge who presided over the consistory (diocesan) court. Finally, just to confuse matters, the titular heads of Oxford and Cambridge were called chancellors.

Chancellor of the Exchequer—The highest post in an administration after that of prime minister. The Chancellor of the Exchequer ran the Treasury Department and prepared the budget.

Chancery—The court of equity law, which sat generally in Westminster Hall, the lord chancellor being its chief judge, assisted by various subordinate chancellors and a master of the rolls. Dickens, who had some unhappy experiences with suits there arising from people plagiarizing *A Christmas Carol*, skewers chancery in *Bleak House*. It was merged with the common law courts in 1873 after numerous, not very successful, attempts to reform it. Ironically, the Chancery Court had started out centuries before as a court through which people who could not get justice in the ordinary common law system might find a remedy that favored justice over mindless legalism.

chandler—Originally, a man who dealt in candles. Later, the corner grocer in poor neighborhoods.

'Change—Short for the Royal Exchange.

chantry—A side chapel or area set aside in churches for the chanting of a mass for the repose of someone's soul (usually that of the donor) in pre-Reformation days. Some of them remained, their original use forsaken, in the Church of England churches after they were taken over from the Catholic church.

chapel—A term in the 1800s that usually meant a Dissenting or nonconformist place of worship, since a Church of England building for worship was either a cathedral or a church, *except that* (1) a private house sometimes had a chapel attached to it; and (2) in especially large parishes a so-called chapel of ease was sometimes built to serve parishioners in the regions of the area more remote from the parish church. Gimmerton Kirk, in the graveyard of which Heathcliff and Catherine are laid to rest, is apparently a chapel of ease.

chaperone—The servant, mother, or married female family friend who supervised eligible young girls in public. At dances the chaperone sat in the corner and made sure her charge did not do anything "improper," and the chaperone was in charge of making introductions to strange young men.

chapter—The group of canons, who, under the leadership of the dean, were in charge of the services in a cathedral and its physical upkeep.

charabanc—A big, light carriage that had two long seats facing forward.

charger—The horse that a cavalry soldier rode.

Charing Cross—The traditional center of London, located at the south end of Trafalgar Square. Named for the thirteenth and final cross which Edward I erected for the funeral procession of his wife to Westminster. To its east lay the City, to its west the West End.

chariot—The name for the fancy carriage used by the very wealthy, especially on long trips, or on state occasions. It was basically a stagecoach with the front half of the body cut off so there was only a single rear seat facing forward.

charity child—A child attending a school founded by a wealthy private benefactor. Charity children often had to sit in conspicuous places in church and wear special badges and colored clothing that proclaimed their status. They were often unmercifully mocked by other children. The charity boy Noah Claypole in *Oliver Twist* takes great delight in tormenting Oliver for being of a status, i.e., a "workhouse" child, more contemptible than his own.

charwoman—The root word for "char" is the same as for "chore." A charwoman was someone who came in and did chores by the day—what today we would call a cleaning woman. In contrast to a maid, who did essentially the same work but lived in. There was a verb, also—to char; Betty Martin, we are told in *Pickwick*, "goes out charing and washing, by the day."

chase—A chase was unfenced land on which one had been granted the right to keep deer for hunting. It was distinguished from a park, which was the same thing but enclosed, and a forest, which was a game preserve for royalty.

chasuble—A piece of clothing worn by a clergyman at communion over the cassock and the surplice. It often bore a cross.

cheapjack—A peddler of cheap metal items like knives, watches, etc., whose skill and sales depended largely on his patter.

Cheapside—An old street in eastern London not far from the river. The name comes from an old Anglo-Saxon word that means to buy and sell.

Chelsea—An area of west London south of Mayfair that was *not* fashionable in the 1800s and was probably chiefly notable for housing the Chelsea Hospital for army veterans.

chemise—The fancy term for a woman's long undergarment—basically like a nightgown—that was the only female undergarment other than the corset for much of the century. The term replaced the word "shift," which was felt to be too indelicate, and which had itself replaced the term "smock."

chemisette—A kind of partial shirt worn tucked down into the front of very low-cut gowns.

chemist—A druggist.

Chesterfield—At the very end of the century a kind of man's coat. Before that, a very plushly upholstered sofa with no woodwork showing. The back and arms usually curved away from the sitter.

cheval glass—A body-length mirror mounted on a pivot.

chiffonier—A popular item of furniture, consisting of a sort of little sideboard.

chignon—A piece of hair, worn in a knot at the back of the neck, popular in the middle of the century. Sometimes the hair was false.

Chiltern Hundreds—A marvelously convoluted device for resigning from Parliament. One could *not* resign from Parliament while it was in session—but then neither could one hold any paid office under the sovereign. Accordingly, if one wanted to opt out of Parliament during a session one applied to become the steward of the Chiltern Hundreds, Chiltern being an area not far from London. One was appointed to this post—which meant one then *had* to resign from Parliament—and then once one was out of Parliament one quit the Chiltern post, too. After relinquishing a choice opportunity to speak in Parliament, the eponymous hero of *Phineas Finn* says, "I must perish . . . I shall apply for the Chiltern Hundreds in a day or two."

chimney corner—The place to sit in the corner near a chimney or—in the very big, old-fashioned fireplaces—a corner or actual seat inside the fireplace, facing or next to the fire itself.

chimneypiece—A mantelpiece or an elaborate moulding all around the chimney.

chimneypot hat—A top hat.

chine—A term applied to the spine of animals like pigs when they were being chopped up for cooking.

chintz—A many-colored cloth with flowers and what-not all over it.

choir—The area of the church—generally in the westernmost part of the chancel—where the singers sat.

choker—Slang word for a big, stiff high collar that was especially favored for wear on fancy occasions or for the clergy's attire.

cholera—A horrible disease that struck England in waves of epidemics beginning in the 1830s. It caused a burning thirst, diarrhea, cramps, and death, often within a day. It was caused by fecal matter in drinking supplies; cities, especially the poorer areas, were hardest hit.

chopping—A fox-hunting term for when the hounds snuffle their way into a covert and tear the fox to pieces instead of scaring him out into the open so that everyone can chase after him.

Christmas box—*See* Boxing Day.

christening—The ceremony of becoming a member of the Church of England as a baby, i.e., being given one's Christian name, while godparents stood by promising to see that one was given a proper religious education. The minister was obliged to dip the child into water at the font in order to do this.

churchwarden—In local parishes, a one-year, unpaid job of some prestige. The churchwarden or wardens were responsible for seeing that the church was kept up and that the congregation behaved themselves. Henchard holds this post as well as the mayoralty of Casterbridge before his precipitous fall.

circulating libraries—When books were expensive and there were no public libraries—as was true in the early 1800s—people often subscribed to a circulating library for an annual fee which entitled them to borrow the best-sellers. The most famous was Mudie's.

City—A term used to refer to the original city of London that was within the old, medieval city walls, running from the Thames on the southeast to the Tower and west to Temple Bar. Since the Bank of England, the Royal Exchange and other commercial activities were located there, "the City" also became, like "Wall Street" in America, a shorthand way to refer to the nation's financial center.

civil list—At one time the list of all the expenses of the civilian branch of the national government. By the middle 1830s, it was merely the list of expenses for the monarch personally and his or her household.

civil service—As opposed to military service. The term first came into use in India for the administrative apparatus of the East India Company. It was later expanded to designate the entire nonmilitary bureaucracy of the British government.

claret—A type of red wine, originally from France, and a great favorite at Victorian dinner parties.

clerestory—The upper "clear story" of windows in a church that admitted light to the nave and transepts below.

clerk—A general term for almost any white-collar employee of an enterprise in the 1800s. The position could range from a low-level middle-aged man who copied documents all day to the equivalent of a general manager or international vice president. An "articled clerk" was a boy apprenticed in a lawyer's office to become a solicitor. "Clerk" was also short for "parish clerk," the layman who kept the parish register of births and deaths and sometimes assisted the clergyman at the services.

climbing boy—The child working for a chimney sweep who actually climbed up inside the chimneys to clean them.

clogs—Shoes with wooden or metal rims on the bottom used mainly by women, for walking in the rain or mud.

close—A kind of alleyway. Also, the name for the immediate area around a cathedral.

close time—With respect to a game animal, close time was the season during which it could *not* be hunted.

closet—Any kind of small room. We think of it as being a small place with a door to hang clothes in, but Jane Eyre sleeps in one.

clubs—The great refuge of the middle- and upper-class male in London in the 1800s. Originating in the gatherings of men in certain coffeehouses in the 1700s, clubs acquired more permanent—and exclusive—quarters on Pall Mall and St. James's Street. Among the more prominent were the Carlton Club, Boodle's, the Traveller's, the Athenaeum and the Army and Navy. In *The Prime Minister,* Trollope described a typical club as a place where "men dined and smoked and played billiards and pretended to read."

coach—Basically, any four-wheel, enclosed vehicle for carrying passengers, whether private or, as in the case of mail and stagecoaches, public.

coal scuttle—The container in which coals were carried to a fireplace and stored next to it.

cob—A tough, sturdily built little horse, much favored for riding by fat people.

cockchafer—A big bug (also called the Maybug) that came out in May and made a big whirring noise when it flew around.

cockloft—A sort of super-attic even above the garret. When the Boffins are troubled by apparitions in *Our Mutual Friend,* they "went all over the dismal house—dismal everywhere, but in their own two rooms—from cellar to cockloft."

coffeehouse—First popular in London in the 1700s, they were places for people to gather, drink coffee, converse and read the newspapers. By the 1800s they had often become dining places where one could also get lodgings and were probably among the classier of such accommodations. Septimus Harding stays and eats at such a place in *The Warden;* Arthur Clennam does the same in *Little Dorrit.*

coffee room—The term for a dining room, especially in a large hotel or inn.

college—One of the residential and instructional units around which the universities of Cambridge and Oxford were organized. The college heads collectively ran their respective universities. Prison was also called "college" in slang. "Little Dorrit's lover, however, was not a Collegian," says Dickens in the novel. "He was the sentimental son of a turnkey." To be hanged was sometimes called "taking your finals at New College," i.e., Newgate prison.

collier—Either a coal miner or someone who buys and sells coal, or else one of the boats used to transport coal.

colonel—The officer who officially commanded a regiment. And since the regiment was the core of the British army for most of the 1800s, a figure of no little military prestige. He ranked above a lieutenant colonel (who often actually ran the regiment day to day).

come out—"What causes young people to come out," says Thackeray in *Vanity Fair*, "but the noble ambition of matrimony." The term—used of young women—meant to become an official member of "society," which meant that one was seventeen or eighteen and had been presented to the sovereign at court. One was thus officially available for marriage.

comforter—A big woolen winter scarf to wear around one's neck if one couldn't afford an overcoat. It is what Bob Cratchit wears—naturally, given what Scrooge pays him—in *A Christmas Carol*.

commander—A position in the Royal Navy with a rather awe-inspiring sound although in fact it was a rank below that of captain. A commander was typically a sort of captain-in-training who served under a permanent captain for a year or so before getting his own command.

commerce—Essentially an old form of poker. Each player got three cards down and then tried to get three of a kind, a three-card straight flush, a three-card flush, a pair, or "point"—the highest number of points.

commercial traveler—A traveling salesman. They often had their own gathering room at inns and were sometimes known as "commercials" for short. Also sometimes called "bagmen," presumably because they carried their wares around in bags.

commit—To have someone put in jail, especially for a relatively short time, as when they were awaiting trial.

common—The area of land in a village that was used by all the members of the village collectively for grazing their sheep or cattle. Many of these lands were "enclosed" by parliamentary acts at the behest of local farmers or landowners who wanted to use them for their own private arable or grazing land.

commoner—An Oxford undergraduate who was not on scholarship. The equivalent status at Cambridge was that of "pensioner." Also, of course, more generally, a commoner was someone without a title.

common law—One of the two types of law (besides church law) practiced in England in the 1800s. It was the oldest body of law, built up from countless decisions, custom and the accreted practices of many years. In London, common law decisions were handed down by the courts of King's Bench, the Exchequer and Common Pleas. Equity was the other great type of law, always compared and contrasted with common law. Its home was the infamous Chancery Court.

Common Pleas—One of the three great common law courts. Only serjeants could argue in it; they were backed up by nonlitigating lawyers called "attorneys." Common Pleas heard disputes between ordinary citizens. It is there that *Bardell* v. *Pickwick* is heard, for example. It was abolished in 1873 and merged into the other high courts.

Common Prayer Book—*See* Book of Common Prayer.

common room—The place where the fellows of a college went after dining and thus, by extension, such a group of fellows.

commons—The name given to meals eaten by students together in university dining halls. Not to get enough to eat was to be on "short commons."

companion—Impecunious gentlewomen who did not want to govern or teach or keep a shop could sometimes find a post being a companion to the widowed or otherwise lonely.

company—The smallest unit of soldiers in the army, a subdivision of a regiment. Generally consisting of 60–100 men and commanded by a captain. "Company" with a capital letter would probably have referred in a London context to one of the ancient livery companies or guilds of the city which, by the 1800s, were turning into prestigious eating clubs.

competency—A term used to describe the sum of money that would allow someone to live independently and, depending on the circumstances, either handsomely or with only the bare necessities.

confirmation—The acceptance of an adult into full membership of the Church of England, in which the candidate, generally having mastered the catechism as a preliminary, "confirmed" the promises made on his behalf by his godparents at his christening to the effect that he would be a good Christian. Children were customarily confirmed in their teens; it was a simple ceremony requiring a laying on of hands by the bishop.

congé d'élire—When the monarch through the prime minister selected a bishop, he did so by formally authorizing the dean and chapter of the cathedral to actually make the selection, i.e., he sent them by letter a "leave to elect" or *congé d'élire*. However, this was purely a formality; the notice was always accompanied by a letter missive that told them *whom* they had to elect.

conservatory—A room in a house for growing plants.

consistory—The diocesan ecclesiastical court. There was one in London that was part of the Doctors' Commons where David Copperfield studied to be a lawyer. Until 1857, such courts handled divorces and wills; thereafter only internal church matters.

Conservatives—The name, fittingly, used for the Tories after about 1830 as the party that in general opposed change and stood with the Church of England and the old ways. Its most prominent leader was Prime Minister Benjamin Disraeli.

console—A small side table with only two legs that was fastened into the wall with supporting brackets. It sometimes had a marble top.

consols—The term was short for "Consolidated Annuities," which were government securities (in the form of annuities) created by combining or consolidating several securities in the 1700s. They paid an invariant 3 percent interest a year, and although one could buy and sell them, they could not be redeemed, like, say, U.S. savings bonds. In the days before a real stock market, they were one of the few things in which one could invest besides land.

constable—An ancient post of authority in local parishes, its incumbent often recognizable by the staff he carried. The justice of the peace chose someone from the parish each year to fill this post, whose duties were to apprehend wrongdoers and keep the peace. In 1829 London made its constables salaried full-time permanent employees—the "bobbies." The countryside was required to do the same in 1856, replacing Dogberry with the bumbling figure on his bicycle who makes his way through so many English murder mysteries—but still called "Constable."

consumption—Pulmonary tuberculosis at an advanced stage. One wasted away, eyes glittering, skin shrunken around one's bones and might be seized with a sudden final outburst of manic energy that engendered the legend that consumption spurred artistic creativity. A widespread killer in the 1800s.

conventicle—The term for a meeting of Dissenters.

conveyancer—A lawyer or copyist who specialized in real estate transactions, i.e., "conveying" or transferring a piece of property from one party to another.

convulvulus—A winding, twisting plant.

cony—An English rabbit.

cook—A fancy household preferred a male French chef; there was—then as now—a predilection for French cooking. Other families made do with a woman, usually addressed simply as "cook," who might by origin be a scullerymaid or kitchenmaid who had worked her way up.

cooper—A man who makes or fixes barrels and similar wooden containers.

copybook—A book full of examples of good handwriting that pupils learning to write were supposed to "copy," i.e., imitate.

copyholder—An ancient type of land tenancy with fewer rights than outright fee simple and more than that associated with a simple lease. Copyholders were so called because their names were supposedly inscribed on a copy of the rent rolls held by the lord of the manor.

coquelicot—A fashionable color for clothes at one point, imitating the poppy, and thus being sort of red and orange.

cord—Rope, especially when it was being used to tie up boxes. Also, corduroy when used for clothing.

coral—A toy made out of coral that infants were given when they were teething.

cordial—A friendly-sounding type of alcoholic beverage that was supposedly medicinal.

corn—*Not* the corn on the cob of the United States. Corn in England—as in the corn factor Henchard of *The Mayor of Casterbridge* or as in the corn laws that were finally repealed in 1846—consisted of cereals, i.e., oats, wheat, barley, or rye, the former three being of vital importance in the English economy.

corn laws—Laws passed during the Napoleonic Wars and after to put a tariff on imported corn in order to protect domestic farmers. These laws drove working people and manufacturers wild because they raised both the price of food of the former and the cost of the wages the latter had to pay the former so they could buy the food. The laws were finally repealed after a big battle in 1846 that was hailed in some quarters as a victory of the new manufacturing classes over the old landed oligarchy.

cornelian—A kind of reddish quartz used for making seals.

corn factor—Someone who bought and sold corn: the occupation of the protagonist of *The Mayor of Casterbridge*.

cornet—The lowest commissioned rank in the cavalry until 1871. The cornet carried the battle flag of the regiment like his counterpart in the infantry, the ensign.

Cornhill—A principal east-west thoroughfare in London.

coroner—The coroner was supposed to investigate all suspicious deaths by empaneling a jury of local men to hear the relevant evidence. His conclusion—if he found there to be foul play—had the force of an indictment. He sometimes went by the title "crowner."

coronet—Just as the royal family got to wear big crowns, members of the peerage got to wear little crowns (which is what "coronet" means). Each rank had a distinctive headpiece: dukes—strawberry leaves (made of precious stones, of course); marquesses—strawberries and pearls; earls—pearls plus leaves; and viscounts—a line of pearls. Barons got six pearls.

corporation—The governing body, usually the mayor and aldermen, and sometimes the council, of an incorporated borough or city.

corps—Generally a regiment.

correspondent—Someone who has regular business dealings with someone else who is usually far away.

corset—The fashionable size for a waist in the 1800s was alleged to be eighteen inches. A corset was the device used to attain this width or something close to it. It consisted of two halves, reinforced with whalebone, that got hooked together in front and then laced up in back. Compressing all that flesh into a small area was not always an easy job. The corset was one reason women needed a lady's maid—someone to stand behind them to pull the laces tight.

costermonger—Street sellers of fruits, vegetables, and fish in London. Some had barrows and wandered through the streets; some had permanent stalls. There were some 12,000 of them in London in the 1850s. A trick of the less scrupulous was to buy a few good cherries, say, and spread them over the top of a bunch of bad ones in order to move the produce that was no good.

cotillion (also cotillon)—A dance that caught on toward the end of the 1800s. Usually danced toward the end of the evening at fancy balls, it was in part a game. It took such forms as La Trompeuse, where the lady walked over to two gentlemen and after asking one to dance, walked off with the other when the first one accepted. Or there was Fish on the Line. The young lady held a fishing rod and two men came over to try and seize the biscuit dangled from the end of it while on their hands and knees.

cottagers—The people at the bottom of the heap in rural areas. Generally, they lived in the cottages owned by the local landowner while working on his estate or practicing their craft as blacksmith or carpenter or whatever in the village. With luck, they could use a few acres out back for a garden or as a place to graze their pig, as do Tess Durbeyfield's parents. In the days when leases ran for generations, their position was

Costermonger.

not so insecure, but as the 1800s wore on and commercial farming flourished, their status became more and more precarious and their condition, often, more degraded.

cottage piano—An upright piano of modest size.

counsel—*See* King's Counsel.

counterpane—A quilt or other similar bed covering with a raised design of some kind.

countess—The wife of an earl in England. The Saxon earl who, along with the sheriff, ran the shire in pre-Norman England kept his title when the Normans changed the "shires" to "counties." His wife, however, became a countess.

counting house—A businessman's office.

count-out—The process used in the House of Commons to ascertain if there were a quorum (forty). (The quorum in the House of Lords was three.)

country—In fox-hunting terms, a country is an area in which a pack may draw.

country-dance—An old-fashioned, often vigorous dance popular in the first half of the century—it is danced in Jane Austen's novels. It was really a kind of square dance. Men and women lined up in two rows opposite one another and then either as couples or lines danced through various "figures."

county family—A family of the nobility or gentry that had had a big estate in a county for many years.

county member—A member of Parliament who represented a county, as opposed to a borough.

courier—A man who journeyed ahead of wealthy people traveling in Europe in order to make—or check on—accommodations and other travel arrangements in the days before telephones and faxes.

coursing—A sport that involved chasing hares or other game with greyhounds.

court—In cities, an alley between two or more buildings. When it appeared in the name of a property, such as Ullathorne Court in *Barchester Towers*, the term referred to a house built around a central courtyard, like Hampton Court.

Court Circular—The officially promulgated word as to what was happening on a daily basis at court, handed out to the newspapers, starting in 1803, at the behest of George III. A sample from 1841: "Her Majesty and Prince Albert fell through the ice at Frogmore on Tuesday last, he skating and she following him around in her sledge. But they were extricated with only a slight inconvenience from the cold water."

Court Guide—A listing of the nobility, the gentry and everyone who had been presented at court. In the days before phone books, it was one way to find the address in London of those of "rank."

cousin—It was okay to marry them, even first cousins.

Covent Garden—The main fruit and vegetable market in London, located near Charing Cross. Near the theater district, it was also a haunt of prostitutes.

covert—Also spelled "cover." The thicket of bushes or shrubs in which a fox or other game would seek refuge when hunted—and from which the hounds tried to oust him so everyone could have fun chasing him across the countryside.

coverture—The legal doctrine that a man controlled and protected his wife.

crape—A kind of black silk that was in great demand for mourning garb. After about 1840 this spelling—in contrast to "crepe"—always connoted a mourning garment.

cravat—Generally a loose kind of fine cloth that was tied around the neck in a bow.

cribbage—A card game, played usually by two people, with a little board with sixty-one holes in it in which pegs were put to keep score.

crinoline—Made of linen and horsehair, it was a support for skirts. The "cage crinoline" was a frame construction for supporting wide skirts that replaced the original, bulkier crinoline fabric and produced a huge, inflated look and made walking through narrow doorways (or avoiding knocking bric-a-brac off tables in small parlors) virtually impossible.

crofter—A renter or owner of a small holding.

cross—To cross a letter or a note was to fill up a page in the normal fashion and then turn it ninety degrees and write across it, a habit originally adopted in the days before the advent of the national penny post in 1840 when postage was very expensive. There were, not surprisingly, complaints about its being hard to read.

croup—An infant's disease, often confused with diphtheria until the 1820s and 1830s, that caused coughing and was often rapidly fatal.

crown—A coin worth five shillings.

crowner—Another term for coroner.

cruet—One of the little glass containers with a stopper in which oil and vinegar were put.

cruiser—The light boats of the British navy. "They are small men of war, employed to sail to and fro in the Channel, and elsewhere, to secure our merchant ships and vessels from the enemy's small frigates and privateers," wrote an 1815 source.

crumpet—A soft kind of muffin made out of egg, milk, and flour, supposedly quite light.

crush hat—So called because that was what one could do to it. Also called an opera hat or Gibus. There were springs inside so that when one wore it to the opera one could remove it and fold it up flat.

cub hunting—The hunting of young foxes in September to train inexperienced hounds and riders before the real fox-hunting season began.

curate—The clergyman who assisted the incumbent of a living. Often desperately poor—and to be distinguished from the "perpetual curate," who had a living and was basically equivalent to a vicar.

curfew—A nightly bell rung at the instigation of William the Conqueror requiring households to extinguish their fires *(couvre + feu)*. The once-mandatory tolling lingered in some parishes even into the 1800s, serving such purposes as to signal the end of the shop day.

curl papers—In the dark days before plastic curlers ladies used papers to obtain the ringlets that were de rigueur during certain decades of the nineteenth century. Sometimes old newspapers were pressed into service to this end.

currant—Little, round shiny berries. There were red, black, and white varieties, sort of like raspberries, that grew wild on shrubs and were edible. There were also "currants" used for cooking that were actually raisins.

curricle—A two-wheel carriage that was fashionable in the early 1800s. It was like a gig except it was pulled by two horses rather than one and it was evidently deemed rather sporty by the younger set.

curtain lecture—An admonishing lecture that a wife gave her husband when they went to bed.

curtsey—An approved way of showing respect, perhaps not much in evidence after the turn of the mid-century except when made by social inferiors like maids to the better off or when made by the better off during presentation at court.

Custom House—An imposing official building on the north bank of the Thames that stood fiscal guard over the entrance to the port of London east of London Bridge. Built between 1814 and 1817; as late as 1871 about half the country's civil service worked in customs collection.

cut—A form of social discouragement that involved pretending not to know or see a person who was trying to be acknowledged. Etiquette books said it should only be used by young ladies trying to discourage unwelcome attentions from gentlemen, but many others "cut" people, too.

cutglass—Glass, usually of a very fine quality, that had been cut and polished, often in such a way that light passing through it would be split into various colors, as if by a prism.

d—Stands for *denarius*, Latin for penny. Hence, used as the abbreviation for pence, as in 5*d*.

dab—A little flat edible fish like a flounder. Also, slang for someone who was an expert at something.

dairymaid—Many large country houses had them. They made butter and milked the cows.

damascene—A damson.

damask—A fancy silk or linen fabric that had raised designs on it, typically of flowers. Used often for table linen.

damson—A kind of small plum a/k/a damascene, although sometimes the damascene was said to be larger and sweeter than the damson.

Davy lamp—A miner's lamp invented by Sir Humphry Davy.

deacon—The lowest of the three orders of clergy in the Church of England. A deacon was a trainee rector or vicar.

deal—Apparently made often of pine, deal was a plank usually measuring about three inches thick and seven or so wide. Generally found in a context suggesting cheap furniture or surroundings.

dean—The man who ran the chapter attached to a cathedral church. He was addressed as "Very Reverend" and the dean's job, as well as the house occupied by a dean, was called a deanery. "The deans often quarrel with their bishops," wrote a contemporary American observer, "especially about the control of the cathedrals. There have been fierce fights over the reredos and the ornaments in the choir." Rather lower in status were rural deans, who were assistants to the archdeacon.

Debrett—An annually published guide to the peerage.

debt of honor—A gambling debt, so called because it was generally not enforceable at law, so that one had to depend for repayment on the "honor" of the person who incurred it.

decant—To pour wine out of the bottle into another container so that the pure liquid can be separated from the dregs and sediment—which remain in the bottle. Decanters were favorite items in Victorian dining rooms.

decree nisi—A provisional divorce decree. The court granted a divorce that was final after six months unless something happened during that time to suggest that it shouldn't be.

demesne—The land attached to a manor house on which the house itself was situated and which was for the occupant's personal use, as opposed to the land farmed by the lord's tenants.

depot—A military term for a place where supplies were stored.

Derby (pronounced "Darby")—*The* great popular horse race in England in the 1800s—eagerly watched by all classes—so popular that Parliament even adjourned for it. Held around the end of May or beginning of June at Epsom Downs about fifteen miles from London. The other great horse race was Ascot—later in the season—but it was considerably more exclusive socially.

diligence—A French stagecoach, sometimes said to be rather heavy.

dimity—A kind of cotton used for wall hangings and dresses.

dining with Duke Humphrey—To go hungry.

dinner—In Jane Austen's time, an era when there was virtually no such thing as "lunch," a meal that followed breakfast. Dinner took place at about three or four in the afternoon and supper came later. Later in the century, after lunch put in an appearance, dinner was moved back to five or six or later by the well-to-do while the lower classes "dined" at midday.

diocese—In the Church of England, the unit of ecclesiastical administration over which a bishop presided. It was divided into parishes, and— along with other dioceses—made up one of the two provinces of the church.

dip—A cheap candle made by dipping a wick a number of times into tallow.

direct—To direct a letter was to address it.

discount—A term used with reference to the buying and selling of bills of exchange by moneylenders and bill brokers. On the one hand, it referred to the practice of buying a bill at a discount, i.e., a moneylender or bill broker purchased a bill from a creditor before it was due to be paid, giving the creditor less money than he would have received when it was finally due, this difference being the "discount." Alternatively, the practice referred to a debtor trying to raise money by writing out a bill directly to the moneylender—only for more than the amount which the moneylender actually gave him. Thus, Mr. Micawber talks of going into the City to "discount" some bills with this second meaning. He would thus write out a bill obligating him to pay a moneylender, say, £50 at some future date, and the moneylender would lend him £30, the discount being the £20 difference.

Dissenters—Members of Protestant churches other than the Church of England, e.g., the Quakers, Unitarians, Methodists, Baptists, etc.

distrain—A term meaning to seize somebody's goods and, if it were deemed desirable, sell them, generally because they hadn't paid their rent. The verb "to distress" was also used with the same meaning in this context.

distress—To distrain.

divan—A public smoking room. Reverend Harding visits one such temple of inhalation in *The Warden* in the course of his trip to London. A contemporary guidebook described for the visitor "the Divan in the Strand, where for 1s. he has the entree of a handsome room, a cup of coffee and a cigar, and the use of newspapers, periodicals, chess, etc."

division—The army unit of organization above a brigade. In the Houses of Parliament, a division was a formal vote on a matter that required the adherents of each side to step into one of the two lobbies adjoining the legislative chamber, where they would be counted.

dock—The place where the prisoner stood during his trial, a usage apparently first popularized by Dickens in *Oliver Twist*.

docks—The big docks in London just east of London Bridge, that is, just before one reached the city coming upriver from the sea. They were the places where the large ships unloaded their cargo, occupying some 450 acres all told, and were built after 1800 by private companies, the East India, West India, and London docks being among the major ones.

doctor—A title used in Jane Austen's novels, usually only to designate a doctor of divinity. It was also applied to physicians, but generally not to surgeons, who were known as "Mr."

Doctors' Commons—The area in London south of St. Paul's Cathedral where the ecclesiastical and admiralty courts were. Here marriage licenses could be obtained and wills were stored. David Copperfield is apprenticed as a law clerk in Doctors' Commons so he can become a proctor (one of the lawyers who assisted the advocates there but didn't argue in court). Doctors' Commons got its name from the fact that an advocate (a lawyer who argued cases there) had to have the degree of doctor of civil law from Oxford or Cambridge to practice, the commons being where the lawyers ate together.

dog cart—So named because it was originally built to carry dogs in small compartments when going shooting—*not* because dogs pulled it. It was a two-wheel open cart with seats back to back, much in use in the latter part of the century as sort of a small all-purpose vehicle in the country for well-off families.

dog rose—A common wild rose, often found in hedges and having red flowers.

don—The colloquial term for a tutor, head of a college or fellow at Oxford or Cambridge.

donkey cart—A small cart pulled by a donkey, obviously, often used by a poor street vendor.

doorpost—One of the two posts framing a doorway from which the door itself was hung.

dormouse—A favorite pet of Victorian children. Small, docile, affectionate, these tree-dwelling animals owed their name to the fact that in the wild they spent much of the winter hibernating. Mouselike in size, squirrel-like in appearance, an ideal choice for a small narcoleptic mammal at the Mad Hatter's tea party.

double first—Someone at Oxford who got first prize both in the classics and mathematics honors exams.

double Gloucestershire—A type of cheese.

dovecote—Certain old estates had roosts for pigeons and doves. In an era when it was difficult to get fresh food in the winter, one ate the pigeons.

dowager—The name given to a widow of rank: thus, the dowager duchess of Granby.

dower—Sometimes also used to mean "dowry," but it generally meant the part of her husband's estate to which a wife was entitled after he died.

A Dormouse.

down—As in the "down" train. "Down" meant one was traveling away from London, which was always "up" from wherever one was in England, even if one were far north of the city. The only exception to this was Oxford and Cambridge, which were always "up" and from which one was "sent down" if one were expelled.

downs—A topographical term that really meant just the opposite. The downs were hilly upland, found especially in the more southerly portions of England. "Down" derives from the Anglo-Saxon *dun*, or hill.

dowry—The wealth a bride was supposed to bring to a marriage. The going rate for a woman of some rank among the aristocracy marrying a person of approximately the same level in the 1870s was about ten thousand to thirty thousand pounds.

drab—A brownish kind of color.

draft—*See* draught.

drag—A private stagecoach, usually pulled by four horses. Also, the brakes on a carriage.

dragoon—Originally, a dragoon was distinguished from an ordinary cavalryman because he rode into battle on horseback and then dismounted and fought on foot. His name has been derived from the pistol he used, which was supposed to send out a flame like a dragon. By the 1800s the dragoons were not very different from regular cavalry. Sergeant Troy in *Far from the Madding Crowd* is a member of the 11th Dragoon Guards.

draper—A man who sold cloth.

draught—Either a check or a bill of exchange. In the context of medicine or alcohol, a draught was an amount of liquid one could toss off in one swallow.

draughts—The game of checkers.

drawers—Underpants, worn by men and women, the men's usually made from flannel or wool. Women's (cut baggy and full) were often made up of two separate legs tied together at the waist and open below (the garments were generally knee length). When they first came in, they were considered quite racy and improper for women to wear inasmuch as previously only men had worn them.

drawing—A fox-hunting term meaning to send the hounds into a covert to find the fox and send him scampering out.

drawing room—A drawing room was used in polite society to receive visitors who came to pay formal calls during the afternoon. It also served as a place for guests to assemble before going in to dinner and as a place to which the ladies would retire after dinner and be joined by the gentlemen after the latter had imbibed their port. In the sense of an event, a drawing room was the name given to one of the occasions at St. James's Palace at which ladies were formally presented to the monarch.

dray—A cart with no sides used for hauling heavy loads.

dress—To dress food was simply to prepare it.

dressing bell—A bell rung in fancy households before dinner to let people know that it was time to dress for the evening meal. Possibly adopted because in large country houses filled with guests it was difficult to get the word out to everyone any other way.

dressing room—A small room, usually attached to a bedroom, in which a husband or wife might dress.

drill—A drill was a little furrow. The name was also given to the tool used for sowing seed in such furrows.

drippings—The grease that dripped out of cooked meat. It was used by the poor instead of butter.

dropsy—A symptom rather than a disease. Limbs swelled up with liquid as a consequence of diseases like diabetes or emphysema.

drover—Someone who drove cattle or sheep to market.

drugget—A carpetlike covering made of wool for floors or tables.

duck—A linen or cotton material used for sails and for sailors' clothing.

ducks and drakes—The English term for skipping stones across the surface of the water. Used to denote throwing away one's chances at something in a similarly carefree and heedless manner. David Copperfield's great-aunt Betsey Trotwood notes of her husband that "he soon made ducks and drakes of what I gave him, sank lower and lower."

duel—Killing a man in a duel was murder in England. Which explains why in *Phineas Finn* the protagonist has to go abroad to fight his opponent. Until about the 1840s, however, convictions were rare, since juries understood that a gentleman simply could not overlook certain slights. "There *are* positions which require Duels, I really think," Her Majesty the Queen observed wistfully at one point, "& many Gentlemen have said the same."

dustman—The man who came around to empty out the dustbins into which London households emptied the ashes from their grates and any other refuse. The dust was then collected into great big heaps which were sifted for valuables and other items.

Dutch—Often used to mean German, as a corruption, presumably, of *deutsch*.

Dutch clock—A clock favored by the poor, consisting basically of a clock face and a pendulum unit.

Dutch oven—A reflecting device that could be put in front of a fireplace to allow baking.

dyspepsia—Indigestion. It made one cranky and so the term came to be applied by analogy to crankiness in general.

earnest money—Money paid as a first installment of part of a bargain, especially by a farmer or the master of a household hiring a servant at a hiring fair.

earth—A fox's den.

earthenware—Something made of clay that had been baked.

Easter term—One of the terms of either the law courts in London or Oxford and Cambridge.

East India—India when under British rule was originally run by a private company, the East India Company, until the British government took over in the wake of the Mutiny in 1857.

East Indiamen—Large, well-appointed ships that bore travelers and cargo back and forth between India and Britain. Never particularly troubled with finding excellent captains, since the captains were permitted to trade on their own accounts and thereby make their fortunes.

eat—This present tense of the word was often used perfectly "properly" by respectable people to mean "ate."

eat one's terms—To study for the bar. One had to show up for a certain number of meals at the Inns of Court in order to be "called to the bar," presumably so that within the small, insular society that then characterized the London legal profession, the senior barristers could get to know one well enough to decide whether or not one should be permitted to become a barrister.

eating house—Cheap restaurants; generally, it seems, a step or so below coffeehouses.

ecarte—At one time a popular gambling game, usually played with two players but often with bystanders betting on the game, a deck being used from which the 2, 3, 4, 5, and 6 were removed.

Ecclesiastical Commission—An official commission created in 1836 to redress imbalances in the salaries of clergy, cathedral endowments and other allocations of money within the Church of England.

elder—A kind of tree. Elder wine, a supposedly medicinal beverage, was made from its berries.

electors—The people who elected a parliamentary candidate in a borough or county. Until 1872, they had to cast their vote by public declaration—no secret ballot nonsense—which meant that the kinds of riotous goings-on that characterized the Eatanswill election in *Pickwick* were not uncommon.

Embankment—A massive public works project in London in the late 1860s. It involved replacing the shore on the north side of the Thames between the old city of London and Westminster with a thick concrete rampart a mile in length and some forty feet high. It was lined with trees and "has magnificent stone terraces with stone stairs to enable wayfarers," wrote an American observer in 1870, "who seek transportation up and down the river, to get on and off the numerous ferry boats that swarm and ply all over the Thames from Richmond to Rotherhithe."

embody—The term used to designate the calling up of the militia, which were summoned during the Napoleonic Wars and then briefly during the 1850s.

ensign—The lowest commissioned rank in the British infantry until 1871, when it was replaced with the rank of second lieutenant. The ensign was the young soldier who carried the flag (or ensign) into battle.

entail—Entail was a legal term meaning that a landed estate was tied up in such a way that the person inheriting it would have only its income—and could not sell or mortgage it. Along with primogeniture, it was the legal basis of the British aristocracy's ability to transmit their great estates intact down through the centuries.

epergne—A great, hideous candlesticklike affair that stood in the middle of Victorian dinner tables and occasionally held flowers or food but was mainly there to look impressive.

Epsom Downs—The location of the Derby, in Surrey, south of London.

equipage—A term generally used to denote a horse and carriage, sometimes also the accompanying servants as well.

equity—One of the two kinds of nonecclesiastical law. Originating as an antidote to the rigidities and unfairness of the common law, equity was administered by the king's chancellor or secretary through what eventually became the Chancery Court. In broad terms, common law looked to the letter of the law, equity more to the spirit. By the 1800s, "Chancery" had become almost synonymous with waste and procrastination.

escritoire—A writing desk with space in it for writing implements and paper.

Epergne.

esquire—A title conferring no rights or privileges but simply an intangible sort of dignity and, theoretically, membership in the landed gentry of one who had no other title. In another view, it was supposedly to be used only by justices of the peace, barristers, military officers and such, although after a while anyone who wanted to seem respectable used it.

Established church—The name given to the Church of England because it was established as the official church of England by parliamentary legislation. In the course of the 1800s there arose a Dissenting movement to *dis*establish it.

euchre—A game of cards popular in the United States played generally with 32 cards (no 2s, 3s, 4s, 5s, or 6s), sometimes with 24 or 28 cards.

Evangelicalism—A movement that arose in the Church of England in the late 1700s to reform what its adherents felt was a church that was becoming dangerously lax. Leaning to Calvinism, it opposed the rather loose sexual mores of the Regency period, alcoholic excess, and frivolity and happiness of most kinds, but no doubt also contributed to many Church of England priests taking their duties seriously for a change. The "national" schools it inspired were a major force in impelling England toward a national elementary school system. Dickens detested the Evangelicals and in the person of characters like Murdstone or Chadband generally made them out to be sour or sadistic hypocrites.

execution—The seizure of a person or his goods pursuant to a court order.

exhibition—A university scholarship obtained through competitive exams.

expectations—A word that in addition to its usual meaning denoted the strong likelihood of inheriting wealth from someone. This gives the title of Dickens's great novel, of course, a double meaning.

express—A special messenger or his message.

extinguisher—A cone-shaped device used to extinguish candles. The Ghost of Christmas Past appears to Scrooge with light shining from its head "which was doubtless the occasion of its using, in its duller moments, an extinguisher for a cap." Scrooge tries to "extinguish" the spirit with it at the end of its visit. There was another, larger kind of extinguisher fastened to the railings of town houses in which linkboys could douse their torches.

facing—A term used to describe the different kind of material put over a cuff or collar on a piece of clothing, or that you see when a cuff or collar is turned over, particularly in the British military when cuffs or lapels were often of a different color from the rest of a uniform.

fag—A term used at English public schools to denote a younger boy who ran errands and did menial chores for an older one. It carried no connotations of homosexual activity. The term seems to have come from a word that meant to do small, tiresome chores and become fatigued thereby. Jane Eyre, for example, speaks in a nonpublic school context of "ceaseless reprimand and thankless fagging."

faggot—A group of sticks tied together to be used for fuel.

fairing—A small present or gift, either won at a fair or given at one.

fall—Sometimes "fall in." A verb used to denote the coming to an end of something such as an annuity or the tenure of an incumbent in a living.

fallow—Farmland left temporarily unplanted.

fancy man—A boyfriend. In the big bad city the term also meant a pimp, but no respectable Victorian novelist would have used the term that way in his or her writing.

Fanny—Nickname for Frances, a popular girl's name.

farden—Slang for a farthing.

faro—A gambling game. Players bet on the order in which cards would turn up when dealt from the top of a deck. The dealer used a faro box—a machine with a spring inside that popped up the cards so that they could be extracted and read.

farrier—A blacksmith, and sometimes one who was a veterinarian as well.

farrow—A litter of pigs.

farthing—A coin worth one quarter of a penny.

father-in-law—*See* in-law.

fell—A desolate area in the hills.

fellow—A member of the fellows of a college at Oxford or Cambridge, the fellows constituting the governing body of the college. To become a fellow necessitated getting honors as an undergraduate, in return for which one received a stipend that was generally for life. Tutors were drawn from among the fellows.

femme de chambre—A lady's maid or a chambermaid.

fen—Low, swampy, ground. The Fens was an area in and around Lincolnshire and Cambridgeshire.

fender—A small protective border around the bottom of a grate to keep sparks and coals from falling out onto the floor. People are always putting their feet up onto it in Victorian novels.

Fenians—Finn was a mythological Irish hero. The Fenians were a revolutionary Irish organization dedicated to freeing Ireland of British rule who borrowed his name.

ferrule—A piece of metal put around or over the end of a ruler or something similar to keep it from weakening or splitting.

fete—A large fancy party. A fete champetre was a fancy party held outdoors.

fichu—A kind of cloth used as a head or shoulder covering by women.

field—In horse racing, the "field" consisted of all the horses running except the one favored. In fox hunting, the "field" meant the riders.

fieldfare—A little thrush of the fields about ten inches long.

figure—As opposed to an isolated dance *step*, a figure was really a sequence of related steps in a dance, typically in a country-dance or quadrille.

filbert—A hazel nut. The dormouse was sometimes called the filbert mouse because it liked them so much. One school of thought says the name comes from St. Philibert, who had his festival in the nut-gathering season. St. Philibert seems to have had poorer luck getting churches and schools named after him than other saints.

fingerpost—English road signs at crossroads were often in the shapes of hands with pointing fingers.

fire screen—A screen used to shield people from the heat of a fireplace. Especially useful at dinner parties in rooms heated only by a fire when one wanted to warm guests on the other side of the room yet not fry those sitting closest to the fire. Also used to keep sparks off the floor. A pastime of nineteenth-century ladies was to paint them decoratively; Elinor Dashwood in *Sense and Sensibility* "painted a very pretty pair of screens for her sister-in-law, which being now just mounted and brought home, ornamented her present drawing-room." There were also small hand screens used for the same heat-shielding purpose as the large ones.

first floor—What the English called the "first floor" is the "second floor" in the United States. The English called the floor level on which one entered from the street the "ground floor" rather than the "first floor."

first rate—*See* rate.

fiver—A five-pound note.

fives—A sport that involved whacking the ball with one's hand against the front of a three-wall court.

flagon—One drank alcohol from it. It had a spout, a handle, and usually a lid.

flag officer—An admiral, vice admiral, or rear admiral, so named because they were each entitled to fly a flag from their respective ship, which—for that reason—was known as the flagship.

flail—The wooden device used to thresh corn in the days before mechanical threshing machines like the one that made life miserable for Tess Durbeyfield. Sometimes everyone stood in a circle with their flail and "flailed away" at the stalks of corn, trying to separate the grain at the end from the rest of the stalk.

flannel—A heavy, warm woolen cloth.

flax—In the 1800s, everyone always describes lovely young girls or handsome boys as having hair like flax. It was the plant from which linen was made. It had blue flowers and seeds that could be turned into linseed oil.

Fleet Prison—A fleet was a small brook. Originally, there was one running down to the Thames where Fleet Street now is. Fleet Prison was a prison housing debtors that was emptied in 1844 and thereafter pulled down.

flip—One of those hearty old English drinks. This one consisted of beer plus some stronger alcohol mixed with sugar and then energized by having a red-hot iron stuck in the middle of it.

flitches—The side of a pig or bacon, which could be hung in chimneys to cure.

flock—Bits of cloth, wool, and the like used for stuffing mattresses and furniture. In *The Mill on the Floss* obviously not a preferred material since when the relatives all gather to discuss Mr. Tulliver's financial downfall, Mrs. Glegg harshly tells her sister, "You must bring your mind to your circumstances, Bessy, and not be thinking o' silver and chany, but whether you shall get so much as a flock bed to lie on."

florin—A silver coin worth two shillings, introduced in 1849.

flounce—A good way to leave a room in a huff, and also a piece of material on a woman's dress that flapped loose after being sewn on at the top.

fly—A horse and carriage that was rented, usually by the day.

fob—A watch fob was a little pocket in the pants in which to keep a watch. When David Copperfield first meets his great-aunt Betsey Trotwood's friend Mr. Dick, the latter "had his watch in his fob, and his money in his pockets."

folio—A piece of paper that has been folded only once, thus producing two large pages. (As opposed to quarto and octavo.) Books were frequently described by their size according to this system of classification.

follower—A would-be boyfriend of a female servant. They were almost always forbidden by employers.

font—The little basin raised on a pedestal used in a church for baptisms.

foolscap—A kind of paper, generally about thirteen by seventeen inches in dimensions, some varieties of which at one time bore a watermark of a fool's cap and bells.

footboard—A board that footmen stood on when riding at the rear of a carriage. Also a board to step on when one got into a carriage, or a board for the driver or coachman to rest his feet on while driving.

Foot Guards—The infantry regiments that stood guard over the sovereign, e.g., at Buckingham Palace. They consisted of the Coldstream Guards, the Scots Guards and the Grenadier Guards and took precedence over all other infantry regiments in the army.

footman—The indoor male servant subordinate to the butler and superior in rank to the boy or page. Typically he cleaned and trimmed the lamps, waited at table at fancy dinner parties and went out with the ladies of the house when they went to pay calls, where it was his job to dash up the steps with a calling card and inquire if anyone was at home while his mistress waited in the carriage. He often wore an old-fashioned livery consisting of knee breeches and silk stockings; footmen were accordingly evaluated quite seriously by the appearance of their calves. If one had more than one footman, one was supposed to make sure they matched in height.

forfeits—A game in which one gave up some small possession after breaking a silly rule and then had to do something that made one look ridiculous to get it back.

form—A wooden bench, such as was typically found in schoolrooms.

four-in-hand—The driving of a carriage pulled by four horses. It became a nostalgic leisure-time activity for the affluent, especially in the later 1800s, after such carriages died out to a great extent as a practical means of transport.

fox's brush—*See* brush.

frank—Until 1840, a member of Parliament could send letters free. This was a worthwhile perquisite before cheap postal rates went into effect that year.

freehold—Basically, out-and-out ownership of land, equivalent to fee simple, as opposed to copyhold and leasehold. Freeholders were the landowners in a community, as opposed to the renters. Before the Reform Act of 1832 the vote was restricted to freeholders whose land yielded them an annual income of forty shillings or more.

freeman—The name sometimes given to those in a borough who had the privileges of borough citizenship such as the right to elect members of the council.

frieze—A coarse-textured wool cloth.

frigate—One of the smaller boats in the old British navy, being of the fifth or sixth rate. Unlike ships of the line, they were used for reconnaissance or for protecting merchant ships. They carried between twenty and forty-four guns.

frock—The standard term for a woman's ordinary or fancy dress until well into the century and applied particularly to dresses made of muslin and other light materials. A frock generally buttoned up the back. Little children had to wear them sometimes, too.

frock coat—A men's daytime coat that became the standard everyday wear for the latter part of the century, by which time it was invariably black. It fell roughly to the knees and was of an even length all around.

front—A small, phony hairpiece worn above the forehead by women.

fruiterer—A fruit seller.

frumenty—A dish made of boiled milk, wheat and seasonings like cinnamon or sugar. It appears at the beginning of *The Mayor of Casterbridge* under the name of "furmity," the dish of "corn in the grain, flour, milk, raisins, currants and what-not" purveyed by the old lady who keeps spiking Henchard's helpings until he sells his wife.

funds—The national debt was sometimes referred to as the "funds," because the government made payments to reduce it out of a whole series of different funds. When the government issued securities against the debt for purchase by small investors, the securities, too, were called the "funds."

furlong—A length equal to 660 feet. That was the average length of a furrow in old farm fields—the word means a "furrow long."

furze—A yellow-flowered, prickly, evergreen shrub growing in desolate areas, also called "whin" or "gorse."

fusiliers—Originally, infantry soldiers armed with fusils. However, as time passed, regiments called "fusiliers" came to be no different from others except that they wore busbies.

fustian—The name for a number of coarse cotton fabrics such as velveteen, corduroy, etc., usually of some darkish color.

gaffer—An old man or a man of high position. In *Far from the Madding Crowd* someone speaks of "a great gaffer like the Lord."

gaiters—Knee-length leggings buttoning up the side that were worn in the country to protect clothes from dirt, mud, and rain. (Shorter ones were called spatterdashes—or spats—because they "dashed away" spatters.)

gallery—The gallery was a raised area at the back of the parish church where, often, the choir sang. In a great country house, it was a long room or hallway generally used to display ancestral portraits. In origin, country-house galleries were simply indoor walking areas for use in inclement weather.

galop—An energetic dance that was later incorporated into the quadrille.

game—Animals that one hunted or shot at for sport, such as pheasant, grouse, hare, partridge, etc.

gaming—Gambling. Nothing to do with the word "game" in the sense of hunted animals.

gamekeeper—The man hired on great estates to breed pheasant or other game for shooting, to trap vermin, to keep poachers off the property, and to take the proprietor and his friends out after game when they journeyed up from London for some days of "shooting."

gammon—An expression meaning "nonsense."

gangway—The gangway was the passageway about halfway down the House of Commons that connected the rear and the front benches. "Above the gangway," i.e., closer to the Speaker, sat the members of the incumbent ministry plus their strong adherents.

gardener—The head gardener on a large estate was generally considered one of the "upper servants" and as such entitled to eat with the steward or the butler when these worthies dined separately from the lower domestic staff.

garret—Basically, an attic.

garner—To store things like corn in a granary.

garter—The Order of the Garter was the highest order of knighthood; its members outranked baronets. It was an honor generally bestowed only on peers. Supposedly, it originated when the countess of Salisbury let slip a garter at a ball and the king picked it up, saying meaningfully, "Honi soit qui mal y pense." Being a Knight of the Garter entitled you to put "K.G." after your name and to wear a fancy star on your chest, a garter, a mantle, and so on.

gas—Gas lights were adjustable. When a room was not in use or the family were out for the evening, the gas lights could be turned down without wholly extinguishing them so as to save money. Gas lighting came in in the early 1800s for streets but was not really suitable for use in homes til late in the century.

gate—To gate an undergraduate at a university was to punish him by confining him within the grounds of his college.

Gazette—A publication whose full name was the *London Gazette,* which came out twice a week and listed government appointments and also bankrupts. "To be gazetted" meant to be appointed to a post somewhere. "To be in the gazette" meant that you were a bankrupt.

general elections—Elections at which all members of the House of Commons had to stand for election, as opposed to by-elections, which were only for one or a few seats, as when someone had died.

general post—The mail that went out of the central London post office to the hinterlands of England. As opposed to the "penny" or "two-penny" local mail *within* London or other large cities, which was organized and run separately.

gentleman farmer—A term that was used to characterize people who formerly might have called themselves yeomen. The gentleman farmer farmed a fairly sizable amount of land but less than that farmed by the gentry and came below the gentry socially. Some gentlemen farmers farmed their own land; others were tenant farmers on great estates. Typically they employed laborers but, unlike a squire, would have no farm tenants of their own. Farmer Boldwood in *Far from the Madding Crowd* is a gentleman farmer; in *The Mill on the Floss* George Eliot tells us that Mr. Glegg belongs to this group also.

gentleman's gentleman—A valet.

gentry—The gentry were the landowners in the country who came just below the nobility in social rank and the amount of land they owned. Their upper reaches consisted of baronets, like Sir James Chettam of *Middlemarch* or Sir Pitt Crawley in *Vanity Fair,* and knights. In the lower reaches of the gentry came the "squires" like Squire Cass in *Silas Marner* or other nontitled folk, who typically had deep family roots in the area and rented out their land to tenant farmers. Unlike the gentlemen farmers or yeomen just below them, the gentry took no part in the actual work of farming themselves. Typically, the gentry were active locally, as justices of the peace, for example, while the great landowners just above them who were members of the peerage spent a good portion of each year in London. Jane Austen draws her main characters almost exclusively from among the gentry.

gibbet—As opposed to a straight hanging, the gibbet involved having one's corpse hung in chains after one died, preferably high off the ground at a crossroads where one could serve as a ghastly deterrent to passersby.

gift—For a living or benefice to be "in" someone's "gift" meant that the giver had the power to say upon whom it should be bestowed.

gig—A one-horse carriage, light, with only two wheels, that became fashionable in the early 1800s as a modest all-purpose country cart, sort of the Model T Ford of its day. Preferred except by the unusually dashing or wealthy to the two-horse curricle, which cost more to maintain.

gill—A quarter of a pint.

gillyflower—A name designating flowers that smelled of clove, they being the wallflower, the stock, and the carnation.

gin—A trap or a snare.

gingham—A strong material made of checked cotton or linen and sometimes used in clothing.

girandole—A candlestick with different branches that was sometimes freestanding and sometimes came out of a wall.

Gladstone—The most famous Liberal prime minister. Known for his antagonism to Disraeli. His name was given to a small traveling bag.

glazier—A man who installed windows.

gleaners—The people who go through a field after the crop has been officially harvested and pick up or glean the bits of wheat or barley that the harvesters have missed. The advent of mechanical reapers, much more efficient than the human kind at harvesting every last little bit, largely killed the practice.

glebe—Sounds like a small Arctic bird. Actually, it meant the land attached to a benefice from which the incumbent was entitled to receive the rents. Jane Austen's clergyman father used his to raise food to feed his eight children.

glee—In music, the glee was a vocal piece for three people or more. In *Jane Eyre*, singers gather around the piano while Jane and her pupil listen: "The solo over, a duet followed, and then a glee."

glen—A low area in between two hills or mountains, sometimes acting as a streambed.

gloaming—Twilight.

globes—Frequently mentioned in a pedagogical context. They consisted of a globe of the earth and a globe of the heavens and were used to teach geography and astronomy.

glowworm—A type of worm. The male has wings but no lights and the female lights but no wings. According to what Hardy says in *The Return of the Native,* on some nights "it is possible to read the handwriting of a letter by the light of two or three." Wildeve and Diggory Venn dice nocturnally for Mrs. Yeobright's guineas by the light of glowworms trapped by the former.

godparent—Someone who promised at a christening that the child would receive a proper religious education and forswore the devil on its behalf so that it could be provisionally made a member of the Church of England.

gooseberry—The berry of a thorny shrub that was edible and could be mixed with cream to make "gooseberry fool." Not to be confused with "playing old gooseberry" with a thing or person, which was to make a mess of it or of their affairs.

Gorm—Lower-class slang for "goddamn."

gorse—*See* furze.

gout—A hereditary disease aggravated by the consumption of too much protein (meat or wine in the 1800s) and resulting in painful swelling of the joints, especially the toes. Sometimes treated as a mild status symbol by the well-to-do since it connoted the financial wherewithal to live high on the hog.

grammar school—Originally schools of this type taught only Greek and Latin language and grammar, hence the name. Most of the great public schools like Harrow and Eton and Rugby were originally grammar schools and then expanded their curriculum in the 1800s and began admitting children from around the nation instead of just their immediate locality.

grange—An isolated farmhouse, usually belonging to a member of the gentry, such as Mr. Linton (Thrushcross Grange) in *Wuthering Heights* or Mr. Brooke (Tipton Grange) in *Middlemarch*. Originally granges were grain storehouses, often attached to monasteries.

grate—The coal used in English fireplaces needed air underneath to burn. Consequently, fireplaces were built with little iron latticeworks of bars in them to hold the coal, frequently with a raised area or hob on the side where kettles and other things could be set to warm. This whole apparatus was the grate. Cleaning the grate was a chore; in fancy households the housemaid or maid-of-all-work cleaned out the grate and laid a new fire each morning and, later, polished the grate with blacklead.

gravel walk—Gravel was evidently the preferred substance for alleys and walkways and driveways in country estates.

Gray's Inn—*See* Inns of Court.

greatcoat—A big overcoat worn out of doors, frequently with several short collars known as capes around the shoulders. Sometimes the term was also used for a pelisse.

great seal—The great seal was the official seal of the realm affixed to major state documents such as declarations of war, and it was in the keeping of the lord chancellor. Actually, it consisted of two halves of a die into which—when they were fitted together—wax could be poured to produce an impression that would then be fixed to the relevant document.

greengage—A green-colored plum.

greengrocer—A man who sold fruits and vegetables.

The Great Seal.

Greenwich—A town several miles downriver from London on the south side of the Thames, perhaps most notable in the 1800s for housing the Royal Naval Hospital for old sailors.

grenadier—Originally, grenadiers were the men in the army who threw grenades. Because of their task they were supposed to be bigger and stronger than everyone else. After it stopped being necessary to lob grenades the tradition was still maintained that the grenadiers should be quite large. The formidable, if pompous, Miss Pinkerton of Miss Pinkerton's Academy, Thackeray tells us in *Vanity Fair,* "was as tall as a grenadier."

Gretna Green—The place in Scotland to which young would-be marrieds eloped, typically when parental consent seemed unlikely and one party was underage. Just across the border from England, one could be married with no waiting period by simply declaring one's desire to do so in the presence of a competent adult—no license or clergyman required. In 1856, however, the requirement of a twenty-one-day residence in Scotland was imposed.

groat—A nickname for the fourpence.

grog—A drink of watered-down rum. Admiral "Old Grog" Vernon, horrified at the amount of alcohol his men were consuming, ordered, circa 1745, that his crews' drinks, traditionally straight rum until then, be cut with water. His nickname, derived from the cloak of grogram he wore, was given to the new, diluted beverage.

groom—The servant in a household who looked after the horses.

groomsmen—The equivalent of the best men and ushers at today's weddings. (Literally, the male analogues of the bride's maids.) If there were only one groomsman, he was the best man.

Grosvenor Square—A part of Mayfair that an 1871 guidebook no doubt truthfully called the most fashionable square in London.

ground floor—The term customarily used by the English to denote the floor entered at street level. What Americans call the "first" floor.

grouse—A small bird that lived on the moors in Scotland, hunted for sport and bearing many names. The red grouse was also known as the moor fowl or moor game, and the black grouse was also known as black game, the heath fowl or the black cock. The grouse season started on August 12 and signaled the end of Parliament and of the London "season" and the beginning of the bird shooting and fox hunting that consumed the fall and winter.

growler—A nickname for the four-wheel coaches that competed with hansom cabs for taxi fares in the latter part of the century. The growlers were not as tippy as hansoms, carried more people and had room for luggage, but they were slower.

gruel—A less-than-exciting dish consisting of corn, in the English sense, mixed with water or milk. It is of this food that Oliver Twist made his immortal request for "more" at the workhouse. It was a staple of institutional diets because in large quantities it was relatively cheap to prepare; the Poor Law commissioners in 1836 based their daily diet for the workhouse around a one-and-a-half-pint ration of gruel a day. It was also supposed to have medicinal properties; Dickens, for example, tells us in *A Christmas Carol* that Scrooge's dismal chambers were furnished with "a little saucepan of gruel (Scrooge had a cold in his head)."

guard chain—A chain attached to something like a watch to keep it from getting lost.

guardians—Under the New Poor Law of 1834, each local parish or area elected a board of guardians to run the union of workhouses in the area.

Guards—*See* Household Guards.

guinea—A coin originally made of gold from Guinea that was worth twenty-one shillings and was last issued in 1813. Mrs. Yeobright in *The Return of the Native* has a little "box full of spade guineas" to divide between Clem and Thomasin; these were guineas that had a design like the spade on playing cards on the back. Luxury items were often priced in guineas long after the coin had stopped being minted.

guinea fowl—A spotted, chicken-size farmyard bird.

haberdasher—In England, a man who dealt in small personal articles like threads and needles.

hack—A hack was a general-purpose, riding horse, i.e., not a hunter. To "hack" on a horse was to ride him along a road at an ordinary speed as opposed to racing him or using him for hunting or military purposes.

hackney coach—A hackney coach was one that could be hired. In London, they served as taxicabs in the early part of the century. Usually they were discarded vehicles of the nobility, sometimes with the family coat of arms still on them.

ha-ha—A landscaping device that consisted of a trench dug at some point in the view where it could not be seen unless one were very close to it. Also called a sunken fence.

half crown—A silver English coin worth two shillings and sixpence. The amount which this coin represented was called a half *a* crown.

half pay—A payment that kept military men on the active list, supposedly ready to be recalled to duty though it was often seen as a preliminary step to retirement.

half price—A term used in connection with London theaters, where one could get in at intermission for half price.

hammercloth—The cloth draped over the driver's seat on a coach.

hand—A term for a factory worker or other kind of workman. A hand was also a measurement, used in describing the height of horses, that was equivalent to four inches.

hansom cab—The cab that everyone loved. Invented in the late 1830s, it had two wheels and the driver sat in back, so the passengers for a change got a clear view of where they were going.

Hants.—An abbreviation for Hampshire county.

ha'penny—A halfpenny.

hardbake—A glazed sweet mass of almonds and sugar or molasses.

hardtack—Biscuits for sailors.

hare—Like rabbits, except they had bigger hind feet and less tender flesh.

harmonium—A kind of primitive organ, worked by foot. The difference between this and similar American organs was that in the former the air was expelled and in the latter it was pulled in.

harrow—As a verb, it described what was done to a field after it was plowed; namely, a harrow (the noun) was drawn over the field, breaking up the clumps of earth that resulted from plowing. The harrow was a frame with iron teeth in it that dug into the ground as it was pulled along.

hartshorn—What it says it was—a deer's antlers. Since deer antlers contained ammonia, they were ground into powder and put into bottles for use like smelling salts. Eustacia Vye is found dead in *The Return of the Native* and "then Thomasin, whose stupor of grief had been thrust off awhile by frantic action, applied a bottle of hartshorn to Clym's nostrils, having tried it in vain upon the other two. He sighed. 'Clym's alive!' she exclaimed."

harvest—The cutting of the corn crop. Corn was always "harvested," while when hay was cut, it was said to be "made."

harvest home—A big feast with food and drink given by the landlord or farmer for all his workers to mark the conclusion of the corn harvest.

hassock—Not to be confused with a "cassock." Originally, hassocks were tufted clumps of earth and grass in swampy areas. They were brought

English harvest home.

into churches to serve as footrests and things to kneel on, and the name was transferred subsequently to manmade furniture serving the same purpose.

hatchment—A shield bearing the coat of arms of someone who had died, displayed first on the front of their house and then in church. In *Vanity Fair*, Thackeray describes two "tall gloomy houses, each with a hatchment over the middle drawing-room window; as is the custom of houses in Great Gaunt Street, in which gloomy locality death seems to reign perpetual."

haw—The red berry of the hawthorn tree.

haymaking—The cutting of a farm's hay, almost always in June, so that it could be gathered and stored for the winter to feed the animals.

heath—The heath was a kind of plant that grew in relatively unfertile soils. When a large quantity grew in one place, that piece of ground was itself referred to as a heath. The name for the plant in northern parts of England and in Scotland was "heather."

heather—*See* heath.

heavy—In military parlance, a unit of soldiers with larger than normal weapons or other equipment was said to be heavy, the soldiers themselves being often larger than the average. The opposite, of course, was "light artillery" or "light cavalry." There was a little-known and relatively successful Charge of the Heavy Brigade as well as the disastrous one of the Light Brigade.

hedgerow—A row made out of a hedge, usually to serve as a barrier to keep cattle or sheep from wandering from one field to the next and often made of hawthorn trees because of their prickly, animal-discouraging properties.

heir apparent—The heir who would inherit a property regardless of any conceivable contingency that might occur.

heir presumptive—The heir who would inherit only if certain contingencies did not occur.

heirloom—An article of personal property which was intended either by law or custom to descend by right to an heir along with the land that he was designated to inherit. *The Eustace Diamonds* concerns whether or not the gems named in the title are heirlooms.

Hessian boots—Long boots worn by the German mercenaries who, inter alia, came over and fought the colonists during the American Revolution. The boots had a tassel on the top. They were popular in England in the early part of the 1800s.

High Church—Before the Oxford Movement, the High Church group was simply the old-fashioned, stuffy faction within the Church of England. After the Oxford Movement, the term was applied to church members who shared the movement's sentiments in favor of ceremony, ecclesiastical organization, and all the things that tended to make the church more like the Catholic church than like the down-home, born-again religion favored by the Evangelicals.

high-lows—A type of lace-up boot.

high sheriff—*See* sheriff.

Hilary term—Hilary was a fourth-century bishop of Poitiers who got himself an English feast day on January 13, which feast day in turn gave its name to university and law terms.

hip—A fruit of a rose, especially the dog rose's red berry.

hiring fair—An annual or semiannual fair held in rural areas at which people hired servants and farm laborers. Gabriel Oak goes to such a fair after his sheep are killed to seek work as a farm bailiff and—when no one wants a bailiff—as a shepherd. His donning of the shepherd's smock frock and making himself a crook to find employment was typical; servants customarily wore distinctive articles of clothing at such fairs so as to make clear the type of position for which they were seeking employment. Hiring fairs were also called "statute fairs" or "mops."

His Grace—Form of address used in writing to a duke.

hob—The place at the side of a grate where one could put things like kettles to keep them warm.

hobbledehoy—A young man or boy in the awkward stage of adolescence.

hobby horse—A particular crotchet or obsession. Also the name given to silly would-be bicycles popular during the Regency that were moved by pushing one's feet along the ground.

hock—German white wine produced at Hockheim.

Hodge—A broken-down form of "Roger," used in a contemptuous or amused way to designate a rural laborer. Maggie Tulliver's silly mother decides to try a stratagem to rescue the family from its desperate financial straits; "imagine a truly respectable and amiable hen," says George Eliot, "by some portentous anomaly, taking to reflection and inventing combinations by which she might prevail on Hodge not to wring her neck or send her and her chicks to market."

hogshead—A measure of liquid equal to 52½ gallons.

holland—A type of clothing made out of linen. Brown holland, a heavier variety, was a favorite material in which to wrap up furniture and the like when one was away from a house for a while. It was also used as a floor covering.

holly—It was favored for Christmas because, as an evergreen, it kept its bright green leaves and red berries.

home counties—Kent, Essex, Surrey, and Middlesex; that is, the counties closest to London, sometimes also including Hertford and Sussex.

Home Rule—A proposal to get the English out of the Irish government and let it be governed by a native Parliament. The proposal caught on in national politics in the 1870s.

home secretary—More properly, the secretary of state for home affairs. The man in charge of dealing with domestic matters, as opposed to the foreign secretary. The home secretary was in charge of law and order and thus ran the prisons and Scotland Yard. He heard pleas for criminals to be pardoned; at the end of *Far from the Madding Crowd* a petition to him results in the commutation of Boldwood's death sentence for shooting Sergeant Troy to life imprisonment. For some unfathomable reason, the home secretary also passed on the eligibility of persons wishing to vend milk from their cows in St. James's Park.

homestead—A home, especially a farm, with its surrounding buildings.

Hon.—*See* Honourable.

Honourable—A title used for all members of Parliament. It was also a "courtesy title," that is, one not accompanied by any legal rights, bestowed on all children of viscounts and barons and on the younger sons of earls. Often abbreviated "Hon." Not to be confused with *Right* Honourable, which would be used by a cabinet member (and any other member of the Privy Council), an earl, viscount or baron, and a peer's eldest son bearing an inferior title of his father's as a courtesy title.

hop—A climbing vine picked in September whose product was used to flavor beer.

horn—Various objects were made in whole or in part out of animal horns for many years, chief among them the "inkhorn" and the panes of the kind of lantern carried by Christian Cantle in *The Return of the Native*, which as he walks disturbs "moths and other winged insects, which flew out and alighted upon its horny panes." On the fateful night his hoard is stolen, we learn of Silas Marner returning through the night to his cottage "with a horn lantern in his hand." The practice of making the opaque side panels of lanterns from horn was known, of course, to

Shakespeare, whose Moon in *A Midsummer Night's Dream* lifts his rustic lantern aloft, proclaiming, "This lanthorn doth the horned moon present."

hornpipe—Originally not a nautical dance at all but merely an old English folk dance done to a horn, usually by one person.

horse pistol—A big pistol carried, unsurprisingly, while riding a horse.

Horse Guards—The cavalry who guarded the monarch as part of the Household troops. They were nicknamed the "Blues," and their barracks in Whitehall became the headquarters of the whole army, so that "the Horse Guards" came to be used synedochally, like "the Pentagon."

hosier—A socks and stockings maker.

hostler—a/k/a "ostler." He took care of the horses of travelers at inns.

house—A colloquial term for the workhouse. Sometimes also used by a sheriff's officer to designate a sponging house when arresting a debtor, as when Pip is arrested for debt at the end of *Great Expectations*. " 'You had better come to my house,' said the man. 'I keep a very nice house.' "

housebreaking—Breaking into a house during the daytime to steal something or commit some other felony. Breaking into a house at night was called burglary.

Household—The royal household or the servants and staff who looked after the royal family. The three top officials were the lord chamberlain, the lord steward and the master of the horse. When Victoria became monarch, the female attendants—led by the mistress of the robes, and

Horse Guards.

her subordinates, the ladies of the bedchamber and the maids of honour—became more important. Such household posts were sought after by high-ranking women and were expected to be awarded by a new prime minister to relatives of members of his party; Lady Glencora Palliser seeks the post of mistress of the robes from her husband. The Household Troops (also known as the Guards) were the army units who by custom were supposed to protect the sovereign. They consisted of the Life Guards and Royal Horse Guards (both cavalry) and the Grenadier, Scots and Coldstream Guards (the so-called Foot Guards or infantry).

householder—A person who occupied a house or other dwelling and was therefore legally eligible under various circumstances to vote.

housekeeper—The top-ranking female servant in a household. She typically hired and fired all the housemaids and made sure they did their work, in addition to which she made household preserves and often supervised the ordering of the food. She was always addressed as "Mrs." whether she were married or not, and generally, like the butler, had her own workroom in which to hold court, gossip, and transact business, and she was rarely without her chain of keys.

housemaid—The maid who did the dirty work of keeping the house cleaned and the bedrooms supplied with water and heat. She carried water up and down stairs for baths, emptied and washed slop basins, cleaned out the grates and polished them, turned down beds, and washed the floors and cleaned the halls, dining room, drawing room, etc., as well. Having a housemaid was probably the next step up for most households from having just a maid-of-all-work. There was a recognized syndrome called "housemaid's knee" that resulted from kneeling on the floors and constantly scrubbing them to get them clean.

housewife (pronounced "huzzif")—A small case for carrying around little clothes-mending items like needles and thread. Sometimes spelled "huswife."

hulks—Notable for their role in *Great Expectations*. They were old ships pressed into use in 1776 as supposedly "temporary" floating prisons, but they were not abolished until 1858. They were located at Woolwich, the Medway, and Portsmouth harbor.

hundred—An ancient English unit of government, being the unit next down from a shire.

hundredweight—A measure of weight equal to 112 pounds and abbreviated cwt.

hunt—The verb was used generally only to apply to fox hunting. (To go after rabbits, pheasant, grouse, partridge, and other game with a gun was always spoken of as "shooting.") The "hunt" as an entity was the local group of sportsmen organized for the purpose of fox hunting.

hunter—A horse that had been bred specifically for fox hunting.

huntsman—The man at a hunt who controlled the dogs and kept them on the scent.

hurdler—A maker of hurdles.

hurdles—Pens or enclosures made from lashed together sticks. They were often used to pen sheep into an area overnight on fields that needed manuring. After the sheep performed each night, the hurdles would be moved the next day to a new location. This would be done until the entire area to be fertilized had been sheep plopped.

hussars—A kind of light cavalryman, originally in the Hungarian army. By the 1800s a hussar in the English army was simply a cavalryman who wore a rather flamboyant kind of uniform.

hustings—The platforms from which, until 1872, candidates for Parliament addressed the voters.

huswife—*See* housewife.

Hyde Park—Located in the West End, the 388-acre park was the most fashionable in London and was where the cream of London society promenaded on their horses to see, to be seen, and gossip. Park Lane, the street on its eastern border, was the most fashionable address in London.

imperial gallon—Virtually the same as a regular gallon. The term "imperial" was used starting in the 1820s to designate the officially adopted uniform system of weights and measures that replaced the hodge-podge of different standards that had been used in the country in a less systematic age.

impropriate—When tithes went to a layman, as opposed to a clerical body.

incumbent—The clergyman occupying a living.

indentures—The documents signed by an apprentice and master when the former agreed to work for—or be "bound" to—the latter. Identical copies of the contract were made on the same piece of paper; it was then torn along a jagged, toothlike ("dentures") edge, leaving each party with a copy that—when fitted together with the other—would prove that it could only have been the counterpart of that one other piece of paper. Hence its name. Indentures were said to be "canceled" when an apprentice was released from them.

independency (or independence)—A term meaning enough money to live on more or less adequately.

India Office—The branch of the British government that handled Indian affairs.

India ink—A kind of paint or ink that was actually from China or Japan and that was made from lampblack and came in sticks.

india rubber—Ordinary rubber. Among other things, it was used for erasers.

induction—One of the steps required to formally install a new clergyman in a living or benefice. In contrast to "institution," induction involved putting him in possession of the actual church buildings.

institution—The act of putting a clergyman into spiritual possession of his living, as opposed to "induction."

inform—To inform or lay an information against someone was to bring a formal criminal complaint against them. This was the usual method of prosecuting and convicting in the 1800s since there were no public prosecutors such as district attorneys. For a while Parliament even provided financial incentives to do so. One did not have to be a crime victim to "inform."

inkhorn—A portable ink container. At one time they were actually made from horns; hence, the name.

in-law—A word sometimes used confusingly. Often it meant just what one would expect, i.e., "father-in-law" was sometimes used to designate one's spouse's father. However, the term was also used to designate a step-relationship. Thus in *David Copperfield* the odious schoolmaster Mr. Creakle tells the young hero after Murdstone has married David's mother, "I have the happiness of knowing your father-in-law," then "pinching my ear with ferocious playfulness." Just to confuse things further, "brother" or "sister" was sometimes used to mean "brother-in-law" or "sister-in-law."

Inner Temple—*See* Inns of Court.

Inns of Court—Four institutions—the Inner Temple, the Middle Temple, Lincoln's Inn and Gray's Inn—located near the western boundary of the City which housed barristers and their law offices, as well as dining halls for the barristers and their law students. Besides serving as offices, dwellings, and law school, the inns had the sole power to determine who should be "called to the bar."

inquest—*See* coroner.

interest—Often used to mean influence with someone or some institution, e.g., "pull."

iron dogs—Andirons.

ironmonger—Someone who sold hardware.

irregulars—Full-time paid soldiers made up a regular army. Part-time volunteers or militia, on the other hand, constituted "irregulars."

jack—A mechanically operated manikin in a clock tower that periodically struck bells to indicate the time.

jackboots—Boots that came up over the knee. In the days before they became associated with dictatorships, cavalrymen wore them because they protected against sword cuts and leg injuries.

jackdaw—A small but clever member of the crow family.

Jack Ketch—A barbaric hangman of the 1600s whose name became a synonym thereafter for the hangman.

jack towel—A long towel on a roller.

japanning—A technique supposedly derived from Japan of applying a black, shiny lacquer to things.

japonica—Various kinds of Japanese plants.

jaunting car—Perhaps more properly called a "jolting car." A two-wheel cart carrying up to four people. "An inside jaunting-car is a bad place for conversation," Trollope observes in *Can You Forgive Her?*, "as your teeth are nearly shaken out of your head by every movement which the horse makes."

Jenny—A nickname for Jane or Janet. In her family, Jane Austen was known as Jenny.

jet—A type of coal which could take a high polish and be made into beads and the like. It was the one kind of ornament acceptable for women to wear in the early stages of mourning. From whence comes our term "jet black," as in the color of hair.

jig—A one-person dance of considerable bounciness; no particular step was dictated.

jobber—A jobber was someone who rented horses. In addition, "job" was the term sometimes given to a position in the government which had been used unethically or improperly for private gain.

jointure—A legal term designating the portion of her husband's estate which a widow was to enjoy after his death. The precise amount formed the subject of negotiations between teams of lawyers in the arrangements for "marriage settlements" which preceded marriages between persons of substance during the period.

jorum—A slang term meaning a big drinking bowl of some kind or else the amount of liquor it could hold.

joseph—An old-fashioned long coat used by women when riding that had buttons down the front.

journeyman—The term applied to someone who had completed his apprenticeship and was thus free to hire himself out by the day (from the French *jour,* meaning "day"). Generally, the term meant someone who had mastered a craft and—upon obtaining sufficient skill and some funds of his own—might be in turn expected to set up as a master. It is clearly a comedown for Henchard in *The Mayor of Casterbridge* that he goes bankrupt and is reduced to working as a journeyman. In *Great Expectations,* we learn that Joe Gargery the blacksmith "kept a journeyman at weekly wages," the infamous Orlick.

junior lordship—In certain departments of government, subordinate positions were called junior lordships. There were three, for example, in the Treasury Department, who were junior to the first lord of the treasury and the Chancellor of the Exchequer.

justice of the peace—The man who received a "commission of the peace" from the sovereign through the lord lieutenant to maintain the local peace and in general regulate affairs in his part of the county. This task he performed by undertaking various administrative and regulatory functions such as the licensing of alehouses, dispensing summary justice to minor offenders against the peace, appointing local parish officials like the constable, and sitting four times a year with his fellow justices in the county at the quarter sessions to decide more serious matters. The post was only open to those with a £100 income; in practice, it was invariably held by a member of the local gentry like a squire or the parish clergyman. Justices of the peace were often referred to as "magistrates." Mr. Brooke in *Middlemarch* is one—so are Edgar Linton and his father in *Wuthering Heights* and Pitt Crawley in *Vanity Fair.*

Kensington—A district of western London just beyond Hyde Park.

kerseymere—A fancy kind of wool cloth.

King's Bench—One of the three superior courts of common law that sat in London, abolished in 1873 when it was combined with the other two into one overall court. It principally heard criminal matters and quasi-criminal civil matters like cases involving "deceit." It sat in Westminster Hall.

King's Counsel—An honor granted to barristers who had served with great distinction and who, at least at one time, were actually supposed to be counselors of the king. The honor conferred the right to write "K.C." after one's name and to wear a gown of silk. It replaced becoming a serjeant as the highest honor a barrister could achieve. During Victoria's reign the honor was, of course, that of Queen's Counsel.

kiss hands, to—Upon assuming office, it was customary for the prime minister to kiss the monarch's hand as a token of fealty. Officially, after all, the term prime minister meant merely the foremost, or "prime," minister of the sovereign.

kitchenmaid—The maid who helped the cook prepare meals, made the cooking fire, etc. Within the household she ranked just above the scullerymaid.

knacker—A man who purchased and slaughtered old horses for the fertilizer, horsehair stuffing, catmeat, etc., that could be made out of them.

knave—In cards the knave was the jack but it was considered lower class to call it that. "He calls the knaves, Jacks, this boy!" says the ever-sweet Estella during one of her early meetings with Pip. "And what coarse hands he has! And what thick boots!"

knickerbocker—A type of men's pants that became fashionable in the latter part of the century. They came down to the knees and bagged out rather fully. They were supposedly named after the illustrations of Dutch merchants with similar pants in Washington Irving's comic history of New York.

knife—The fork was something of a latecomer to the English table as an instrument for getting food into the mouth. The knife was long favored for this purpose instead.

knifeboard—In omnibuses the knifeboard consisted of two benches placed back to back and running the length of the roof.

knight—The lowest of the titled ranks in England. A knight was allowed to put "Sir" in front of his name and his wife was addressed as "Lady ————." The knight ranked below a baronet; the knight, unlike peers and baronets, could not pass the title on to his child. There were various orders of knighthood such as the Order of the Garter and the Bath which gave one a higher social status than did plain knighthood alone.

knock up—To bang on somebody's door in order to wake them up. In inebriated ecstasy at the prospect of marrying Becky Sharp, Joe Sedley confides to Dobbin in the Vauxhall Gardens that "he would marry her next morning at St. George's, Hanover Square; he'd knock up the Archbishop of Canterbury at Lambeth: he would, by Jove! and have him in readiness."

£—The sign for the monetary unit, the pound.

Ladies' Mile—A riding road in Hyde Park for women.

lady—Someone's "lady" in colloquial usage was his wife. As a title, "Lady" was used in the following ways: (1) for the wife of a baronet or knight, e.g., Sir Henry Churchill, "Lady Churchill"; (2) for the wife of a peer below the rank of duke, e.g., the earl of Derby, "Lady Derby"; (3) for the wife of a duke or of a marquis's younger son who had the courtesy title "Lord," e.g., Lord Henry Russell, "Lady Henry Russell"; and (4) for the daughter of a duke, marquis, or earl, e.g., George Russell, the earl of Derby, "Lady Mary Russell."

ladybird—Not a bird at all but what we call the ladybug. Also called a ladyclock.

Lady Day—March 25, the day the Angel Gabriel is said to have announced the birth of Jesus to the Virgin Mary. One of the quarter days. Until 1752, it was used as the start of the year for purposes of official business.

lady's maid—The woman who took care of her mistress's clothes and grooming, dressing her, packing and laying out her clothes, and mending them with small repairs if necessary. She was considered an "upper servant" and could not be fired by the housekeeper. Often better educated than the average maid, she was also resented by the housemaids. Her lot was not necessarily easy; lady's maids were generally supposed

Lady Day.

to be young—when they got too old they might well find themselves out of work on the grounds of age alone.

Lambeth—An area across the Thames from Westminster where Lambeth Palace, the official residence of the archbishop of Canterbury, was located.

Lammas—August 1, the date of an old church festival at which bread from the harvest was sanctified.

lancers—A type of cavalry distinguished by the fact that they indeed carried nine-foot lances made of bamboo. They gave their name to an apparently vigorous form of the quadrille.

landau—A kind of open, fancy carriage with four wheels popular in the first part of the century. It had a hood at each end and two seats opposite each other.

lanthorn—An old-fashioned lantern whose panes were made of animal horn rather than glass. *See* horn.

lappets—Basically, parts of a garment like a cap or a coat that hung down.

lapwing—A member of the plover family that was also sometimes called the "pewit" because of the call it made.

larder—The place where, as a rule, perishable goods like meats were kept in a great house, as opposed to the pantry, which stored nonperishable food. Larder, of course, comes from the same root as the word "lard." *Pride and Prejudice* mentions "such cold meat as an inn larder usually affords."

latititudinarian—Someone who did not believe that the forms of religion made that much difference.

lattice—A window crisscrossed with little bars.

laudanum—Opium in a solution of alcohol.

lawn—A type of fancy linen that was used, inter alia, in the sleeves of bishops of the Church of England as part of their clerical attire.

lay an information—*See* inform.

leader—In a newspaper, it was an editorial. In a team of horses, the leaders were the ones in front (as opposed to the "wheelers"); in a tandem pair, the leader was the horse in front.

leads—A rooftop made out of lead.

league—An old-fashioned, not very precise measurement of distance equal to roughly two to four miles.

Lent—The forty-day period between Ash Wednesday and Easter.

letter of credit—A letter from a banker or similar figure to another banker or businessman, asking him to give money to the person presenting the letter. Used by travelers abroad in the days before American Express.

levee—A formal reception held for the presentation of men to the sovereign or to the sovereign's representative. A "drawing room" was the equivalent ceremony for the presentation of women.

leveret—A young hare.

Liberal—The party that advocated reform and free trade and, together with its opponents, the Conservatives, dominated nineteenth-century English politics. It was the descendant of the Whig party and its most famous leader was Prime Minister William Gladstone.

liberty—The liberty of a city was an area, as in London, that was outside the formal city limits but was still subject to the authority of the mayor and the rest of the corporation.

library—A male preserve in most houses, sometimes serving as the place of business, as when, say, the male head of the house had tenants to receive. Poor Mr. Bennet of the eligible daughters in *Pride and Prejudice* is besieged in his library by his absurd relative Mr. Collins: "In his library he had always been sure of leisure and tranquillity; and though prepared, as he told Elizabeth, to meet with folly and conceit in every other room in the house, he was used to be free from them there."

license to marry—The way to get married if one did not want to get married by the banns. There were three different kinds of licenses by mid-century. The archbishop of Canterbury could provide a "special license" to get married anywhere, any time, and a local minister could grant a much cheaper license that permitted marriage in the parish. Finally, beginning in 1836, one could also get a license to have a simple civil ceremony at the local registrar's office or a ceremony in a nonconformist place of worship.

lieutenant—In the army, he was the officer who assisted a captain in running a company. He and the second lieutenant were known as subalterns. In the navy, lieutenant was also a junior post, the first real position of any authority or importance—it required passing the lieutenant's exam after serving six years as a midshipman. Both the army and navy ranks are to be distinguished from the post of lord lieutenant.

lieutenant colonel—The rank just below colonel. He was often the man who actually ran the regiment that the colonel nominally commanded.

lieutenant general—A subordinate to a general.

Life Guards—Along with the Horse Guards, the Life Guards composed the cavalry units that guarded the royal family.

lifeholder—Someone who leased land for periods of time measured either by his life or the lives of others.

life interest—A life interest in a piece of property was a right to that property which gave the holder the right to enjoy it only during his lifetime, i.e., he typically could not sell or mortgage it, or do anything else that would prevent it from passing intact and unencumbered to the succeeding generation.

life preserver—A wooden truncheon, sometimes with lead in the end of it, used by criminals and sometimes by guardians of the law, too. The ghastly Miss Murdstone is at one point engaged to serve as Dora's protector, leading David Copperfield to observe that "Miss Murdstone, like the pocket-instrument called a life-preserver, was not so much designed for purposes of protection as assault."

light—*See* heavy.

lighter—A barge used to load or unload things from a ship like a collier.

Limehouse—An area in east London around the docks.

line regiment—One of the regular regiments of the army, as opposed to the Household Guards on the one hand or supplementary troops such as the militia on the other.

linen—A generic term for fine shirts and underwear, since linen was the material generally used to make them before cotton became popular. The material had the advantages of being cool and strong. There were different kinds. Lawn and cambric—the latter favored for handkerchiefs—were fine varieties used by the rich. The poor used coarser types of linen.

link—A torch made with pitch that was carried by "linkboys" ahead of carriages to light their way through the city streets at night.

linnet—A brown and gray songbird, except that it turned red in summer.

linsey-woolsey—Material of mixed wool and linen. Also, low-grade wool.

list—The edge of a cloth, from which things like slippers were sometimes made.

Liverpool—A major port for shipping from the West Indies and the non-English side of the Atlantic.

livery—A distinctive uniform worn by servants in the service of a particular master, e.g., the knee breeches and powdered wigs worn by footmen.

livery company—Livery companies were descendants of the guild and craft organizations which had once played a leading role in the economy and governance of London. By the 1800s for the most part they had degenerated into prestigious chowder-and-marching societies with various affluent and distinguished personages among their membership.

livery stable—A place to rent horses.

living—A benefice.

loam—A very fertile kind of soil, made of clay, sand, and rotting vegetation. *Middlemarch* is set in the fictitious county of Loamshire.

lobby—In the Houses of Parliament, it designated first of all, a large hallway where members could receive the general public; this is where, in *Phineas Finn*, the eponymous hero is pursued by a bill collector. In addition, there were two other lobbies adjacent to each House into which members went when they were to be counted in a formal division of the House.

lodge—A house by the gate at the entrance to an estate, often inhabited by someone like a gardener or gamekeeper, who would unlock the gate to let in expected visitors. Depending on the size of the estate, these lodges could be quite a distance from the actual house; in *Mansfield Park*, we are told the lodge gate is a mile from the Bertrams' mansion. In addition, lodges for shooting were often built in the woods for people to stay in while they were out pursuing small animals.

long clothes—The baby clothes with an extraordinary long skirt or train that infants were subjected to during parts of the nineteenth century.

loo—A card game that could theoretically be played by any number, but five to seven was supposedly best. The idea was to win each trick with the high card or highest trump one could play out of the hand of three one was dealt.

lord—A member of the peerage. It was also a form of address, e.g., the earl of Derby was addressed as "Lord Derby." The title was also a "courtesy title" given to eldest sons in the peerage, as if they were real peers, e.g., "Lord Granby," and to younger sons in the peerage, but only with their Christian names and surnames added, e.g., "Lord George Ridley."

lord chancellor—The most powerful member of the legal profession. He had precedence of everyone in the country—including the peerage—except the royal family and the archbishop of Canterbury. He was the chief judge of the Chancery Court, a member of the cabinet, and nominally presided over the House of Lords from his woolsack. His position was originally that of secretary to the king and he remained keeper of the great seal. Sir Thomas More and Cardinal Wolsey, from the era when churchmen still held the post, were perhaps the most famous lord chancellors. Chancellors, like other cabinet members, lost their job when administrations changed; they were usually made peers when they became lord chancellor.

lozenge—The shape a coat of arms was required to assume on the carriage of a spinster or widow, who could not use a coat of arms in the shape of a shield, as a male heir could.

lord lieutenant—Historically the lord high sheriff and the earl were the king's men in each county. In the 1600s, however, a lord lieutenant was designated to command the county's fighting force for the Crown. His powers dwindled thereafter but he remained a significant power within the militia until the 1870s, and he was the man who told the Crown whom in the county it should appoint as justices of the peace. The post was apparently held usually by high-ranking members of the peerage, e.g., the duke of Omnium, Plantagenet Palliser. The marquis of Steyne in *Vanity Fair* is also a lord lieutenant.

Low Church—People like the Evangelicals who didn't believe in ceremony, ritual, hierarchy, and elaborate dress for the clergy in the Church of England.

lucifer matches—An intermediate form in the history of matchdom that succeeded the first "Promethean" matches, circa 1805, which necessitated dipping a treated match into a bottle filled with asbestos and sulfuric acid, which would cause it to ignite, probably rather dramatically. The lucifer match came along around 1830 and was handy because it lit simply by friction. It was followed by the safety match twenty years later which one couldn't ignite unless one had the box, too.

lumbago—Rheumatism of the back.

lumber room—Basically, a place to store old furniture and other similar disused items. Not a repository for lumber in the sense of boards and planks.

lych-gate—A covered gateway at the entrance to a churchyard where people at a funeral rested the coffin while waiting for the minister.

M.C.—*See* master of the ceremonies.

M.F.H.—Master of fox hounds.

M.P.—A member of Parliament.

macaw—A cheerfully colored member of the parrot family.

macintosh—Rubberized waterproof clothing invented by one Charles Macintosh in the 1820s. It was slow to catch on, in part because it originally smelled bad. In the latter part of the century coachmen wore white ones at night so oncoming vehicles could see them and avoid a collision.

madeira—A sweet white wine sometimes prescribed for medicinal purposes. It came from the island of the same name some four hundred miles northwest of the African coast.

magic lantern—Like a slide projector. One lit an oil lamp or candle and placed a mirror behind it so the light would be reflected toward a wall and then passed colored glass slides in front of it to obtain a magnified picture. The slides were supposed to be displayed in sequence to tell a story. To get movement—a twinkling star was one effect—one turned a handle to move the slide; to show wild animals moving through the jungle one pushed a lever to illuminate one slide through another.

magistrate—Another term for a justice of the peace, who was addressed as "Your Worship" by the humble, except that justices were usually only unsalaried county gentry, while magistrates included stipendiary or police magistrates as well, that is, justices of the peace who had been put on salary, usually in big cities, in order to cope with a volume of crime greater than that of rural districts.

maid-of-all-work—She washed the dishes, cooked, swept the floor, emptied the grates, kept the lamps clean, hauled coal, looked after the children, did needlework, made the beds, etc., in those households which could afford only one servant. Usually only young girls were hired for the post. A maid-of-all-work was the maid that the poorest of upwardly mobile families would have when they couldn't afford a real housemaid but needed that one mark of gentility that came from having a servant.

mail coach—Until the railroads, the fastest regularly scheduled transportation in England. The mail coach in 1784 replaced the notoriously inefficient postboys who wandered along, sometimes on horseback, delivering the mail in their own good time. The mail coaches carried not just mail but a limited number of passengers; they were a faster and classier means of transportation than a regular stagecoach and were so good at meeting their schedules that people quite literally set their watches by them in rural areas. The railroads ultimately snatched away all their business.

major—The rank in the army immediately underneath that of lieutenant colonel and superior to that of captain.

major general—Just above a brigadier general and just below a lieutenant general.

malt—Barley put in water (so that it would sprout) and then heated up, to be used in making beer.

mangel-wurzel—Also called the mangold. A root crop popularized in the 1800s as a source of winter fodder for livestock. The crop produced more edible matter per acre than turnips or swedes did but was difficult to grow in areas colder than southern England.

mangle—The hand-operated clothes presser of the nineteenth century. One put a piece of clothing between two cylinders placed on top of each other and then turned the crank, which drew the garment in between them, and the mangle flattened it.

man-of-war—A ship, particularly a big one, that was built or used for warfare.

manor—Certain land after the Norman invasion was granted by the king to men, "lords of the manor," to be farmed by their tenants, the local villagers.

man-traps—They were steel traps like those used for catching animals, except these were big—some weighed up to eighty pounds—and were used by landowners with game on their property to catch poachers, which they often did, sometimes (some traps had steel teeth) inflicting considerable injury in the process. They were outlawed in 1827.

mantua-maker—A term for a dressmaker based on the name of an old-fashioned type of gown. By the middle of the century a somewhat archaic usage.

marchioness—The name given to the wife or widow of a marquis or to a woman granted the status of marchioness in her own right.

marines—The Royal Marines. They were soldiers who kept order aboard naval vessels and participated in the hand-to-hand shipboard fighting in naval battles.

marine store shop—Not unlike a rag-and-bone shop except it tended to trade more in marine goods, often having customers, e.g., sailors, in waterfront areas.

market day—The day on which markets were held in a locality, i.e., when people might go into town to sell their pigs and stock up on what they needed, especially in rural areas where stores were few and far between.

market town—Any town that regularly held a market.

marl—A type of soil that contained clay and could be used as fertilizer.

marquis—The second highest rank in the peerage, coming just below a duke. One was known as the "marquis of ——" and addressed formally as "Lord ——." The plural could be either "marquises" or "marquesses."

Martin's Day—Martinmas, November 11. Martin's summer was the term used for a period of terrific weather in late autumn, corresponding to the American Indian summer.

master—A term with several meanings. First, a master was a skilled craftsman who had passed the journeyman stage and consequently worked for no one but himself and was entitled to train apprentices and hire journeymen. Second, the term referred to a teacher at a school. Third, until 1814 the rank of commander in the Royal Navy was known as master and commander. Fourth, master was the title given to the heads of certain colleges at Oxford and Cambridge. Finally, the man who ran the workhouse was called its master.

master of fox hounds—Also called master of hounds. The man who organized and oversaw the fox hunting of a particular pack. To be distinguished from the huntsman.

master of the ceremonies—The man at public balls and assemblies in charge of organizing the dances, introducing people to one another, and in general supervising the goings-on. Sometimes abbreviated M.C. The most celebrated M.C. was probably Beau Nash at Bath.

mastiff—A great big watchdog with floppy ears and a big head.

May Day—May 1. The day on which to go out in the woods just before dawn with one's sweetheart and, supposedly, pick branches and garlands with which to decorate the maypole tree that graced the village green for the occasion. One then danced around the maypole.

Mayfair—The fanciest residential area of London, about a half a mile square in size. It was located in the West End and bounded by Oxford Street on the north, Bond Street on the east, Piccadilly on the south, and Hyde Park on the west. Within it were located, inter alia, Pall Mall and Grosvenor and Berkeley Squares. The district was so named because of an annual fair held there at one time each May.

mayor—The senior official in a town, e.g., Casterbridge, frequently selected from among the aldermen or councilors. He served for a year and generally acted as a magistrate as well. It is presumably in recognition of his *having* so served as magistrate that ex-mayor Henchard is pressed into service to hear the case of the old woman whose tale of his wifeselling proves his undoing.

mead—A drink made by putting yeast into a mix of honey and water.

mechanic—Any skilled craftsman who worked with his hands.

meet—The gathering at the beginning of a day's fox hunting of the hunters and hounds.

meeting house—Church of England services were always held in a church or a cathedral. Religious meetings of Dissenters customarily occured in a "chapel" or a "meeting house."

member—A member of Parliament.

merchantman—A nonmilitary ship.

merino—A superior kind of wool derived from a sheep brought from Spain to England in the 1700s.

Methodism—A popular, lower-middle-class nonconformist Protestant sect that was a product of the teachings of John Wesley. It stressed Bible reading, large, open-air meetings, and hymn singing (from whence the latter custom worked its way into Church of England services) and forbade drinking, gambling and similar wicked activities.

mews—Mew comes from the Latin *mutare*, meaning "to change," and the mews were the place in London where the king's hawks were at one time confined while they molted or "changed." The royal stables then replaced the hawks' lair and thereafter any lane or open area where a group of stables was situated was referred to as a mews.

mezzotint—A way of scraping steel or copper plates to make them rough. Parts were then scraped to provide what would be the light parts in the finished print.

Michaelmas—The feast of St. Michael, a leader of the angels and their army. "And there was war in heaven: Michael and his angels fought against the dragon" (Rev. xii). This feast was held on September 29 and was one of the quarter days. Michaelmas term was a law term and also a term at Oxford and at Cambridge.

Middlesex—The name of the county in which London north of the Thames was located. (South lay the county of Surrey.)

Middle Temple—*See* Inns of Court.

midshipman—The lowest rung of the ladder in the officer class of the British navy. A midshipman was a boy between the ages of eleven and fifteen who was taken on board a vessel, usually through his family's knowing the captain or through the exertion of some other kind of influence. The boy was then set to learn the ways of the navy for the next six years. At the end of that time he was eligible to take the exam for lieutenant. Those who failed could—and often did—remain midshipman literally for decades. Naturally, the position was not very impressive to the girls; in *Mansfield Park* Fanny Price's brother laments in this connection, "One might as well be nothing as a midshipman."

Midsummer Day—It fell on June 24, which was also the feast of John the Baptist. It was a quarter day, too. The wild, magical atmosphere we associate with it from *A Midsummer Night's Dream* probably has as much if not more to do with the practices and customs of May Day.

militia—An organization that had its roots in the obligation of all citizens in feudal days to come to the military aid of their sovereign. By the early 1800s it was a defensive force that was selected by lottery from the men in each parish (one could buy one's way out by hiring a substitute, though). It trained for twenty-eight days a year and was "embodied," or called up, when there was a threat of invasion, something that seemed a real possibility during the war with Napoleon. After Napoleon's defeat, the militia were quiescent until a brief movement to reactivate them in the fifties was made when Napoleon III unnerved the English in a similar fashion. The militia could not be sent out of England to fight without their consent and the consent of Parliament.

milliner—A maker of women's hats and sometimes other items of dress.

milch cow—One that was giving milk.

ministry—The ministry of a given "government" was composed of the cabinet plus another thirty-five or so men who occupied positions of responsibility in the chief executive departments, such as junior lords of the treasury.

minor canon—One who helped conduct the choir at a cathedral. Unlike other canons, he did not belong to the cathedral chapter.

minute—A memorandum from a government department ordering something to be done.

miss—When used with only the surname in talking about one of several sisters, it meant the eldest.

mister—Used of a medical man, it generally meant a surgeon or apothecary. A physician was usually "Dr."

mittens—These were popular items for ladies. Unlike contemporary mittens for cold days outdoors, these were cut off part way along the fingers, leaving the tips bare, and extended up the the arm toward the elbow. They seem to have been made frequently of lace or net.

mizzle—A word meaning to depart. It also meant to drizzle.

mobcap—An ugly piece of indoor headgear for women that was standard, at least in the earlier part of the century. "I mean a cap, much more common than now," says David Copperfield in describing his aunt's dress, "with sidepieces fastening under the chin."

mock turtle—Turtle soup and flesh became very popular in England at the beginning of the century. So popular that those who couldn't afford it decided they wanted at least an imitation—hence "mock turtle" was born. It was usually made out of a calf's head.

monitor—Under certain systems of elementary education, particularly in the national schools, a monitor was appointed by the teacher to keep order and—in addition—teach the younger pupils. This supposedly freed the teacher up for other duties in what was billed as a tremendous economy—under one version of the system, one teacher would thus purportedly be able to instruct 500 students.

Monument—The Monument was a 200-foot high tower located in London just south of London Bridge, designed by Christopher Wren in commemoration of the Great Fire of 1666 and the subsequent rebuilding of London.

moor—A wild, rather desolate area like the part of Yorkshire where *Wuthering Heights* is set. Frequently covered with heather or heath and, in fact, not terribly different from the heath that turns up in Thomas Hardy's novels, except that "moor" was a term more likely to be used in the north of England or with reference to boggy or marshy areas. A moor was also an area kept specifically for shooting game like grouse, generally found in northern England or Scotland.

morning—A term that in Jane Austen's day often meant the period of time between breakfast and dinner, a meal which was often not consumed until three or four in the afternoon. The usage survived in the term "morning calls," those ceremonial visits paid by the genteel to ladies "at home" in their drawing rooms between 3 P.M. and 5 P.M.

Morning Post—The London paper that chronicled the goings-on of the fashionable world and the court.

morning room—A place used by a family as a sitting room in the morning.

morocco—Goatskin, used in the 1800s to cover books. It was often prepared with dog excrement or "pure" that was collected off the London streets daily by the very poor. Sometimes imitation leather made from sheep was also called morocco.

Most Reverend—Form of address to an archbishop.

muck—To us, the term generally designates some kind of heavy, unpleasantly clinging mud. Actually, muck was sheep or cattle dung, a mainstay, of course, of farming in the days before artificial fertilizer.

Mudie's—The famous circulating library of the mid-century. One paid a sum to belong and then could borrow best sellers rather than having to buy them.

Morning room, Windsor Castle.

muff—A popular women's accessory among the upper and middle classes for keeping the hands warm.

muffin man—A street vendor known for the bell he carried. At the unruly Eatanswill elections in *Pickwick* the mayor loftily calls for silence and instructs the crier to call for it, too. "In obedience to this command the crier performed another concerto on the bell, whereupon a gentleman in the crowd called out 'muffins'; which occasioned another laugh."

mull—To mull wine or another beverage was to stick a red-hot poker into it after it had had sweetening and spices added.

muslin—One of the finest kinds of cotton. It was very thin and was the favorite material for dresses in Jane Austen's day. The more daring girls wore them with damped down chemises underneath. It was very popular for the first few decades of the century.

mute—A person hired to come to a funeral and mourn.

mutton—The flesh of sheep. Sheep, it should be emphasized, are grown-up lamb. Hence their meat was apt not to be as tender as lamb.

My Lord—The correct form of address to bishops of the Church of England and any peer below the rank of duke, as well as a lord mayor and certain judges.

nankeen—A yellowish kind of cotton originally made in China or imitations of it. Named after the port of Nanking in China.

national school—A misleading term. The name national schools makes them sound like government institutions but they were actually schools set up by the Church of England's National Society for Promoting the Education of the Poor in the Principles of the Established Church throughout England and Wales that was founded in 1811, their purpose being to teach children to read the Bible. Along the way, however, the society's schools became the main source of primary education for the lower classes in England and started receiving government subsidies in the 1830s. Thereafter they were for many years the almost exclusive providers of education for those who were not well-to-do. Tess Durbeyfield, we are told, attended a national school and passed her "standards," which is one reason she no longer speaks only the dialect.

nave—The main, lengthwise axis of the church, along which the congregation entered, facing the altar. The eastern end of the nave was called the chancel.

navy list—The list of officers in the navy.

navvy—The laborers who worked on the building of the canals in the early 1800s were called inland navigators. When they later went to work on the railroads, the nickname "navvy" stuck. They were the most skilled of railroad workers and tackled the roughest and most dangerous jobs. They also had a reputation as somewhat colorful dressers.

negus—Colonel Francis Negus cooked up this drink, which consisted of sugar mixed with water and a wine such as sherry or port. Apparently, a popular drink for balls and dances.

net—A favorite material for making mittens, it looked like what it sounds like, i.e., a net of tiny ropes. Net was used in various parts of dress and ladies seemed to have "worked" at it in their spare time.

newel—The central column around which a circular staircase wound. The newel *post* was the post at the bottom of the stairs from which a banister ascended.

Newgate Prison—For years the main (and perhaps most formidable) prison in London, the site of public executions and the place where condemned criminals, e.g., Fagin in *Oliver Twist*, spent their last hours. It connected with the Old Bailey by a passageway, and on the Sundays before executions it was the custom in the early part of the century for a sermon to be preached in the prison chapel at which the condemned was seated next to his coffin, the public—until 1826—being charged a shilling a head to attend this edifying spectacle.

Newgate Calendar—In the late 1700s biographies of some of Newgate Prison's more notorious inmates began to appear. Newgate Calendar was the name given to their issuance in collected form.

Making net, or netting.

nightjar—The "goatsucker," a night bird of somewhat sinister reputation and appearance—under one name it was known as the "lich" or "corpse" bird—that made a kind of whirring sound.

nob—Someone with a good deal of status. Used often in conjunction with "snob," in the sense snob initially had of someone of *no* status or pretensions.

nobility—A somewhat loose term, but used generally to refer to the peerage, sometimes with a correlative reference to the "gentry."

"nolo episcopari"—Literally, "I do not want to become a bishop" When chosen bishop one was supposed to make this reply at least twice, and the post was supposed to be pressed upon one at least three times. The third time one was supposed to keep one's mouth shut and accept the post unless one really did *not* want the job in which case one said "nolo episcopari" a third time and was not made a bishop.

nonconformists—The nonconformists were the Protestant sects like the Quakers and the Unitarians and the Baptists and the Methodists outside the Church of England who did not "conform" to the teachings of the Church of England. They could not hold office in a borough until 1828, they could not get an Oxford or Cambridge degree until the 1850s and they had to pay local church rates to support the local Church of England parish church's upkeep even in the 1860s. Sometimes, the term was used as a synonym for "Dissenters," although a distinction between the two is sometimes made on the grounds that nonconformists also sought the disestablishment of the Church of England.

normal school—One that trained teachers.

note of hand—A promissory note.

nullifidian—A nonbeliever.

nursemaid—A girl, usually in her teens, hired to look after the young children in a household, dressing them, feeding them, exercising them, and so forth. Often believed to be a target for amorous policemen or soldiers since nursemaids alone of female servants were assured of getting out of the house each day when they took their young charges for an airing in the park.

nursery—A special room in well-to-do homes in which children from infancy until the age of about three or four played and ate. Jane Eyre sleeps there—age ten—at the beginning of her eponymous novel. "In first-rate homes," said a contemporary source, "a room may be attached, to serve as a place for cooking the babies' food, and washing and drying their clothes, and washing and bathing all the children."

oakum—The tarred strands of which ropes were composed. In prisons it was deemed a suitably mindless and pointless punishment to put people to work picking oakum apart, which, given its tarry condition, was not such an easy task. The resulting substance would then theoretically be used to caulk ships, except that after a certain point in the 1800s ships were no longer caulked this way. The prison task went on anyway. Workhouses also favored this endeavor—Oliver Twist is set to work in the workhouse picking oakum.

oatcake—In Scotland, Ireland, and the northern parts of England, one is not surprised that of the corns, wheat and barley did the poorest while oats did the best. Consequently, Mr. Lockwood finds in the kitchen parlor "a frame of wood laden with oatcakes" when he enters Wuthering Heights.

oil light—Whale oil was used for street lighting in London until the early 1800s, when it began to be replaced by coal gas. Oil lights were apparently less bright than gas.

oilskin—A cloth treated with oil to make it waterproof. Used as floor covering or raingear.

offices—The kitchen or stables or other parts of a large house where the work of the household was done—as opposed to the bedrooms, dining room, etc., lived in by the family.

Old—*See* Old Style.

Old Bailey—*See* bailey.

Old Style—The way of reckoning dates before 1752, when the English switched from the Julian to the Gregorian calendar and permanently "lost" eleven days. (Thursday, September 14, 1752, came the day after Wednesday, September 2, 1752.) Nothing else changed, e.g., the day of the year on which a quarter day fell. Thus, Lady Day would have fallen on March 25 both in 1751 and in 1753. But when *Tess of the d'Urbervilles* makes reference to "Old Lady Day," occurring in the 1890s it means April 6 under the *New* Style, i.e., where the *Old* Style March 25 would fall *plus* the eleven days needed to bring it into line with *New* Style reckoning.

ombre—An old-fashioned (even in 1800) card game played by three players. Only forty cards were used; the 8s, 9s, and 10s were omitted from play.

omnibus—The forerunner of the bus, only it was pulled by horses. The first one appeared in London in 1829 and soon there were large numbers of them as the city grew and commuters found them a convenient way to get around. They ran fixed routes, were generally small and cramped inside, and had floors strewn with hay. Their conductors were known colloquially as "cads." The first ones carried about twenty-two passengers; by the 1880s a circular staircase leading up to the roof had been added, and they carried twelve inside and fourteen on top. There were about 1,500 omnibuses in London by 1850.

operative—A factory or mill worker.

opium—A bitter-tasting, pain-killing drug made out of the juice of poppies.

Opposition—The party that was *not* running the national government at the moment. Opposition members sat on benches across the aisle in the House of Commons from the members of the party in power.

orange girl, orange woman—Among the poorest of the London street sellers, they were often young girls. The capital required to get started was very little—fifty oranges could be bought in the early 1860s for 15*d.* to 18*d.* Oranges were more of a treat then than now—the price went up a good deal at Christmas and in May during the peak season for fairs and races.

orderly—A military term. The orderly was a private or a noncommissioned officer who carried messages for a higher officer.

orders—To take orders was to become a clergyman in the Church of England. The church consisted of three orders—deacons, priests, and bishops.

ordinary—A place to eat where meals at a fixed price were served.

oriel—A sort of bay window on the upper floor of a building.

ormolu—From the French word for gold. A piece of furniture or similar item made to look like gold through the use of gold leaf or a substance resembling gold.

osier—A willow tree whose twigs or branches could be woven into baskets.

ostler—Also spelled "hostler," which see.

ottoman—Not usually a footstool but rather a proto sofa from the early 1800s that was like an upholstered bench, generally with no arms or back.

ouzel—The name of two different birds. The ring ouzel was a blackbird with white on its chest that frequented moors and mountain areas. The water ouzel was a wren that liked mountain brooks and had coloring similar to the ring ouzel.

out—*See* come out.

outdoor relief—The name given to any official means of helping the poor (Christmas turkeys, a dole, etc.) that kept them from becoming workhouse inmates, i.e., that kept them *out*side the *doors* of the workhouse. The most controversial outdoor relief was the so-called Speenhamland system, where the poorhouse authorities paid the difference between local farm wages and a living wage. Outcry against this resulted in the oppressive Poor Law of 1834 to which Oliver Twist was subjected.

outhouse—Any detached building that was part of a complex surrounding a dwelling.

outside—An outside was someone who rode on the outside of a stagecoach, which was generally cheaper than the inside, but, of course, exposed to the elements.

overseers—Short for overseers of the poor. These were the people in a parish chosen annually by the justice of the peace to look after the poor. The New Poor Law of 1834 replaced them with a board of guardians, e.g., the "board" before which poor Oliver Twist is brought at the beginning of his adventures.

Oxford Movement—A movement at Oxford University in the 1830s and 1840s led by John Keble and E.B. Pusey, among others, who published religious tracts (the movement was also called the Tractarian Movement) setting forth their view of the need for the church to return to first, i.e., semi-Catholic, principles. John Henry Newman *did* become a Catholic subsequently. They were the epitome of High Church. Oxford specialized in the training of Tory clergy during this period—it was not an illogical place for such a movement to originate.

packet—A ship carrying mail regularly from one place to another and also, sometimes, passengers.

packman—A peddler, usually carrying ladies' goods like linen and cotton in his pack.

paddock—A horse pasture. Also, in racing, a place where the horses and their jockeys gathered prior to the race.

page—A boy hired to run errands and answer the door and serve generally as a junior-grade footman.

palace—The name given to the residence of a bishop of the Church of England. The archbishop of Canterbury lived in Lambeth Palace, across the Thames from Westminster.

Pall Mall—A fancy street in the West End of London, notable for being the site of many fashionable clubs. It was named after a French game resembling croquet that was at one time played on Pall Mall.

palsy—Any kind of paralysis, including those like Parkinson's, which could produce shaking.

panels—The square or rectangular pieces of raised or sunken wood set in an old-fashioned wall.

pannier—A large round basket that was slung on either side of a horse to carry goods to market.

pannikin—A little metal drinking cup, usually made of iron.

pantalettes—Undergarments in the form of long pants worn mostly by little girls from the 1820s through the 1850s, the frilled bottoms of the pants descending below the level of skirt and petticoats so as to be visible.

pantaloon—The name for the pants that were worn, beginning in the early 1800s, in competition first with breeches and then with tights. The name was later shortened in the United States to pants.

pantomime—A favorite theatrical diversion for children, especially at Christmas. It combined music, dancing, drama, and all sorts of things, with elaborate costumes, and at the end there was always a broad comic routine involving Harlequin, Columbine, the old man (Pantaloon), and the clown.

pantry—A place for storing food that wouldn't go bad rapidly. The butler's pantry was the place where the "plate" was kept, often in a locked safe.

paraphernalia—Things like jewelry and clothing. Virtually alone of a woman's possessions, they did *not* become her husband's property when she married.

parish—The local unit of ecclesiastical jurisdiction in the Church of England. Also—sometimes coterminous with this religious unit and sometimes not—a unit of local government administration dating back at least to Elizabethan days whose officials were responsible to the local justice of the peace for relief of the poor, maintaining law and order, keeping the local roads repaired, and seeing that church property was kept up. The parish officials charged with these duties were the constable, the overseers of the poor, the surveyor of highways, and the churchwardens. There was generally a parish workhouse, too; *Oliver Twist* was actually subtitled *The Parish Boy's Progress*. To be "on the parish" meant to need poor relief.

park—The term park originally denoted a fenced-in area containing deer. By the early 1800s it meant an enclosed area—sometimes several square miles in extent—with trees and lawns and sometimes sheep or deer, kept primarily for purposes of the sublime view and grandeur rather than profit or cultivation. *Mansfield Park* is, of course, the story of one such environment, where, as sometimes happened, the name was given to the entire estate. Parks were favorites of the gentry. Some of their estates, e.g., Thrushcross Grange, incorporated a park without its being reflected in the name of the estate.

Park Lane—The ritziest street address in London. Park Lane was the street in Mayfair that ran along the eastern border of Hyde Park.

Parliament—The House of Commons and the House of Lords.

parlor—The formal or "best" room in a modest home. In a grander home, it seems to have been either a sitting room or a formal room for company, a little more impressive than a sitting room, perhaps not as grand as a drawing room. In a tavern, the parlor as compared with the taproom was usually the room for the more upper-class traveler or drinker.

parlormaid—A sort of substitute for the butler, she was hired in families that couldn't afford or didn't want such a male servant. Often hired for her appearance—and therefore reputedly quite pretty. She answered the door and waited on table as a butler would have in a grander household.

parson—Another name, sometimes affectionate or mildly contemptuous, for the local parish rector or vicar. Also, a dissenting or nonconformist cleric.

parterre—An area in a garden with different-size plots of flowers connected by various walkways and paths.

pasteboard—Basically cardboard. Calling cards were made from it, and pasteboard was sometimes used as a slang term for visiting card.

pastille—A little roll that could be set afire to disinfect or fumigate a room. Also a small sweet lozengelike object, sometimes medicinal in nature.

pastor—A minister.

pastry cook—A shop that sold pastries, but it also often had tables at which customers could eat ices and sip wine as well or have soups and other light food.

patent—The monarch sometimes gave something to one of his subjects with a "letter patent," that is, a letter that was open, available for the whole world to see, as opposed to a "closed" letter. Hence, a "patent of nobility" was a royal grant of noble status of which the whole kingdom was made aware. The "patent" of an invention was the grant of a right to an invention.

patience—The card game of solitaire.

patron—A person who had the right to appoint a clergyman to a living.

pattens—What women wore on their shoes in Jane Austen's day to keep them from getting muddy or wet in the great outdoors. Pattens were little circular rings strapped on under the shoes to raise the foot up a few inches out of the mud or slush. They ceased to be fashionable with the quality by mid-century, but continued to be used in the country. There are not infrequent references to the racket they could make on city pavements when it was wet out. David Copperfield is transported by an evening at the theater and exits only to find he has "come from the clouds, where I had been leading a romantic life for ages, to a bawling, splashing, link-lighted, umbrella-struggling, hackney-coach-jostling, patten-clinking, muddy, miserable world." In 1850, Kensington Gardens was apparently off-limits to "servants in livery, women in pattens or dogs."

peck—A measurement of dry goods equal to a quarter of a bushel or to two gallons.

Peel—Sir Robert Peel. As home secretary he came up with the "bobbies" or "peelers," i.e., the London police force. As Tory prime minister he saw to the repeal of the Corn Laws. He was killed in a freak accident when he was thrown from his horse.

Peeler—The nickname given the members of the new Metropolitan Police Force (Scotland Yard and all that) which replaced the old Bow Street Runners. They were called peelers because they were founded in 1829 by Sir Robert Peel. For the same reason, they were also called bobbies.

peer—A nobleman, that is, a duke, marquis, earl, viscount, or baron, all such titles being hereditary and entitling the owner to a seat in the House of Lords.

peeress—Either the wife of a peer or a woman who had noble status in her own right.

pegtop—A style of men's trousers popular around the middle of the century. It was very broad at the hips and narrow at the feet, like the children's spinning pegtop toy. The trousers were usually fastened under the shoes with straps.

pelerine—A kind of collar that was like a cape, with hanging ends in front, worn by women.

pelisse—A kind of overcoat worn by women over the thin frocks of the early 1800s, buttoning in front and usually about three-quarter length.

Pembroke—A four-legged table with two sides that could be swung up and placed on additional legs.

pence—The plural of penny, usually used to mean the amount of pennies, as in "that will cost you 3 shillings 4 pence," whereas the actual physical units of payment were called "pennies," as in "he dropped six pennies down the drain." A shilling consisted of 12 pence, a pound of 240 pence.

Peninsular—Relating to the Peninsular War, the campaign fought by the duke of Wellington from 1808–14 in Spain and Portugal to drive Napoleon out of that peninsula. Widely seen as a major turning point in the Napoleonic Wars, and for years the pride of the old veterans who had served there.

pensioner—An ex-soldier or sailor. In-pensioners were old veterans resident in the Royal Hospital at Chelsea (army) or Greenwich (navy), while out-pensioners were veterans lacking such an official residence. At Cambridge University, pensioner had an altogether different meaning, referring to a nonscholarship student.

perpetual curate—A parish clergyman basically equivalent to a vicar. To be distinguished from an ordinary curate, who did not have his own parish.

petticoat—An undergarment worn by women in the 1800s over the basic underwear—the shift or chemise—and under the dress, sometimes, as in the middle of the century, in several different layers. At times petticoats were considered supplementary skirts rather than underwear, and it was not considered scandalous for them to be seen. Later on, at mid-century before the cage crinoline came in, sometimes as many as five or six were worn at a time.

petty sessions—The periodic meetings between a local justice of the peace and one or more of his counterparts from elsewhere in the county to dispense justice in relatively minor matters.

pewter—A material made of tin and lead much favored for mugs and dishes by the poor.

phaeton—Basically, any light, four-wheel carriage with open sides drawn by one or two horses. Sometimes, the term was applied to a carriage that was driven by its owner rather than by a coachman.

phial—A vial.

physic—Drugs. To "take physic" was to take drugs the "physician" had prescribed.

physician—The most prestigious member of the medical profession in the early part of the century, the physician dealt only in internal disorders, i.e., those things for which he could prescribe physic, as opposed to wounds, falls from horses and other things. For these the less socially prominent surgeon would be called in. There was an abundance of physicians in London, while other kinds of medical men (such as surgeons) were more likely to practice in the countryside. Physicians were generally called "Dr." while a surgeon was simply "Mr."

pianoforte—The piano. Many young ladies were taught to play it, music being thought to be a suitable feminine accomplishment, although it was not considered gentlemanly for a man to know how to play. When he first encounters Jane Eyre, Rochester with his customary urbanity asks her to play and remarks with a subsequent snarl, "You play a *little*, I see; like any other English schoolgirl." There were two subspecies of uprights, called the cottage piano (diagonal strings) and the cabinet piano (vertical strings).

Piccadilly—A long, fancy street in the West End, said to have been named after a tailor whose shop there in the 1600s manufactured high ruff collars called piccadillies.

pier glass—A piece of ornamentation popular in the early part of the century that consisted of a long mirror placed in between two windows.

pigeoncote—*See* dovecote.

pillar letter box—Cylindrical mailboxes that came into use in the 1850s. Anthony Trollope, a post office employee in addition to being a writer, claimed to have invented them.

pillion—A cushion or saddle for women riding on a horse behind someone. At the beginning of *Silas Marner* we are told how social events were not brief, one-evening affairs in the days of long and arduous travel: "When ladies had packed up their best gowns and top-knots in band-boxes, and had incurred the risk of fording streams on pillions with their precious burden in rainy or snowy weather, when there was no knowing how high the water would rise, it was not to be supposed that they looked forward to a brief pleasure."

pinafore—Supposedly derived from "pin" and "before," since it was a white coverall or apron that was at one time actually pinned over a dress in the front to keep it from getting dirty. These are the horribly proper white frilly aprons that all solemn little girls in late Victorian photographs are wearing over their dark dresses as they stare dubiously into the camera.

pinchbeck—Phony or cheap.

pin money—An allowance given to a woman upon her marriage—frequently bargained for explicitly as part of the marriage settlement between the families of a prospective husband and wife—to be spent on small household items or for personal adornment.

pinner—Dialect for "pinafore."

pint pot—So called because that was what it held. Usually for beer.

pip—A seed, or else one of the marks, e.g., a club, heart, etc., on a playing card, showing what suit and number it was.

pipe—Wine was sometimes sold by the pipe, which was a unit of 105 gallons.

pipe clay—Clay used for making pipes. Also used for cleaning pants in the army, whence the term "pipe clay" acquired the military meaning of making something spic and span.

pipkin—A little clay dish of some kind.

pippin—An apple grown from seeds or pips, and not from grafts.

piquet (also spelled "picquet")—A card game for two people played with thirty-two cards and no 2s, 3s, 4s, 5s, or 6s , with the players trying to obtain the highest number of cards of one suit, a flush, three or four of a kind, and so forth.

pitch and toss—A game where everyone threw a coin at a particular target. The person whose coin landed closest then threw all the coins up and got to keep the ones that came down "heads." Then the person whose coin was second closest did the same with the coins that were left, and so on until no coins were left.

plantation—Any area where trees had been planted.

plate—Silverware. In the days when most personal property consisted either of land or tangible objects such as carriages or horses, and few people owned stocks or bonds, plate was especially valued. It was the butler's job to look after it and he sometimes kept it in a safe and slept in the same room with it. When families left London, they sometimes left their plate in the custody of their banker.

pleurisy—An inflammation of two sacs in the chest called the pleura that could produce a hacking cough or sometimes a sharp pain.

Plough Monday—The first Monday after Twelfth Day and traditionally the day on which the new agricultural season was supposed to begin. Indeed, ploughing on "good" days in late autumn or early winter was desirable for a spring wheat crop. For Plough Monday, ploughboys blackened their faces and went through the village with their plows as the villagers called out "Speed-the-plough."

plums—There were real plums like damsons in England in the 1800s but they were *not* put into the famous Christmas plum puddings. The "plums" in Christmas plum puddings were raisins. Plum cake was also made with raisins. At other times of the year, confusingly, real plums might be used for some desserts like plum pudding.

pluralist—In the good old days one could hold more than one benefice or living in the Church of England, a curate often being retained to discharge one's duties in the parish or parishes where one was nonresident. In 1838 legislation was passed to put an end to this practice.

poachers—The men who tried to take game from the property of private landowners. They were the targets of various harsh Game Laws which made some poaching punishable by transportation. Until 1827 landowners were legally permitted to have their gamekeepers set up mantraps and spring guns to catch, kill, or maim poachers.

pocket borough—The name given to a parliamentary borough that was said to be so much under the control of some powerful individual that it was "in his pocket." The Reform Bill of 1832 was meant to outlaw pocket boroughs.

pocket pistol—A flask for alcohol carried in the pocket.

pole—The long bar projecting from the front of a carriage to which the horses of a team of two or more were attached on either side. On single-horse vehicles the horse was constrained by the shaft on either side of him.

police court—A local, "street" court in London run by a police magistrate (in effect, a paid justice of the peace) that could convict people for minor offenses without a trial, or, in the case of more serious offenses, direct that they be handed over to the Old Bailey for trial.

police magistrate—The name given to justices of the peace in London who were made permanent, salaried officials, beginning in 1792, to cope with the growing amount of crime in the city. Until 1839 they supervised local constables from their "police office" as well as trying certain offenses there. After 1839 control of the police was taken from them, and their sole function was judging.

police office—Before the advent of the bobbies in 1829, a police office was one of the local offices headed by police magistrates in London who heard cases and directed the work of the constables attached to that office. After 1839, the constables were put in separate local police offices or stations under the control of Scotland Yard, while the judging by the magistrates continued in what were now called police courts.

polka—A dance from Czechoslovakia that became popular in fashionable English society by mid-century. The basic rhythm was *one-two-three-AND*. One version of its origins—*polka* means "half" in Czech—is that it was invented by a farmgirl in a very small room where she could only take half steps.

pollard—A tree cut off above the bole so that it would grow in straight, thin shoots all around the area where it had been lopped off. This was frequently done to willows near rivers, apparently to obtain willow branches for making baskets and other wicker items.

pomade—A kind of perfumed hair ointment, originally, apparently, made partly from apples.

pony—Slang for £25.

pony carriage—Ponies were frequently driven by ladies or by children, who were supposed to be incapable of managing horses. In the original, nonoptimistic ending of *Great Expectations*, which Bulwer-Lytton persuaded Dickens to change, Pip meets Estella driving down Piccadilly at the helm of her pony carriage.

poorhouse—The name for publicly supported homes for the destitute, especially in the era before the workhouse began to replace it. Places of residence for the poor funded by *private* monies were called almshouses.

Poor Law—The original Poor Law dated from Elizabethan days and called for the overseers of the poor in each parish to provide relief for the poor, the sick, the aged and needy children. The New Poor Law of 1834 aimed at making the workhouses in which the poor were sometimes lodged extremely unattractive to what it imagined to be hordes of lazy and undeserving poor. The consequent regimentation and grimness of life inside the workhouse soon became such as to make them a byword among the poor for misery. Under this new system, a central board of commissioners in London oversaw the work of local, elected boards of guardians that took the place of the overseers.

poplin—A material that, like muslin, was popular for thin dresses at the beginning of the century. It was made of silk and worsted.

porch—A building entrance that consisted of a covered passageway. "Hareton, drive these dozen sheep into the barn porch," Heathcliff orders at the start of *Wuthering Heights*. It most generally turns up in references to parish churches, where it was often on the south, nonwindy side. "Porch" in this sense bears no relation to the wide, outside area for relaxing in the United States for private houses.

porridge—A concoction of oatmeal and either milk or water, made by boiling the dry food in the liquid.

porringer—A bowl or similar container out of which to eat porridge or something equally liquid and hot.

port—A favorite after-dinner drink of the gentlemen when the ladies had retired to the drawing room after dinner. A sweetish Portuguese red wine.

porter—There were two kinds of porters. First, there were the ones who carried things around, as the ticket porters did in London. They were called ticket porters because they were originally specially licensed, or ticketed, to do so. And then there were the men who slumbered in little gatehouses—basically doormen—at the entrances to various institutions such as the Inns of Court or Sue Bridehead's training college at Melchester. The kind of dark beer that was favored by the former sort of porter acquired its name from them. It looked formidable but was not very strong.

portmanteau—A traveling bag.

post—Originally the system by which horses for the king's journeys and mail were provided. Then it was realized that postboys could carry the mail for everyone else, too, which they began to do. In addition, the relays of horses used to provide fresh nags for postal carriers were rented out to members of the public who, say, did not want to take their own horses all the way from Bath to London. This renting of horses and/or carriages for long journeys split off from the mail service but, confusingly, also continued to be called the post. It was something only the well-off could afford; the pompous Lady Catherine de Bourgh in *Pride and Prejudice* travels post. One could substitute one's own chariot for the rental post chaise, but, in any case, one rented the horses which would have to be changed at intervals along the way. They were steered by postillions, men who rode directly on one or more of the horses.

postboy—The term given to the often lackadaisical boys who delivered the mail on foot or on horseback in the days before the crackerjack express mail coaches came along in 1784. The term was also applied to the postillions—usually extraordinarily superannuated for "boys"—who rode post-horses hired by travelers.

post captain—In the early 1800s, the title was used to distinguish captains in the Royal Navy who held permanent positions as captain on ships of at least twenty guns both from acting captains and from officers of lesser rank such as commanders who might captain a vessel of inferior size.

post chaise—A small, closed carriage used for traveling post.

postern—A back entrance or back way in.

postillion—Rich people who did not want to drive their own carriages over a long distance had two choices. They could hire a coachman, who drove the carriage from his seat thereon, or they could use a postillion, who actually rode one of the horses in order to direct the team. Post-horses were invariably ridden by postillions; the men sported red or blue jackets, pants, and colored top boots.

post-obit—From the Latin words for "after" and "death". A post-obit was a kind of bond, or promise to pay, wherein one agreed to pay someone money upon the death of someone else from whom one was expecting to inherit money.

pot—As in a pot of beer. The word meant something to drink out of—like a mug—and was also a rough measure of quantity, being in the neighborhood of a quart to a half-gallon.

potboy—A boy at a tavern who brought drinks to tables and also delivered beer ordered by customers not on the premises.

pothouse—A tavern or an alehouse.

poulterer—A chicken retailer; also, he usually sold game, including hares, sometimes those illegally obtained by poachers.

poultice—A warm, soft, gooey mass of bran or meal or herbs put onto a cloth like muslin and then applied to the skin to make a sore better or to warm someone.

pounce—A fine powder made out of something such as the pulverized resin of the Moroccan sandarac tree, used either for stopping the spread of ink on paper or to get a parchment ready to be written on.

pound—As a unit of money, the pound was worth 240 pence or 20 shillings. In addition, the pound as a location was the place where runaway cattle were detained or held if they had been seized for their owner's debt.

Prayer Book—The Book of Common Prayer.

prebendary—Cathedrals were often endowed by donors. A canon or other cleric attached to the cathedral who received a prebend, i.e., money from such an endowment, was called a prebendary. The clerics often had stalls in the cathedral, the term "prebendal stall" coming eventually to refer to the actual grant itself.

precentor—A cleric charged with conducting music at a cathedral; in some cathedrals, he was called a minor canon.

preferment—A job or position that represented a definite step upward financially or socially. To prefer someone to a post was to appoint them to it.

premium—The sum of money that it was customary for an apprentice or his family or guardian to pay to a master when the boy was apprenticed to him.

present—To "present" a clergyman "to" a vacant living or benefice meant that the layperson who owned it asked the bishop to officially install the layperson's candidate in the post. To be presented at court meant attending a formal drawing room or levee at which one was formally brought forward to meet the sovereign, a necessary step for girls "coming out" and for those who wished to be invited to court balls and concerts.

press—A cupboard or closet, often with shelves in it, for storing clothes or other items.

Prince Consort—A prince married to a reigning queen. Prince Albert, Victoria's husband, was the Prince Consort.

Princess Royal—The oldest daughter of a reigning monarch. When George III was king, his daughter Charlotte was Princess Royal.

private secretary—A secretary. The adjective "private" evidently distinguished him from the secretary of a group or organization.

Privy Council—Originally a body of genuine advisers to the Crown, it had become by the 1800s a collection of 250 or so distinguished scientists, writers, contemporary and former cabinet members and the like, sort of an academy of notables. Certain actions could be taken and certain orders given by the sovereign only "in council." In correspondence, a Privy Council member was "the Right Honourable."

privy seal—It was the monarch's private seal, unlike the great seal, which was that of the monarch acting in his public capacity. Instructions from the monarch to the lord chancellor to take certain official actions—like declaring war—required the chancellor to affix the great seal, which was in his custody, to the relevant document, but the chancellor could only do so upon receiving royal instructions impressed with the privy seal. The lord privy seal, to whom was entrusted custody of the privy seal, was a cabinet member, a political appointee whose job was to devote himself to his political party's affairs in the time he did not spend once or twice a week putting the privy seal on a document or two.

prize money—The only way to get rich in the navy. Prize money was the money or other loot obtained from capturing a vessel and dividing up the proceeds among the capturing crew or crews. The ordinary crewmembers got a quarter of the proceeds, lesser-ranked officers like the midshipmen got a quarter, lieutenants and masters got an eighth, and the captain got the rest (unless his ship was part of a squadron, in which case the admiral got a third of the captain's share).

proctor—One of the officials at Oxford and Cambridge in charge of undergraduate discipline.

prog—Slang for food.

province—One of the two administrative units into which the Church of England divided England. The northern province was ruled by the archbishop of York, the southern by the archbishop of Canterbury.

provost—A title given to the heads of some of the colleges at Oxford and Cambridge.

pub—Usually, a tavern or an inn.

public ball—Any large, open-to-the-public dance, such as a hunt ball or a charity ball. Distinguished on the one hand from a private ball—by invitation only in a private home—and on the other from the assemblies, which were generally like private balls in being restricted to the upper crust but were originally held in a subscription series and devoted to conversation as much as dancing.

publican—An alehouse or pub keeper or owner.

public school—e.g., Eton, Harrow, or Rugby. Such schools before 1800 were originally for *any* children in the immediate locality and hence "public" in the true sense. When they became more exclusively institutions for the rich, they were still distinguished from private boarding schools like Dotheboys Hall in *Nicholas Nickelby,* which were run by their headmasters or founders for profit.

pump room—The room at watering places like Bath where you drank and/or bathed in the supposedly curative mineral waters. Also, of course, as we see in *Northanger Abbey,* such a room served as a place to meet and gossip.

pupil-teacher—The name of the apprenticeship system in the national schools. A pupil would apprentice himself to a teacher who would supervise him and educate him while the pupil in turn taught others under the teacher's supervision. After 1846, the pupil-teacher route became one of the pathways to the training college normal school.

purse—What a gentleman carried to hold his coins so as not to spoil the line of his tights with unsightly bulges when he was wearing the fashionably tight trousers of the early part of the century. We know Marley is a man of the old school because he appears to Scrooge in tights and numbers purses among the objects of greed and miserliness that are fettered to his spectral self.

pursy—Fat and short of breath.

Puseyite—An adherent of E.B. Pusey, a professor of Hebrew at Oxford, who was one of the leaders of the Oxford Movement.

putrid fever—Typhus fever.

quadrille—Originally a card game played by four people with forty cards that was the fashionable predecessor of whist. Also, the dance that became popular in the mid-century, which had five figures, or sets of movements. It was basically a slowed-down square dance, involving four couples who started from the four points of an imaginary diamond. Even by the mid-century the dance had slowed down practically to a walk. It was used as the lead-off dance at almost all dances and balls, the waltz and the polka following.

quality—"The quality," says Trollope in *Barchester Towers,* is how "the upper classes in rural districts are designated by the lower."

quarter—One of the four parts of the year demarcated by the quarter days. Also, a quarter was a measurement of volume equal to eight bushels. Finally, it was the name of a measurement of weight equal to twenty-eight pounds.

quarter days—Four days which were traditionally used to mark when rents were due, periods of employment terminated and the like. The quarter days were Lady Day (March 25), Midsummer (June 24), Michaelmas (September 29), and Christmas (December 25).

quarterdeck—On a ship it was the deck behind the main deck, usually only running from the stern to the sternmost mast and sometimes raised a step or more above the main deck. As a rule, it was for use only by the passengers and officers.

quartered—A reference to a coat of arms, which was often divided into four or more areas, generally in order to display the arms of different branches of the family, e.g., those of the husband and those of the wife.

quartern—A quartern was an old-fashioned way of designating one quarter of various measurements, i.e., a stone, an ounce, a pint, or a peck. A quartern loaf of bread weighed about four pounds. Apparently, they cut bread thick in those days, for a contemporary writer observes that it yielded only sixteen slices.

quarter session—A joint sitting of all the justices of the peace in a county, held at least four times a year, to decide on the weighty matters of criminal and civil justice they could not handle independently. Cases that were too complicated or capital in nature, however, were held off for the assizes.

quarto—A book size named for a sheet of paper that had been folded twice and thus yielded four leaves (eight pages). It was approximately as high as it was wide.

quay—A dock or other place built out of stone to unload ships.

Queen's Counsel—*See* King's Counsel.

Queer Street—To be "in Queer Street" meant to be hard up for money.

quickset—A hedge made from cuttings of hawthorn and similar shrubs.

quid—A sovereign. Slang.

quinsy—Basically, tonsillitis.

quiz—Someone or something that was peculiar; someone who mocked others.

Quorn—One of the oldest and most prestigious of the fox-hunting packs in England. Named for Quorn Hall in the Midlands where the pack was first bred in the mid-1700s.

R. A.—Member of the Royal Academy, a combination official art school and exhibition hall founded by George III.

race—A channel of water, generally artificially produced, directed toward some point like a mill where its power would be harnessed.

radical—The name applied in the early part of the century to extreme liberals like Jeremy Bentham. It was also applied to certain members of Parliament active in the agitation for the Reform Act of 1832.

rag-and-bone shop—A shop that bought and sold rags that could be made into paper (since much clothing was then linen) and bones that could be ground up and made into manure. In addition, they sometimes bought other rather odiferous things like drippings. Mr. Krook in *Bleak House* is a rag-and-bone man.

ragbag—Among the perquisites of some servants was the right to maintain a ragbag into which they could throw the household's discarded linen for sale at their own profit, presumably to rag-and-bone shops.

rank—A person of rank was a person of considerable social standing.

ranker—A rank was a line of ordinary soldiers lined up next to one another, just as "file" meant that they were lined up in front of each other. (Hence, the "rank and file" were the ordinary soldiers). A "ranker" was an officer who had advanced from the ranks instead of buying his commission. There were also "gentleman rankers"—immortalized by Rudyard Kipling in verses later set to music by Cole Porter for Yale persons. These were gentlemen who disgraced themselves in civilian life and sought refuge and anonymity among the ranks rather than among the army's officers.

Ranters—A term used for Primitive Methodists, a denomination started in the first decade of the 1800s.

rapeseed—The seed of the rape plant, which is a cousin of the turnip. It was used as feed for sheep.

rasher—A not very thick slice of ham or bacon.

ratcatcher—A great occupation for the not so well educated who enjoyed work with some mild excitement to it. A ferret was made to sneak down the holes after the rats and then drive them out into the open where a terrier seized them by the scruff of the neck and did them in. Alternatively, ratcatchers simply poisoned the rats. It was not a marginal occupation; some very fancy London nurseries were attacked by rats owing to the deplorable conditions of the drains and sewage system.

rate—Until the middle of the century, the rate of a ship-of-war was based on the number of guns the vessel carried. First-rates carried 100 guns or more, second-rates between 100 and 75, and so on down to sixth-rates, which carried 20 to 28 guns. In an altogether different context, a "rate" was a local parish tax or assessment levied for various purposes, such as the care of the poor (the poor rate), the upkeep of the local church (the church rate), and so forth. It was distinct from the tithe, which went not to the government but to the local rector or vicar or perpetual curate. The rates should not be confused with various nationally imposed government taxes, e.g., on glass, windows, newspapers, dogs, hats, etc.

reading desk—A lectern in a church used for reading part of the Sunday service, often, apparently, placed underneath the pulpit.

read—An expression meaning to study, as in to "read law," i.e., with a senior lawyer. Also, chapter 23 of *Barchester Towers* is called "Mr. Arabin reads himself in." This referred to the practice of an incumbent reading the Thirty-nine Articles aloud to his congregation upon assuming his new office.

reader—An old-fashioned position indicating a senior status among the lawyers belonging to one of the Inns of Court.

rector—A parish clergyman entitled to all the tithes, as opposed to a vicar or a perpetual curate, who only got some of them. He was addressed as "Reverend."

recusant—Someone who refused to attend Church of England services. A name originally given to Catholics and Dissenters; subsequently applied more generally to people who wouldn't obey authority.

Red Book—The term sometimes referred to a book containing the names of everyone who worked for the government. In the second half of the century it was also the name given to a book that listed the nobility and gentry, along with their addresses.

reddle—A kind of red chalk used for marking sheep to identify their owners. Useful because it would wash off and not permanently color the wool that was sheared from them.

reel—A Scotch dance that involved at least two couples and usually the execution of some kind of a figure eight.

refectory—The dining hall of a large institution like a monastery or school.

Reform Act—The Reform Act of 1832 sought to put an end to rotten boroughs and the underrepresentation of middle-class voters. This was done by extending the franchise and by more evenly redistributing parliamentary seats among the boroughs. Previously, political power had rested almost exclusively with the nobility and gentry, who thereby controlled Parliament and the affairs of the nation. Thus, the borough of Old Sarum was represented in Parliament although it had no inhabitants, while the big new, industrial cities of the north like Birmingham and Manchester had no representation at all. The Reform Act was a gigantic shock to the whole system of rule by the titled landowners who had governed the country more or less unchallenged until then. The Second Reform Act in 1867 extended the franchise to many workers in towns. (Women got the vote in the 1900s.)

Regency—*See* regent.

regent—A person who reigned on behalf of a monarch who for some reason could not. George III went permanently insane in 1810. His son, the Prince of Wales, later George IV, thereupon became prince regent. The period from then until his father's death in 1820 subsequently acquired the name of the Regency period.

regiment—*The* permanent and important unit in the British army throughout the nineteenth century. It usually numbered some 750 to 1,000 men and was made up of eight to ten companies, each commanded by a captain. Sometimes, too, a regiment was grouped into one or two battalions. In name the colonel was the commander of the regiment; in practice, it was generally the lieutenant colonel who ran things.

register—In 1800 every church in England maintained a register in which were recorded the births and deaths of all the inhabitants of the parish. In addition, each married couple signed the register in the vestry right after the wedding ceremony. The entries served the purpose not only of making the birth or marriage valid in the eyes of the church but making it civilly legal as well. This latter function was taken over by the registrar beginning in 1836.

registrar—The local official who came into existence in 1836, who had to be notified of all births and deaths within the county. He could also issue marriage licences for civil and nonconformist marriages.

regular—The regular army were the permanent soldiers who could be sent anywhere, anytime to fight. The irregulars were the militia and volunteers who were limited in pay, responsibility, or military commitment.

rent-roll—The landlord's list of his rents and rental properties.

repeater—An old-fashioned watch, very popular in the days before good matches because when one pushed the handle on it, it struck the last hour or quarter hour, thereby enabling one to tell the approximate time in the dark without having to go through the production involved in striking a light with a tinderbox.

reredo—The screen in front of the choir or behind the altar in a church. In a home, the stone or brick back of a fireplace.

resurrectionist—A body snatcher. Before 1833, the only corpses that could be used for dissection in the teaching of anatomy were those of executed criminals. There were not enough to fill the demand. Accordingly, doctors informally arranged with resurrectionists to bring them bodies they had spirited away in the dead of night from churchyards. Some, like the infamous Burke and Hare, upon running short of specimens, went a step further and hastened some of their fellow citizens involuntarily into the corpse stage. In a contemporary poem, a ghost told her former lover that the famous surgeon Sir Astley Cooper had been successful in having the resurrectionists steal her corpse: "The cock it crows—I must be gone—/ My William, we must part;/But I'll be yours in death although/Sir Astley has my heart."

retainer—A servant who had been with a family for years and years.

reticule—A little bag in which ladies carried their personal toilet articles and the like when the tight, thin muslin dresses with no pockets made it impossible to carry any personal effects actually on their person. Sometimes called a "ridicule."

reversion—A legal term meaning that after one had the use of something or other the right to it would revert back to someone else. Usually meaning a right to some fancy position or the enjoyment of an estate after, say, the death of the current occupant.

ribbon—One was entitled to wear a blue ribbon as part of the getup that went with membership in the Order of the Garter.

rick—A haystack or cornstack. Sometimes they were thatched to protect them from the rain and put on staddles to keep them from rats and moisture.

Right Honourable—The formal way to address earls, viscounts, barons, and privy councillors. Also used to a peer's eldest son bearing as a "courtesy title" an inferior title of his father.

Right Reverend—Term of address to a bishop.

Riot Act—Yes, there actually was such a thing as "reading the Riot Act," namely, the Riot Act of 1714. In the good old days when there was trouble brewing—or actually in progress—a justice of the peace or similar worthy got up and read to the assembled rabble the instructions of the act to disperse, specifically, that any twelve or more persons still causing a ruckus an hour after the Riot Act was read aloud to them would be guilty of a felony.

robin redbreast—Not the same as the American robin, who was a thrush and about twice the size of his cousin in England. It was considered bad luck to harm a robin. Robin redbreast was also the colloquial name for the Bow Street Runners because of their red vests.

Stacking wheat on ricks.

"(Sir) Roger de Coverley"—A jolly type of country dance used to finish off dances and popular at Christmas. It involved the first man and last lady and last man and first lady from two lines of parallel men and women swinging out and then back, then swinging round, then weaving their way through the lines and then promenading, etc. The dance is known in the United States as the Virginia reel.

roly-poly pudding—Jam or fruit all rolled up in a sheet of pastry and cooked.

rook—A relative of the crow, except that the crow lived on dead animals while the rook ate grain, insects, slugs, and snails. In northern Britain rooks were called crows. They nested in big groups called rookeries.

rookery—Literally, a nesting place for a lot of rooks. For what it's worth the actual full title of *David Copperfield* was "The Personal History, Experience and Observation of David Copperfield the Younger of Blunderstone Rookery which he never meant to be published on any account." "Rookery" also was used to denote an urban slum of many people and buildings jammed together.

root—Root crops were turnips, Swedish turnips, mangel-wurzels, and potatoes. The first three were viewed in the 1800s as a key to successful "modern" farming because they put nutrients back into depleted fields and provided winter feed for livestock.

rotten borough—A parliamentary borough that had very few or almost no inhabitants, due usually to gradual population decline over the years, yet still managed to return members to Parliament. The most notorious was perhaps that of Old Sarum in Wiltshire; it had five voters and *no* inhabitants. Rotten boroughs were one of the targets of the First Reform Act of 1832. Those who benefitted from them—they were, after all, easy to control—saw it in a somewhat different light. "Rotten! be hanged"— says Sir Pitt Crawley in *Vanity Fair*—"it produces me a good fifteen hundred a year."

Rotten Row—A walkway for horses in the southern part of Hyde Park much favored by the fashionable elite. In 1871 the time to catch the fashionable in action was from noon to two or five to seven in May through July.

roundabout—A merry-go-round.

rounders—A game like baseball. There were two teams and one whacked a ball and then ran around the bases. Unlike baseball, someone could put a player out by throwing the ball at him and hitting him.

round game—A card game at which any number could play, like Pope Joan, as opposed to a game like whist where there was a maximum number of players.

round robin—A letter of complaint or petition signed by a group.

Royal Exchange—'Change, as it was called, was the meeting place in the City for merchants in different trades, who would gather there and walk about with their fellow merchants in the specific area allotted to their line of commerce. It also housed Lloyd's, the famous insurance firm. As certain trades outgrew the 'Change, they left and formed their own, like the Corn Exchange and, in 1801, the Stock Exchange.

rubric—The portions of the Book of Common Prayer that were printed in red. The rubric provided the instructions for the clergyman on how to conduct the services.

rubber—In games like whist, a rubber was a set of three or more games, where the idea was to win the best two out of three or three out of five.

Rules—Areas around prisons like the Fleet and the King's Bench that certain prisoners, particularly debtors, could inhabit with permission from the appropriate authorities. One prisoner commuted to his work every night under this arrangement for some time as editor of the *Times*.

run—A fox-hunting term denoting the chase of a fox by the field and ending in a death. If the fox were caught quickly, there could be more than one run in a day's hunt.

rural dean—A clergyman who assisted the archdeacon in overseeing the affairs of a diocese.

rushlight—Ordinary rushes dipped in drippings or similar material so they could be set alight. Used as candles by the poor and also as nightlights, since, unlike a candle, when they burned down, the "wick" just disintegrated, thus lessening the danger of fire.

rusticate—To punish by sending away from Oxford or Cambridge, usually only as a temporary suspension. To "send down," by contrast, was to expel permanently.

s.—The abbreviation for shilling. From the Latin *solidus*.

Sabbatarians—*Very* strict observers of Sunday who tried to close down shops and other "irreligious" activities on the Lord's Day. Often, they were Evangelicals and the like. One of their particular bêtes noires, as the fulminations of Mrs. Proudie in *Barchester Towers* make clear, was the impious running of trains on Sunday by the railroad companies. There was also a parliamentary proposal to prevent the poor from using bakehouses to cook hot Sunday meals.

sack—A dry white wine from Spain or the Canary Islands.

sackcloth—A cloth for making sacks. Coarse and made usually of hemp or flax.

sack coat—The ancestor of the sport coat, it started becoming popular in the 1870s. Like the frock coat, it was of uniform length all around, but in front it stopped short just below the hips, and it hung straight down in back instead of being form fitting.

sacristan—The man who looked after the sacred chalices and similar consecrated ware in a church, like those used in the communion services. The vessels were kept in what was called a sacristy.

saddler—A saddlemaker.

sago—A pasty sort of substance made out of certain kinds of palm trees and used for food.

St. Giles—A notoriously wretched London slum in the mid-century with a substantial Irish and Jewish population. Along with Covent Garden, it was a center of prostitution.

St. James's Palace—The official royal residence until 1837 when the new queen, Victoria, moved to Buckingham Palace. St. James's was used thereafter for drawing rooms and levees. (Buckingham Palace became the site of royal concerts and balls.)

St. Martin's Day—*See* Martin's Day.

saloon—Any large, grand room for receiving visitors in a great house. In *Pride and Prejudice*, Elizabeth Bennet et al. are "shown through the hall into the saloon" at Mr. Darcy's Pemberley. "In this room they were received by Miss Darcy."

salver—One of those little silver trays that people put their visiting cards on in the hallway or that the servants used for handing around biscuits at various private social gatherings.

sal volatile—A kind of smelling salt made with ammonium carbonate.

sandals—Used for footgear by ladies in the early part of the century, they were slipperlike shoes that fastened over the instep with a strap.

sapper—Among the forerunners of the army engineers. They were in charge of building fortifications that would make it possible to advance toward a besieged fortress without being blown to smithereens.

sash—A popular accompaniment to the muslin frock, especially for little girls.

saveloy—A kind of strongly seasoned, dry sausage.

savoury—A spiced dish served at the start or conclusion of a dinner.

sawpit—*See* sawyer.

sawyer—A man who sawed things. There were top sawyers and bottom sawyers. When wood was sawed in a sawpit, the bottom sawyer stood in the pit below ground holding one end of the saw while the top sawyer stood on the ground above holding the other.

schoolroom—The place where children in a well-off home had their lessons, generally until they went away to school or "came out," and which, a contemporary source advised, should be large enough so as to enable the children "to take their dancing lessons in it, and to serve for them to play at battledore and shuttlecock in it, or take other exercise during inclement weather." Typically, it was on one of the upper floors of the house. The expression "in the schoolroom" used of a young girl meant that she had not yet "come out."

scout—A man servant at Oxford.

screw—An old worthless horse. Also, an old tightwad or miser. Becky Sharp writes to Amelia Sedley that people call her employer Sir Pitt Crawley "an old screw; which means a very stingy, avaricious person." Prison guards were sometimes called screws, too.

scrivener—A copier or secretary.

scullery—The place where dishes were washed and stored or a back kitchen.

scullerymaid—The girl who washed dishes and who was at the very bottom of the servant hierarchy. The generic term for male or female scullery workers was "scullion"—it was used as a term of abuse.

sealing wax—Beeswax and later a mixture that included shellac and turpentine; used for sealing letters. Red was to be used only for business letters, other colors for social correspondence, and black for mourning.

seals—Small ornaments, worn on a watch chain, and including a seal used to seal letters plus similarly shaped items. It is one of the possessions of Scrooge's that he and the Spirit of Christmas to Come find the ghoulish charwoman and her cronies haggling over in the rag-and-bone shop in Scrooge's prevision of his death.

season—The London social season, in which the fashionable high life of the nobility dominated the city. Although families returned from their country houses to London in February, the *real* season—of balls, parties, sporting events like Ascot and so on—ran only from May through July.

second-rate—*See* rate.

secretary of state—The title given to the heads of various executive departments in the national government such as the Foreign Office, the Home Office, and so on, who were known informally as the home secretary, the foreign secretary, etc. In 1801 only the Home Office and the Foreign Office had a secretary, plus there was one for war and the colonies. A secretary of state for war was added in 1854 and one for the colonies and then one for India in 1858 after the government took control of the subcontinent from the East India Company. They were all members of the cabinet.

sedge—Plants similar to grass. They grew in marshy areas and on river banks.

see—The post of bishop in a diocese.

seedcake—A sweet cake made usually with caraway seeds.

sell out—To leave the army by selling the commission one had purchased to someone.

sell up—To sell all the goods belonging to someone in settlement of their debts.

seminary—Originally, a place of religious instruction but applied by the 1800s to private schools for young ladies.

senior wrangler—In the math honors exams or "tripos" at Cambridge the top students were called wranglers. The student who ranked higher than all the others was the senior wrangler.

sennight—A contraction of "seven night," meaning a week. Used by the pompous Mr. Collins in *Pride and Prejudice*.

send down—To expell from a university. To "rusticate," by contrast, was usually only to suspend temporarily.

sergeant major—Not the same as "sergeant," who was the man who drilled a company and ranked just above a corporal. The sergeant major was in charge of discipline and drill for an entire regiment.

serjeant—In 1800, the serjeants were the lawyers with the most prestige. They were the litigators in the courts of Common Pleas, King's Bench and Exchequer, corresponding to the barristers who argued in the Chancery Court. For a long time one could not be a common-law judge without being a serjeant first, and they had their own "inn"—Serjeants' Inn—separate from the Inns of Court. However, the barristers eventually edged them out for top position, and the status of serjeant became less prestigious than the new honor of King's or Queen's Counsel. The position of serjeant was abolished altogether after mid-century.

servants' hall—The place where the servants ate and congregated in a household when they were given a special room for the purpose. (In smaller houses, they generally used the kitchen.) Thackeray makes use of the term to tell us how Becky Sharp conquered the servants at the Sedleys' in the course of her efforts to trap Joe Sedley—"the Servants' Hall was almost as charmed with her as the Drawing Room."

session—A session of Parliament meant its annual meeting, usually from January or February till about the middle of August. An "adjournment" was a brief cessation of business during a session. To "dissolve" Parliament meant that the existing Parliament went out of existence either during or after the session as general elections were held to elect new members.

sessions—The period in which a court sat; in rural areas, sessions would probably have generally meant the quarter sessions.

set—A group of dancers. When country-dances were performed, if there were too many couples to fit in the two long straight parallel lines which the dance demanded, the dancers would be divided up into several sets. The term could also mean the figures in a quadrille.

settee—An indoor chair on which at least two people could sit.

settle—In taverns and rustic homes, a wooden bench with a high back capable of seating several people. It was often drawn up facing the fire, and the high back served to protect against cold drafts. As a verb, "to settle" meant to make some legal arrangement by will or contract or similar device for the use or custody of property or money.

settlement—Applied to a legal arrangement of property, it was used principally in two connections. First, it was employed to denote the *marriage settlement* of a well-off woman, in which lawyers for her side met with lawyers for the groom prior to the marriage to ensure that at the least she would get pin money, a jointure and portions for their children. Second, a *strict settlement* was an arrangement by which a landed estate was entailed against the possibility of a male heir selling or mortgaging it, e.g., to pay his debts. In an entirely different, *non*property context, settlement under the Poor Law meant that one could not get relief in a parish without meeting certain criteria of "settlement" there, e.g., that one was born in the parish, had been apprenticed there, or—in a woman's case—had married a resident.

Seven Dials—An infamous criminal district in London of seven streets converging in the area of St. Giles.

sexton—A contraction of sacristan, but the sexton acquired different duties as his name changed. The sexton was the man who rang the bells and dug the graves at a churchyard. The sexton in *Tess* charges the heroine "a shilling and a pint of beer" to bury her child. Uriah Heep observes to David Copperfield that "my father's former calling was umble. He was a sexton."

shawl—A favorite accompaniment to dresses and frocks for a good portion of the century. There was an art to how it was to be draped.

sheriff—The high sheriff was originally the king's principal representative in a shire. Along with the earl, he basically ran things, especially the peacekeeping establishment, which is why the sheriff of Nottingham was Robin Hood's nemesis. In the twelfth century the position abruptly lost its prestige when it was turned into a one-year job. Thereafter, the sheriff's authority dwindled away until by the end of the 1800s he was basically a country gentleman in charge of entertaining the assize justices when they came around on circuit. The sheriff was also in charge of executing writs and carrying out certain official county functions through his assistants, the bailiffs. In London the sheriff's officers were the ones who ran the sponging houses to which people arrested for debt were taken.

shift—The basic item of women's underwear, a long kind of nightgownlike garment which—except for the corset—was all the underwear women wore until the advent of drawers in the 1860s. "Shift" actually replaced the original term "smock" because smock was thought to be too indelicate. Then shift was thought to be improper, and people started calling it a "chemise" instead.

shilling—An English silver coin worth twelvepence. Twenty shillings equaled a pound.

shilling number—A monthly installment of a novel (*Pickwick* was published thus), each costing a shilling; a popular form of serialized publication for a good part of the century.

shipbreaker—Someone who tore apart old boats and sold the resulting scrap.

ship-of-the-line—A warship large enough to take part in the "line of battle" in which ships then fought. Hence a ship usually of sixty guns or more, i.e., a "fourth-rate" or better.

shire—The unit of regional government run by the earl and the sheriff (shire reeve) on behalf of the monarch into which all England was divided when the Normans arrived. The Normans substituted the term "county" for "shire" but the old name lingered in a number of the counties such as Hampshire, Lincolnshire, etc. "The shires" in foxhunting circles referred to Midlands shires, which were said to have the best fox hunting in the country, particularly Rutland, Northamptonshire, and Leicestershire.

shopman—A man who owned a shop or worked in one.

short commons—At Cambridge University food was referred to as "commons." "Short commons" was insufficient food.

shorts—Knee breeches.

shove-halfpenny—A children's game basically equivalent to shuffleboard, except it could be played on a table instead of the floor and one shoved coins instead of big disks.

shovel hat—"His shovel-hat," observes Trollope in *The Warden*, "declared the profession as plainly as does the Quaker's broad brim." It was the hat worn by Church of England clergy, turned up on either side and sticking out in the front and back like a shovel.

sideboard—Originally, a rather modest piece of furniture, that stood in a dining room, on which one could put extra dishes. It grew drawers and spaces as the century wore on and became a storage place for plate, silverware, and similar articles.

Sir—The title by which baronets and knights were addressed.

sitting room—The room where family members sat and were comfortable, as opposed to a drawing room, for example, where visitors would typically be received or entertained more formally after dinner. Rented apartments seem generally to have consisted at a minimum of a bedroom and a sitting room.

sizar—At one time, the name given to scholarship students at Cambridge.

'sizes—Short for "assizes."

skimmington, skimmity—A rural pastime that involved parading people or effigies of a quarreling wife or husband past the home of the feuding couple for everyone's general amusement and edification.

skittles—Basically, bowling. One set up nine skittles or pins and then tried to knock them down with a ball.

slop basin—The basin into which the housemaid cleaning a bedroom would empty waste water.

slops—The word referred to loose clothing bought by sailors. Also, slop-work was cheap, slapped-together sweatshop work, e.g., slop furniture. Slops was also the name for a feeble kind of broth given to sick people. "Have you given him any nourishment?" Mr. Brownlow asks his house-keeper when poor Oliver Twist is ill. "Any slops, eh?" "He has just had a basin of beautiful strong broth," she replies haughtily. Slops was also household waste water.

small beer—A kind of weak, low-quality beer.

small clothes—Knee breeches.

smalls—*See* small clothes.

smelling bottle—A bottle filled with smelling salts (usually a compound containing ammonia) to be used in case of fainting.

smock—The original term for a "shift" or "chemise."

snob—Until Thackeray got hold of the term and changed its meaning in his *Book of Snobs* in 1846, it meant someone of no social standing, as opposed to a "nob."

smock frock—As an outer garment a smock frock was worn by the agricultural working poor till well into the century. It was like an ordinary smock, except heavier. Hardy observes in *Tess* (1891) when the ubiquitous Alec Durberville turns up in one that it is "now worn only by the most old-fashioned of labourers."

snipe—A bird with a long bill that lives in marshes.

snuffers—Scissorslike instruments used for periodically trimming the wicks on tallow candles, which would otherwise start burning poorly. To "snuff" a candle was to trim its wick to make it burn better. To extinguish it was to "snuff it out." The snuff was the burning or burnt part of the wick. "The candles went on flickering and guttering, and there were no snuffers," says Esther Summerson of a visit she makes to the chambers of Conversation Kenge in *Bleak House*, "until the young gentleman by and by brought a very dirty pair."

solicitor—A lawyer who handled such matters as wills and estate problems and hired barristers to represent his clients in the Chancery Court when courtroom work was called for. Solicitors lacked the prestige of barristers and could not, themselves, appear in court, but like Mr. Tulkinghorn, "attorney-at-law and eke solicitor of the High Court of Chancery," could develop a good deal of influence and make a nice living. When paying for a barrister's services, one always paid the solicitor—never the barrister directly.

Somerset House—A building in the Strand in London that housed various government offices, most notably the Board of Inland Revenue, the tax office.

Southwark—The area immediately across the Thames south of London, known sometimes as "the Borough."

sovereign—A gold coin worth a pound, first issued in 1817.

spade guinea—*See* guinea.

spatterdashes—Basically long gaiters. Spatterdashes came up high on the leg. Extremely short spatterdashes fastened under the feet were called "spats."

special pleader—Someone who wrote up "pleadings" or petitions submitted in a court case by a lawyer, an occupation sometimes followed by a student at the Inns of Court who had not yet been "called to the bar."

spencer—For women, a kind of short jacket. For men, an overcoat without tails, also on the short side.

splinter bar—The crossbar at the end of the pole hitched in front of a carriage to which the horses were attached so that they could pull it.

sponging house—A house maintained by a sheriff's officer where debtors were put up after they had been arrested for debt and where they were given a chance to pay it before going to prison. Also spelled "spunging house."

spooney—A fool, sometimes with the connotation of a person made foolish by love.

sprat—A baby herring; also, a small seafish; also, slang for a sixpence.

spring van—Vans were generally used for hauling around goods and sometimes poor or working people. A spring van was so elegant that it actually had springs to smooth the ride. "The modern spring van," wrote a mid-century observer, "is, as it were, the landau, or travelling carriage of the working classes. . . . They were about 14 feet long, with removable seats, an awning on top and side curtains that could be rolled up or kept down depending on the weather and could be pulled by anywhere from one to four horses."

spunging house—*See* sponging house.

squadron—Part of a fleet of ships in the navy detached from the main fleet. The navy was divided into the red, white, and blue squadrons, each with its own complement of admirals, rear admirals and vice admirals; thus, one would refer to "an Admiral of the Blue." In the army, a squadron was the unit in the cavalry corresponding to a battalion in the infantry, that is, the next biggest unit down from a regiment. It had anywhere between 100 and 200 men in it.

squire—Simply a term of courtesy for a member of the gentry whose family had lived for generations in an area and who had tenant farmers on his property. Squires were often justices of the peace.

staddle—A platform made out of stone or wood on which hay or corn was put after it was cut or harvested to keep it away from moisture and rats.

stagecoach—A coach that traveled in stages, i.e., stopping periodically to change horses or to allow the passengers to eat or rest. They were commercial vehicles, usually running on some kind of regular schedule.

stair rod—The metal rods clamped along the base of each riser on stairs to keep the stair carpet in place.

stake—To stake a horse—as Dunstan Cass does in *Silas Marner*—was to impale it on a fence or hedge of some kind.

stall—Synedoche at work. Since prebendaries sat in a cathedral stall, a stall came to signify the position that a prebendary held. "Dr. Grant," we learn at the end of *Mansfield Park*, "through an interest on which he had almost ceased to form hopes, succeeded to a stall in Westminster."

standard—The first attempt to establish a nationwide system of requirements for the education of elementary school children was made with the minute passed in the Privy Council's committee on education in 1846. It created six standards—one for each age, beginning with six- and seven-year-olds up through age twelve (standards I–VI), at the end of which children had to show that they could read a simple paragraph and take dictation of a simple paragraph, plus do some arithmetic. The girls also had to demonstrate some facility in needlework as well. Tess Durbeyfield, Hardy says at one point, had passed her sixth standard.

stand up—To stand up with someone was to dance with them.

stanhope—A light, two- or four-wheel carriage that had no top, named after the Honourable and Reverend Fitzroy Stanhope (1787–1864).

statute fair—*See* hiring fair.

stay—A stay was one of the two halves of a corset; hence, stays, or a "pair of stays," were an entire corset.

staylace—One of the laces used to tighten a corset. They were sold on the streets of London by elderly poor women (it required little capital to start the business), whose customers were servant girls, working-class girls, and the daughters and wives of small shopkeepers. On occasion staylaces were cut by doctors after ladies had fainted away from wearing them too tight—the desirable female waist measurement was at one time very modest, although probably not the eighteen inches sometimes spoken of as the theoretical ideal.

steamers—In 1848 there were 33,000 sail boats and 1,100 steamships in Britain. The river steamers in the Thames at first disturbed people with their large wakes (they averaged eight to nine miles per hour). They were used in large part by middle class and working people to commute to work from the suburbs.

steeplechase—Some gentlemen socializing together one night apparently decided to ride for sport straight toward a distant steeple—letting nothing get in their way. Hence, steeplechase became the term for a horseback ride or race that went straight across country over all obstacles.

sterling—As in "one pound sterling." The term came from the old Norman penny made of silver that was known as a sterling. Thereafter any object of the same degree of purity was called "sterling."

steward—In very elaborate households, the steward was the head of the male servants or at times chief of the male and female servants alike. He presided over the running of the entire establishment—keeping the accounts, ordering supplies, supervising staff. In a less grand establishment a butler headed the male staff. There were also land stewards in the eighteenth century, who managed the farming and pasturage of the great estates. In the 1800s they were generally superseded by professional agents.

stewpond—A special fishpond kept by manor houses in medieval days so as to have a supply of fresh food.

stile—A set of steps in a fence through or over which a human could climb to get out of a field or pasture but which would be impassable to sheep or cattle.

stillroom—The place in a house—if not still used as a still—where preserves and wine were kept and where coffee or tea was made.

stoat—The ermine. Most of the year he was brownish and was called a stoat. In the winter he turned white and was called an ermine.

stock—A tightish, stiff collar worn by men, especially soldiers (a character in *The Return of the Native* refers to a "stock sawing my jaws off"). In clerical dress it was the black shirtfront over which the white bit of collar was fastened. Horticulturally speaking, stocks were tall flowers that grew in cottage gardens.

stole—A long narrow scarf worn by clergymen that was draped over the shoulders so that it hung down to the knees in front on either side.

stone—A measurement of weight equal to fourteen pounds.

stovepipe hat—A top hat (a/k/a chimneypot hat).

strait waistcoat—A straitjacket.

strand—The shore of a river or ocean. There was a three-quarter-mile-long street in London running from Charing Cross to Temple Bar that was one of the two big east–west thoroughfares in London called the Strand because it had originally marked the northern boundary of the Thames.

straw plaiting—Weaving together straw into the straw bonnets then fashionable; a cottage industry for many years among the rural poor.

stud—A collection of horses kept for a special purpose such as breeding or racing.

stuff—A name for different kinds of fabrics, but most commonly those made of wool.

subaltern—In the army, a subaltern was a junior officer. Subalterns were ensigns (a rank later redesignated as second lieutenant) and lieutenants. They were the young officers who assisted a captain in running his company.

suet pudding—Suet was the hard fat of an animal around its kidneys and loins, which, in some conditions, could be turned into tallow. Suet pudding was a pudding made of flour and suet that was generally boiled in cloth.

sugarloaf—The hardened, crusty form in which sugar was generally available for much of the 1800s. It had the shape of a cone—a shape it acquired when the sugar was stacked up to dry and the liquid drained away from it during the production process.

sugarplum—A roundish piece of flavored candy made mostly out of sugar.

sunk fence—*See* ha-ha.

surgeon—A man who fixed broken bones, wounds, and any other kind of external injury—something which physicians did *not* do. Surgeons were of lower social status than physicians. They were generally addressed as "Mr." rather than "Dr.," a title usually reserved for physicians.

surplice—A loose, flowing, ankle-length garment with big droopy sleeves, generally worn over the cassock by clergymen when conducting a service. Toward the latter part of the century wearing a cassock came to connote High Church leanings.

Surrey—The name of the county on the southern side of the Thames opposite London where Southwark was.

surtout—A man's overcoat that looked like a frock coat.

swallowtail coat—A man's coat, so called from the shape of the long tails that tapered down in back.

Swede—Also called the Swedish turnip. A root crop grown for winter fodder.

sweep—A chimney sweep. They treated their "climbing boys" abysmally in the early part of the century, presumably one reason for the grim characterization of the sweep Gamfield, who seeks to acquire Oliver Twist as an apprentice.

sweetmeat—A sweetmeat was a candy, particularly a candied fruit, although also a hard, fruit-flavored candy.

swing glass—A mirror similar or identical to a cheval glass.

tags—Little hanging ornaments of dress.

take orders—To become a clergyman of the Church of England.

take silk—A barrister could wear a silk gown once he became, according to the gender of the reigning monarch, either King's Counsel or Queen's Counsel.

take up—To pay an obligation like a bill of exchange.

tallow—Fat from oxen or sheep, which was used for making soap or candles and for various other purposes.

tambour—A hoop filled with material on which embroidery was done.

tandem—A team of two horses harnessed one behind the other (as opposed to side by side) were said to be driven in "tandem." Like the bicycle.

tankard—A big drinking mug, usually for beer, often with some kind of cover on it.

tanner—Slang for a sixpence.

taper—A small wax candle.

taproom—The room in a tavern or inn where ordinary laborers or working people were served, as opposed to the parlor, which often had fancier decor and was for the genteel.

tar—Colloquial word for a sailor. Also, an ingredient mixed into cold water with a supposed medicinal aim. Mrs. Gargery doses Pip with it at the beginning of *Great Expectations*.

tarts—In addition to being the little fruit pastries one thinks of, they could also apparently be deep-dish pielike foods.

tea caddy—A box that tea was kept in. They were sometimes locked in the days when tea was very costly.

teapoy—A three-legged stand that became a table used for serving tea, in part apparently through a misapprehension of the word's origins, which lie actually in Persian and Hindu words that in conjunction mean "three-legged."

Temple—An area in London once the site of buildings occupied by the Knights Templar, and, by the 1800s, by two of the four Inns of Court, i.e., the Inner Temple and Middle Temple.

Temple Bar—It stood north of the Temple at the eastern end of the Strand where the Strand became Fleet Street. It was a gate that marked the formal entrance to the City of London. The sovereign had to request the right from the lord mayor of London to pass through it when he or she wanted to enter the city.

tenant—Many exceedingly prosperous farmers farmed as tenants of greater landowners rather than as landowners on their own. Thus, the term in agricultural circles was by no means synonymous with reduced economic circumstances. Both Farmer Boldwood and Bathsheba Everdene in *Far from the Madding Crowd*, for example—together disposing of some two thousand acres and a good many farm workers—were tenant farmers.

tenner—A ten-pound note.

term—The name given to the academic sessions of Oxford and Cambridge, e.g., Michaelmas, Easter; also given to the periods during which the law courts were formally in session in London. In 1873 the law terms were redesignated "sessions" or sittings. To "eat one's terms" was to be a law student at the Inns of Court, since for many years to dine there a certain number of times was the only requirement for becoming a barrister.

terrace—A row of houses along a slope, usually of the same style and all attached to one another; more or less synonymous with cheap middle-class housing.

Test Act—Legislation passed prior to 1800 which kept Catholics from holding public office, including Parliament. Repealed in 1829 by the Tory administration led by the duke of Wellington.

thimblerigger—The man who worked the old shell game where the spectator tries to figure out which one of the three shells the pea is under.

third class—The lowest class of railroad travel (except the parliamentary). Third-class cars were originally without roofs or seats.

third-rate—*See* rate.

Thirty-nine Articles—The thirty-nine different statements, which, taken together, made up the basic credo of the Church of England. Adherence to them was required of all students entering Oxford until the 1850s, and a clergyman "read himself in" to a new parish congregation by reading the articles aloud from the pulpit.

thorn tree—Often a reference to the hawthorn.

throne—The seat of a bishop in his cathedral.

throstle—The song thrush, a popular caged bird.

ticket-of-leave man—Certain convicts were excused from having to serve their whole sentence under an "order of license," known colloquially as a ticket-of-leave. If they misbehaved, they went back in jail.

ticket porter—A porter in London "licensed" to carry goods, parcels, etc. Originally, as with many London occupations, being a porter was a regulated monopoly (like belonging to a guild), so the porters carried small badges or tickets to show that they had an official right to carry things.

tidewaiter—A customs official who boarded boats after waiting for them to come in on the tide.

tiffin—A light, midday snack customary in India that involved chutney, etc. Joe Sedley, collector of Boggley Wallah for the East India Company, buys a pineapple in *Vanity Fair*, ever mindful of his stomach's needs. "Let's have it for tiffin," he says, "very cool and nice in this hot weather."

tights—The thin skintight pants worn by gentlemen in the early part of the century, so tight that they had to carry separate purses in which to keep their money. Marley, old-fashioned spook that he is, shows up to visit Scrooge dressed in "his pig-tails, usual waistcoat, tights and boots" with "heavy purses wrought in steel" among the impedimenta he drags after him in punishment for his misdeeds.

tilbury—A two-wheel, rather light carriage with no top, popular before 1850.

tilt—In a waggon or cart, the tilt was the cloth covering the "covered" part of a "covered waggon."

Times—Ultimately the most influential newspaper of its day. It started life as a fairly feisty, rough-and-tumble paper—at one point not atypically calling a competing paper a "squirt of filthy water." Then it became respectable and magisterial—Trollope parodies it in several novels as the "Jupiter" in allusion to its nickname of the "Thunderer." It was supposed to be nonpartisan, and it published the entire text of parliamentary debates and reports. It had a circulation of about 60,000 in 1861 and was read by the movers and shakers of its day.

tinderbox—The way to start a fire in the days before matches. One took the flint out of the box and struck a piece of metal against it, hoping the spark would fly into the small pile of cotton rags in the box and set them alight. Whereupon one had to light a match from the smoldering rags and then light one's fire or candle with that. Pip remarks on the aural difficulty of household theft in the days of the tinderbox when he tries to sneak food out of the Gargerys to Abel Magwitch in the dead of night: "There was no doing it in the night, for there was no getting a light by easy friction then; to have got one, I must have struck it out of flint and steel and have made a noise like [a] pirate rattling his chains."

tinker—An itinerant fixer of pots and pans. The trade was often associated with the gypsies, and there clung to it a sinister and unsavory air.

tippet—An article of apparel (often made from a dead furry animal) that was slung over the shoulder so it hung down the chest on either side of one's neck.

tithes—An amount paid in kind to the local parish clergyman by each farmer or tradesman equal to one tenth of his year's produce. In 1840 the payment of tithes was "commuted" to one of money.

toffee—Taffy.

Tokay—A sweet and rich Hungarian white wine. Favored for dessert.

top—At a dance or ball, the place in the room where the orchestra was, generally opposite the door. The top couple was the couple at the top of the two lines of men and women who made up a country-dance "set." They led off the figures. It was considered an honor to be asked to be top couple.

top boots—High boots used basically for riding, with a lighter colored area at the top that at one time had been simply the inside of the boot top turned down.

top sawyer—Since the top sawyer in a sawpit is the man who works on top and gets the better part of the job, the term came to denote someone in a good or superior position. Describing the spring wind whirling through the streets of London, Dickens writes in *Our Mutual Friend:* "Every street was a sawpit, and there were no top-sawyers; every passenger was an under-sawyer, with the sawdust blinding him and choking him."

Tory—The conservative party in English politics, as opposed to the more liberal Whigs. In general, the Tories supported the king, the Church of England and the old way of doing things. They changed their name to the Conservatives in the 1830s and 1840s while the Whigs became the Liberals.

tosspot—Someone who drank a lot.

town traveler—A commercial traveler who worked in the town where the home office was located.

tracery—The metal or stone work joining together the different parts of the top of a stained-glass window.

Tractarian—*See* Oxford Movement.

tradesman—A shopkeeper or anyone else who bought and sold things. One could not be in trade and still mingle with the quality, e.g., be presented at court. ". . . the selling of goods by retail is a shameful and infamous practice," says Thackeray with heavy irony in *Vanity Fair*, "meriting the contempt and scorn of all real gentlemen."

training college—A college that trained teachers for the national schools. If one successfully completed the college's program, one was supposedly in better shape to take the exam for the certificate that permitted one to teach. McChoakumchild in *Hard Times* is the dreadful product of this system, and Eugene Headstone in *Our Mutual Friend* is also a training-college graduate. Thomas Hardy presents a rather unsympathetic portrait of the Melchester Training College for Women that Sue Bridehead attends in *Jude the Obscure*—one night, of course, she simply runs away from it.

tram—A streetcar.

transept—In a church built in the shape of a cross, the transept was the section perpendicular to the nave and bisected by it to form the two arms of the cross. Sometimes each such arm was itself designated a transept.

transportation—The practice of shipping English criminals overseas for punishment, which flourished until the mid-1800s. Sentences of seven years or life were not uncommon. Until 1776, criminals were transported to the American colonies; thereafter, to Australia. Some 140,000 people were transported to Australia between 1810 and 1852, the overwhelming majority for theft. Ultimately transportation was replaced with hard labor in England.

trap—A little light carriage that had springs.

treacle—Originally a sweet, medicinal compound. There was a "treacle" Bible (1568), so called because it translated Jer. viii, 22, "Is there no tryacle in Gilead, Is there no phisitin there?" By the 1800s it had become merely what Americans call molasses.

treadmill—A nasty device consisting of a great iron cylinder made to revolve by the marching of convicts around the steps fixed on to it, which descended under their feet as they did so. The idea was to have convicts doing something as senseless as possible; also, it was exhausting, especially because it was worked by several convicts at once, whose movements had to be constantly coordinated to keep them going properly. The device was finally banned in 1898.

Treasury—Basically the center of political action within the government, it was nominally run by the Board of Treasury, which consisted of the first lord of the treasury, the Chancellor of the Exchequer, and the three junior lords of the treasury. Since the position of first lord was always held by the prime minister, the Chancellor of the Exchequer became the *de facto* head of the department. He prepared the budget and was chief financial officer of the government. Meanwhile the junior lords spent their time assisting the parliamentary (or patronage) secretary to the treasury, who was the party's patronage man and the "whip" in charge of seeing to it that members voted. The prime minister and the leaders of his party in the House of Commons always sat on the front bench to the right of the Speaker, which was called the Treasury Bench.

trick—In a game like whist, a "trick" was the name given to a single round of cards won by one of the players.

tripos—The final honors exams in certain subjects at Cambridge, especially math and classics, so called because the examiner had at one time sat on a small three-legged stool.

troop—The smallest unit of military organization in the cavalry, corresponding to a company in the infantry.

trooper—A private in the cavalry.

truck system—Paying one's employees in something other than cash.

truckle bed—The same thing as a trundle bed, i.e., one that could be slid under something else during the day time.

tucker—A piece of lace in lady's garments to cover the upper part of the chest.

tuft—In one of the more obvious class distinctions at Oxford, the nobility wore special little tassels on their caps to denote their aristocratic status. People who sucked up to them were known as "tuft hunters."

tumbler—A big drinking glass. They originally had pointed bottoms so one couldn't put them down until one had finished everything in them. Later a tumbler was merely a big drinking container with a normal, flat base.

turbans—A popular ladies' fashion in the early part of the century consisted of wearing imitation Middle Eastern headdress.

turbot—A big flatfish. One mid-century etiquette advisor lauded the changeover from dinner service *à la française* (putting all the plates on the table so the guests could serve themselves) to dinner *à la russe* (footmen handing everything around discreetly from diner to diner) because it meant one didn't have to eat turbot so much anymore. It had been served frequently before because it looked more impressive on the table than a lot of silly little fish.

turf—Chopped-up slabs of grass and earth, sometimes sold in London for use in birdcages. Sections six inches in diameter went for two to four pence a dozen. "Turf" also meant the sport of horse racing.

Turkey carpet—A rug supposedly or actually imported from Turkey that was made of wool and looked like velvet.

turnips—They were grown as feed for sheep and cattle on the one hand and as a crop that rested fields usually planted with crops like corn. A major ingredient in the "revolution" in farming from the old, prescientific way.

turnkey—A jailer.

turnpike—An old-fashioned way of funding local road repair through private enterprise. The theory was to create local turnpike trusts, administered by commissioners who would use the toll money they collected to keep the part of the road subject to their toll in good repair. Ultimately there were over 1,100 trusts and 23,000 miles of turnpike road. Sample tolls were 2½ pence a mile for a stagecoach in winter, 3 pence in summer. The ever-righteous Mr. Bold in *The Warden*, perhaps straining

386 ..... Glossary

at gnats, goes after a local turnpike woman, "rode through the gate himself, paying the toll, then brought an action against the gate-keeper and proved that all people coming up a certain by-lane, and going down a certain other by-lane, were toll-free."

turtle—A very genteel, much fancied dish, either as flesh or soup, among the quality, so much so that it spawned the imitation foods called "mock turtle." A staple of official banquets.

turves—Plural of turf.

tutor—A Fellow at Oxford or Cambridge who had taken on the responsibility for teaching one or more undergraduates.

twelfth cakes—Cakes made for Twelfth Night. They contained a coin or bean that made the finder the "king" or "queen" of the celebration.

Twelfth Night—January 5, the night before the twelfth day after Christmas, on which day Christmas festivities traditionally ended. January 6 was Epiphany.

two-penny post—The local mail delivery system within London and certain other large cities, which was run for many years as an enterprise separate from the national mail system.

typhus—A disease transmitted by body lice and found typically in dirty places.

under—*See* upper.

union—Short for the workhouse, because workhouses in a given local area were often built after 1834 by a group or union of several individual parishes. In a different context entirely, Union referred to the act that brought together England and Scotland in 1603 and 1707 or the act that united England and Ireland in 1801.

up—In trains or coaches "up" always meant toward London. With respect to the universities, "up" always meant toward Oxford or Cambridge (e.g., to "go up") just as to be "sent down" meant to be expelled from one's university and to "go down" meant to leave it.

upper—In a large household, the upper servants had more seniority than the servants below them and, in the case of the butler and the house-keeper, the right to order all the others around. Upper servants included the butler, the housekeeper, and the lady's maid. Unlike the other servants, the butler and housekeeper generally each had their own room, the butler his pantry and the housekeeper her own room from which to direct the affairs of the household, and they were entitled to respect, e.g., the housekeeper was always addressed as "Mrs.," that the other servants did not merit. With*in* a category of servants who reported to the upper servants, e.g., housemaids, upper was used, confusingly enough, in a different sense to denote a difference in tasks. A large household, for example, might have an upper and under housemaid; the former responsible for getting flowers and arranging decorations, the latter for polishing, cleaning and scrubbing; neither housemaid, however, would be an upper *servant* like the housekeeper. In the context of national politics, the upper house in Parliament was the House of Lords.

usher—An assistant to the headmaster of a school or one of the teachers.

vacation—The interval between terms of either the universities or the high court sessions in London.

vail—A tip expected from a departing guest by the servants in that household who had waited on him.

valet—Called the gentleman's gentleman, a not inappropriate title in view of his status as an upper servant. His job was to get his master's clothes out, to keep his shoes and hats in good shape, to stand behind him at dinner if required, and accompany him on his travels—the male equivalent of being a lady's maid.

van—A covered-over, lightweight version of the heavy waggons used for hauling goods around. Sometimes used for transporting people, too.

Vauxhall—A cheerful, eleven-acre pleasure garden across the Thames from London that flourished until the mid-1800s.

vellum—A parchment made out of sheep or goat skin used for extra good writing paper.

velveteen—A fabric that looked like velvet but was actually made from cotton.

Venerable—A term of respect used in addressing an archdeacon of the Church of England.

verger—The man who looked after the inside of a church.

vermin—Animals that killed game or the eggs or young of game. Vermin included stoats, owls, weasels, otters, foxes, hawks, and badgers. It was among the tasks of gamekeepers to prevent vermin from killing the young pheasant and other creatures breeding on their masters' estates.

Very Reverend—Form of address to a dean of the Church of England.

vestry—A room in a church where sacred vessels were kept and where the clergyman dressed for the service; it was where the bride and groom signed the parish register immediately after the wedding ceremony. It was also where the vestry, a group of men from the parish, met to look after the parish's or the church's affairs and, in particular, to set the church rate and, in some parishes, designate the churchwardens.

vicar—A parish priest appointed to a living owned by someone else. As a consequence, the vicar shared the tithes with the owner, while a rector, an incumbent who had exclusive rights to a living, got all the tithes. In the 1800s, vicars were considered of slightly less status than rectors.

victoria—A low, open carriage with four wheels, very popular for ladies' driving, e.g., in Hyde Park, from about the mid-century on. Usually seating only one or two people.

vinaigrette—A little box made of silver or a similar metal containing vinegar and having holes in the top. It was used to revive fainting ladies.

ving-et-un—The same as the card game 21, that is, one tried to get as close to 21 with the value of one's cards as possible without going over that amount.

viscount—The peer who ranked just under an earl and just above a baron. His wife, perhaps unsurprisingly, was a viscountess and he was a "Right Honourable" and was addressed as "Lord ————."

visiting card—The calling card with one's name on it that one left when paying a call or when merely leaving one's card.

visitation—An inspection tour of a parish or diocese by a bishop or archdeacon.

wafer—A little round thing made out of flour and gum or a similar substance, which one could dampen and then place on a letter to seal it.

waggon—The great, heavy, lumbering vehicle—sometimes with eight wheels or more and ten or more horses—used to transport goods in prerailroad England, especially when speed was no object (they traveled at a speed of only a few miles per hour). When David Copperfield gets into a stagecoach after overeating, there are jokes about "the greater expediency of my travelling by waggon."

waggonette—A four-wheel light carriage used for fun trips, e.g., picnics, and general middle-class use in the country. It seated some six people on two seats facing in toward the center of the vehicle and was popular after the mid-century.

wainscoting—Wainscot was a kind of fancy oak imported from Russia, Holland or Germany. The term "wainscoting" was applied to panels that were originally made out of such oak.

waistcoat—A vest.

waistband—The part of a skirt or pair of pants around the waist in which money was sometimes kept.

Walker—An expression that meant "nonsense!" Used in conjunction with "Hookey" for the full effect. "Do you know what my great grandfather's name was?" says Miss Mowcher in *David Copperfield* to Steerforth. "No," he replies. "It was Walker, my sweet pet," says Miss Mowcher, "and he came of a long line of Walkers, that I inherit all the Hookey estates from."

ward—A child looked after by a guardian. Wards in Chancery were children either directly looked after by the court itself or for whom it appointed a guardian. Chancery wards could not marry without the court's consent.

warden—The head of a prison or a hospital or similar institution, as in the Trollope novel of that name. Not to be confused with a churchwarden.

wardrobe—A big wooden cupboard either for hanging clothes in or else with shelves or drawers for putting them in. It usually stood in a bedroom.

warrant officer—An officer in the Royal Navy like a boatswain or carpenter or surgeon whose position was attained by warrant rather than by commission.

washballs—Little round balls of soap used for washing or shaving.

washhand stand—A table in a bedroom that held a washing basin, pitcher of water, soap dish, and other washing paraphernalia. Generally, it would be refilled by the maid several times a day, as needed, before meals and before the chamber's occupant retired for the night.

washhouse—A building in which to wash clothes.

washing stand—Same thing as a washhand stand.

watch—Men appointed in each parish, usually only in towns, to walk the streets at night, periodically calling out the time and the weather and supposedly keeping criminals at bay. They were usually elderly, ineffectual individuals, and it was considered sport in London at one time for young men to tip over the street booths in which the watchmen sat when not making their rounds.

watch and ward—To keep watch over someone.

watch guard—A chain or ribbon attached to a watch to keep it from disappearing.

water butt—A barrel that was put under the eaves to catch rain water for washing, etc.

water cart—A cart used to keep the dust down on dirty streets. It carried water in a barrel or similar container that was released through a tiny series of holes onto the roads as the vehicle was driven through the streets.

watering place—Places like Bath and fancy seaside resorts where one went in order to drink or bathe on the theory that the water would cure one of some ailment. (Gout was a popular ailment at Bath.)

watermen—They were of two kinds. The ones on the Thames rowed people out to boats or across the river for a fee. The watermen on land were men who stood at cab stands and gave water to the horses.

weeds—Mourning garments, the word "weed" meaning simply clothes.

weepers—Various kinds of funeral garb, including a black band on a man's hat and the long black veil which widows wore. On those days when she anticipated that her husband might leave her not as much money as she would like, Mrs. Gregg in *The Mill on the Floss* "resolved that she would have scarcely any weeper on her bonnet and would cry no more than if he had been a second husband." In the latter part of the century the term also came to refer to long sideburns.

weir—Either a dam, usually constructed in order to channel water for a millwheel, or a series of stakes and nets in a body of water aimed at trapping fish.

Wellington, duke of—The great British war hero who defeated Napoleon in the Peninsular War and at Waterloo and subsequently became a Tory prime minister, responsible for passing the Catholic Emancipation Act in 1829.

Wesleyanism—*See* Methodism.

wetnurse—Somebody hired to breast-feed a child not her own.

West End—The western and fancy part of London (as opposed to the City and the East End), reaching from Charing Cross west to the western boundary of Hyde Park. It included Buckingham Palace, Mayfair, and St. James's Park.

Westminster—Before London expanded so enormously during the nineteenth century, there lay to its west the city of Westminster. This was the home of the monarch and it also housed Westminster Abbey, the royal palaces of Whitehall and St. James, and the Palace of Westminster, where the courts and Parliament met. (Due to its meeting place, Parliament was sometimes spoken of in verbal shorthand as "Westminster.") As London grew, Westminster was absorbed into it.

whalebone—Used to reinforce corsets but not made of a whale's bone. Actually, whalebone consisted of long thin strips in a whale's jaw that acted like teeth to strain out its food. Whalebone was springy and tough enough to serve as a corset stiffener (and also as umbrella ribs).

wharfinger—Someone who owned or ran a wharf.

wheeler(s)—The horse(s) harnessed closest to a carriage, i.e., its wheels, the "leaders" being farther away.

whey—As in "eating her curds and—." Whey was the runny substance that separated from milk when the curds coagulated, as in the course of making cheese. In *Tess of the d'Urbervilles* Tess falls asleep to "the measured dripping of the whey."

Whigs—The liberal faction in English politics. Opposed to the Tories, they represented, broadly speaking, the middle class, manufacturers, and Dissenters. They changed their name in the 1830s and 1840s to Liberals.

whin—Another name for furze or gorse.

whippers-in—The term given to the assistants of the huntsman in fox hunting who helped him keep the hounds together. In Parliament, whippers-in or whips were party members who tracked down their colleagues in the party so they would be on hand for crucial votes in Parliament. The parliamentary, or patronage, secretary to the treasury was the leading whip for the party in power; his main assistants were the junior lords of the treasury.

whist—That quintessential nineteenth-century English card game. The ancestor of bridge. Four people, that is, two couples, with the partners sitting opposite each other, were each dealt thirteen cards. They then fixed a trump suit. Then one person put down a card and the next player had to play the same suit or—if he couldn't—he played the trump suit or discarded. When all four people had played, the person who dealt the highest trump or the highest card of the suit took that trick of four cards. Points were scored on the basis of tricks played and, sometimes, on the number of honors (high trump cards) held. A game was either 5 or 10 points depending on whether it was "short" or "long" whisk. The best two out of three games was a rubber.

Whitehall—A district in Westminster named for an old royal palace that did, indeed, have a white hall in it. It was the location of the Admiralty, the Treasury, the prime minister's residence at 10 Downing Street, and the Horse Guards, i.e., the army headquarters.

whitesmith—A worker in tin or sometimes in other metals. Sometimes a worker in metal who just did cosmetic work on it as opposed to "forging" it.

whiting—A good-tasting small fish. Also, pulverized fine chalk used for cleaning or whitewashing.

Whitsun—In the church calendar, the seventh Sunday after Easter. Also known as Pentecost.

wicket—A small gate sometimes used in preference to the larger gate that it was part of or next to. In cricket, depending on the era in question, a wicket referred to either two or three stakes in the ground that had either one or two pieces of wood on top that a bowler tried to hit.

Wilberforce—There were two eminent figures in the 1880s who bore this name, the first, the great Evangelical reformer William Wilberforce (1759–1833), whose career was most notable for his attack on the slave trade. Mr. Brooke in *Middlemarch,* liberal spirit that he is, points out that "I knew Wilberforce in his best days." The other Wilberforce (1805–73) was the somewhat oleaginous bishop of Oxford known as "Soapy Sam." In describing in *The Warden* various of Dr. Grantly's children who are named after prominent contemporary clergy, Trollope describes Samuel, "dear little Soapy as he was familiarly called," "a cunning boy, and those even who loved him best could not but own that for one so young he was too adroit in choosing his words, and too skilled in modulating his voice."

wilderness—An area in a park or garden that had trees in it, sometimes growing wild and sometimes planted in a kind of maze. In *Mansfield Park* the protagonists journey to Sotherton, where, after a tour of the house, "a considerable flight of steps landed them in the wilderness, which was a planted wood of about two acres, and though chiefly of larch and laurel, and beech cut down, and though laid out with too much regularity, was darkness and shade, and natural beauty." Landscaping for a romantic, "natural" effect was very popular in the early 1800s.

willow pattern—A popular pattern for blue china dishes that showed a mandarin and his house with a river, a boat, a bridge, and two lovers.

wimble—Something used for boring holes, like an auger or a gimlet.

Windsor—A town on the Thames west of London that has housed a palace of the royal family for many years and which Queen Victoria increasingly favored for her residence near London, rather than Buckingham Palace, after her husband died.

withy—A withy was a willow tree. It was also a twig or branch not necessarily of willow that was suitable for making into baskets or twisting and tieing things with.

woodbine—A climbing plant like honeysuckle, ivy, or convulvulus.

woolsack—The lord chancellor sat on a square sack filled with wool while presiding over the House of Lords. To be elevated to the woolsack was therefore to become lord chancellor.

Woolwich—Woolwich and the Tower of London were the two main arsenals for the British army. Woolwich was also where engineers and artillery officers trained.

workbox—Sewing, embroidery, and similar kinds of needlework were referred to as "work." A "workbox" or "workbag" was thus a sewing basket or kit. There were also "worktables."

workhouse—Or the "union" or sometimes just plain "the house" for short. The publicly supported institution to which the sick, destitute, aged, and otherwise impoverished went, the theory being that they would get food and shelter there in exchange for work. After 1834, apparently in an effort to make sure lazy people did not take advantage of the workhouses, they were made grim beyond belief. Husbands and wives were separated once inside their walls, children were taken from their parents, and all inmates had to wear a dismal uniform. No cards, no tobacco—the work consisted of breaking stones or picking oakum, and after 1833, unclaimed workhouse bodies were given to anatomists for dissection. The poor hated and feared the workhouse. Before 1834 the workhouses were run by overseers of the poor selected by the local justice of the peace. After 1834, they were run by elected boards of guardians.

worsted—Worsted was the name of the place in Norfolk where this woolen material was first made. Sometimes the term referred to a very fancy kind of wool yarn.

wrangler—Wranglers were the top honors students in math at Cambridge. The person with highest honors was the senior wrangler.

wuther—It is actually an intransitive verb and it describes—among other things—exactly what Emily Brontë says it does in her novel: " 'Wuthering heights' is the name of Mr. Heathcliff's dwelling. 'Wuthering' being a significant provincial adjective, descriptive of the atmospheric tumult to which its station is exposed in stormy weather." "Wuther" is a dialect form of "whither," which is applied to something like the wind when it roars or rushes sharply at something.

yellow—In election campaigns and the like, yellow was the color of the Whigs. The Tories favored blue.

yellow fever—A tropical disease spread by mosquitoes, which produced flulike symptoms in mild cases, kidney failure, liver failure and death in severe ones.

yeoman—The small independent farmer with some land of his own, say, 300 to 1,000 acres in the estimate of one expert, typified by Mr. Gregg in *The Mill on the Floss*. (As George Eliot explicitly tells us.) As the century wore on, the yeomen often styled themselves "gentleman farmers." They were the social group next below the gentry in the countryside. Unlike the gentry, they typically had no tenants on their property and sometimes even worked it themselves. Historically, they represented the sturdy, independent Englishman, e.g., the yeoman archer at Agincourt, who was the stout bulwark of traditional English freedoms and the mainstay of the countryside. With economic change and the increasing growth of large estates in the nineteenth century, much of the class died out.

yeomanry—The mounted, i.e., wealthier, group within the militia.

yew—A dismal evergreen tree—poisonous, appropriately enough—which was a favorite in English churchyards, apparently because, being evergreen, it was thought to symbolize immortality.

Your Grace—The correct form of address to dukes and duchesses by those below the nobility and gentry in rank and the correct form of address to a bishop by everyone.

Your Worship—The correct form of address to a magistrate, e.g., a justice of the peace.

Bibliography

ADAMS, ROBERT M. *The Land and Literature of England: A Historical Account*. New York, London: W.W. Norton & Co., 1983.

ADAMSON, GARETH. *Machines at Home*. Harmondsworth: Puffin Books, 1974.

ADAMSON, JOHN W. *English Education, 1789–1902*. Cambridge: Cambridge University Press, 1930.

ANDERSON, GREGORY. *Victorian Clerks*. Manchester: Manchester University Press, 1976.

AUSTEN-LEIGH, JAMES EDWARD. *A Memoir of Jane Austen, by Her Nephew J. E. Austen-Leigh*. London: R. Bentley, 1870.

BADEAU, ADAM. *Aristocracy in England*. New York: Harper & Bros., 1886.

BANKS, J. A. *Prosperity and Parenthood: A Study of Family Planning Among the Victorian Middle Classes*. London: Routledge & Paul, 1954.

BEALES, DEREK. *From Castlereagh to Gladstone, 1815–1885*. New York, London: W. W. Norton and Co., 1969.

BECKETT, J. V. *The Aristocracy in England, 1660–1914*. Oxford, New York: Blackwell, 1986.

BEETON, ISABELLA. *The Book of Household Management*. London: S.O. Beeton, 1861; New York: Farrar, Straus & Giroux, 1969.

BENINGFIELD, GORDON. *Hardy Country*. London: A. Lane, 1983.

BENTLEY, NICOLAS. *The Dickens Index*. Oxford, New York: Oxford University Press, 1958.

BONHAM CARTER, VICTOR. *Farming the Land*. London: Routledge & K. Paul, 1959.

————. *The English Village*. Harmondsworth: Penguin Books, 1952.

BOVILL, E. W. *English Country Life, 1780–1830*. London, New York: Oxford University Press, 1962.

————. *The England of Nimrod and Surtees, 1815–1854*. London, New York: Oxford University Press, 1959.

BREWER'S DICTIONARY OF PHRASE & FABLE. New York: Harper & Bros., n.d.

BRIMBELCOMBE, PETER. *The Big Smoke: A History of Air Pollution in London Since Medieval Times*. London, New York: Methuen, 1987.

BRITTON, J. *The Original Picture of London, enlarged and improved: being a correct guide for the stranger, as well as for the inhabitant, to the metropolis of the British empire, together with a description of the environs. . . .* London: Longman, Rees, Orme, Brown, and Green (etc.), 1830.

BROWN, C. K. FRANCIS. *A History of the English Clergy 1800–1900*. London: The Faith Press, Ltd., 1953.

BROWN, JULIA PREWITT. *A Reader's Guide to the Nineteenth-Century English Novel*. New York: Collier Books, 1986.

BURNETT, JOHN. *A History of the Cost of Living*. Harmondsworth: Penguin Books, 1969.

————. *Plenty and Want: A Social History of Diet in England from 1815 to the Present Day*. London: Nelson, 1966.

————. *Useful Toil: Autobiographies of Working People from the 1820s to the 1920s*. Suffolk: Penguin Books, 1977.

BURTON, ELIZABETH. *The Early Victorians at Home, 1837–1861*. London: Longman, 1972.

BYRDE, PENELOPE. *A Frivolous Distinction: Fashion and Needlework in the Works of Jane Austen*. Bath: Bath City Council, England, 1979?

————. *The Male Image: Men's Fashion in Britain, 1300–1700*. London: B. T. Batsford, 1979.

CAMPBELL, LADY COLIN (GERTRUDE ELIZABETH). *Etiquette of Good Society*. London: Cassell & Co., 1892.

CHADWICK, OWEN. *The Victorian Church*. New York: Oxford University Press, 1966–70.

CHAMBERS, J. D., AND G. E. MINGAY. *The Agricultural Revolution, 1750–1880*. New York: Schocken Books, 1966.

CHAPMAN, R. W. (ED.). *The Novels of Jane Austen*. London: Oxford University Press, 1933–69.

COLLINS, PHILIP. *Dickens and Crime*. London: Macmillan; New York: St. Martin's Press, 1965.

————. *Dickens and Education*. London: Macmillan; New York: St. Martin's Press, 1963.

CRITCHLEY, T. A. *A History of Police in England and Wales*. London: Constable, 1978.

CROWTHER, M. A. *The Workhouse System, 1834–1929: The History of an English Social Institution*. Athens, Ga.: University of Georgia Press, 1982.

CRUCHLEY, GEORGE F. *Picture of London comprising the history, rise and progress of the metropolis. . . .* London, 1850.

CUNNINGTON, CECIL. *English Women's Clothing in the Nineteenth Century*. London: Faber and Faber, 1937.

CUNNINGTON, CECIL, PHILLIS CUNNINGTON, AND CHARLES BEARD. *A Dictionary of English Costume (900–1900)*. Philadelphia: Dufour Editions, 1960.

CUNNINGTON, PHILLIS. *Costume of Household Servants, from the Middle Ages to 1900*. New York: Barnes & Noble, 1975.

————, AND CATHERINE LUCAS. *Occupational Costume in England, from the Eleventh Century to 1914*. New York: Barnes & Noble, 1967.

DARRYL, P. (PASCHAL GROUSSET). *Public Life in England*. London, New York: G. Routledge and Sons, 1884.

DAVIDOFF, LEONORE. *The Best Circles: Society, Etiquette and the Season*. London: Croom Helm, 1973.

DAVIDSON, CAROLINE. *A Woman's Work Is Never Done: A History of Housework in the British Isles, 1650–1950*. London: Chatto & Windus, 1986.

DOWELL, STEPHEN. *A History of Taxation and Taxes in England from the Earliest Times to the Year 1885*. London, New York: Longmans, Green, and Co., 1888.

DRABBLE, MARGARET (ED.). *The Oxford Companion to English Literature*. Oxford, New York: Oxford University Press, 1985.

DRAPER, JO. *Thomas Hardy's England*. London: J. Cape, 1984.

DUFFY, IAN. *Bankruptcy and Insolvency in London During the Industrial Revolution*. New York: Garland, 1985.

DUNLOP, O. J. *English Apprenticeship and Child Labor: A History. . . .* New York: Macmillan, 1912.

ENCYCLOPAEDIA BRITANNICA. 11th edition. Cambridge: University Press, 1910–11.

ETIQUETTE FOR GENTLEMEN: WITH HINTS ON THE ART OF CONVERSATION. London: Tilt and Bogue, 1841.

EVANS, BARBARA. *Everyman's Companion to the Brontës*. London: Dent, 1985.

EVANS, HILARY, AND MARY EVANS. *The Party That Lasted 100 Days: The Late Victorian Season*. London: Macdonald and Jane's, 1976.

FARWELL, BYRON. *Mr. Kipling's Army*. New York, London: W. W. Norton & Co., 1987.

FREEMAN, SARAH. *Mutton and Oysters: Food, Cooking and Eating in Victorian Times*. London: Gollancz, 1989.

GASH, NORMAN. *Politics in the Age of Peel; A Study in the Technique of*

Parliamentary Representation, 1830–1850. London, New York: Longmans, Green, 1953.

GAY, PETER. *The Tender Passion*. New York: Oxford University Press, 1986.

———. *The Bourgeois Experience: From Victoria to Freud*. New York: Oxford University Press, 1984.

GEORGE, DOROTHY. *London Life in the XVIIIth Century*. London: K. Paul, Trench, Tubner; New York: A.A. Knopf, 1925.

GILLIE, CHRISTOPHER. *Longman Companion to English Literature*. London: Longman, 1972.

GIROUARD, MARK. *A Country House Companion*. New Haven: Yale University Press, 1987.

———. *Life in the English Country House: A Social and Architectural History*. New Haven: Yale University Press, 1978.

———. *The Victorian Country House*. Oxford: Clarendon Press, 1971.

GLOAG, JOHN. *Victorian Comfort, A Social History of Design from 1830–1900*. London: A. and C. Black, 1961.

———. *Victorian Taste: Some Social Aspects of Architectural and Industrial Design from 1820–1900*. London, A. and C. Black, 1962.

GREENOAK, FRANCESCA. *All the Birds of the Air: The Names, Lore, and Literature of British Birds*. London: Deutsch, 1979.

GREY, J. DAVID (ED.). *The Jane Austen Companion*. New York: Macmillan, 1986.

GROVE, MRS. LILY. *Dancing*. London: Longmans, Green, 1895.

THE HABITS OF GOOD SOCIETY: A HANDBOOK OF ETIQUETTE FOR LADIES AND GENTLEMEN. . . . London: J. Hogg & Sons, 1859.

HALEVY, ELIE. *A History of the English People in 1815*. London, New York: Ark Paperbacks, 1987.

HARRISON, BRIAN. *Drink and the Victorians: The Temperance Question in England, 1815–1872*. Pittsburgh: University of Pittsburgh Press, 1971.

HARRISON, J. F. C. *The Early Victorians, 1832–1851*. New York: Praeger, 1971.

HARTCUP, ADELINE. *Below Stairs in the Great Country Houses*. London: Sidgwick & Jackson, 1985.

HARTLEY, DOROTHY. *Food in England*. London: Macdonald, 1954.

———. *Lost Country Life*. New York: Pantheon Books, 1979.

———. *Water in England*. London: Macdonald, 1964.

HASWELL, JOCK. *The British Army: A Concise History*. London: Thames and Hudson, 1975.

HEYWOOD, VALENTINE. *British Titles: The Use and Misuse of the Titles of Peers and Commoners, with Some Historical Notes*. London: A. and C. Black, 1951.

HIBBERT, CHRISTOPHER. *London: The Biography of a City*. London: A. Lane, 1977.

———. *The English: A Social History, 1066–1945*. New York, London: W. W. Norton and Co., 1987.

——— (ED.) *The London Encyclopaedia*. London: Macmillan, 1983.

HOLCOMBE, LEE. *Wives and Property: Reform of the Married Women's Property Law in Nineteenth-Century England*. Toronto, Buffalo: University of Toronto Press, 1983.

HOLDSWORTH, WILLIAM. *A History of English Law*. London: Methuen, 1903–72.

———. *Charles Dickens as a Legal Historian*. New Haven: Yale University Press, 1928.

HORN, PAMELA. *Labouring Life in the Victorian Countryside*. Gloucester: Sutton, 1987.

———. *Life and Labour in Rural England, 1760–1850*. Houndmills, Basingstoke, Hampshire: Macmillan Education, 1987.

———. *The Rise and Fall of the Victorian Servant*. Dublin: Gill and Macmillan, 1975.

———. *The Rural World, 1780–1850: Social Change in the English Countryside*. London: Hutchinson, 1980.

HOSKINS, W. G. *The Making of the English Landscape*. Harmondsworth: Penguin Books, 1970.

HOUSE, HUMPHRY. *The Dickens World*. Oxford, New York: Oxford University Press, 1979.

HOWARD, D. L. *The English Prisons: Their Past and Their Future*. London: Methuen, 1960.

HOWITT, WILLIAM. *The Book of the Seasons; or, The Calendar of Nature*. London: Henry Colburn and Richard Bentley, 1831.

———. *The Rural Life of England*. London: Longman, Brown, Green, and Longmans, 1844.

———. *The Year-book of the Country; or, The Field, the Forest, and the Fireside*. London: H. Colburn, 1850.

HUGGETT, FRANK E. *Carriages at Eight: Horse-Drawn Society in Victorian and Edwardian Times*. Guildford: Lutterworth Press, 1979.

———. *Life Below Stairs: Domestic Servants in England from Victorian Times*. London: J. Murray, 1977.

ITZKOWITZ, DAVID. *Peculiar Privilege: A Social History of English Fox-Hunting, 1753–1885*. Hassocks: Harvester Press, 1977.

JACQUES, EDWARD. *Charles Dickens in Chancery, being an account of his proceedings in respect of the "Christmas Carol" with some gossip in relation to the old law courts at Westminster*. London, New York: Longmans, Green and Co., 1914.

KAY-ROBINSON, DENYS. *Hardy's Wessex Reappraised*. New York: St. Martin's Press, 1972.

400 . . . . . Bibliography

KITSON CLARK, G. *The Making of Victorian England.* New York: Atheneum, 1982.

LAMBERT, ANGELA. *Unquiet Souls: The Indian Summer of the British Aristocracy, 1880–1918.* London: Macmillan, 1984.

LAWSON, JOHN, AND HAROLD SILVER. *A Social History of Education in England.* London: Methuen, 1973.

LLOYD, CHRISTOPHER. *A Short History of the Royal Navy, 1805 to 1918.* London: Methuen & Co., Ltd., 1943.

———. *The Nation and the Navy: A History of Naval Life and Policy.* London: Cresset Press, 1954.

LOWELL, ABBOTT L. *The Government of England.* New York: Macmillan, 1908.

MACALPIN, DANIEL. *The Law relating to Money-Lenders & Borrowers; being a treatise on bills of sale, personal security, and monetary dealings with "expectant heirs."* London: Reeves and Turner, 1880.

MAITLAND, F. *The Constitutional History of England: A Course of Lectures.* Cambridge: Cambridge University Press, 1908.

MAKOWER, FELIX. *The Constitutional History and Constitution of the Church of England.* London: S. Sonnenschein & Co., Lim.; New York: Macmillan, 1895.

MALCOLMSON, ROBERT. *Popular Recreations in English Society, 1700–1850.* Cambridge: Cambridge University Press, 1973.

THE MANNERS OF THE ARISTOCRACY, BY ONE OF THEMSELVES. A GUIDE TO THE ETIQUETTE OF DINNERS, WEDDINGS, AT HOMES, HOSTESS AND GUEST, TOWN AND COUNTRY VISITS, ETC. London [Ward & Lock's Useful Handbooks], 1881?

MARSDEN, HILDA. "The North of England in the Novels of the Brontës." Ph.D. dissertation. University of London, 1967.

MARSHALL, DOROTHY. *The English Domestic Servant in History.* London: published for the Historical Association by G. Philip, 1949.

MARSHALL, J. D. *The Old Poor Law, 1795–1834.* Houndmills, Basingstoke, Hampshire: Macmillan, 1985.

MAYHEW, HENRY. *London Labour and the London Poor: A cyclopaedia of the condition and earnings of those that will work, those that cannot work, and those that will not work. . . .* London: Griffin, Bohn, 1861.

McCAUSLAND, HUGH. *The English Carriage.* London: Batchworth Press, 1948.

McGREW, RODERICK. *Encylopedia of Medical History.* London: Macmillan, 1985.

MINGAY, G. E. *The Gentry: The Rise and Fall of a Ruling Class.* London, New York: Longman, 1976.

———. *Rural Life in Victorian England.* London: Heinemann, 1977.

——— (ED.). *The Victorian Countryside.* London, Boston: Routledge & Kegan Paul, 1981.

MITCHELL, R. J., AND M. D. R. LEYS. *A History of the English People.* London: Pan Books, 1967.

MITCHELL, SALLY (ED.). *Victorian Britain: An Encyclopedia.* New York: Garland, 1988.

MITTON, G. E. *Jane Austen and Her Times.* London: Methuen & Co., 1905.

MUNSCHE, P. B. *Gentlemen and Poachers: The English Game Laws, 1671–1831.* Cambridge, New York: Cambridge University Press, 1981.

MYATT, FREDERICK. *The Soldier's Trade: British Military Developments, 1660–1914.* London: Macdonald and Jane's, 1974.

NICHOLSON, BARBARA. *The Oxford Book of Garden Flowers.* London, New York: Oxford University Press, 1964.

———. *The Oxford Book of Wild Flowers.* London, New York: Oxford University Press, 1977.

THE OXFORD ENGLISH DICTIONARY. Oxford: Clarendon Press, 1933 (2d. ed.). Oxford: Clarendon Press, 1989.

PAGE, NORMAN. *Speech in the English Novel.* Houndmills, Basingstoke, Hampshire: Macmillan, 1988.

PALGRAVE, R. H. *Dictionary of Political Economy.* London, New York: Macmillan, 1894–99.

PALMER, ARNOLD. *Movable Feasts: A reconaissance of the origins and consequences of fluctuations in meal-times, with special attention to the introduction of luncheon and afternoon tea.* London, New York: Oxford University Press, 1952.

PERKIN, HAROLD. *The Age of the Railway.* London: Panther, 1970.

PETERSON, M. J. *The Medical Profession in Mid-Victorian London.* Berkeley: University of California Press, 1978.

PHILLIPPS, K. C. *Jane Austen's English.* London: Deutsch, 1970.

———. *Language and Class in Victorian England.* New York: Blackwell; London: Deutsch, 1984.

PINION, F. B. *A Hardy Companion: A Guide to the Works of Thomas Hardy and Their Background.* London, Melbourne: Macmillan; New York: St. Martin's Press, 1968.

QUENNELL, MARJORIE AND CHARLES. *A History of Everyday Things in England.* London: B.T. Batsford [1950–54].

RADZINOWICZ, LEON. *A History of English Criminal Law and Its Administration from 1750: The Movement for Reform, 1750–1833.* New York: Macmillan, 1948.

READER, W. J. *Professional Men: The Rise of the Professional Classes in Nineteenth-Century England.* New York: Basic Books, 1966.

REED, JOHN. *Victorian Conventions.* [Athens]: Ohio University Press, 1975.

ROBBINS, M. *The Railway Age.* London: Routledge & Paul, 1962.

ROBINSON, HOWARD. *The British Post Office: A History.* Princeton: Princeton University Press, 1948.

ROLT, L. T. C. *Victorian Engineering*. London: A. Lane, 1970.

ROSE, PHYLLIS. *Parallel Lives: Five Victorian Marriages*. New York: Knopf, 1983.

ROTHBLATT, SHELDON. *The Revolution of the Dons*. New York: Basic Books, 1968.

RUSSELL, ANTHONY. *The Clerical Profession*. London: SPCK, 1980.

SALA, GEORGE. *Twice Round the Clock; or, The Hours of the Day and Night in London*. London: Houlston, 1861.

SANGER, CHARLES P. *The Structure of "Wuthering Heights."* London: L. & Virginia Woolf, 1926.

SHANLEY, MARY LYNDON. *Feminism, Marriage and the Law in Victorian England 1850–1895*. Princeton: Princeton University Press, 1989.

SHEPHERD, THOMAS. *London and Its Environs in the nineteenth century, illustrated by a series of views from original drawings*. London: Jones & Co., 1829.

SIMOND, LOUIS. *An American in Regency England: The Journal of a Tour in 1810–1811*. London: Maxwell, 1968.

SKELLEY, ALAN. *The Victorian Army at Home: The Recruitment and Terms and Conditions of the British Regular, 1859–1899*. London: Croom Helm, 1977.

STOCQUELER, J. H. *The Military Encyclopaedia: A technical, biographical, and historical dictionary, referring exclusively to the military sciences, the memoirs of distinguished soldiers, and the narratives of remarkable battles*. London: W.H. Allen & Co., 1853.

STONE, LAWRENCE. *The Family, Sex and Marriage in England 1500–1800*. New York: Harper & Row, 1977.

TAINE, HIPPOLYTE. *Notes on England*. New York: Holt & Williams, 1872.

TATE, W. *The Parish Chest: A Study of Parochial Administration in England*. Cambridge: Cambridge University Press, 1951.

THE NATURAL HISTORY OF COURTSHIP BY "PUNCH." Philadelphia: Carey & Hart, 1844.

THOMPSON, F. M. L. *English Landed Society in the Nineteenth Century*. London: Routledge & Kegan Paul, 1963.

————. *The Rise of Respectable Society: A Social History of Victorian Britain, 1830–1900*. Cambridge, Mass.: Harvard University Press, 1988.

TIMBS, JOHN. *Curiosities of London.* . . . London: D. Bogue, 1855.

TODD, ALPHEUS. *Parliamentary Government in England: Its origin, development, and practical application*. London: S. Low, Marston & Company, limited, 1892.

TRAILL, H. D., AND J. S. MANN. *Social England: A record of the progress of the people in religion, law, learning, arts, industry, commerce, science, literature and manners, from the earliest times to the present day*. New York: Putnam. 1902–9.

TRISTAN, FLORA. *Flora Tristan's London Journal, 1840.* Boston: Charles River Books, 1980.

TURBERVILLE, ARTHUR. *Johnson's England: An Account of the Life & Manners of his Age.* Oxford: Clarendon Press, 1933.

WALKOWITZ, JUDITH. *Prostitution and Victorian Society: Women, Class and the State.* Cambridge, New York: Cambridge University Press, 1980.

WANG, CHI-KAO. *Dissolution of the British Parliament, 1832–1931.* New York: Columbia University Press; London: P.S. King & Son, Ltd., 1934.

WATERSON, MERLIN. *The Servants' Hall: A "Downstairs" History of a British Country House.* New York: Pantheon, 1980.

WEBB, SIDNEY, AND BEATRICE WEBB. *English Local Government from the Revolution to the Municipal Corporations Act.* London, New York: Longmans, Green and Co., 1906–29.

WEEKS, JEFFREY. *Coming Out: Homosexual Politics in Britain from the Nineteenth Century to the Present.* London, New York: Quartet Books, 1977.

WEISS, BARBARA. *The Hell of the English: Bankruptcy and the Victorian Novel.* Lewisburg: Bucknell University Press, 1986.

WHITAKER'S ALMANAC. London, 1869–99.

WILSON, THOMAS. *The Treasures of Terpsichore; or, A Companion for the Ballroom. Being a collection of all the most popular English country dances, arranged alphabetically, with proper figures to each dance.* London: printed for the author; and to be had of Messrs. Sherwood, Neely, and Jones, 1816.

WOODHOUSE, R. I. *What Is the Church? or, Plain Instruction About the Church, Especially in England.* . . . New York: D. Appleton & Co., 1887.

WOODWARD, E. L. *The Age of Reform, 1815–1870.* Oxford: Clarendon Press, 1949.

YOUNG, G. M. *Victorian England: Portrait of an Age.* Garden City: Doubleday, 1954.

YOUNG, G. M. (ED.). *Early Victorian England, 1830–65.* London: Oxford University Press, 1934.

ZUPKO, RONALD. *British Weights and Measures: A History from Antiquity to the Seventeenth Century.* Madison: University of Wisconsin Press, 1977.

Index